Westminster Abbey Reformed

Westminster Abbey Reformed

1540–1640

Edited by

C.S. Knighton and
Richard Mortimer

ASHGATE

Published by

Ashgate Publishing Limited
Gower House
Croft Road
Aldershot
Hants GU11 3HR
England

Ashgate Publishing Company
Suite 420
101 Cherry Street
Burlington, VT 05401–4405
USA

Ashgate website: http://www.ashgate.com

British Library Cataloguing in Publication Data

Westminster Abbey reformed: 1540–1640
   1. Westminster Abbey–History–16th century 2. Westminster
   Abbey–History–17th century 3. Reformation–England–
   London–History
   I. Knighton, C.S. II. Mortimer, Richard
   283.4'2132

Library of Congress Cataloging-in-Publication Data

Westminster Abbey reformed: 1540–1640 / edited by C.S. Knighton and
Richard Mortimer.
    p. cm.
   Includes bibliographical references and index (alk. paper).
   1. Westminster Abbey–History. 2. England–Church history–16th century. 3.
   England–Church history–17th century. 4. Reformation–England. I. Knighton,
   C.S. II. Mortimer, Richard.
   DA687. W5 W37 2003
   283' .42132–dc21   2002024921

ISBN 0 7546 0860 3

This book is printed on acid-free paper

Typeset by Manton Typesetters, Louth, Lincolnshire, UK.

Printed by MPG Books Ltd, Bodmin, Cornwall.

Contents

Preface

We are indebted to the Dean and Chapter of Westminster for permitting access to their muniments, and for quotations from them to be published. We are grateful to all our contributors for their varied and scholarly essays, and for their patience. Our thanks are warmly given to Ashgate Publishing for accepting this book and smoothing its path to publication. We have also been helped and encouraged in many ways by Dr Tony Trowles, Librarian of Westminster Abbey, and Christine Reynolds, Assistant Keeper of the Muniments.

It is with sadness that we record that Jennifer Loach, who was to have given us an essay on royal funerals, died shortly after accepting that commission.

C.S.K.
R.M.

For my own part I am grateful to my editorial colleague for joining with me in this project, not least because it has taken him so far and so frequently from the period of his own specialization. My paper on Henry VIII's foundation has benefited from the very helpful comments of Miss B.F. Harvey, to whose guidance I have long been indebted. The essay on Dean Williams derives from a paper delivered at Lincoln Cathedral in 1982; in its developed form it has been usefully scrutinized by Dr Foster and Dr Milton, and I am grateful to them. I am also much obliged to Mr M.G. Underwood, Archivist of St John's College, Cambridge for access to the records in his care.

Westminster, February 2000   C.S.K.

Notes on Contributors

Editors:

C.S. Knighton, MA, PhD, DPhil, FSA, is an editor for the Public Record Office, and has published calendars of the state papers of Edward VI and Mary I. The muniments of Westminster Abbey provided the principal material of his original research, and he has edited the first Act Book of the dean and chapter of Westminster.

Richard Mortimer, MA, PhD, FSA, FRHistS, has been Keeper of the Muniments of Westminster Abbey since 1986. He is the author of a standard text book on Angevin England, and he has edited several collections of charters, including those of Westminster Abbey's dependent cell at Sudbury.

Contributors:

Andrew Foster, BA, DPhil, FRHistS, is Research Director at University College, Chichester. Archbishop Richard Neile was the subject of his doctoral thesis, and he has developed this interest in a series of studies of the early seventeenth-century church. He has also contributed to the official history of Chichester Cathedral.

Dale Hoak, AM, PhD, FRHistS, is Chancellor Professor of History at the College of William and Mary at Williamsburg, Virginia. He gained his doctorate under the supervision of Sir Geoffrey Elton at Cambridge, and has published numerous studies of mid-Tudor government.

Stanford Lehmberg, AM, PhD, LittD, FSA, FRHistS, taught at the University of Texas and has recently retired from the chair of history at the University of Minnesota. He studied at Cambridge under Sir Geoffrey Elton, and has published monographs on Henry VIII's parliaments and surveys of cathedral history in the early modern period.

David Loades, MA, PhD, LittD, FSA, FRHistS, taught at the Universities of St Andrews, Durham, and Wales (Bangor). He is now Professor Emeritus of the University of Wales and Honorary Research Professor of the University of Sheffield. He is Director of the British Academy Foxe Project. His many publications include a biography of Mary I and the authoritative study of her reign.

J.F. Merritt, MA, PhD, is Research Fellow in the History Department at the University of Sheffield and Director of the Stuart London project there. She has written extensively on the social, cultural and religious history of early modern London and Westminster.

Anthony Milton, MA, PhD, is Senior Lecturer in History at the University of Sheffield. He has published a monograph on religious thought in early Stuart England, and is working on a biography of Peter Heylyn, canon of Westminster.

The Reverend Ashley Null, MDiv, STM, PhD, an Anglican clergyman of the diocese of Western Kansas, is a visiting scholar in Church History with Frau Professor Dr Dorothea Wendebourg at the Humboldt University of Berlin, where he is preparing a critical edition of Cranmer's 'Great Commonplaces'. He has already published a monograph on Cranmer's doctrine of repentance. He is also a Visiting Fellow in the Faculty of Divinity at Cambridge.

List of Abbreviations

Works listed here and cited elsewhere in this volume are published in London or by issuing societies unless otherwise stated.

Certain standard reference works, and some of the more frequently mentioned books about Westminster Abbey, are cited throughout by these short titles. All other works are cited in full at their first occurrence within the volume. Short titles occurring in more than one contribution are given below.

Acts, 1543–1609, 1609–42	*Acts of the Dean and Chapter of Westminster, 1543–1609*, ed. C.S. Knighton (Westminster Abbey Record Ser. i, ii, 1997–9); *1609–42* (to be published in the same series)
APC	*Acts of the Privy Council of England*, new ser., ed. J.R. Dasent (1890–1907), and continuing (1921–)
Atherton *et al.*, *Norwich Cathedral*	*Norwich Cathedral. Church, City and Diocese, 1096–1996*, ed. I. Atherton, E. Fernie, C. Harper-Bill and A. Hassell Smith (1996)
Baker, *Hist. St John's*	T. Baker, *History of the College of St. John the Evangelist, Cambridge*, ed. J.E.B. Mayor (Cambridge 1869)
BIHR	*Bulletin of the Institute of Historical Research*
BL	British Library, London
Bodl.	Bodleian Library, Oxford
Burke, *St Margaret's*	*Memorials of St Margaret's Church, Westminster*, ed. A.M. Burke (1914)
Carpenter, *House of Kings*	*A House of Kings. The History of Westminster Abbey*, ed. E.F. Carpenter (1966)
CCCC	Corpus Christi College, Cambridge
CCR	*Calendar of Close Rolls*
CJ	*Journals of the House of Commons*
Cobban, *King's Hall*	A.B. Cobban, *The King's Hall within the University of Cambridge in the Later Middle Ages* (Cambridge 1969)
Collinson *et al.*, *Canterbury Cathedral*	*A History of Canterbury Cathedral*, ed. P. Collinson, N.L. Ramsay and M.J. Sparks (Oxford 1995)

Cox, *Letters of Cranmer*	*Miscellaneous Writings and Letters of Thomas Cranmer*, ed. J.E. Cox (Parker Soc. 1846)
CPR	*Calendar of the Patent Rolls*
CSPD	*Calendar of State Papers, Domestic Series*
CSP Span.	*Calendar of State Papers, Spanish*
CSP Ven.	*Calendar of State Papers, Venetian*
CUL	Cambridge University Library
DNB	*Dictionary of National Biography* (original edn except where *ODNB* stated)
EcHR	*The Economic History Review*
EHR	*The English Historical Review*
Fincham, *Early Stuart Church*	*The Early Stuart Church, 1603–1642*, ed. K.C. Fincham (1993)
Foster, *Alumni Oxon.*	*Alumni Oxonienses. The Members of the University of Oxford, 1500–1714*, ed. J. Foster (Oxford 1891–2)
Foster, 'Clerical estate'	A.W. Foster, 'The clerical estate revitalised', in Fincham, *Early Stuart Church*, 139–60
Foxe, *Actes and Monuments*	J. Foxe, *Actes and Monuments of these latter and perillous dayes, touching matters of the Church* (1563)
Guildhall	Guildhall Library, London
Hacket, *Scrin. Res.*	J. Hacket, *Scrinia Reserata. A Memorial offer'd to the great deservings of John Williams* (1693)
Harvey, *Estates*	B.F. Harvey, *Westminster Abbey and its Estates in the Middle Ages* (Oxford 1977)
Harvey, *Living and Dying*	B.F. Harvey, *Living and Dying in England, 1100–1540. The Monastic Experience* (Oxford 1993)
HBC	*Handbook of British Chronology*, ed. F.M. Powicke and E.B. Fryde (Royal Historical Soc. Guides and Handbooks, no. 2, 2nd edn 1961)
Heylyn, *Cyprianus*	P. Heylyn, *Cyprianus Anglicus: or, the History of the Life and Death of ... William ... Archbishop of Canterbury* (1668)
Heylyn, *Examen*	P. Heylyn, *Examen Historicum* (1659)
Hist. Parl.	*The History of Parliament. The House of Commons, 1509–1558*, ed. S.T. Bindoff (1982); *1558–1603*, ed. P.W. Hasler (1981)
HJ	*The Historical Journal*
HMC	Historical Manuscripts Commission

HMC, *Cowper MSS*	*The Manuscripts of the Earl Cowper, K.G., preserved at Melbourne Hall, Derbyshire* (HMC, 1888–9)
HMC, *Salisbury MSS*	*Calendar of the Manuscripts of the Most Hon. the Marquis of Salisbury, K.G., etc. preserved at Hatfield House, Hertfordshire* (HMC, 1883–)
JBAA	*Journal of the British Archaeological Association*
JBS	*Journal of British Studies*
JEH	*Journal of Ecclesiastical History*
Knighton, 'Collegiate foundations'	C.S. Knighton, 'Collegiate foundations, 1540 to 1570, with special reference to St Peter in Westminster' (Cambridge PhD dissertation 1975)
Knighton, 'Provision of education'	C.S. Knighton, 'The provision of education in the new cathedral foundations of Henry VIII', in Marcombe and Knighton, *Close Encounters*, 18–42
Laud, *Works*	*The Works of the Most Reverend Father in God, William Laud*, ed. J. Bliss and W. Scott (Library of Anglo-Catholic Theology, lviii–lxiv, 1847–60)
Lehmberg, *Cathedrals under Siege*	S.E. Lehmberg, *Cathedrals under Siege. Cathedrals in English Society, 1600–1700* (Exeter 1996)
Lehmberg, *Reformation of Cathedrals*	S.E. Lehmberg, *The Reformation of Cathedrals. Cathedrals in English Society, 1485–1603* (Princeton 1988)
Le Neve (1854)	J. Le Neve, *Fasti Ecclesiae Anglicanae*, ed. T.D. Hardy (1854)
Le Neve, *1300–1541, 1541–1857*	J. Le Neve, *Fasti Ecclesiae Anglicanae, 1300–1541*, comp. H.P.F. King *et al.* (1962–7); *1541–1857*, comp. J.M. Horn *et al.* (1969–)
Letters of Chamberlain	*The Letters of John Chamberlain*, ed. N.E. McClure (American Philosophical Soc. Memoirs, xii, Philadelphia, 1939)
LJ	*Journals of the House of Lords*
LMA	London Metropolitan Archives (incorporating the former Greater London Record Office)
Loach, 'Ceremonial'	S.J. Loach, 'The function of ceremonial in the reign of Henry VIII', *Past & Present*, no. 142 (Feb. 1994), 43–68

Lockyer, *Buckingham*	R. Lockyer, *Buckingham. The Life and Political Career of George Villiers, first Duke of Buckingham, 1592–1628* (1981)
LP	*Letters and Papers, Foreign and Domestic, of the reign of Henry VIII*, ed. J.S. Brewer, J. Gairdner and R.H. Brodie (1862–1932) [cited by entry no.]
LPL	Lambeth Palace Library
Marcombe and Knighton, *Close Encounters*	*Close Encounters. English Cathedrals and Society since 1540*, ed. D. Marcombe and C.S. Knighton (Nottingham 1991)
McConica, *Collegiate University*	*The Collegiate University*, ed. J.K. McConica (History of the University of Oxford, iii, Oxford 1986)
MacCulloch, *Cranmer*	D.N.J. MacCulloch, *Thomas Cranmer. A Life* (1996)
MacCullough, *Tudor Church Militant*	D.N.J. MacCullough, *Tudor Church Militant. Edward VI and the Protestant Reformation* (1999)
McCullough, *Sermons at Court*	P.E. McCullough, *Sermons at Court. Politics and Religion in Elizabethan and Jacobean Preaching* (Cambridge 1998)
Nichols *Chron. Jane and Mary*	*The Chronicle of Queen Jane, and two years of Queen Mary*, ed. J.G. Nichols (Camden Soc. xlviii, 1850)
Nichols, *Literary Remains*	*Literary Remains of King Edward VI*, ed. J.G. Nichols (1857)
n.s.	new style (here only as year of grace counted from 1 January)
O'Day and Heal, *Continuity and Change*	*Continuity and Change. Personnel and Administration of the Church in England, 1500–1642*, ed. M.R. O'Day and F.M. Heal (Leicester 1976)
ODNB	*Oxford Dictionary of National Biography* (forthcoming)
o.s.	old style (here only as year of grace counted from 25 March)
OW	Old Westminster
Pearce, *Monks*	E.H. Pearce, *The Monks of Westminster* (Notes and Documents relating to Westminster Abbey, no. 5, Cambridge 1916)

Powell, *Pory*	W.S. Powell, *John Pory, 1572–1636. The Life and Letters of a Man of Many Parts* (Chapel Hill NC, 1977)
PRO	Public Record Office, London
Robinson, *Abbot's House*	J.A. Robinson, *The Abbot's House at Westminster* (Notes and Documents relating to Westminster Abbey, no. 4, Cambridge 1911)
Robinson and James, *MSS of Westminster Abbey*	J.A. Robinson and M.R. James, *The Manuscripts of Westminster Abbey* (Notes and Documents relating to Westminster Abbey, no. 1, Cambridge 1909)
Rosser, *Medieval Westminster*	A.G. Rosser, *Medieval Westminster, 1200–1540* (Oxford 1989)
ROW	*The Record of Old Westminsters. A Biographical List of all those who are known to have been educated at Westminster School*, comp. G.F. Russell Barker, A.H. Stenning *et al.* (1928–)
Rymer, *Foedera*	*Foedera, Conventiones, Litterae, et cujuscunque generis Acta Publica*, ed. T. Rymer (1727–35)
Shrewsbury, *Plague*	J.F.D. Shrewsbury, *A History of Bubonic Plague in the British* Isles (Cambridge 1971)
SJC Archives	St John's College, Cambridge, Archives
Soden, *Goodman*	G.I. Soden, *Godfrey Goodman, Bishop of Gloucester, 1583–1656* (1953)
Somerville, *Savoy*	R. Somerville, *The Savoy: manor, hospital, chapel* (1960)
SR	*The Statutes of the Realm*, ed. A. Luders *et al.* (1810–28)
SRP	*Stuart Royal Proclamations*, ed. J.F. Larkin and P.L. Hughes (Oxford 1973–83)
Stanley, *Historical Memorials*	A.P. Stanley, *Historical Memorials of Westminster Abbey* (5th edn 1882)
Statutes (1)	Statutes of the Henrician cathedrals as given in *The Foundation of Peterborough Cathedral, A.D. 1541*, ed. W.T. Mellows (Northamptonshire Record Soc. xiii, 1941 for 1939)
STC	*A Short-Title Catalogue of Books printed in England, Scotland, and Ireland and of English Books Printed Abroad 1475–1640*, comp. A.W. Pollard and G.R. Redgrave, 2nd edn by W.A. Jackson, F.S. Ferguson and K.F. Pantzer (1986–91)

Strype, *Cranmer*	J. Strype, *Memorials of the Most Reverend Father in God Thomas Cranmer* (Oxford 1840)
Strype, *Smith*	J. Strype, *The Life of the Learned Sir Thomas Smith* (Oxford 1820)
Tanner, *Library*	L.E. Tanner, *The Library and Muniment Room* (Westminster Abbey: Westminster Papers, no. 1, 1935)
TLMAS	*Transactions of the London and Middlesex Archaeological Society*
TRHS	*Transactions of the Royal Historical Society*
TRP	*Tudor Royal Proclamations*, ed. P.L. Hughes and J.F. Larkin (1964–9)
Tyacke, *Anti-Calvinists*	N.R.N. Tyacke, *Anti-Calvinists. The Rise of English Arminianism* (Oxford 1987)
Venn	*Alumni Cantabrigienses. A Biographical List of the University of Cambridge*, ed. J. and J.A. Venn, part 1 (–1751) (Cambridge 1922–7)
Vernon, *Life of Heylyn*	G. Vernon, *The Life of the Learned and Reverend Dr. Peter Heylyn* (1682)
WA Library	Westminster Abbey Library
WAM	Westminster Abbey Muniments
WAM Reg.	WAM, Register (Lease) Book
WCA	Westminster City Archives
Westlake, *Westminster Abbey*	H.F. Westlake, *Westminster Abbey. The Church, Convent and College of St Peter, Westminster* (1923)
WHR	*Welsh History Review*
Widmore, *Westminster Abbey*	R. Widmore, *An History of the Church of St. Peter, Westminster, commonly called Westminster Abbey* (1751)
Williams, *Work of Williams*	*The Work of Archbishop Williams*, ed. B. Williams (Abingdon 1979)
Wing	*Short-Title Catalogue of Books printed in England, Scotland, Ireland, Wales and British North America and of English Books printed in other countries, 1641–1700*, comp. D. Wing, 2nd edn by Wing, T.J. Crist, J.J. Morrison and C.W. Nelson (New York 1972–88)
Woodward, *Theatre of Death*	J. Woodward, *The Theatre of Death. The Ritual Management of Royal Funerals in Renaissance England, 1570–1625* (Woodbridge 1997)

Wriothesley, *A Chronicle of England during the reigns of*
  Chronicle *the Tudors, from A.D. 1485 to 1559, by*
Charles Wriothesley, Windsor Herald, ed.
W.D. Hamilton (Camden Soc., new ser. xi,
xx, 1875–7)

Yates and Welsby, *Faith and Fabric. A History of Rochester*
  Faith and Fabric *Cathedral, 604–1994,* ed. W.N. Yates and P.A.
Welsby (Woodbridge 1996).

Technical Note

The year of grace (except within quotations) is deemed to begin on 1 January, but otherwise dating by Old Style is not adjusted. The year of account (from Michaelmas to the eve of the next) is represented by the form '1542/3'; very often tenure of office is known only from accounts of such duration.

In quotations from MS sources, contractions and abbreviations have been silently expanded where interpretation is clear, and the letter forms u/v and i/j have been adjusted to modern usage. Punctuation and capitalization have occasionally been modified.

As far as possible, we distinguish the *Abbey* (meaning Westminster Abbey, as a place and institution before and after the Reformation) from the *abbey* (meaning the Benedictine monastery there). Similarly, the *Sanctuary* is a location, *sanctuary* is the institution; and in the Abbey church, the area before the high altar is known as the *sacrarium*. For the continuing offices within the collegiate church we have used the titles now current; therefore *canons* not *prebendaries* (the term favoured in the sixteenth and seventeenth centuries); likewise *minor canons* not *petty canons* (though where it is not possible to separate these from the *lay vicars*, we call them all *singingmen*). We are grateful to our contributors for accepting these conventions, which in some cases differ from styles they have used elsewhere.

Westminster Abbey from Reformation to Revolution

C.S. Knighton

There is, as is popularly said, a lot of history in Westminster Abbey; indeed, the stock has quite notably increased during the time that this book has been in the making. As the scene of coronations, royal funerals and weddings, and the mausoleum of the nation's great, it is of course one of the best known buildings in the world, and much has been written on these subjects. The Abbey's architectural and artistic history has also been extensively recorded and described. Among its less familiar treasures is a remarkable archive, which documents a thousand years in the Abbey's domestic history, and that of the widespread lands it once owned. The muniments, as this collection is known, arguably more comprehensive than those of any comparable institution, are the building blocks of the Abbey's history. From them it is possible to reconstruct much of the administrative routine and wider economy of the place, and to illuminate the careers and concerns of those who lived here. For the Benedictine monks who occupied the church of Westminster from Anglo-Saxon times until 1540, this has been accomplished in two magisterial studies by Barbara Harvey.[1] After 1540 the nature of the archive changes considerably, as obedientiary rolls give way to chapter acts and treasurers' accounts as the chief sources of information. The post-Reformation muniments will never tell us of the living and dying of deans and canons in such penetrating detail as has now been done for their monastic predecessors. The secular clergy, by definition, live a less regimented life than the regulars, and the archives they generate are consequently less structured. Nevertheless a great deal of material exists, and much of it has received little attention from professional historians outside the Abbey's own ranks. It would be foolish and impertinent for the present writers to pose as Miss Harvey's continuators, but we aim in a modest way to follow her in the application of the modern practice of historical scholarship to the Westminster past.

---

[1] B.F. Harvey, *Westminster Abbey and its Estates in the Middle Ages* (Oxford 1977) and *Living and Dying in England, 1100–1540. The Monastic Experience* (Oxford 1993).

The room where the Abbey muniments are housed is itself of considerable interest, since it forms a gallery high up in the South Transept (in fact built over the east walk of the Cloisters), open on two sides to the Abbey church. Those who are privileged to work there must accustom themselves to the chatter of the visitors below (much reduced in recent years by the thoughtful arrangements of the dean and chapter). They will, however, from time to time be edified by prayer and music. The Muniment Room may well have been constructed as a royal gallery; it has undoubtedly been the repository for the Abbey's records for 600 years.[2] Its very remoteness has played a large part in preserving the archive intact, for it is relatively safe from fire, flood, all but the more adventurously disposed rodents, and (one must add) from human interference. Not until it was connected by a staircase to the Library in the 1930s was it possible to reach the Muniment Room with any ease. Only since then has the collection been conveniently accessible to scholars.

The first to make systematic use of the muniments was Richard Widmore, appointed Abbey Librarian in 1733, as which he remained until his death in 1764. His chief work was the history published in 1751;[3] for this he used some documents which are no longer extant, but for which (as can be otherwise demonstrated) he can be trusted as an authority. The extent to which his book retains its usefulness will be evident from the several citations which appear below. A.P. Stanley, dean 1864–81, virtually created the Abbey as we now think of it, the focal point of the nation's religious dedication. He also gave the Abbey its most enduringly popular book, the *Historical Memorials*,[4] which went into five editions under his hand, and retains (as again our citations show) an independent value. Stanley was not (and would not have claimed to be) a professional historian, still less a palaeographer, and in some points of detail his work is unreliable. In 1923 H.F. Westlake produced a more scholarly history, soundly based in the muniments of which he was custodian. Westlake was the first Westminster historian to regard the post-Reformation collegiate foundation as worthy of serious study, and not (as even

---

[2] See principally L.E. Tanner, *The Library and Muniment Room* (Westminster Abbey: Westminster Papers, no. 1, 1935) and, for a summary of the archive, *idem*, 'The nature and use of the Westminster Abbey muniments', *TRHS*, 4th ser. xix (1936), 43–80. Lawrence Tanner was keeper of the muniments 1926–66, and gave a more personal account of his work in *Recollections of a Westminster Antiquary* (1969).

[3] R. Widmore, *An History of the Church of St. Peter, Westminster, commonly called Westminster Abbey* (1751).

[4] A.P. Stanley, *Historical Memorials of Westminster Abbey* (1868). The present volume cites the 5th edn (1882) which included the author's final revisions.

Stanley seems to suggest) an addendum to the great monastic era that went before.[5]

Other scholarly work of this period continued to concentrate on the monastery; a series of 'Notes and Documents relating to Westminster Abbey' was established during the decanate of the distinguished medievalist Armitage Robinson. Robinson's own volume concerning the Abbot's House (now the Deanery) included some material on the post-Reformation history of the house. Robinson joined with M.R. James in cataloguing the library MSS (quite distinct from the muniments), and this included a full account of the collection. Archdeacon Pearce's census of the monks (based principally on the obedientiary rolls) provides biographical detail for such of the brethren who continued at Westminster as members of the secular foundation after 1540.[6]

The present work may be said to have its origins in two publications of the 1960s. On 28 December 1965 the Abbey began a year of celebrations to mark the 900th anniversary of Edward the Confessor's foundation. In the course of that memorable year a splendid new history was produced (as Stanley's *Memorials* had marked the previous centenary). The new book, *A House of Kings*, was edited by Edward Carpenter, already himself part of the Abbey's history and in time to become its dean; most of the other contributors were canons of Westminster and lay officers of Westminster Abbey.[7] The text opened with the nearest thing protocol allows to a preface by Her Majesty The Queen. The volume was handsomely produced, elegantly written, and ostensibly well documented – but not, alas, supported with a critical apparatus by which facts can be checked, opinions tested, and further research followed.

Two years before *A House of Kings* appeared, A.G. Dickens published the first edition of a book which was to have a profound impact on the professional study of the English Reformation.[8] Dickens directed attention away from the legislated Reformation, the idea that England became a protestant nation because the Tudor monarchs and their ministers decreed that it should be so. Dickens's reformation was not an act of state but an expression of popular will, and the natural

---

[5] H.F. Westlake, *Westminster Abbey. The Church, Convent and College of St Peter, Westminster* (1923).

[6] J.A. Robinson and M.R. James, *The Manuscripts of Westminster Abbey*. Robinson, *The Abbot's House at Westminster*. E.H. Pearce, *The Monks of Westminster*: (Notes and Documents relating to Westminster Abbey, nos 1, 4 and 5, Cambridge 1909, 1911 and 1916).

[7] *A House of Kings. The History of Westminster Abbey*, ed. E.F. Carpenter (1966).

[8] A.G. Dickens, *The English Reformation* (1964).

development of deep-rooted traditions of dissent in many localities. Not that there was anything startlingly novel in this; it was, as has been pointed out, what the first historian of the English Reformation, John Foxe, had said four hundred years before.[9] What gave a special sharpness to Dickens's interpretation was his use of documentary evidence from ecclesiastical archives, sources which had (for early modernists at any rate) hitherto been little used by mainstream historians. The fact that such records had been enthused over by their clerical custodians and local antiquaries had tended if anything to deter the more austerely constitutional and political historians from exploring them. That changed in the years after 1964, to a large extent because of Dickens. Not everyone would agree with his interpretation of the English Reformation, but it was now clear that historians needed to go to the local ecclesiastical records and see what they told us about the actualities of the Reformation, or indeed non-Reformation of the English church. Many did, thanks to the coincidental expansion of university research in the 1970s and 1980s, and the improved accessibility of the records themselves. In many cases diocesan and capitular authorities, unable to provide suitable facilities, deposited their archives in county record offices. Westminster Abbey's muniments (happily retained *in situ*) were among those which came to be more fully investigated. Since 1972 scholars working in these areas have had, in the Reformation Studies Colloquium, a forum for exchanging their findings and launching their opinions. Several of those contributing to this volume have become known to one another through these meetings.

The Reformation so greatly affected the history of Westminster Abbey (indeed, no other church was affected so frequently) that we must regret the Dickens-inspired revolution in Reformation historiography did not occur in time to influence *A House of Kings*. There have more recently been several collective histories of cathedrals, beginning with the volume on York Minster which set the benchmark.[10] By comparison

---

[9] C.A. Haigh, 'The recent historiography of the English Reformation', *HJ*, xxv (1982), repr. in *The English Reformation Revised* (Cambridge 1987), 19–33, especially pp. 21–2; also editor's introduction, especially pp. 1–7. Citations below are (where possible) to the original edition of J. Foxe, *Actes and Monuments of these latter and perillous dayes, touching matters of the Church* (1563).

[10] *A History of York Minster*, ed. G.E. Aylmer and R.E. Cant (Oxford 1977). *Wells Cathedral. A History*, ed. L.S. Colchester (Shepton Mallet 1982). *Winchester Cathedral. Nine hundred years, 1093–1993*, ed. P.M.J. Crook (Chichester 1993), which chiefly concerns the fabric, the institutional history having been given in F. Bussby, *Winchester Cathedral, 1079–1979* (Southampton 1979). D. Welander, *The History, Art and Architecture of Gloucester Cathedral* (Stroud 1991). *Chichester Cathedral. An Historical Survey*, ed. M. Hobbs (Chichester 1994). *A History of Lincoln Minster*, ed. D.M. Owen

with these publications, Westminster Abbey's official history now seems decidedly lightweight. It would be ungracious to criticize the editor's (and, no doubt, the dean and chapter's) decision to invite contributions chiefly from within the collegiate body past and present. The fact that York and Canterbury, and the others, have engaged outside professionals could be said to reflect well on the distinguished band of authors whom Dr Carpenter could number among his Westminster colleagues in the 1960s. Parts of *A House of Kings* are indeed very good. Dom Hugh Aveling's account of the medieval monastery, of which Dom Aveling's own community of Ampleforth is the descendant, can still be read with pleasure even though it has been so substantially replaced by Barbara Harvey's work. The following section, 'The Reformation and its aftermath', cannot, however, be commended to future readers. Arthur Tindal Hart, alone of the *House of Kings* team, could claim no particular association with Westminster Abbey. He was a country parson of the (now virtually extinct) learned sort, whose several books on Anglican history earned him a Cambridge DD. His contribution to *House of Kings* has been admired, and was undoubtedly based on a reading of the Chapter Acts and some of the other principal documentary sources. Unfortunately the author's deployment of this material has been found so defective where it has been checked, that large doubts must be cast on its general reliability. Quotations and examples have not infrequently been extracted from various places, and remixed into a lively but wholly unchronological collage. It is not unlike the Confessor's shrine, lovingly reassembled by Abbot Feckenham in Queen Mary's reign – but not always the right way up. It is also unacceptably introspective, quite failing to place Westminster's affairs within the wider context of the Reformation, and specifically neglecting Westminster's place in the more general scheme of Henry VIII's cathedral foundations.

But large edifices like *A House of Kings* are not easily or suddenly made. We may expect that in 2065/6 the dean and chapter will

---

(Cambridge 1994). *A History of Canterbury Cathedral*, ed. P. Collinson, N.L. Ramsay and M.J. Sparks (Oxford 1995). *Norwich Cathedral. Church, City and Diocese, 1096–1996*, ed. I. Atherton, E. Fernie, C. Harper-Bill and A. Hassell Smith (1996). *Faith and Fabric. A History of Rochester Cathedral, 604–1994*, ed. N.G. Yates and P.A. Welsby (Woodbridge 1996). *Hereford Cathedral. A History*, ed. G.E. Aylmer and J. Tiller (2000). With these scholarly studies of living institutions, there must also be included *Coventry's First Cathedral. The Cathedral and Priory of St Mary*, ed. G. Demidowicz (Stamford 1994), which achieves much for a cathedral which has no standing fabric and no archive. The earlier *A History of St. Paul's Cathedral and the Men associated with it*, ed. W.R. Matthews and W.M. Atkins (1957) was the model for *House of Kings* – having the same publisher, and Dr Carpenter and Dr Hart among its contributors – but it did include, for C.N.L. Brooke's opening chapter, detailed bibliographical notes.

commission a new book, to commemorate the Abbey's own millennium. The present volume is conceived with that larger replacement distantly in view. Our concern is the century between the Reformation and the puritan revolution – in Westminster terms, between the erection of the first collegiate church in 1540 and the disintegration of the second on the eve of the Civil War. We do not thereby assert the much contended theory that the events of 1640 followed inevitably from those of 1540; these dates simply define a period in Westminster's history which is poorly served in the official account, and where recent research has been particularly fruitful. Nor do we attempt a consecutive history of those years, but instead discuss various aspects of the Abbey's life and function, and the careers and influence of some of those who served there. Since our chapters reflect the specific research interests of those who have contributed them, it will be necessary to set them within the general framework of the Abbey's history.

The outlines are briefly stated. In 1540 the monastery was dissolved and in its place was erected a cathedral, governed by a chapter of secular clergy, providing a centre for the simultaneously created diocese of Westminster. In 1550 the cathedral lost its *raison d'être* when the diocese was dissolved and reunited with London. In 1552 a special act of parliament declared that the Abbey was still a cathedral, but only a secondary one for the bishop of London. In 1556 Queen Mary dissolved the secular chapter and replaced it with a new Benedictine community. This was in turn dissolved by Elizabeth I in 1559, who in the following year founded the collegiate church which still exists, though in common with all other such bodies it was temporarily abolished during the republican rule of 1649–60. At Westminster, as elsewhere in the areas adhering to parliament, the dean and chapter lost control of its church in the early months of the Civil War.[11]

When the dissolution of the monasteries was in prospect, the future status of Westminster Abbey excited particular interest. The social planner Thomas Starkey, writing c. 1530, thought that Westminster, along with the other great houses, should be turned into a kind of compulsory training camp where the sons of the nobility could learn the political and martial arts.[12] Starkey was thinking chiefly of the uses to which monastic wealth in general might be put; it is doubtful if the use of the Abbey church itself was in his mind. Not all the redevelopment proposals were as drastic as Starkey's, but most rec-

---

[11] Le Neve, *1541–1857*, vii, 65–6.

[12] *Thomas Starkey. A Dialogue between Pole and Lupset*, ed. T.F. Mayer (Royal Historical Soc., Camden 4th ser. xxxvii, 1989), 124–5.

ommendations stressed the potential for preaching, almsgiving, and other social usefulness. But none of this requires a building as large and elaborate as Westminster Abbey, nor an endowed corporation of higher clergy, still less a body of clerics, laymen and choristers maintained for the performance of a choir office. Yet that is precisely what was established at Westminster and in five other former abbeys, while all but two of the existing cathedral priories were converted into secular cathedrals in the same fashion. These together are known as the Henrician or 'new' foundations, in distinction to the nine existing secular cathedrals of the 'old' foundation. As has often been said, the English Reformation had little effect on the institutional structures of the church, and this applies with special respect to the cathedrals. Smaller dioceses were an obvious need; dioceses needed bishops, bishops needed cathedrals, and cathedrals were felt to need vergers, bellringers, choristers, and many more supporting staff. The debate about the purpose of these great churches was carried on throughout the century from Reformation to Revolution, and of course it is still a matter of lively concern. The English cathedral service has developed a tradition and following which provides its own justification, but it remains an essentially catholic form of worship, quite at odds with the intentions of sixteenth-century reformers. The consequence has been a typically English compromise, the Anglican *via media*, catholic and reformed. For some the effect has been of the deans and chapters having to 'camp out in the shells' of the great medieval churches.[13] And the purpose of it all continues to puzzle outsiders; when Mikhail Gorbachev visited St Paul's Cathedral he asked what so much space was *for*. The answer he received ('to worship God in') begs rather than answers his very fair question.[14] It could equally well be asked of post-Reformation Westminster Abbey.

There was no certainty that Westminster Abbey would have a post-Reformation existence. Henry VIII's dissolution of the monasteries involved the complete destruction of one medieval cathedral (Coventry) and his son's dissolution of the chantries saw the end of the great royal collegiate church of St Stephen in Westminster. Tudor governments did not carry a heritage ministry, and neither architectural merit nor royal foundation conveyed any protected status. Henry VIII's treatment of his living relatives does not suggest he held the tombs of his ancestors – even his parents – in any large regard, though no doubt Westminster Abbey's function as royal mausoleum played some part in its

---

[13] N. Taylor, *Looking at Cathedrals* (1968), 1.

[14] A.B. Webster, reviewing *Sir Christopher Wren. The Design of St Paul's Cathedral* in *The Tablet*, 21 July 1991.

preservation. Rather more important was its role as coronation church (on which Professor Hoak writes here). There may even have been some genuine feeling that Westminster could usefully be split off from London to form one of the new, smaller dioceses. Westminster certainly features in all the official draft schemes for the new foundations, and although its career as a cathedral church was brief, it was essential to its survival. Nevertheless it must be stressed that during this phase Westminster was in no constitutional respect different from the other cathedrals then established. The formal documents by which it was founded, endowed and regulated were in the common form sent to Chester, Peterborough, and the other new sees. There were some distinctive features of the Westminster foundation. The unusually wide spread of its landed estate meant that it was not so rooted in its locality as other cathedrals; this might help to explain why it took so much longer to complete the refoundation at Westminster, and it certainly added to the burdens of administration once the dean and chapter were fully in charge. Westminster also had a larger share in the subsidizing of university education which was originally a general responsibility for the Henrician cathedrals. As well as providing exhibitions for students, the Westminster foundation had supported the teaching posts later known as the regius professorships. The process by which the new Westminster Cathedral was established, and the early days of its administration, are the subject of the first essay in this collection. The death of Henry VIII provides a convenient terminus, and prompts the reflection that the king deserves to be better remembered as the founder of collegiate Westminster.

The first secular chapter included two men eminent in the history of the English Reformation, Nicholas Ridley and Edmund Grindal. But neither the future Marian martyr nor the future Elizabethan primate was active in the Abbey's internal affairs while they held their stalls. The most distinguished of the original canons to be much involved in the administration was John Redman. As warden of the King's Hall, Cambridge, he played a leading part in the restructuring of Henry VIII's educational policy in the last year of the king's life. Instead of studentships and professorships funded by distant deans and chapters, there would be two great new colleges – Christ Church, Oxford, and Trinity, Cambridge. Redman became the first master of Trinity, into which the King's Hall was incorporated, and he fostered the association between Westminster and Trinity which, together with a corresponding link with Christ Church, would later be made a formal concordat. Redman himself was not just a top-flight academic administrator, but a thoughtful and influential theologian, and it is this aspect of his career which is Dr Null's principal concern. His essay here is the first substantial analysis of Redman's views, so significant in his own day that the summary he gave while he lay dying in his Westminster house would be keenly disputed between contending factions. Sir William Cecil, the secretary of state, was instrumental in the publication of a report which showed that Redman died a solid protestant, firmly against transubstantiation and the doctrine of purgatory, regretting his earlier reservations about the central Lutheran doctrine of justification by faith. In Mary's reign some of Redman's earlier writings were published in support of the catholic cause, and the debate continued into Elizabeth's reign. Dr Null's pioneering examination of the texts brings into focus the sharpness of Redman's mind, and reveals a theology which can be fitted into no particular confessional divide. Redman died in 1551, before the second Edwardine Prayer Book gave the Church of England its decidedly protestant imprint. The last services he would have heard in the Abbey would therefore have been those of the 1549 Book, with which he must have had a large measure of sympathy. Redman's eclectic Anglicanism, as Dr Null hints, can offer a useful model for modern ecumenists.

Redman's career extended into the second phase of reformed Westminster Abbey, for since April 1550 it had been a cathedral without a diocese. The dean and chapter and their inferiors went about their business regardless, somewhat after the fashion of a decapitated chicken, and the fictional status of secondary cathedral to London, announced in 1552, had no effect whatsoever on day-to-day affairs. This was the position when Mary I came to the throne in 1553, and which she continued; though before her coronation in October 1553 she had replaced the protestant dean, Richard Cox, with her catholic nominee, Hugh Weston, and in the following April a larger purge removed the remaining protestants from the chapter. Westminster's status as a secular cathedral was implicitly and retrospectively legitimized in the eyes of the universal church by Paul IV's bull *Praeclara charissimi* of 21 June 1555; as part of the deal to return England to papal obedience, all the Henrician and Edwardine dissolutions and refoundations were accepted as fact. By this date Mary had probably already decided that the secular chapter of Westminster would be replaced by a restored Benedictine community, the would-be members of which had appeared at court in March 1555. But it was a complicated process, and Mary's government had more pressing concerns, so it was not until Michaelmas 1556 that Dean Weston and his colleagues resigned to make way for Abbot Feckenham and his monks. There seems to have been no suggestion that the revived monastery might retain its cathedral status and so continue to provide the bishop of London with a secondary chapter – as the cathedral priories of Bath and Coventry had done for bishops with secular chapters at Wells and Lichfield. So Westminster Abbey became an abbey again.[15]

None of the constitutional changes to the Abbey between 1540 and 1556 had any bearing on the legal status of the sanctuary, which now rested on a statute of 1540 and was a civil responsibility of the successive regimes at the Abbey itself. Abbot Feckenham chose nevertheless to give prominence to the institution and included the sanctuary men in the public processions which marked the inauguration of the monastic observance. He also emphasized the humanitarian role of the institution of sanctuary, suggesting that it had lapsed during the years of schism, which were all the more to be deprecated in consequence. Not unnaturally there has been an assumption that the Marian refoundation did actually involve the resurrection of a defunct and rather disreputable practice. Professor Loades, in the first full treatment of the Westminster sanctuary during this period, demonstrates that Feckenham's claims, and the statements of subsequent commentators deriving from them, are quite erroneous. The sanctuary as it existed in Marian Westminster owed nothing to the grants of King Lucius and other marginally less implausible evidence which Feckenham cited before an incredulous parliamentary committee. It was the legislation of Henry VIII which kept sanctuary alive at Westminster during the restoration of monasticism, and some years beyond. In the formal sense the institution of sanctuary was whittled away into insignificance; but as Professor Loades observes, in more general terms sanctuary was not a legal creation, but a custom which developed and faded in relation to its social usefulness.

Although the dean and the canons departed in 1556 to make way for the incoming monks, the rest of Henry VIII's collegiate body remained intact. The inferior clergy, lay choristers, scholars, almsmen, bellringers and the rest continued on the payroll; many of the same individuals served throughout this interlude and then in the Elizabethan college. Those most directly affected by the monastic restoration were the members of the choir, since the performance of the daily office would have devolved on monks themselves; the secular musicians resumed (we suppose) the function of Lady Chapel choir as had existed before 1540. Professor Lehmberg has reviewed the history of the musical foundation at Westminster for the whole period from 1540 to the Civil War; his analysis of the tenures of the minor canons and lay vicars demonstrates the continuity of service which they gave. This is always a significant factor; members of the chapter often move on, or may be rarely resi-

---

[15] Since the constitutional status of the Marian abbey, and the implications of this for the successor collegiate church, are matters on which Dr Mortimer and I are not agreed, the subject is not discussed here; my views will be expressed elsewhere.

dent, while the men of the choir not uncommonly remain a daily presence for the whole of their professional lives. Westminster's famous musical tradition owes much to such continuity. Its greatest flowering lies just beyond the scope of this volume; but, as Professor Lehmberg reminds us, Blow and Purcell built on what had been achieved in our period. Pre-eminent of the organists before the Civil War was Gibbons, whom in a later chapter we meet briefly at the console. Among his predecessors, Robert White and Edmund Hooper have left the most substantial testimony to their direction of Westminster's music. We are also introduced to a host of other musicians, many of them hitherto wholly unfamiliar, a few of them not all that well behaved, who contributed to the cultural life of the Abbey, and to the wider community beyond its walls.

Music is also heard, naturally, in Professor Hoak's essay on the coronations of Edward VI, Mary I and Elizabeth I, and a good deal of the ceremonial is seen. These three occasions do not actually mark out the left-right-left march of the English Reformation as neatly as the Abbey's own constitutional history does, because Edward and Elizabeth, no less than Mary, were consecrated with catholic rites. Each coronation was nevertheless an occasion for defining the political structure of the regime it hallowed. Hoak's special interest is in Edward VI, and he makes use of a previously unrecognized account of the 1547 service. He sees Cranmer playing a crucial role here; not merely as the celebrant, but in revising the coronation oath in keeping with the royal headship of the church lately established by Henry VIII. This process was completed by Sir William Cecil, who contrived for himself a walk-on part in Elizabeth's coronation to hand over what was undoubtedly a text he had refashioned. Hoak also sets the mid-Tudor coronation ceremony in the context of aspirations to a monarchy of 'Great Britain'. He therefore contributes to the current debate on the origins of unionism (which may be said to have left no stone unreturned).

The Abbey's place in its own locality has too often been overlooked, but Dr Merritt's contribution reminds us emphatically that the Abbey is in Westminster. She takes up where Dr Rosser's comprehensive survey of the medieval vill concludes,[16] and unravels much of what hitherto was confused or simply unsuspected about relations between the Abbey and its neighbours. The most significant of those was, of course, the monarch, and the crown's influence bears as directly on Westminster's civic history as on its ecclesiastical affairs. A key role was played by the high steward, notionally an officer of the dean and chapter, but because

---

[16] A.G. Rosser, *Medieval Westminster, 1200–1540* (Oxford 1989).

the office was almost always held by the chief minister of the crown, in practice an agent of royal involvement in the city. The status of city was conferred in 1540, as it was for all the other towns where new cathedrals were erected. But as Dr Merritt stresses, it was a city in name only, with none of the institutions of self-regulation which that designation implies to the modern mind. It has always been supposed that a statute of 1585 created a new civic authority for Westminster: indeed, the present City Council traces its descent from this measure. Dr Merritt will have none of this. She argues that the 1585 act merely perpetuated the system by which the dean and chapter ran the town as their own back yard, as the abbot had done before. Only when the West End outgrew the limits of its medieval government was the dean and chapter's hold on civic affairs relaxed.

Between the monastery dissolved in 1540 and the cathedral body then erected by Henry VIII there had been considerable continuity of personnel. Abbot William Boston was transformed into Dean William Benson, and six other monks followed him into the chapter, while several others received lesser posts. None of the monks of the Marian abbey would join the successor college, and the interregnum between Midsummer 1559 and May 1560 was therefore a greater hiatus than the changeover in 1540. Two of the canons ejected by Mary would return to Westminster as members of the Elizabethan foundation, but in other respects a new start was made. William Bill, the first dean of this second collegiate church, died after only a year in office, but not before drafting the statutes which are the guidelines for the Abbey's present constitution.[17] Bill's successor, Gabriel Goodman, stayed for forty years, and gave Westminster an era of stability in marked contrast to the upheavals of the twenty years before.[18] Goodman's churchmanship was of a moderate cast; perhaps, like Redman, he could be called an Anglican *avant la lettre*. He was the friend and trusted agent of William Cecil, Lord Burghley, whose tenure as the queen's chief minister almost exactly matched Goodman's period of office. The fact that, despite this connexion, Goodman was several times passed over for the episcopate, should occasion no surprise. Goodman's donnish, perhaps rather dull, manner would probably have made him little use at Chester, Salisbury or York, but these were ideal qualities for Westminster. It may be said that he helped to elevate the deanery to the status it would achieve in

---

[17] We await a biography of Dean Bill which is being prepared by the Reverend J.St H. Mullett; we regret that, for technical reasons, we were unable to include here (as we had hoped) a discussion by Mr Mullett of the tapestries given by Bill to the Abbey.

[18] For Goodman see R. Newcome, *A Memoir of Gabriel Goodman ... with some account of Ruthin School* (1825).

the nineteenth century, from which no promotion could reasonably be made.[19] Goodman's immediate successors were, as Dr Merritt notes, all made bishops. But then, in the Jacobean church, a mitre was a much more respectable attainment than it had been under Elizabeth, who regarded the episcopate as a fairly low grade in the civil service. James I, after his disagreeable experience of presbyterianism in Scotland, was an enthusiastic promoter of an order in which he saw his own divine authority reflected. For their part the bishops were flattered that the new monarch took them seriously. Even so, it is instructive to find that Dean Neile thought long before accepting a bishopric and, with charac-teristic efficiency, commissioned a financial assessment of his prospects before making his decision. He was also reluctant to lose a place which gave him such ready access to court and the political world. These considerations applied even more keenly to Dean Williams, who (as we see) coveted and enjoyed the deanery as much for the house it provided as for anything else, and held on to the office even when he had been advanced to the archbishopric of York.

Neile's time as dean saw progress in many departments, all of it so carefully documented in Neile's own Memorial Book that Dr Foster is able in large measure to allow his subject to speak for himself. Neile's record has, of course, been familiar to previous Westminster historians. Now Dr Foster has introduced an analysis based on his own prolonged study of Neile's career and his place in the early Stuart church. Once again the Cecil connexion is a predominating factor. Robert Cecil, first earl of Salisbury, who succeeded his father as high steward of Westmin-ster as he had done as the crown's chief minister, had been Neile's boyhood companion; Neile was later his chaplain, and owed all to the Cecil family, themselves Westminster residents. Neile's own roots were in Westminster, and he was the first of five deans who have been educated at Westminster School.[20] Neile indeed typifies the Westminster character; he was no dazzling intellectual like his predecessor Lancelot Andrewes, but a man of affairs, with an easy public manner and a sound sense of the way the world works.

That Neile was able to accomplish so much during his five years as dean was also due to the co-operation and confidence of his colleagues in the chapter. In the late 1620s and throughout the 1630s there was no such harmony, as the Abbey was divided by an internal conflict which seems to prefigure the real war which was about to erupt in the nation

---

[19] From the Restoration to 1802 all deans became bishops; between 1666 and 1802 the deans held the bishopric of Rochester *in commendam*. Dean Wilberforce was the last to vacate Westminster for a bishopric (1845): Le Neve, *1541–1857*, vii, 70–1.

[20] The others being Dolben, Atterbury, Pearce and Vincent.

at large. The two principal combatants in Westminster's troubles are the subjects of the concluding essays here.

Peter Heylyn would have a considerable long-term influence as a champion of what came to be called Anglo-catholicism. His more immediate impact was at Westminster, where he led the opposition to Dean Williams, a role in the chapter he inherited from his mentor William Laud. Dr Milton's examination of this controversy is part of a major reassessment of Heylyn's career. At Westminster it is Williams who, because of his undoubted benefactions to the Abbey and School, has generally been more sympathetically remembered. Dr Milton is able to take an impartial view, from which a more attractive picture of Heylyn emerges. But not entirely; Dr Milton is obliged on occasion to refer to Heylyn's hypocrisy and sanctimoniousness. Heylyn's oleaginous deference to Archbishop Laud, England's Cyprian, remains central. Just as many of those to whom Laudianism is congenial find Laud the man difficult to admire, so the merits of Heylyn's ecclesiology are obscured by his unappealing personality, a sort of prototype for the Reverend Obadiah Slope.

The image of John Williams endures in a very particular way at Westminster. Everyone who comes to work on the muniments first passes through the Library, where a full-length portrait of Williams occupies a dominating position. He does not look much like a clergyman, still less a bishop; rather, his hand rests on the purse emblazoned with the royal arms, symbol of the office of lord keeper. Williams was unique in combining, albeit briefly, the roles of dean of Westminster and head of government. Williams himself found the arrangement very satisfactory, and it undoubtedly enhanced his status within the collegiate body. But he was not destined to enjoy his political office after the death of his patron, James I; and soon afterwards he effectively lost control of his deanery as well. His story has often been told before, as first it was by his disciple John Hacket,[21] and much of it belongs to the general political and ecclesiastical history of his time. The account below has been documented as fully as possible from the Abbey's muniments, and also examines in detail the scholarships and fellowships which Williams established at his old Cambridge college. Williams saw himself in the tradition of the great episcopal patrons of education who had founded schools and associated university colleges. Williams's benefactions were on a decidedly more modest scale, and even then were inadequately endowed. There have been doubts about other aspects of

---

[21] J. Hacket, *Scrinia Reserata. A Memorial offer'd to the great deservings of John Williams* (1693).

Williams's generosity, but his demonstrable and continuing presence in the Library secures him the gratitude of all who have the privilege of working among the Abbey's books and papers.

This collection ends at the bleakest point in Westminster Abbey's history, its lawful ministers dispersed, its music silenced, and its traditions dishonoured. But happily it escaped the fate of its French counterpart in a worse revolution, and in 1660 the collegiate church could be restored along with the monarchy from which it draws its life. The settled order which has prevailed since that time adds definition to the century from Reformation to Revolution which we study here. Our title is deliberately ambiguous: the Abbey had to be re-formed more than once to take its place in the English church, reformed and catholic. It is also, as a royal peculiar, set apart from the normal ecclesiastical structure. Although the Abbey has never ceased to belong to its immediate neighbourhood, the removal of diocesan responsibilities created in 1540 has enabled it the more readily to fulfil a national and international role.

CHAPTER ONE

King's College

C.S. Knighton

Fundatorem specialem serva regem nunc Henricum
From the anthem *Christe Iesu pastor bone*
adapted by John Taverner as a prayer for Henry VIII

Henry VIII is conspicuously not at home in the house of kings. Alone of the Tudor monarchs he is buried elsewhere; and of the six wives, only Anne of Cleves, who gave him no joy, has a tomb in the Abbey. Henry's heraldry and motifs may be seen here, but without suggesting that he had any particular role in the history of the place. Yet he preserved it when it was in his power to destroy it, and for that reason he deserves to be named with Edward the Confessor and Henry III as one of its principal founders and benefactors. What Queen Elizabeth did in 1560 was to re-create a collegiate foundation much the same as the one her father had established twenty years before. As far as the school, an integral part of that Henrician foundation, is concerned, Elizabeth did no more than confirm arrangements which had continued unchanged during the restoration of monasticism from 1556–9. The school today regards Elizabeth as foundress, calls its magazine *The Elizabethan*, and every third year celebrates her accession anniversary with a Commemoration of Benefactors at which her father's name is not mentioned. Henry nevertheless remains Westminster's undistributed middle: he was the destroyer of the monasteries; Westminster Abbey stands. There is not the smallest doubt that, had he willed it, England's finest Gothic church would have been knocked down and carried away in trucks. Why this did not happen has already been suggested; some account is now given of how it did not happen.

Since the end of the fourteenth century Westminster Abbey had sustained a relatively stable number of 46 monks (including the abbot and prior).[1] When the abbot and convent surrendered on 16 January 1540, only 25 signatures were appended to the deed, though three others are known to have still been in the community.[2] In common with general

---

[1] Harvey, *Living and Dying*, 73–4.
[2] PRO, E 322/360 (*LP*, xv, 69). For the monks' careers see Pearce, *Monks*. John Ambrale *alias* Ambrose and Henry Thacksted did not sign the surrender deed but are

practice in the Henrician refoundations, as many of the monks as were willing and suitable were found places in the new cathedral. William Boston, the last abbot, became the dean; discarding, as did all his colleagues, his name in religion along with the habit, he reverted to his family name of Benson. Denis Dalyons, the last prior, and five other monks became canons. Richard Gorton, a DD and fourth in seniority among the monks, would doubtless have been offered a canonry also, but he died in the interregnum between surrender and refoundation.[3] Four of the more junior monks were found places as minor canons (equivalent to vicars choral in the old secular cathedrals); another became gospeller (a new post soon to become redundant when the liturgy was simplified). Four more monks were provided with university studentships (another innovation of the new foundations which was not long in being).[4] Those for whom no status could be found were dismissed with pensions.[5]

In the months preceding the dissolution many religious houses had been making financial provisions of their own by assigning the rights of next presentation to parochial livings in their gift. Such *pro hac vice* grants were widely made by Westminster Abbey in the 1530s; by this means livings could be held in trust by the grantees for monks who might find themselves (at the dissolution or in anticipation of it) needing employment as secular clergy.[6] As early as 1537 three monks of Westminster received faculties to change their habits and hold secular

---

described as former monks in the erection book of the new foundation: WAM 6478, f. 3. Thacksted is unknown save from this reference: cf. Pearce, 190, 192. George Springwell did not sign the surrender but received a pension: PRO, E 315/245, f. 57 (*LP*, xv, 69(2)). Pearce, 183.

[3] Gorton was dead by 12 July 1540: *LP*, xv, 943(73).

[4] WAM 6478, ff. 3–4. For the university studentships see below, pp. 35–6.

[5] Seven ex-monks with no further duties at Westminster received pensions of between £3 6s 8d and £10 *per annum* on 21 January 1540. First payment was due at Lady Day, but marginal notes of smaller sums probably indicate immediate disbursements: PRO, E 315/245, f. 57 (*LP*, xv, 69(2)). In all £141 2s 2d was paid at the time of the dissolution to ex-monks and to almsmen and women on the foundation of Henry VII: PRO, E 323/1, pt 2, m. 22d (*LP*, xiv, II, 236 (p. 74)). Ex-prior Dalyons and John Alleyne were given pensions of £10 and £2 respectively in addition to the canonry and lectorship they severally acquired in the new foundation: PRO, E 315/235, ff. 85, 85v-86 (*LP*, xvi, 1500 (p. 718)).

[6] WAM Reg. II, ff. 277, 286v, 292, 296v, 297, 299, 300, 301, 305, 314v. Cf. G. Baskerville, 'The dispossessed religious after the suppression of the monasteries', *Essays in History presented to R.L. Poole*, ed. H.W.C. Davis (Oxford 1927), 453 n. 1, which notes that John Lathbury, ex-monk of Westminster, received three livings by *pro hac vice* grants. One of them is among those issued by Westminster Abbey (Todenham, Glos.: WAM Reg. II, f. 301) and would explain why his name was removed from the list of university students on the cathedral foundation: WAM 6478, f. 3v.

benefices.[7] On 3 April 1538 the abbot and convent granted the presentation to the rectory of Launton (Oxon.) to Robert Smallwood and William Russell *pro hac vice*; both were prominent citizens of Westminster and lay officers of the abbey. On 20 December 1540 they duly exercised the advowson in favour of ex-prior Dalyons. A similar grant for the vicarage of Aldenham (Herts.) had been made to John Moulton, the abbot's steward and subsequently long-serving receiver to the dean and chapter. He presented Thomas Baxter, another ex-monk and future canon, on 9 November 1540.[8]

Although Westminster was the first of the main group of new foundation cathedrals to be erected, it was almost the last to receive its endowment. In all other cases endowment followed within a few weeks or even days of foundation: Winchester, for example, was refounded on 28 March 1541 and endowed on 1 May. At Westminster the interval was from 17 December 1540 to 5 August 1542.[9] There is no clear reason for this exceptional delay save that of simple financial advantage to the crown. Westminster Abbey had in the first place a vast material treasure to be taken into the king's hands; but it would seem that the

---

[7] LPL, Reg. Fl/Vv, ff. 125, 148v (*Faculty Office Registers 1534–1549*, ed. D.S. Chambers (Oxford 1966), 90, 107); dispensations for John Clerke and John (*recte* Richard) Gorton 20 March 1537, for John Randall 10 September following. Randall is described as '*nuper monacho dimisso monasterii Sancti Petri Westm*'' and '*habitu sui ordinis prorsus relicto*' clearly indicating that he had already abandoned religion. The calendar (p. 107) mistakenly renders the entry 'monk of the dissolved h[ou]se of Westminster'. Gorton ('Goorson') and Clerke ('Clarke') were recommended to Cromwell as 'good monkes ... of ryght jugment' by Hugh Latimer in November 1536: *Three Chapters of Letters relating to the Suppression of Monasteries*, ed. T. Wright (Camden Soc. xxvi, 1843), 147.

[8] Lincolnshire Archives, Lincoln, PD 1538/49; Episcopal Reg. 27, ff. 198, 247v. For Russell and Smallwood see D.R. Ransome, 'Artisan dynasties in London and Westminster in the sixteenth century', *Guildhall Miscellany*, ii (1964), 240–2. *Hist. Parl. 1509–58*, iii, 233, 238. Rosser, *Medieval Westminster*, 397, 399.

[9] *LP*, xvi, 379(30), 678(53), 878(1); xvii, 714(5). Tables of the surrender, foundation and endowment dates of the main group of Henrician refoundations are given in C.S. Knighton, 'Collegiate foundations, 1540 to 1570, with special reference to St Peter in Westminster' (Cambridge PhD dissertation 1975), 12, 25. Cf. *The Statutes of the Cathedral Church of Durham*, ed. A.H. Thompson (Surtees Soc. cxliii, 1929), pp. xxxi–xxxviii; S.E. Lehmberg, *The Reformation of Cathedrals. Cathedrals in English Society, 1485–1603* (Princeton 1988), 81–3; D.M. Owen, 'From monastic house to cathedral chapter: the experiences at Ely, Norwich and Peterborough', in *Close Encounters. English Cathedrals and Society since 1540*, ed. D. Marcombe and C.S. Knighton (Nottingham 1991), 8–9. The earlier and irregular foundation at Norwich (1538) is discussed by R.A. Houlbrooke and by I. Atherton and B.A. Holderness in Atherton *et al.*, *Norwich Cathedral*, 507–10, 665–8.

most serious part of this operation (the plate) was secured by 16 March 1541.[10] Westminster was not, however, rich only in gold and silver, jewel and fabric; it was furnished handsomely with broad acres. To the core estate in Westminster itself the Confessor had given manors in Worcestershire and Gloucestershire which developed into a solid block of 'western lands'. Later kings and other benefactors built up a realty extending into half the counties of England, from the South Downs to the Humber and from within sight of the Welsh hills to the mudflats of Essex.[11] In 1535 the clear income was assessed at £3,470 2s ¼d from which the maintenance of certain royal anniversaries and the running of the college of St Martin-le-Grand are deducted by Miss Harvey to show a true net income of £2,827.[12] During the whole period from January 1540 to August 1542 the church of Westminster and its estates remained wholly within the control of the court of augmentations, the government department set up to receive monastic property. Although the dean and chapter were legally constituted in December 1540, until they received their second patent 20 months later they could make no leases, appoint no estate officials and exercise no ecclesiastical patronage. Throughout this period the finances were managed by John Carleton, a particular receiver of augmentations, who was to become the dean and chapter's steward of lands. He had long served the monastic administration, and was himself one of the abbey's tenants.[13] He was assisted by Moulton, an even more important agent of administrative continuity, and by Thomas Mildmay, an auditor of augmentations who would likewise serve the dean and chapter.[14]

---

[10] PRO, E 315/249, f. 53v (*LP*, xvi, 745 (p. 361)). The principal inventory is PRO, LR 2/111, ff. 1–55 of which the contents of the church (ff. 1–34v) were printed in full in M. Walcott, 'The inventories of Westminster Abbey at the dissolution', *TLMAS*, iv (1873), 313–56; the contents of the conventual buildings etc. (ff. 35–55), of which Walcott gave only selections, were printed in full in Robinson, *Abbot's House*, 30–50. PRO, E 117/11/59 (*LP*, xiv, I, 889) is a duplicate of the first section of the Abbot's House inventory (Robinson, pp. 30–40). PRO, E 117/10/30, ff. 1–1v is a further list of church ornaments delivered to the king.

[11] Harvey, *Estates*, 26–31; cf. maps on pp. 471–4.

[12] *Valor Ecclesiasticus temp. Henrici VIII*, ed. J. Caley and J. Hunter (1810–34), i, 424. Harvey, *Estates*, 62–3.

[13] WAM 6478, f. 4v; 22710, 22717; Reg. II, ff. 292, 296v, 297, 301–2. W.C. Richardson, *History of the Court of Augmentations, 1536–1554* (Baton Rouge 1961), 49, 81, 221.

[14] Moulton occurs as joint-receiver with Carleton in 1540/1, though in October 1542 he is called merely Carleton's servant: WAM 37041, m. 30d. PRO, SC 6/Hen. VIII/2414, insert at f. 10. He had been Abbot Boston's steward; he succeeded Russell as receiver-general to the dean and chapter in effect from 1543 and by patent from 1544: WAM 33332, 37043, f. 2. *Acts 1543–1609*, nos 24 & n. 48, 31. For Mildmay

Under the augmentations management the Westminster estates were provided with a centralized financial system, replacing the multiple accountability which had characterized the greater monasteries, and which continued in the old secular cathedrals. The monastic obedientiary system, in which revenue and expenditure were channelled through several independent departments headed by senior monks, had since the fourteenth century frequently been modified by concentrating these offices in the (supposedly) most competent hands.[15] At Westminster, Abbot Boston had held the obedience of keeper of the new work (that is, the building of the nave) in the years 1532/3 and 1533/4, and the separate obediences of cellarer and keeper of the Lady Chapel 1535/6. In 1536/7, and perhaps previously, he was domestic treasurer.[16] The last appointment was in accord with, if not actually consequent upon, directions from Cromwell as vice-gerent, confirmed by the king 11 July 1536, permitting the abbot to assume direct control of the house's finances.[17] The interregnum between dissolution and refoundation enabled the crown's offices to advance this process. The new foundations which emerged had simpler and more efficient procedures, in line with those of late medieval collegiate churches and the university colleges.[18]

The first ministers' accounts for the Westminster estate under crown management were for the year to Michaelmas 1540, and so included the last quarter of the monastic regime. Receipts from the formerly distinct portions of the abbot and the convent were pooled, and listed by counties (conforming to augmentations standard). The only relic of the monastic system was in the urban rents in London and Westminster, which were still structured under the defunct titles of prior, sacrist, almoner, domestic treasurer, keeper of the Lady Chapel, chamberlain,

---

see WAM 6478, f. 13v; *Hist. Parl. 1509–58,* ii, 600–1. Richardson, *Augmentations,* 55 and *passim.*

[15] M.D. Knowles, *The Religious Orders in England* (Cambridge 1948–59), ii, 328–30. Cf. Harvey, *Estates,* 93. R.B. Dobson, *Durham Priory, 1400–1450* (Cambridge 1973), 67–8. For contrary trends cf. Dobson in Collinson *et al., Canterbury Cathedral,* 127–9; A. Oakley in Yates and Welsby, *Faith and Fabric,* 48.

[16] Pearce, *Monks,* 190.

[17] WAM 12787. Cf. Westlake, *Westminster Abbey,* ii, 199–200.

[18] For the old foundations see K. Edwards, *The English Secular Cathedrals in the Middle Ages* (2nd edn, Manchester 1967), 216–43; D.N. Lepine, *A Brotherhood of Canons serving God. English Secular Cathedrals in the later Middle Ages* (Woodbridge 1995), 180–1. For collegiate systems cf. A.K.B. Roberts, *St George's Chapel, Windsor Castle, 1348–1416. A study in early Collegiate Administration* (Windsor [1947]), 219–36; A.B. Cobban, *The King's Hall within the University of Cambridge in the later Middle Ages* (Cambridge 1969), 112–47.

and keeper of the new work.[19] These divisions remained in the accounts until at least Michaelmas 1542.[20]

Up to this point the court of augmentations was also responsible for paying for the upkeep of the church and the salaries of its ministers. Seven quarterly accounts of payments to the chapter and other members of the collegiate body run from Christmas 1540 to Michaelmas 1542.[21] From these we learn something of the arrival of outside appointees to join the ex-monks and others who remained from the monastic establishment. Only one member of the new chapter who had not been a monk was paid for the first quarter of the new foundation (to Lady Day 1541); this was Gerard Carleton, the administrator's brother, who was himself one of the first to handle internal disbursements.[22] Only half the complement of twelve minor canons was present at the foundation; likewise only six of the twelve singingmen (lay vicars) and four of the ten boy choristers. It would be a year before all these places were filled. The lay singers already in place at Christmas 1540 must have transferred from the abbey's Lady Chapel choir.[23]

There were also departures. Four lay brethren were still on the payroll at Christmas 1540; two were gone by March, and the others cease to be named after Michaelmas 1541. The 1540–2 accounts also name (in all) nineteen almsmen and women who were on the foundation of Henry VII; the actual establishment for a priest, twelve men and three women. The priest, Thomas Ballard, and twelve of the men would become almsmen on the new foundation, but there was no place for the women. Two of them, Anne Jurye and Agnes Byrd, are actually listed with the almsmen in the first collegiate treasurer's account (Michaelmas–Christmas 1542) but their names are deleted and no payment is recorded there. They received pensions of £6 13s 4d apiece, the same rate as their former stipends, paid out of those Westminster Abbey revenues which were *not* returned to the dean and chapter in 1542.[24] It is instructive to see that these humble

---

[19] PRO, SC 6/Hen. VIII/2415 (2416 and 2417 in this series are drafts). For the abbot's lands see B.F. Harvey, 'The leasing of the abbot of Westminster's demesnes in the later middle ages', *EcHR*, 2nd ser. xxii (1969), 17–27. For the grouping of former monastic lands into county receiverships cf. G.R. Elton, *The Tudor Revolution in Government* (Cambridge 1953), 206–7.

[20] PRO, SC 6/Hen. VIII/2414 is for 1541/2. 1540/1 is covered in WAM 37041, with receipts for the following year marginated. WAM 37038 is a summary of receipts 1539–42.

[21] PRO, LR 2/111, ff. 56–76.

[22] *Ibid.*, f. 56. Cf. WAM 37039 and *Acts 1543–1609*, no. 98 n. 29.

[23] See Lehmberg, below, pp. 94.

[24] WAM 37045, f. 4. PRO, SC 6/Hen. VIII/2421, m. 5d. Cf. Harvey, *Living and Dying*, 215 n. 3. The duties of Henry VII's almsfolk are in *CCR 1500–9*, nos 389(xi), 390 (pp.

women, to whom a useful role was given as an adjunct to the Benedictine monastery, were unacceptable in the collegiate foundation.

Three drafts for the complete new collegiate body survive. These 'erection books' (to which equivalent documents exist for a number of the other new foundations) list the proposed holders of offices, and are therefore distinct from and developments of the draft 'schemes' listing the offices only.[25] There are considerable variations between the earlier of the two schemes for Westminster and the eventual establishment. The most striking apparent change is in the dean's stipend, which rises from £50 *per annum* in the first scheme to £232 10s in the second, and which was the sum actually settled. The latter figure comprises £40 *corpus* (the basic stipend) and a 10s quotidian (a daily allowance notionally given for 365 days). It is likely that the quotidian was accidentally omitted in the first draft, and the revision may therefore have been slightly downwards. Equivalent reductions were made for the other members of the chapter: the canons' allocation was reduced from £480 (i.e. £40 each *per annum*) to £339 (i.e. £28 5s each, which is known from later usage to be computed at 365 quotidians of 1s and a £10 minimum *corpus*).[26] Sixty scholars were originally projected, but only forty were established. The budget for the university studentships was also cut from a suggested £200 to an eventual £166 13s 4d *per annum*. However there was an increase in the number of and allocation for minor canons, from 8 to 12, in all from £80 to £120 *per annum*. The creation of these additional places for inferior clergy is a reminder that the Henrician foundations took place within a liturgical and ecclesiastical framework untouched by protestantism. Intercessory prayer was actually given an increased budget, and education a reduced one, as the foundation was shaped.

146–7, 151–4). For the subsequent foundation cf. L.E. T[anner], 'The queen's almsmen', *One. Westminster Abbey Occasional Paper*, no. 23 (Dec. 1969), 9–10.

[25] For Westminster the two main schemes are PRO, E 314/24, ff. 5–6, 36–7 (*LP*, xiv, II, 429), printed in H. Cole, *King Henry the Eighth's Scheme of Bishopricks* (1838), 4–6, 34–5. The erection books are: (1) BL, Add. MS 40061, ff. 2–7v; (2) PRO, E 315/24, ff. 81–86v (*LP*, xvi, 333); (3) WAM 6478. Books (2) and (3) are identical and appear to have been drawn up between 5 and 25 March 1541; book (1) dates from about Christmas 1540: Knighton, 'Collegiate foundations', 37–40. Lists of the erection books for the group of new foundations are in PRO, E 315/24, f. 80v; SP 1/154, f. 94v (*LP*, xiv, II, 429, 430(2)). The only dated example appears to be that for Winchester, 28 April 1541 (cf. dates of foundation and endowment above, n. 9), printed in *Documents relating to the Foundation of the Chapter of Winchester, A.D. 1541–1547*, ed. G.W. Kitchin and F.T. Madge (Hampshire Record Soc. i, 1889), 54–8. Lehmberg, *Reformation of Cathedrals*, 90, gives a tabular synopsis of the two main schemes for Westminster and the establishment in books (2) and (3).

[26] Cf. *Acts 1543–1609*, i, pp. xxix–xxx.

That the liturgical observance was unbroken throughout this period of change is demonstrated by accounts of payments by the crown for the necessaries of worship from 16 January 1540, the day the abbey surrendered. In each of the three following quarters 5,000 communion wafers were bought at 8d the thousand, and in all three quarters a total of 45 gallons of red wine for masses. Box and palm for Palm Sunday, rushes for the floor of the choir on Easter Day, and wax for candles, particularly at the obit of Henry VII on May 11 are among the purchases. The most expensive acquisitions were a 'legend and processionalles' for which John Bray, fishmonger, and several London stationers were paid £4 15s.[27] The Henry VII obit took place as usual again in 1541 and 1542, attended by the lord chancellor. By this time the dean and chapter were in existence, but the government remained the paymaster.[28]

The extent to which the crown may have enjoyed financial advantage by deferring so long the endowment of the new dean and chapter is uncertain. The benefit cannot have been so direct and ample as was to be had from keeping a bishopric vacant, a device to which Queen Elizabeth was particularly disposed.[29] Any such saving in the first two years in this case must have been quite incidental.[30] The history of the other new foundations shows no significant delay between foundation and endowment; there was no general policy in withholding the latter until all or most vacant posts were filled. Two features of the Westminster refoundation, however, distinguish it from its cousins. One is the extraordinary geographical spread of the estates surrendered by the abbey and, in very large part, restored to the successor foundation. It is possible that this placed an exceptional administrative burden on the officials of augmentations, though no evidence can be offered to support this suggestion. The second distinction of the Westminster foundation was in its support of the ten university readers in addition

---

[27] PRO, E 314/22/1.

[28] PRO, E 315/250, ff. 44–44v; E 323/2B, pt 1, m. 76 (*LP*, xvii, 258 (p. 135); xviii, II, 231 (p. 124)). Cf. *Acts 1543–1609*, no. 78 n. 26; but the anniversary celebrated was that of the king's burial not of his death: *CCR 1500–9*, no. 389(iv) (p. 142). Cf. WAM 37573.

[29] J.E.C. Hill, *Economic Problems of the Church. From Archbishop Whitgift to the Long Parliament* (Oxford 1956), 15–17. F.M. Heal, *Of Prelates and Princes. A Study of the Economic and Social Position of the Tudor Episcopate* (Cambridge 1980), 277, 276.

[30] Stipends had reached the figure allowed in the erection book (£296 17s 6d per quarter) by Midsummer 1542: PRO, LR 2/111, ff. 56–76. University readers and students did not reach their full complement until Michaelmas 1543, resulting in a saving of *c.* £350: WAM 6478, ff. 2, 3; 37043, ff. 11v, 12. The court of augmentations authorized a sum of £200 in February 1544 to cover legal and administrative expenses: PRO, E 315/104, ff. 77v–78. The total saving to the crown can be estimated between *c.* £668 and *c.* £983.

to their quota of students. The readers' stipends amounted to £400 *per annum*, almost a fifth of the whole allowance for the foundation. The protracted and piecemeal fashion in which these posts were filled might well have contributed to uncertainties about the funding needed for Westminster, and have delayed the endowment patent as a consequence.[31]

There were therefore two phases to the Westminster foundation; from the surrender to the foundation (January–December 1540), and from then until the endowment (August 1542). It has been shown that even in the first of these periods the *opus dei* did not, as some have supposed, cease to be performed.[32] Nor were these months empty of incident.

The most notable occasion within the precinct of the Abbey between dissolution and refoundation had been the joint session of the convocations of Canterbury and York which ratified the nullity of the king's marriage to Anne of Cleves. These proceedings took place in the Chapter House on 7–9 July 1540, and among those present were the former abbot and three of the ex-monks who would join him as founding members of the secular chapter (Dalyons, H. Perkyns and Baxter). Also there were several of the other future canons, but so were most of the senior clergy in the country. More significant is the first certain appearance here of Thomas Thirlby as 'elect of Westminster'.[33] He had not been the original choice, because Richard Sampson had minuted on one of the draft schemes of the new foundations (late 1539 or early 1540) that he accepted translation from his existing see of Chichester.[34] It has been supposed that Sampson was actually so promoted; but this rests entirely on the report of the French ambassador Charles de Marillac,

---

[31] During the Westminster funding of the readerships only Thomas Wakefield's appointment to the Hebrew chair at Cambridge can be pinpointed: PRO, SP 1/164, f. 77 (*LP*, xvi, 365); Sir Richard Rich, joint-chancellor of augmentations to John Carleton authorizing payment of the stipend from revenues of the house of Westminster 29 December 1540. Wakefield's patent (not enrolled) was dated 9 November: F.D. Logan, 'The origins of the so-called regius professorships: an aspect of the Renaissance in Oxford and Cambridge', in *Renaissance and Renewal in Christian History*, ed. D. Baker (Studies in Church History, xiv, Oxford 1977), 276. For Oxford see G.D. Duncan, 'Public lectures and professorial chairs', in *The Collegiate University*, ed. J.K. McConica (History of the University of Oxford, iii, Oxford 1986), 343–5, 352–3, 354–5, 356, 358–9.

[32] Cf. contrary assumptions in Westlake, *Westminster Abbey*, i, 208; A. Tindal Hart in Carpenter, *House of Kings*, 110.

[33] PRO, E 30/1470, ff. 3, 4v (*LP*, xv, 861). Thirlby's elevation is further evident from his vacation of the prebend of Yetminster I in Salisbury Cathedral by 15 July: *LP*, xv, 942(90).

[34] PRO, E 314/24, ff. 35–35v.

writing on 1 June 1540 that 'en ung mesme jour le doyen de la chappelle, évesque de Chichester fut faict de Valmaister (*sic*), en print possession avec toute solempnité' a few hours before he was taken to the Tower accused of treason. Sampson was arrested by 28 May.[35] He was saved by Cromwell's fall immediately afterwards, but nothing more is heard of him in connexion with the see of Westminster. Whatever Marillac's account describes, it cannot be Sampson's enthronement as bishop of Westminster because at this time there was no such see. It is wholly implausible that the new see (and cathedral) had been erected by May 1540, then the whole process abandoned and the documentation lost, to be repeated in December. In none of the other new foundations which were also new sees (Bristol, Chester, Gloucester, Peterborough and Oseney) was there any apparent anticipation of the single patents by which bishoprics and cathedrals were founded and the bishops, deans and canons nominated. Until then, their prospective bishops (whether they were to be translated or newly raised to the episcopate) could only be 'elect' in the sense that the king had chosen them; there were no chapters in place to make formal election.[36] By appointing the new foundation bishops in his letters patent, Henry VIII anticipated the enactment in the next reign by which the charade of capitular election was abolished, albeit temporarily.[37] The Westminster chapter therefore never exercised this function.

Two days after his eventual appointment, on 19 December 1540, Thirlby was consecrated in Henry VII's chapel.[38] The bishopric was

---

[35] *Correspondance politique de MM. de Castillon et de Marillac, Ambassadeurs de France en Angleterre (1537–1542)*, ed. J. Kaulek (Paris 1885), 187 [editor's *sic*] (*LP*, xv, 737). Cf. J.G. Ridley, *Thomas Cranmer* (1962), 201; T.F. Shirley, *Thomas Thirlby. Tudor Bishop* (1964), 30–1. Against this it is argued that Thirlby appears to be named to Westminster in April 1540: H.A. Kelly, *The Matrimonial Trials of Henry VIII* (Stanford CA 1976), 267 n. 8, citing *LP*, Add., 1457 [PRO, SP 1/243, f. 49]; but the date in *LP* is editorial, and Thirlby's name is supplied where the MS is torn (so is not necessarily original). Note also that Marillac, writing on 11 June, refers to Sampson still as bishop of Chichester: Kaulek, 190, given in *CSP Span.* vi, I, 539. Cf. G.R. Elton, 'Thomas Cromwell's decline and fall', repr. in *Studies in Tudor and Stuart Politics and Government* (Cambridge 1974–92), i, 219 & n. 2.

[36] For the southern province see Le Neve, *1541–1857*, vii, 69; viii, 9, 40, 75, 115. For Chester cf. R.V.H. Burne, *Chester Cathedral. From its founding by Henry VIII to the Accession of Queen Victoria* (1958), 1–2. The new bishops of Chester and Oxford were translated from other sees. No episcopal vacancies occurred in existing sees while their cathedrals were without chapters; the surrender of Rochester priory may have been delayed to avert such complication: Yates and Welsby, *Faith and Fabric*, 58. Cf. Thompson, *Statutes of Durham*, p. xxxix.

[37] 1 Edw. VI c. 2 (*SR*, iv, I, 3–4).

[38] LPL, Reg. Cranmer, ff. 260v-261. Guildhall MS 9531/12, f. 251. Shirley in *Thirlby*, 34 wrongly locates the consecration in St Stephen's Chapel, Westminster.

endowed on 21 January 1541.[39] The record of his administration begins on 7 February, and includes (22 June) a commission for trial of criminous clerks to take place in the Abbey, and to which six of the new canons were appointed.[40] But the new bishop's association with his cathedral and its chapter would be slight. He moved into the former Abbot's House (so that the ex-abbot had to make the next-best residence his Deanery) where he was connected to the collegiate plumbing.[41] He had little use of it, because throughout his tenure of the see he was chiefly employed on diplomatic service abroad. He was not even present in the Abbey for the coronation of Edward VI.[42] His absenteeism, albeit honourable, undoubtedly contributed to the failure of the diocese of Westminster to establish itself as a useful unit. Its administration remained in part in the hands of officials of the diocese of London from which it had been created, and to which in 1550 it would return.[43]

Dean Benson, as he had become, has left scarcely more of a mark on the Abbey. His reputation has been poor, largely because as abbot he is thought to have connived at a loosening of monastic discipline by way of preparing for surrender. Doubtless this is true. He has also been criticized for entering into a disadvantageous exchange of property with the crown in 1536. But when lay magnates, even one so close to the king as the duke of Suffolk, could be painfully squeezed by Henry's handshake, Benson cannot be blamed for the surrender of some of the Westminster estate for less valuable country lands.[44] He was, moreover, a lifelong friend of Cranmer, Hugh Latimer and other reformers, which does not suggest that he was an ignoble figure.[45] His appointment as abbot in 1533 broke a succession of internal promotions dating back to 1222, which must have unsettled the Westminster community. He was no longer an 'obscure monk of Peterborough',[46] but the abbot of Burton-upon-Trent, having already received the distinction of being the first

---

[39] WAM LXXXII (*LP*, xvi, 503(33)). WAM 6484A is an abstract. Robinson, *Abbot's House*, 24–6, prints and comments on an extract.

[40] Guildhall MS 9531/12, ff. 243, 251.

[41] *Acts 1543–1609*, no. 11.

[42] *CSPD EdVI*, no. 10.

[43] For some detail of Thirlby's administration see P. Ayris, 'Preaching the last crusade: Thomas Cranmer and the "Devotion" money of 1543', *JEH*, xlix (1998), 684–5, 697–700.

[44] Harvey, *Estates*, 337–8. A. Tindal Hart in Carpenter, *House of Kings*, 107–10. Cf. H. Miller, *Henry VIII and the English Nobility* (Oxford 1986), 218–19, 248–9. S.J. Gunn, *Charles Brandon, Duke of Suffolk, 1484–1545* (Oxford 1988), 135–7.

[45] D.N.J. MacCulloch, *Thomas Cranmer. A Life* (1996), 20, 94, 136, 364, 369, 613.

[46] A. Tindal Hart in Carpenter, *House of Kings*, 107.

head of that house to sit in the House of Lords.[47] It seems likely that he was moved to Burton and summoned to parliament precisely in order to make him eligible for transfer to the abbacy of Westminster when this became available. Here we may detect the hand of Cranmer as well as that of Cromwell; the two old Cambridge friends rose to their respective eminences together, Cranmer being consecrated to Canterbury on 30 March 1533, and Benson being elected abbot of Westminster on 10 April.[48]

At some point between the surrender and the following summer Benson asked Cromwell to relieve him of his office:

> ... devyse suche wayse that I may be delyvered from the cure and to me the unportable borden in governance of this house in suche sorte as the kynges majestyes indignation be avoyded from me ... my feblenes is suche by reason of dyverse most grevouse dyseases that I know well taryng here I shall not only have a very short paynfull bodlye lyeff, but also put my soule in dawnger.

He cared not how little pension he might receive, 'so y may have the kynges hyghnes my gracyouse lord, for as Paule sayth *scio habundare et scio penuriam pati*'.[49] This must date after 16 January 1540 because he signs himself as Benson and 'quondam of Westminster', and it has to be before Cromwell's arrest on 10 June. In fact it may well have prompted Cromwell's memorandum as to what the king 'will have ffeder don' with the former abbot of Westminster.[50] Benson did (by 1541/2) obtain a pension of £110 16s 8d in addition to his deanery.[51] What the letter to Cromwell does show is that Benson remained head of the Westminster community. This was in keeping with the general instructions for the conversion of abbeys or priories into cathedrals or colleges; in some cases the former abbot or prior (be he prospective dean or bishop) was

---

[47] J.E. Powell and K. Wallis, *The House of Lords in the Middle Ages* (1968), 568. Pearce (*Monks*, 189) was misled by Benson's connexions with Peterborough to suppose him to have been abbot there. But it is clear that he migrated from Peterborough Abbey to Burton where he was elected abbot 21 March 1531 (date of petition for king's assent to election): *LP*, v, 166(53), 278(25). Cf. *CPR 1548–9*, 159.

[48] The petition of the prior and convent for the king's assent to Benson's election is dated 10 April 1533: *LP*, vi, 417(21); date of petition assumed as in case of Burton (above) to be that of election itself. Temporalities were restored the following day. Pearce (*Monks*, 189–90) knew only the date of Benson's oath to uphold Henry VII's foundation, 12 May [*LP*, vi, 472].

[49] PRO, SP 1/157, f. 59 (*LP*, xv, 70), printed in *Original Letters illustrative of English History*, ed. H. Ellis (1824–46), 3rd ser. iii, 272–3. The quotation (from Philippians 4: 12) is imprecise.

[50] BL, Cotton MS Titus B.I, f. 435v (old f. 427) (*LP*, xv, 322); undated.

[51] PRO, E 315/235, f. 74 (*LP*, xvii, 1258 (p. 694)).

constituted warden of an interim establishment.[52] This is most evident at Peterborough, where the ex-abbot and future bishop, John Chamber, was in administrative charge of the church for the whole period from surrender to refoundation.[53] At Westminster, as has been shown, financial control was entirely in the crown's hands during the equivalent period, and it cannot have been 'governance' of this nature which Benson sought to relinquish. Perhaps he was merely asking to decline the deanery which was in prospect.

It cannot be said that his eventual application to this task was vigorous. The record he left, in the Chapter Act Book he kept in his own hand, is untidy and haphazard.[54] He was, however, apparently resident more or less permanently, despite a dispensation to be absent for all but three months in the year while receiving his 10s quotidian as if present.[55] In January 1543 he was, perhaps unknowingly, recommended by Sir Edward North (joint-chancellor of augmentations) for a canonry at Peterborough should one become vacant by promotion to the deanery there.[56] The opportunity did not arise, and Benson had no other benefice. He must, however, have been adequately supported by his stipend and pension, as when he died in 1549 he left over £600 in cash. As well as his decanal residences he had private houses in Long Ditch, Westminster and at Peterborough, and his will includes bequests to Cranmer, Thirlby, Latimer and Paul Fagius.[57] The first dean of Westminster was a man of consequence and respectable association.

Of the six ex-monks who joined Benson in the secular chapter from December 1540, all but one were gone within six years.[58] John Rumney

---

[52] PRO, E 36/116, ff. 8v-10v (*LP*, xiv, I, 1189). The interim structures varied from place to place; in some an informal college was formed: Knowles, *Religious Orders*, iii, 390–2. But the substance of these arrangements should not be over-stated, or the subsequent change to cathedral establishment appears an alteration not a progression, as implied in the case of Gloucester: G. Baskerville, *English Monks and the Suppression of the Monasteries* (1937), 183–4.

[53] *The Last Days of Peterborough Monastery*, ed. W.T. Mellows (Northamptonshire Record Soc. xii, 1947 for 1940), pp. xc–xcviii, 33–49, 114–28, printing Chamber's accounts.

[54] *Acts 1543–1609*, i, p. xxxvii & n. 84.

[55] *CPR 1547–8*, 163–4.

[56] PRO, SP 1/182, f. 204 (*LP*, xviii, II, App. 2).

[57] PRO, PROB 11/32, ff. 290–291v. For his Peterborough property see Mellows, *Peterborough Monastery*, 71 & n. 5, 79, 88; *The Foundation of Peterborough Cathedral, A.D. 1541*, ed. W.T. Mellows (Northamptonshire Record Soc. xiii, 1941 for 1939), pp. xxvii, xliv.

[58] For biographical data generally see Le Neve, *1541–1857*, vii, 69 x 83. Knighton, 'Collegiate foundations', 374 x 407. *Acts 1543–1609*, i, pp. xl–xli.

was dead before the end of 1541, Baxter died in 1542, Dalyons and Harvey in 1544. Thomas Elfred resigned in 1546 and died later in the year, asking to be buried by the old procession way.[59] The only survivor of this group was Humphrey Perkyns, who retained his stall until deprived for marriage in 1554. He returned in 1560 as a canon of the second collegiate church, as which he died in 1577. He, Baxter and Dalyons had been monk-students at Oxford. Perkyns (then called Charity) associated with Robert Joseph, the humanist letter-writer of Evesham Abbey.[60] The other three ex-monks were without such background; indeed, they constitute the majority of non-graduate canons of Westminster that there have ever been.[61] More significantly these three had no other livings after they became canons. Even the Oxford-educated ex-monks had only parochial livings derived from Westminster's own patronage. The relatively quick disappearance of these men from the chapter contrasts with patterns elsewhere: at Durham, for example, the ex-monastic element lent a mediocre character to the new foundation for a generation.[62]

By contrast the canons appointed to Westminster in 1540 from outside were already highly placed. Simon Haynes was dean of Exeter and a canon of Windsor; John Redman was warden of the King's Hall at Cambridge and much else besides; Edward Leighton, a canon of the successive foundations of Cardinal and Henry VIII's College, Oxford, was also clerk of the closet; Anthony Bellasis was a chancery master with a string of benefices, chiefly in the north; William Britten was a prebendary of Lincoln. Gerard Carleton was the only one of this group

---

[59] LMA, DL/C/355, ff. 96v–97.

[60] *The Letter Book of Robert Joseph*, ed. J.C.H. Aveling and W.A. Pantin (Oxford Historical Soc., new ser. xix, 1967 for 1964), 233–4, 272. Perkyns was DD, Baxter *alias* Essex BD. Dalyons, though at Oxford, apparently did not graduate. He is accorded BD (1522) in Foster, *Alumni Oxon.* ii, 368, followed in Pearce, *Monks*, 183, but only the *supplicat* (1519) is given in *Register of the University of Oxford*, i, *1449–63, 1505–71*, ed. C.W. Boase (Oxford Historical Soc. i, 1885), 111. No degree information appears in A.B. Emden, *A Biographical Register of the University of Oxford, A.D. 1501 to 1540* (Oxford 1974), 159; *q.v.* pp. 113, 193 for Perkyns (Cheryte) and Baxter (Essex). No degree is given Dalyons in the foundation charter, and on institution to Launton (Oxon.) 20 Dec. 1540 he is called only 'Magister': Lincolnshire Archives, Episcopal Reg. 27, f. 198. Cf. Le Neve, *1541–1857*, vii, 76.

[61] Only two subsequent canons were non-graduate: Alphonso de Salinas (1554–6) and William Young (1560–79). The 1544 statutes required all canons to be graduate, but the ex-monks were appointed before this rule was made; see *Statutes (1)*, 82.

[62] D. Marcombe, 'The Durham dean and chapter: old abbey writ large?', in *Continuity and Change. Personnel and Administration of the Church in England, 1500–1642* ed. M.R. O'Day and F.M. Heal (Leicester 1976), 130, 135–7. Cf. R. Houlbrooke in Atherton *et al.*, *Norwich Cathedral*, 514–15, 518.

not previously beneficed above parish level; in 1543 he would add the deanery of Peterborough to his holdings.[63]

Of these, Leighton's was perhaps the most turbulent career. After his spell in Wolsey's College he appears to have become brother then prior of the collegiate hospital of St John in Ludlow. By 1532 he was back at what would become Christ Church. In 1540 he was sent to Calais to preach Henry VIII's gospel to the French. From there he wrote on 14 April asking Cromwell to fulfil a promise made two years before for the rectory of Islip. Cromwell and another had been given the right of next presentation to this Westminster Abbey living by the abbot and convent in 1531. Cromwell (who had other problems with the Calais mission) never acted on Leighton's behalf, and Islip went to another man. Although continuing to enjoy the king's favour (as the appointment to Westminster in December 1540 demonstrates) Leighton was obliged, in November 1544, to assign his Westminster stipend to two London mercers. Despite or because of this he was in prison for debt two years later; he then simply sold his canonry to Edward Keble, chaplain to the earl of Hertford.[64] Leighton subsequently alleged that Keble had forged the deed, thereby defaulting on his payment. Leighton failed to prevent Keble being installed in his place, and so lost his canonry and his cash. He lived just long enough to see Keble's patron, who had become duke of Somerset and lord protector, ejected from office. Keble then found trouble of his own.[65]

As the ex-monastic membership of the chapter decreased, its collective distinction rose. Among the canons of the first collegiate church, Nicholas Ridley (1545–53) and Edmund Grindal (1552–4) are pre-eminent. Neither played a significant part in the Abbey's life; indeed Ridley seems not to have attended a single chapter meeting during his tenure. For such men the Westminster stall was a temporary posting on the path to higher command. There would always be a distinction in the chapter between them and those to whom the canonry was their career peak. It was from the latter group that the domestic officers of treasurer and steward were most often chosen, and to whom much of the routine business fell. Those with administrative experience would be pressed into service as available – especially in dealings with higher authority. Thus, at an early chapter meeting (29 March 1543) Dean Benson had to decide an issue with his old monk-colleagues Elfred and Perkyns, and

---

[63] For Redman see below, pp. 38–74.

[64] PRO, SP 1/159, ff. 82–3 (*LP*, xv, 514). WAM Reg. II, f. 277. Lincolnshire Archives, Episcopal Reg. 27, f. 198v. *Acts 1543–1609*, no. 28.

[65] WAM 9418 (Leighton to Bernard Sandiforth, canon, 13 May 1547). For Keble's nemesis see below, p. 83.

one other present, 'by causse ther wher no mo of prebendaris at home'. Elfred and Perkyns served as treasurer in three of the first four years of internal management (1542–6), and Elfred is the first known sub-dean. But it was Redman, Britten, and the equally competent Thomas Reynolds who were deputed to negotiate with the court of augmentations in the matter of an improved endowment.[66]

The endowment charter finally passed the great seal on 5 August 1542.[67] It provided a theoretical rental income of £2,598 3s 5d, against which were allowed certain bailiffs' fees, compensation for houses in the precinct to be occupied by the canons and which could therefore not be let, £60 for the observation of Henry VII's anniversary, £296 19s 4½d for tenths and certain other charges. From the residue the domestic stipends and fixed allowances, £2,167 10s in all, were payable, leaving approximately £23 clear which the dean and chapter was allowed for casual expenses and as compensation for decayed rents.[68]

Approximately 85% of the properties, accounting for £2,164 2s 2d of the rental, had belonged to Westminster Abbey. The remainder came from other dissolved houses: Merton (Surrey), Mountgrace (Yorks.), Pershore and Evesham (Worcs.), Newstead (Notts.), Grimsby (from both the Austin friars and the Austin canonesses), Haverholme and Bardney (Lincs.). In most cases these new accessions were close to old Westminster properties. The dean and chapter's estates, therefore, while not so extensive as those of the abbey, were equally diverse. It was particularly important to secure information about the new properties, and an early search was made for 'evydence' relating to the former Mountgrace lands.[69] A further complication was that some of the abbey's original archives had been abstracted by augmentations officials during the interregnum; according to Dean Benson's later recollection, Thomas Mildmay had failed to return one of the registers.[70]

Only when the estate came within the dean and chapter's control could their business properly begin. An early start was made by surveying the immediately surrounding houses on 23 October 1542. Most were conventionally described as 'ruinous' and some, more alarmingly, as 'ready to fall'. A further survey of the Westminster tenements was

---

[66] *Acts 1543–1609*, nos 3, 31, 41, 46. WAM 37045, 37060, 37064.

[67] WAM LXXXV (*LP*, xvii, 714(5)). The dean and chapter paid £4 for an enrolment: WAM 37043, f. 12v. Valors are in WAM 6478, ff. 6–14v; PRO, SP 1/243, ff. 141–145v (*LP*, Add., ii, 1478(2); PRO, E 315/24, ff. 87–93v (*LP*, xvi, 333(2); PRO, E 315/426.

[68] WAM 6478, ff. 6–14v; the calculation is imperfect.

[69] WAM 37047, f. 5.

[70] PRO, C 24/27, f. 6. Cf. *Acts 1543–1609*, no. 9.

made on 25 November.[71] Inspection of the country properties would have to wait for the spring. Meanwhile, and only now, some elementary equipment was acquired. A chapter seal was bought for £12, paid in two instalments, 6 January and 27 June 1542. Parchment was bought for a register of leases, and this was bound in the course of the financial year (1542/3).[72] The first entry is a lease of 12 February 1543, but the earliest is one of 7 September 1542, just over a month after the chapter had the authority to make such a grant. It was in favour of Griffin Tyndale, an augmentations auditor who had drawn up the Westminster erection book.[73] At about the same time the chapter acquired a ready-bound paper volume of 300 pages which became their first Act Book.[74] The first meeting this now records is of 3 March [1543]. Because preceding pages have been cut away, we cannot tell when meetings began or were first recorded; a later entry refers back to one of 2 March. Since the rear of the volume was begun as a register of sealing fees on 10 February 1543, it is reasonable to assume that the main series of acts began at about the same time.[75] The 3 March entry prescribes three daily masses and a weekly chapter. It is not to be supposed that the dean and chapter, having been in office for over two years, had only just turned their minds to the ordering of the liturgy. Their attention may have been focused by reforms then under discussion in convocation.[76] But it may simply be that, having opened their Act Book, they decided to use it to codify existing practice.

The first estate business occurs in the Act Book on 5 March, when auditing of accounts is the chief concern. Bellasis was appointed surveyor and instructed to set out with the steward of the lands in the second week in April to hold manorial courts and compound with copyhold tenants. After briefly noting that sermons should be given in the Abbey every Sunday (and this does not appear to be a retrospective ruling), the chapter ordered that the new seal, the charters and other archives should be kept securely in the treasury.[77]

Bellasis made a preliminary trip to Godmanchester (Hunts.) and Grantham (Lincs.) in mid-March, but his first main progress did not

---

[71] WAM 37036.

[72] WAM 37046, ff. 2v, 4v, 6v, 7.

[73] WAM Reg. III, ff. 1–2v, 3v–5. WAM 6478, f. 7v.

[74] WAM Chapter Act Book I, printed in *Acts 1543–1609*. For description of the MS and dating of its opening entries see *ibid.* i, pp. xxi, xxiv–xxv.

[75] *Ibid.* i, 7, 8, 108.

[76] Cf. S.E. Lehmberg, *The Later Parliaments of Henry VIII, 1536–1547* (Cambridge 1977), 184. MacCulloch, *Cranmer*, 301. Bellasis was the chapter's proctor in convocation: WAM 37046, f. 4v.

[77] *Acts 1543–1609*, no. 2.

begin until 1 May. This took him to Steventon (Berks.) by the 8th, and then on into the main western estate. Moving from one tenant's house to another (since the provision of such hospitality was generally an obligation), he was at Pershore from 14–18 May, reaching Worcester by the 24th. On his return he stayed again at Pershore and Evesham and passed through Islip, reaching Westminster in time for supper on 30 May. He kept an increasingly detailed account of his expenses, since everything (including 3d for apples and oranges at Tewkesbury and 5d for sugar and strawberries at Evesham) would be deductible. On 8 July he set off again to visit properties in Huntingdonshire, Rutland, Leicestershire and Lincolnshire, reaching Grimsby on 22 July, where sole, plaice and other fish enlivened his diet. He returned on or after 6 August, having spent £39 1s 9d on these three journeys.[78] For Master Bellasis this was a considerable time spent in a task for which he was somewhat over-qualified, and in the next two years there was a reappraisal of the chapter's administrative offices.

In these early years there is some ambiguity in the use of the terms treasurer, surveyor and receiver. Bellasis was called surveyor-general and receiver, while Elfred was surveyor of Westminster and Harvey surveyor of London.[79] Elfred was also, in 1542/3, partly responsible for the internal payments in what came to be specifically the treasurer's office, though he is called only 'paye maister' and acted with William Russell, clerk of the works.[80] Russell died in July 1543 and the final quarter's payments were made by John Moulton.[81] On 8 March the chapter had directed the dean and Bellasis to enter into negotiations with Moulton for a new appointment. On 2 October Moulton duly received a patent as receiver for life with a fee of £40 *per annum*. This post was confirmed on 20 January 1545, when a treasurer was also appointed. Thereafter the post of canon receiver became superfluous, and in 1549 the chapter would decide that no election to it was to be made during Moulton's tenure. After his death the receivership was briefly exercised by canons until a new appointment was made; but Moulton's prolonged tenure of the post clearly established it as a lay not a capitular office.[82]

The restructuring of offices in 1544/5 is also in consequence of the arrival of the king's statutes. These had been promised to all the new

---

[78] WAM 37048, ff. 5–11v.

[79] WAM 37046, ff, 4, 4v. *Acts 1543–1609*, nos 2, 6. Harvey's duties also took him to France to settle accounts for soldiers supplied to the duke of Norfolk's forces: WAM 37047, f. 7.

[80] WAM 37045, 37046.

[81] WAM 37043, ff. 2, 9–12v.

[82] *Acts 1543–1609*, nos 21, 31, 97, 212, 215.

foundation cathedrals in their foundation charters. The drafting of a uniform model set of statutes had been committed to the bishops of Chichester (George Day) and Worcester (Nicholas Heath) and the dean of Oxford (Richard Cox). None of these men had much experience of the old secular cathedrals, and the forms they devised reflect their backgrounds in university administration. Most of the cathedrals received their sets in the summer of 1544: Chester on 4 June, Ely and Winchester on 20 June, Rochester on 30 June, Worcester on 21 July.[83] A.H. Thompson, who was the first to make a comparative study of these documents, supposed that the apparent lack of Henrician statutes for Norwich and Oxford was the result of their special circumstances, and he suggested that Westminster was also omitted from the general distribution for 'other reasons'.[84] Henrician statutes have since been found at Norwich and Oxford, but there are still none for Westminster.[85] That they were expected is clear from the chapter's expressed concern on 10 February 1544 that 'there be as yet no certayn statutes' whereby 'certayn urgent busynesse dayly doth occur'. The internal accounts for 1544 record payments for 'the firste boke of the statutes for the colledge of Westm' (4s), then 'the secunde boke of statutes' (6s 8d), and finally 'wryttyng the boke of the statutes another tyme' (5s). And between the two latter entries, with one other intervening item, is a payment of 1s 7d 'for the bokes for the latenye in englysshe'.[86] The

---

[83] Thompson, *Statutes of Durham*, pp. xxxix–xl, dates for Chester and Worcester p. xl. The Winchester set is printed (from a near-contemporary copy) in Kitchin and Madge, *Documents*, 113–66 with translation and comment. Extracts from the Ely set (from an Elizabethan copy) are in D.M. Owen, *The Library and Muniments of Ely Cathedral* (Ely 1973), 12, and *The King's School, Ely*, ed. D.M. Owen and D. Thurley (Cambridge 1982), 35–43. For Rochester see Yates and Welsby, *Faith and Fabric*, 61 & n. 21. The most convenient edition is that for Peterborough, printed with translation and collation to Gloucester set in Mellows, *Peterborough Cathedral*, 75–121. This is referred to as *Statutes (1)* in my edition of the Westminster Acts and in the present volume. See generally Thompson, *Statutes of Durham*, pp. xxxviii–li; Lehmberg, *Reformation of Cathedrals*, 91–4.

[84] Thompson, *Statutes of Durham*, p. xl.

[85] For Norwich see R.A. Houlbrooke in Atherton *et al.*, *Norwich Cathedral*, 530; F. Meeres, *Guide to the Records of Norwich Cathedral* (Norwich 1998), 24. The set here is in the common format, but may not actually have been of effect since the dean and chapter had in their 1538 foundation been empowered to make statutes of their own. For Oxford see J.E.A. Dawson, 'The foundation of Christ Church, Oxford and Trinity College, Cambridge in 1546', *BIHR*, lvii (1984), 211 & n. 21; J.K. McConica, 'The rise of the undergraduate college', in McConica, *Collegiate University*, 33–4. These statutes, again in the common format, are believed to apply to a transitional foundation (1545–6) on the site now Christ Church.

[86] WAM 37047, ff. 5v, 8; 37048, f. 12v. Some of these entries appear to relate to the 35th year of Henry VIII (ending April 1544) but the adjacence of the references to the

English litany was issued in June 1544.[87] It therefore seems very likely that the Westminster statutes were delivered at much the same time as the others, and there is no reason to suppose that they differed in any marked way from the common form. On 15 December 1545 the chapter is said to have assembled 'according to the statutes' and proceeded to elect a vice-dean, receiver and treasurer from among themselves.[88]

In 1545 a major change in the king's educational policy ended the funding of university places by the new cathedral foundations. This obligation had been confirmed by the 1544 statutes; the decision to rescind it was probably taken after Cranmer (who had been having difficulties with his own new chapter at Canterbury, and that of Oxford), met Bishops Day, Heath and Thirlby at Lambeth in December 1544.[89] The co-opting of Thirlby to this group may have had prompt effect at Westminster, where by 1 February the chapter had received a letter from the king. In response they sent a deputation to Thirlby, Day and the chancellor of augmentations (North). On 13 March, clearly in consequence of this negotiation, the chapter sealed a grant of land to the crown in exoneration of their support for the twenty students at Oxford and Cambridge.[90] It does not seem that the three bishops and North had been formally appointed to oversee such transactions, though they would shortly be commissioned to deal with related matters.[91] But it was to them that the dean and chapter addressed a certificate, professing ignorance of the students' studies, and confident that their

---

litany (WAM 37047, f. 8; 37048, f. 13) points to the summer of 1544. Cf. MacCulloch, *Cranmer*, 328–30.

[87] It is likely that Westminster's purchase was of Berthelet's musical edition (*STC* 10619–21): Durham Cathedral acquired MSS of the litany in 3, 4 and 5 parts from the precentor of Westminster Abbey in 1544: *Extracts from the Account Rolls of the Abbey of Durham*, ed. J.T. Fowler, iii (Surtees Soc. ciii, 1901), 726.

[88] *Acts 1543–1609*, no. 46. That this entry indicates the reception of Westminster's Henrician statutes was first noted by J.A. R[obinson], *Notes regarding the earliest form of the Statutes of the Collegiate Church of St Peter, Westminster* (privately printed 1906), 3–4.

[89] MacCulloch, *Cranmer*, 336–7, amplifying my earlier account of the studentships: 'The provision of education in the new cathedral foundations of Henry VIII', in Marcombe and Knighton, *Close Encounters*, 25–35. The statutory provision is in *Statutes (1)*, 100–1 (but not in the translation of the relevant chapter at p. 119, having been deleted from the Peterborough MS from which this text is taken).

[90] *Acts 1543–1609*, nos 33, 39. In annotating the first entry I wrongly identified the bishop of Chichester as Day's predecessor Sampson.

[91] On 28 July 1545 Day, Heath, Thirlby and North were appointed by patent to enquire into the new foundations' spending on alms and road repairs; in 1546 the same four were empowered to nominate almsmen in all the king's foundations, for which task the king had no leisure: *LP*, xx, I, 1335(2); xxi, I, 970(16).

financial obligations to them had been discharged.[92] In July 1546 the chapter made further surrenders to the crown, ending their funding of the ten readerships.[93] In all £567 18s 11½d in rental was returned in 1545–6.[94]

In common with other chapters, Westminster felt it had been short-changed in these deals. Their loss in rental was a mere £1 5s 7½d; to this they added £10 8s 4d which they had paid to certain of the university students after Michaelmas 1544 (to which the surrender had been backdated) but before letters of discharge had been received from the crown. These claims formed part of a general submission for recompense for unleviable rents, charges not provided for in the erection book, and miscellaneous expenses – almost £400.[95] Deputations were sent to the court of augmentations on 29 April 1545 and 21 June 1547.[96] It was not until a new chancellor was appointed in 1550 that the cathedrals' complaints generally were considered; a small grant to Ely appears to have been the only result.[97]

For Westminster the ending of the university studentships and readerships cannot have been a 'heavy surrender', nor was it simply a cut in the crown's education budget.[98] Many of those who had been on the cathedrals' payrolls (at Westminster over half of those who can be traced) and much of the endowment passed directly to the king's new foundations, Christ Church, Oxford and Trinity College, Cambridge, in 1546–7. The Westminster readerships became the regius professorships.[99] Connexions between Westminster, Trinity and Christ Church, developed in the 1540s, would be made formal in 1560.

---

[92] WAM 43048; undated. Payments to most students had ended at the previous Michaelmas, but some had received further moneys up to the next Lady Day. Another account confirms that this was Lady Day 1545: WAM 37064, f. 4.

[93] WAM 18400; Reg. III, ff. 76v–77v.

[94] WAM 12960.

[95] WAM 6481–3, 43933; four drafts of the same petition with slight variations; confirming payments to students as in WAM 43048.

[96] Acts 1543–1609, nos 41, 64. The complaint related only to the lands surrendered for the students in March 1545. The 1546 surrender was considered fair.

[97] CSPD EdVI, no. 432. CPR 1550–3, 173–4.

[98] A. Tindal Hart in Carpenter, House of Kings, 117. Cf. Knowles, Religious Orders, iii, 389; J. Simon, Education and Society in Tudor England (Cambridge 1966), 184.

[99] Knighton, 'Provision of education', 32–5. For the Canterbury students see my note in The Cantuarian, xlix (1985), 110–13. For Rochester see Yates and Welsby, Faith and Fabric, 66. For Worcester see M. Craze, King's School, Worcester, 1541–1971 (1972), 19–21. Cf. Logan, 'Regius professorships', 276–8; Dawson, 'Foundation of Christ Church and Trinity', 213–14; Duncan, 'Public lectures', 344–7.

Henry VIII lived just long enough to see his university colleges founded, but not to complete the tomb he intended for himself in the Abbey. This he had planned to be even more magnificent than that of his parents, and since 1530 it had been under construction in the Abbey precinct.[100] Henry would, however, be taken from Westminster to Windsor for burial. In the Abbey the only immediate requirement was a 'herse' (meaning an empty catafalque) erected at a cost of £20 for the memorial services.[101] The tomb was still in progress in the 1550s, and Edward VI in his will directed its completion.[102] It remained in an outbuilding in Mary's reign, but the queen may have diverted craftsmen from this project to one to which she attached greater importance: the restoration of the Confessor's shrine.[103] Henry's other daughter had her own reasons for deciding not to finish the tomb, the components of which eventually followed the king's remains to Windsor. Henry VIII's disappearance from Westminster Abbey was complete.

---

[100] A. Higgins, 'On the work of Florentine sculptors in England in the early part of the sixteenth century; with special reference to the tombs of Cardinal Wolsey and King Henry VIII', *Archaeological Journal*, li (1894), 164–91, 367–70, which presents much of the available documentation. Cf. P.G. Lindley, *Gothic to Renaissance. Essays on Sculpture in England* (Stamford 1995), 51 n. 19, 57 n. 46.

[101] WAM 37060, f. 2. For Henry's funeral: *CSPD EdVI*, no. 16. S.J. Loach, 'The function of ceremonial in the reign of Henry VIII', *Past & Present*, no. 142 (Feb. 1994), 56–68.

[102] *APC*, iii, 347, 380. The first is the council's thanks to the dean and chapter of Westminster for stowing the king's treasure in their dorter, and licensing them to repair 'their howse where his Hieghnes father's tombe is a working and wherin Modena dwelleth' (28 August 1551); the second order requires Modena to be restored to the house, from which the 'preestes' of Westminster had expelled him (5 October 1551). The latter inadvertently refers to 'Henry the vij^thes' tomb. Cf. M. Biddle, 'Nicholas Bellin of Modena. An Italian artificer at the courts of Francis I and Henry VIII', *JBAA*, 3rd ser. xxix (1966), 106–21; *Acts 1543–1609*, nos 94, 112, 123 (the first two references here to the tomb house are misreadings corrected *ibid*. ii, 328). Edward VI's instruction for his father's tomb to be 'made upp' is in minutes for his will, printed in *The Chronicle of Queen Jane, and of two years of Queen Mary*, ed. J.G. Nichols (Camden Soc. xlviii, 1850), 102.

[103] In 1556/7 payment was made for repairing the house where the 'tombe of copper standeth' at Westminster: E.B. Jupp, *An Historical Account of the Worshipful Company of Carpenters of the City of London*, ed. W.W. Pocock (1887), 169; followed in W.R. Lethaby, *Westminster Abbey and the King's Craftsmen* (1906), 236n., and in H.J. Dow, *The Sculptural Decoration of the Henry VII Chapel, Westminster Abbey* (Edinburgh 1992), 95 (both supposing the reference to be to Henry VII's tomb, but noted as referring to Henry VIII's by Dean Robinson ['J.A.R.'] in MS correction to WA Library copy of Lethaby). The suggestion that Modena transferred to the shrine is made in L.E. Tanner, 'The shrine of Edward the Confessor and Nicholas da Modena' (unpublished paper 1954: WAM, Dykes Bower Papers, Box 3; another copy, dated 1956: WAM 64299), 5–7.

CHAPTER TWO

John Redman, the Gentle Ambler

Ashley Null

Within the walls of Westminster Abbey, that great shrine to the national collective memory of centuries of English worship and worthies, the fierce religious divisions of Tudor times are today quietly sealed up in their respective royal tombs. Edward, Mary, Elizabeth, and even their cousin Mary, queen of Scots, all lie within the same house of God, achieving in death the Christian unity they lacked in life. The centuries have worn away the sharp divisions of their day so that in our era their common interment in the Abbey serves to underline the message of Christian ecumenism. How ironic, then, that even as time has helped to heal the wounds of that turbulent period, the years of the Abbey's continued use have also effaced its memorial to an eminent Tudor theologian who attempted a middle way between the religious extremes of his day and won the respect of all concerned. Nothing of his burial inscription in the North Transept remains today to remind Abbey visitors of this man's life and witness. Yet, his reformed catholicism rather than the committed protestantism of Thomas Cranmer would seem more in keeping with those who would wish to see Anglicanism as a theological equipoise. He is Cranmer's younger Cambridge contemporary, John Redman, DD, an original canon of the refounded Abbey.[1]

Redman was one of the new Cambridge men whom John Fisher had hoped his promotion of Christian humanism would help the university to produce. Born in 1499, Redman was a relative of Cuthbert Tunstall, a well-placed ecclesiastic twenty-five years his senior who was also a humanist friend of Thomas More. At Tunstall's suggestion, Redman applied

---

[1] William Camden recorded two tributes for Redman's grave in *Reges, Reginae, Nobiles, et alii in Ecclesia Collegiata B. Petri Westmonasterii sepulti* (1600), sigs [I4]r–K[1]v. The first, a lengthy poem, was almost certainly affixed to the table which is recorded as being set over Redman's grave in 1553 (WAM 37413, f. 1v). The second, shorter description would then have been the actual inscription on the grave. H.M. Nixon, then librarian, fixed the approximate time of their disappearance in a letter of 17 November 1976 (WA Library file R/8163). Apparently, Redman's grave was still marked as late as 1682, since Henry Keepe mentions the canon's burial in the north transept in his *Monumenta Westmonasteriensia*, 174. By 1715, however, Jodocus Crull wrote in *The Antiquities of St. Peter's* (2nd edn, p. 289) that Redman was among those whose monuments were no longer extant.

himself from boyhood to studies, eventually spending some time at Oxford, before moving on to Bishop Fisher's newest centre for humanist learning in Cambridge, St John's College.[2] Fisher wanted to improve the training of clergy so that they would be able to commend the Christian faith to their people by clear instruction and personal example. Integral to his reforming programme was the intertwining of scholasticism and humanism. The *tres linguae* (Latin, Greek and Hebrew), the *bonae literae* (classical literature), scriptural exegesis and patristic writings were all useful for establishing and effectively communicating the wisdom of the past. However, the rigour of scholastic logic was still necessary for defining and defending the details of the church's doctrinal interpretation of that legacy.[3] Fisher intended St John's to be the ultimate embodiment of his theological ideal, a college founded for the training of preaching priests who were to improve the quality of parish life by sharing the fruit of their scholastic-humanist learning with the people.[4]

As befitted an institution whose statutes were ordered by a future saint, the daily routine of St John's was one of austere sacrifice devoted to scholarship as a religious vocation. Members of college rose between 4 and 5 am, had Chapel between 5 and 6, and spent the hours between 6 and 10 in either common lectures or private study. At 10 there was a meagre lunch of 'a penye pyece of byefe amongest iiii. Havyng a fewe porage made of the brothe of the same byefe, wyth salte and otemell, and nothynge els'. After lunch they resumed teaching or learning until 5 pm when they had a similar second meal. Afterwards they returned to study until 10 pm. Then, 'beyng wythout fyre' they would 'walk or runne up and downe halfe an houre, to gette a heate on their feete whan they go to bed'.[5] In this environment Redman took his BA in 1526. He then pursued further studies at Paris, taking his MA in 1528.[6] Afterwards,

---

[2] Venn, iii, 436. Cf. 'Cognatione proxime attingit CUTHBERTUM TONSTALLUM episcopum Dunelmensem: ejus consilio in studio literarum a puero versatus est. Cantabrigiae et Oxonii aliquot annnos vixit': *The Whole Works of Roger Ascham*, ed. J.A. Giles (1865), i, 294.

[3] Fisher, *Opera* (Würzburg 1597), col. 871.

[4] R.A.W. Rex, *The Theology of John Fisher* (Cambridge 1991), 213 n. 4. Cf. D.R. Leader, *A History of the University of Cambridge*, i, *The University to 1546* (Cambridge 1988), 284–90.

[5] Such was the description of Thomas Lever, a senior fellow of St John's, preaching at Paul's Cross on 14 December 1550 to solicit funds from London merchants: *Thomas Lever ... Sermons 1550*, ed. E. Arber (1870), 121–2.

[6] For Redman's Paris MA see Register 15 (*Liber procuratorum nationis alemanniae*, 1521–52), la Bibliothèque de la Sorbonne (Archives de l'ancienne Université de Paris), f. 141; Register 91 (*Liber receptorum nationis alemanniae*, 1494–1530), la Bibliothèque de la Sorbonne (Archives de l'ancienne Université de Paris), ff. 249v–250. Cf. 'Post Lutetiam vidit: ubi diu commoratus tandem rediit in Angliam ante vicesimum [recte, tricesimum?]

he returned to Cambridge, having his MA incorporated in 1530 and becoming a fellow of St John's College in November of the same year.[7] Once back home Redman gained a great reputation for the depth of his learning, the vigour of his preaching, the sanctity of his living and the firmness of his commitment to catholic doctrine.

Redman's Qualities

Redman quickly established himself at Cambridge as a leading specialist in Greek and Ciceronian Latin, becoming the fount for the succession of outstanding classicists which Cambridge began to produce in the 1530s. According to one of their number, Roger Ascham, it was Redman's academic excellence and its university-wide esteem that inspired the young John Cheke and Thomas Smith to emulate his example and become masters themselves in the intricacies of classical literature rather than those of the schoolmen. Together, Redman, Cheke and Smith promoted the study of Cicero, Aristotle, Plato and Demosthenes, gaining many followers.[8] When Cheke and Smith developed a different system for pronouncing Greek that clearly distinguished between vowel sounds as suggested by ancient sources, ever the scholar, Redman approved and adopted the method in his own public lectures.[9] Yet, he was not surpassed by his distinguished protégés. In keeping with Fisher's vision for St John's, Redman came to give himself wholly over to the study of theology. He proceeded BD in 1534 and DD in 1537,[10] becoming famous in his day as a faithful expositor whose scholarship was painstaking and prudent.[11] According to Ascham, Redman was so gifted and industrious in these matters that he surpassed nearly all in wit, wisdom, and words.[12] As a result, he became equally renowned as a

---

jam annum aut plus eo': Ascham, *Works*, i, 294. For the dispute whether or not to grant MA degrees to Redman and George Buchanan because they did not hold BA degrees from Paris see Register 15, ff. 144–145v.

[7] *Grace Book B*, ii, ed. M. Bateson (Cambridge Antiquarian Soc., Luard Memorial ser. iii, 1905), 131, 155–6. Venn, iii, 436. *ODNB*.

[8] Ascham, *Works*, i, 294–5. Cf. J. Strype, *The Life of the Learned Sir Thomas Smith* (Oxford 1820), 9–10. J. Strype, *The Life of the Learned Sir John Cheke* (Oxford 1821), 151.

[9] *LP*, xvii, 611. Strype, *Smith*, 13–14. Strype, *Cheke*, 18.

[10] *Grace Book B*, ii, 187, 203.

[11] 'Eloquii interpres sacri, praecoque fidelis / Illius, et prudens assiduusque fuit': Camden, *Reges*, sig. [I4]v.

[12] 'REDMANNUS ... totum se sacrarum literarum studio tradidit, tot praesidiis ingenii, doctrinae, eloquentiae munitus, ut omnes fere superaret': Ascham, *Works*, i, 295.

preacher. The epitaph on his Abbey memorial compared his speech to thunder and his learned preaching in the pulpit to the sounding of a heavenly trumpet.[13] Ascham was no less impressed, confessing that Redman's brilliant skill at fashioning sermons to help his hearers live the Christian life was probably the best that he had ever heard.[14]

Despite such accomplishments, however, what impressed Redman's contemporaries the most was the consistency between what he preached and how he lived. The Abbey poem developed this theme at length. 'What he taught in word, he performed in deed. What his mind loved inwardly, his godly tongue spoke outwardly ... He not only taught Christ but also lived him.' He was rightly famous, for he was just, holy, of a child-like guilelessness, a man who gave no heed to worldly concerns, but scorned wealth, keeping himself poor by richly providing for those in need. If his preaching voice was like thunder, the virtuous light of his godly life shone as brilliantly as lightning.[15] Should this effusive epitaph seem more hagiography than honest history, even John Foxe, never unduly favourable to religious conservatives, substantially agreed. Noting that during Henry's reign Redman savoured 'somewhat more of superstition, then of true religion, after the zeale of the Phariseis', he still recorded with evident respect that Redman was 'not so malignant or harmefull, but of a civile and quiet disposition, and also so liberal in wel doing, that few poore scholars were in the universitie, which fared not better by his purse'.[16]

Perhaps the most impressive surviving testimonies to Redman's character come from his Cambridge colleagues. Having shared with him the close quarters of university life with all its opportunities for vanities and vice, they would have been in the best position to be familiar with his failings. Many in Cambridge considered Redman's sermon at Bucer's funeral in 1551 to be the supreme example of his charity. Paying his theological opponent what must be the ultimate compliment for a scholar,

---

[13] 'Sacro e suggestu fandi doctissimus vnus / Caelesti est visus saepe sonare tuba ... sermo eius tonitru ...': Camden, *Reges*, sig. [I4]v.

[14] 'Tam praeclarus artifex in concionibus suis ad formandam Christianam vitam, qualem ego profiteor me vix unquam audivisse': Ascham, *Works*, i, 295.

[15] 'Quod verbo docuit, re praestitit, illud amauit / Mens intus, sonuit quod pia lingua foris. / Contemptor mundi, contemptor diuitiarum, / Pauperibus diues, pauper eratque sibi. / Vir iustus, sanctus, puerili simplicitate / Praeditus, et magni nomine dignus erat. / Regno in caelesti magnus namque ille vocatur / Cuius doctrinae consona vita piae. / Redmanum hac ratione potest quis dicere magnum, / Quod docuit si quidem praestitit assidue. / Christum non docuit solum, sed vixit eiusdem / Quem docuit vultu voce docensque simul. / Sermo eius tonitru, fulgur pia vita vocari, / Virtutis lucens lumine digna fuit': Camden, *Reges*, sig. [I4]v.

[16] Foxe, *Actes and Monuments*, 1308.

Redman said that Bucer sought verity more than victory and considered himself a winner if truth triumphed, bearing defeat with equanimity.[17] In trying to explain such generosity to his correspondent Johann Sturm, Ascham related that Redman had a pleasant disposition, being humble, sociable, and good to all, even his enemies, but being troublesome or harsh to none.[18] As a fellow Johnian and a protestant himself, Ascham had good reason to know, especially since he and Redman had at one time come into conflict over patronage opportunities for their respective pupils.[19] When near the end of his life Ascham looked back at St John's in the 1530s, he attributed the quality of the graduates not so much to Fisher's statutes as to two men, John Cheke and John Redman and 'their only example of excellency in learning, of godliness in living, of diligence in studying, of counsel in exhorting, of good order in all things'.[20]

As Fisher would have hoped, however, Redman's famed equanimity did not prevent him from being a lifelong advocate for catholic principles in the English church. The first extant evidence we have for this side of Redman also comes from Foxe, who summarized an exchange of letters between the young scholar and Hugh Latimer when both were at Cambridge. About fourteen years Redman's senior, Latimer's original antipathy towards any deviation from scholastic orthodoxy, including humanist learning, would have made for strained relations with the young classicist, even when they agreed upon doctrine. The situation could only have worsened when Thomas Bilney converted Latimer to the evangelical party in 1524, and his vigorous preaching attracted notoriety. Evidently, Redman thought his reputation as a leading humanist permitted him to rebuke a more senior scholar who had adopted the new theology, most likely because this 'new learning' claimed his field of study for support.[21]

Redman dismissed any such notion out of hand, telling Latimer 'you neither haue any thing at al in the word of god to make for you nor yet

---

[17] '[N]unquam illum fuisse victoriae magis quam veritatis cupidum ... victrixque si triumpharet veritas, se victum aequo animo tulisse': M. Bucer, *Scripta Anglicana* (Basel 1577), 880–1 (Nicholas Carr to John Cheke). *The Chronicle and Political Papers of King Edward VI*, ed. W.K. Jordan (Ithaca, NY 1966), 54.

[18] 'Usus est semper suavissimis moribus, modestissima vita, communis et bonus omnibus etiam adversariis, nemini molestus aut durus': Ascham, *Works*, i, 295.

[19] Ascham smoothed over any estrangement by telling Redman, 'I know your moderation to be more ready to forgive even in the most serious of offences': *ibid.*, i, 38–40.

[20] *Ibid.*, iii, 142.

[21] Foxe, *Actes and Monuments*, 1308. This exchange probably took place after Redman returned from Paris and before Latimer left Cambridge in 1531 to be the vicar of West Kington, Wiltshire.

the testimony of any autenticall writer'.[22] The only possible explanation for evangelical doctrine was not 'new learning', but rather that a wicked spirit had tickled Latimer's ear. Redman advised his protestant colleague that, at least for charity's sake, if not for the sake of his soul, to remember that he was but a man. Therefore, he should not lean on his own understanding but seek not to offend the church by being party to rending it asunder. True to Fisher's model, Redman appealed to the doctrinal authority of the catholic church because he could not yet conceive of any intrinsic conflict between its traditional teachings and the new humanist methodology.

Redman's Rubicon

For catholic humanists in Cambridge the advent of royal supremacy severely challenged such a comfortable assumption. Faced with this crisis, Fisher remained loyal to his own theological principles and, thus, to the pope. He gained a cardinal's hat from Rome, but received a martyr's crown from Henry VIII. Fisher's university, however, showed no such resolve. Choosing accommodation rather than conflict, the dons formally acquiesced on 2 May 1534.[23] Redman joined them, proceeding BD in the same year. His conformity and scholarly attainments soon led to professional advancement in Cambridge. Possibly as early as 1536, and certainly by 1538, he was elected the Lady Margaret professor. It appears he also acted as public orator between the resignation of George Day in 1537 and the appointment of Thomas Smith which took effect in 1538.[24]

In 1535, however, Redman was one of three senior fellows from St John's to visit Fisher while awaiting execution in the Tower. Evidently, they came to encourage him by paying their respects, even as they sought to have him finalize their statutes before his impending death.

---

[22] *Ibid., Actes and Monuments*, 1308.

[23] Leader, *History of Cambridge*, 329.

[24] Venn, iii, 436. Richard Rex suggested the likelihood of the earlier date for the Lady Margaret professorship in a lecture in Cambridge 1 March 2002 marking the 500th anniversary of the chair. Redman's name appears on a list of orators begun in 1559 in the University Letter Book (CUL, University Archives, Lett. 1, p. 356/f. 163v). Although the university Grace Books record no stipend for him as orator, there is a gap of some months between Day's last payment as orator at the end of the academic year 1536/7 (he having become master of St John's on 27 July) and Smith's first payment as orator for the latter half of 1537/8: *Grace Book B*, ii, 206, 216; cf. *ibid.*, pp. 221–2, 227–8, 232–3; T. Baker, *History of the College of St. John the Evangelist, Cambridge*, ed. J.E.B. Mayor (Cambridge 1869), i, 110.

For someone as noted for his life matching his doctrine as Redman, he must have found the visit with Fisher bittersweet at best, especially if the desired revisions had been prompted by the new political realities, as has been suggested.[25] Face to face with Fisher, Redman must have been only too aware that his own subscription meant that either he had broken with his mentor's theological method or at least with his theological resolve. Either way, by agreeing in principle that the teaching authority of the catholic church could err, Redman had crossed the Rubicon. Rather than using his scholarship to defend eternal truths, from now on he would have to look to his learning to discern what was truth.

That Redman came to embrace the renunciation of papal authority as a matter of conviction rather than mere compromise seems a justifiable enough conclusion from his last work, *The Complaint of Grace*. Although unpublished in Redman's lifetime, a version of the manuscript was printed about 1556 which tactfully omitted a significant anti-papal section. William Crashaw, that hammer of catholic textual alterations, noticed the discrepancy and restored the following passage in his 1609 edition:

> In this time, the Bishop of *Rome* would needs be peerelesse: they would suffer none to be equall with them, or to be like unto them. Nay, rather they would be in power alone, authoritie and preheminece [*sic*] and all the universall Church under their subjection: ... Alas ... how by their fault the Church is defaced ... [T]hrough their avarice and pride all good rule hath beene broken, and all good order dissolved, and both the Scripture and the wholesome Canons troden under feet.[26]

Redman's humanist emphasis on historical inquiry led him to conclude that the later church, especially during the time of the imperial papacy of the last 'foure or five hundred yeares', had departed from the polity of the early church and had significantly twisted the interpretation of scripture and the Fathers in the process.[27] *The Complaint of Grace* does not specify what these distortions were, but John Jewel in his own apologetic work mentions one example offered by Redman, that Pope Zosimus had corrupted the canons of the Council of Nicaea in order to bolster his claim of oversight and jurisdiction over the

---

[25] E. Surtz, *The Works and Days of John Fisher* (Cambridge, Mass. 1967), 189, 484 n. 24.

[26] Redman, *The Complaint of Grace*, ed. William Crashaw (London 1609), 57–8. For Crashaw see P.J. Wallis, 'The library of William Crashawe', *Transactions of the Cambridge Bibliographical Society*, ii (1954–8), 213–28, especially pp. 216–18.

[27] Redman, *Complaint of Grace* (1609), 60.

churches and bishops of Africa.[28] This chain of corruption from polity to doctrine eventually led to morals. The final effect of the papal pursuit of power was that the laity 'went pittifully astray', since 'the guides themselves began ... to walke abroad in the wide way which leadeth to perdition'.[29]

Significant corruption of spiritual authority, however, did not necessarily mean complete invention. While Redman embraced the royal supremacy as an alternative to papal authority, he did so in a manner as consistent as possible with his catholic principles. In 1540, the year of the traditionalists' resurgence in Henrician ecclesiastical politics, Redman was appointed to a doctrinal commission to prepare a more acceptable replacement for the protestant-leaning Bishops' Book whose statutory authority of three years had now expired. In his reply to a theological questionnaire he received as a part of this assignment, Redman carefully defended a separate, legitimate sphere for the clergy, albeit under royal authority.[30] Of course, he affirmed the sovereign's right to order the church by appointing clergy to such offices as he thought appropriate. Nevertheless, unlike Cranmer, he insisted that something more than mere appointment by the prince was necessary for a person to become a priest or bishop. From the beginning of the primitive church, Redman argued, the Holy Ghost had ordained that ministers in the church were to be consecrated by imposition of hands and prayer, not only for the confirmation of their faith, but 'for the obtayning of ferthr grace requysite in the same'. Therefore, princes could appoint a person to the office of bishop, but only the apostles and their successors had the authority to consecrate that person. Although it was the responsibility of the godly prince to ensure that priests did their duty, the power to ordain a person to the priesthood rested exclusively with the episcopate.[31]

Evidently, Redman's balanced approach to the supremacy was pleasing enough to the king, for at the end of the year 1540 he was appointed a canon in Westminster and made archdeacon of Stafford.[32] By 1542 he had vacated his Lady Margaret professorship, becoming the archdeacon of Taunton, with its annexed prebend of Milverton I, as well as the new

---

[28] *The Works of John Jewel*, ed. J. Ayre (Parker Soc. 1848), iii, 126–7.

[29] Redman, *Complaint of Grace* (1609), 59.

[30] R.W. Dixon, *History of the Church of England* (Oxford 1878–1902), ii, 234, 303–6. R.A.W. Rex, *Henry VIII and the English Reformation* (1993), 155–6.

[31] LPL, MS 1108, ff. 111–12; reprinted in G. Burnet, *The History of the Reformation of the Church of England*, ed. N. Pocock (Oxford 1865), iv, 469–86.

[32] Le Neve, *1300–1541*, x, 20; *1541–1857*, vii, 72. Redman held Westminster's second prebend; for his involvement there see *Acts 1543–1609*, i, pp. xx, xl, and nos 18, 24, 29, 33, 41, 84, 184 (f. 273), 185 (ff. 278, 278v *bis*).

warden of King's Hall, Cambridge.[33] In the same year Redman was also appointed to a committee of convocation responsible for preparing a new translation of the Bible, although the work was to be abandoned.[34] Naturally, when the king questioned Westminster about its sponsorship of university scholars in 1545, Redman along with his fellow canon Thomas Reynolds was detailed to respond on behalf of the dean and chapter.[35] One year later Henry VIII incorporated King's Hall into his new collegiate foundation of Trinity College and granted Redman his greatest preferment, appointment as its first master.[36]

Redman's *Via Media*

Having come to identify the true catholic church with the patristic period rather than current practice, Redman now operated in a theological world with fewer fixed boundaries, for traditionalist and evangelical scholars offered contradictory interpretations of what exactly ancient Christian faith and practice was. He aptly described the chaotic result in *The Complaint of Grace*:

> [Y]ea the chiefe amongst them ... be so divers in their opinions and judgements, that there be now almost as many kindes of faith, as there were sorts amongst the Philosophers ... One sort runne headlong, another draweth back, and not without cause: for if al should runne alike, all were like to fall on heape, and marre themselves. The new sort spurre and pricke with all their might: The old sort, holde the bridle with no lesse strength.[37]

Significantly, Redman's solution was not to argue merely for the continuation of medieval catholic faith and practice in the English church, albeit without papal affiliation. Like Erasmus, he was willing to attempt a reformation of scholastic doctrines as well as personal morals, and, true to his humanist training, he chose as his new plumbline a pragmatic, patristic emphasis on godly living:

> I would wish that these new spurres should be put to hold the bridle, and keepe in the horse head, and leave their wanton spurring, for feare of casting over both horse and man. And I would wish, that the olde bridle-holders, would begin to spurre more

---

[33] *LP*, xviii, I, 66(30). Le Neve, (1854), iii, 654; (1962–), *1300–1541*, viii, 17; *1541–1857*, v, 16. Venn, iii, 436. Cobban, *King's Hall*, 289–90.

[34] Dixon, *History*, ii, 286.

[35] *Acts 1543–1609*, no. 33. Knighton, 'Provision of education', 26–34.

[36] Cobban, *King's Hall*, 289–90. W.W. Rouse Ball, *Cambridge Papers* (1918), 3–25.

[37] Redman, *Complaint of Grace* (1609), 68.

quickly, not with such newe sharpe spurs and pricks, as moove
debate or nourish controversie, or contentions in opinions: but
such gentle spurres (after the old ancient making) as would moove
the horse, (I meane the people) to amble a good gentle pace in the
commandements of God, such prickes as would stirre to repentance, and true amendement of life.[38]

If Fisher was wrong to believe that the English church only needed a
reformation of morals, not doctrine, the protestants were equally wrong
to emphasize a reform of doctrine without proper regard for the moral
consequences. Redman wanted to move on from those aspects of medieval Christianity which he thought undermined personal holiness, but
he had no desire to gallop headlong into the antinomian teachings of
the evangelical party. Here is the coherence of Redman's life and doctrine. He argued for the importance of godly living as the true test of
right doctrine, and he disciplined his behaviour to embody what he
believed.

We first see something of Redman's moderate, moralist approach to
doctrinal revision in his description of penance from the 1540 theological questionnaire. While acknowledging that no text in either scripture
or the Fathers specifically linked the number seven to the term 'sacraments', Redman argued that each was well attested individually as a
sacrament in both. Indeed, he suggested that it would be better to add
the washing of feet as a sacrament well attested in both scripture and
the Fathers, rather than subtract any of the traditional seven.[39] However, his defence of the traditional number of sacraments did not mean
that he always understood them in the traditional way.

According to John Fisher, the catholic church taught a two-fold
method of forgiveness for post-baptismal sins: 'either through great and
bitter sorrow, not having yet received the sacrament of absolution or
through the reception of the sacrament, with some sorrow preceding'.[40]
In the first case, penitents assisted by prevenient grace persisted in
regret and good works until a certain level of intensity was reached. At
that point God would mercifully choose to accept their penitence as
sufficient for forgiveness, although never as inherently worthy of the
divine gift of pardon. Nevertheless, since penitents would never know
for certain that their sorrow had reached the necessary degree, they
could always trust the sacramental means for assurance of pardon. This
second way for forgiveness was also noticeably easier, requiring only
some regret on the penitent's part and relying on the priest's power of

---

[38] *Ibid.*, 68–9.
[39] LPL, MS 1108, f. 110. Burnet, *History of the Reformation*, iv, 445–63.
[40] Fisher, *Opera*, col. 385.

the keys to make up the difference. For those who argued that merely requiring attrition (the lower standard of sorrow) for sacramental penance encouraged spiritual laxity, Fisher countered that accommodating human weakness was only being faithful to the gospel, because Jesus would not break a bruised reed or quench a smouldering wick.[41] In either case, however, sacramental penance was still required for salvation, since true penitence, known as contrition, always included the intention to confess to a priest.

Erasmus rejected this two-track approach to justification. He thought that confession was abused by those who came without earnest sorrow and serious intention to change.[42] For forgiveness of sins came not by sacramental action *ex opere operato*, nor because of external works of satisfaction *per se*, but rather through godly sorrow and love in the penitent's heart.[43] Therefore, the proper purpose of auricular confession was to help people learn to hate their sins while also encouraging in them a confident trust in Christ's promise of forgiveness so that they would love God, rather than merely fear his punishment.[44] Because individual confession to a priest could be an effective means of promoting true penitence and faith, Erasmus argued that sacramental penance was expedient, a beneficial custom that ought to be retained in the church, but not necessary for salvation.

When the duke of Norfolk sought to reassert traditional catholic teaching through the act of Six Articles (31 Hen. VIII c. 14), he wanted auricular confession to be declared necessary for salvation, thus clearly repudiating the protestant teaching of justification by faith alone. Cranmer, however, persuaded the king to accept Erasmus's position that in scripture and the Fathers the practice was considered helpful, but not required. In the end, the act read that auricular confession was expedient and necessary to be retained, the word order indicating that the sacrament's function in the life of the church was pastoral comfort, not as a condition for salvation. Tunstall bitterly opposed this abandonment of traditional teaching, sending the king a memorandum to that effect afterwards, which Henry truculently dismissed.[45]

A year later the theological questionnaire of 1540 reopened the debate, asking whether John 20:23 ('Whosoever sins you forgive, they are forgiven') required confession to a priest for the forgiveness of mortal

---

[41] Fisher, quoting Matthew 12:20, *Opera*, col. 339.

[42] *Desiderii Erasmi Roterodami opera omnia*, ed. J. LeClerc (Leiden 1703–6), v, 155E.

[43] *Ibid.*, v, 157E.

[44] *Ibid.*, v, 147C–152B, 155D.

[45] See G. Redworth, 'A study in the formulation of policy: the genesis of the act of Six Articles', *JEH*, xxxvii (1986), 42–67.

sin. In the same questionnaire that Redman defended the traditional number of sacraments, he failed to repristinate clearly the traditionalist position of his relative Tunstall. According to Redman, although private confession was not expressly commanded, it could be deduced from the scripture text in question that sacramental penance was a necessary medicine 'for the quyeting of theyr conscience to seke if they may convenientlye have siche a prieste as is mete to here theyr confession'.[46] Both qualifications sound distinctly Erasmian, for focusing on a quiet conscience based the necessity of penance on pastoral rather than soteriological grounds, and stipulating a 'mete' priest suggested that clerical learning was more important in the sacrament than the pronouncement of absolution. Redman's fuller discussion of justification in a treatise he presented to Henry VIII in 1543 merely confirms this interpretation.[47] In *De Iustificatione*, Redman argued that confession of sin was necessary, but he stressed the need for true penitence, trust in forgiveness and love for righteousness, while never mentioning priestly absolution.[48] On the key issue of justification, evidently Redman's concern for Christian morals had led him by the early 1540s to move beyond Fisher's traditionalist catholic humanism to embrace the more progressive position of Erasmus.

Yet, if Redman abandoned sacramental absolution *ex opere operato* out of fear of encouraging moral laxity, he equally had no desire to adopt solifidianism with its antinomian implications. According to Roger Ascham, justification was the chief issue which separated Redman from English protestants precisely because of his concerns over morality.[49] Redman made his *via media* position perfectly clear to Henry VIII in *De Iustificatione*, arguing that his reformed catholicism was more scripturally accurate than the competing protestant claims. Since Redman was among the six of those involved in the 1540 questionnaire who were eventually delegated the task of revising the Bishops' Book, *De Iustificatione* was probably composed as part of this task, although he could have written the manuscript in his capacity as a royal chaplain.[50] Redman's treatise

---

[46] LPL, MS 1108, f. 113. Burnet, *History of the Reformation*, iv, 488.

[47] According to Ascham, Redman presented a manuscript to the king in that year: Ascham, *Works*, i, 46.

[48] 'Habes ergo in quibus consistit iustificatio, in agnitione et confessione peccatorum per poenitentiam, in fiducia misericordiae per Christum, in renovatione voluntatis ad studium iustitiae per spiritum sanctum': Redman, *De Iustificatione* (Antwerp 1555), 10.

[49] 'De justificatione autem solius fidei, nonnihil a nobis discrepavit, et id semper laude et sine aculeis, non tam (uti ego de illo existimo) quod dubitavit de veritate illius doctrinae, quam quod metuit de licentia vitae ...': Ascham, *Works*, i, 295.

[50] For the relationship between the committee on doctrine and the King's Book, see Rex, *Henry VIII*, 156.

may well have played a key role in the debate behind the new formulary which was published in 1543 and known as the King's Book. A copy of the manuscript with its title in Cranmer's handwriting can be found amongst his papers at Lambeth Palace, and it was Henry VIII's custom to give theological works to people who opposed the position taken by the author for their comments.[51] Cranmer's persistent protestantism would have found much that needed to be challenged in Redman's description of justification as based on the historic catholic principles of choice, change, and grace.

The heart of the difference between Redman's position and that of Cranmer was the role of the will in salvation. Cranmer and the English evangelical party stressed salvation as a gift determined by God's choice, not humanity. Grounding salvation in predestination, they argued that those who were given saving grace would naturally respond and embrace the initiative of God in their lives, like a withering plant soaking up the gift of water. Redman simply refused to discuss predestination, since the subject was a mystery beyond the comprehension of human beings. Instead he concentrated his discussion on vocation', justification and glorification, insisting that the freedom of human choice was integral to this process.[52] No one had the power to choose the good without grace, but grace did not have the power to determine an individual's choice.[53] This was the true catholic position, confirmed by the writings of the saints and accepted from the beginning of the church. According to Redman, preachers should never proclaim grace in such a way as to suggest that human decisions had no effect, but only that they were ineffectual apart from grace. With grace, however, people were able to do all things through the God who strengthened them.[54]

Redman's insistence on choice was reflected in his adherence to the ancient understanding of justification as a process of intrinsic transformation. The justified were those who continued to choose to co-operate

---

[51] LPL, MS 1107, ff. 137–59; For Henry's manner of soliciting opinions, especially concerning those writings which he had not the patience to read himself, see *Miscellaneous Writings and Letters of Thomas Cranmer*, ed. J.E. Cox (Parker Soc. 1846), 341.

[52] 'Omissa illa archana et inscrutabili predestinatione, et fidelium ante mundi constitutionem electione, de qua nihil aliud loqui possumus quam exclamare cum Paulo, o altitudo, etcaet. Ad inferiora illa descendamus, vocationem, Iustificationem, et glorificationem': Redman, *De Iustificatione*, 1.

[53] '[N]on quod sine nostrae voluntatis motu et assensu iustificatio in nobis fiat, sed quod Deus ex sola gratia voluntatem nostram praeueniens et praeparans': *ibid.*, 16.

[54] 'Hoc autem secundum catholica dogmata quae ab initio sanctorum scriptis confirmata in Ecclesia recepta sunt credimus ... sic praedicandam gratiae vim vt liberum arbitrium non quidem nihil esse, sed absque gratia inefficax esse, cum gratia autem nihil non posse confiteamur, iuxta illud, Omnia possum in eo qui me confortat': *ibid.*, 16–17.

with grace, so that they developed a personal holiness which would eventually save them from God's wrath: 'To be justified is for the ungodly to become righteous, to be freed from sin, to progress in righteousness and to be absolved from judgement'.[55] Like Erasmus, Redman thought that this holiness consisted of being joined to Christ through trusting in God's promised forgiveness and loving to serve righteousness.[56] Stephen Gardiner helpfully referred to this as holding on to Christ with both hands.[57] Since justification was a process of gradual transformation towards the perfect holiness of Christ, the just could become more just through deeper faith and love as well as the good works which sprang forth from them.[58]

For Cranmer and the English evangelical party, however, on-going human sinfulness meant that no one could develop a personal right-eousness sufficient to withstand God's judgement. Hence, justification had to be based on an external righteousness untouched by human frailty, that is, the unchanging righteousness of Christ. God promised to credit sinners fully with Jesus's perfect holiness in the very moment they put their trust in Christ's atoning sacrifice on the cross as the sole basis for the forgiveness of their transgressions. Since divine pardon was based on what Christ had done and given freely to those who believed, human works contributed nothing to gaining salvation. The justified were those who held on to Christ by faith alone. And since only those predestined by God to eternal life ever came to have this saving faith, once individuals were justified, they could be certain of their future home. Of course they did good works, but always out of gratitude for

---

[55] 'Iustificari est ex impio iustum fieri, a peccato liberari in iustitia progredi, et in iudicio absolui': *ibid.*, 1.

[56] 'Ita vere sumus iustificati, si Christo simus configurati, qui traditus est propter delicta nostra, et resurrexit propter iustificationem nostram, vt nos peccatis mortui, iustitiae per ipsum viuamus', *ibid.*, 10; 'Tunc enim vere iustificamur vbi gratia Christi cordibus nostris aspirante, peccata vere agnoscimus, et coniecta fiducia in abyssum misericordiae domini Iesu Christi, per illius spiritum ad iustitiae dilectionem ac studium, mentibus renouamur': *ibid.*, 16.

[57] Andreas Osiander described his 1541 debate with Gardiner on justification as follows: 'Cum concederemus Deum justificare, et Christum esse justitiam, et fide eatenus nos justificari, quatenus fides tanquam manus donum Dei per evangelium oblatum apprehenderet, voluit charitatem, tanquam alteram manum in apprehendo, adjungere': *Corpus Reformatorum*, ed. C.G. Bretschneider *et al.* (Brunswick 1834–1900), iv, 140–1 (letter to Justus Jonas).

[58] 'Eiusmodi autem proficiens iustificatio fit indies per opera fidei, id est, bene in fide operantes in iustificatione indies progrediuntur, et crescunt': Redman, *De Iustificatione*, 27; 'Opera fidei et charitatis faciunt vt melius ac certius Dei misericordiam apprehendamus … iustificatio autem nostra est ex vera apprehensione misericordiae. Bona igitur opera ad iustificationem inutilia non sunt': *ibid.*, 28.

their assured salvation, not as the grounds for maintaining it. Thus, justification for Cranmer was an event which happened in an instant of belief, assuring sinners of eternal peace with God despite their lack of perfect personal holiness.

In Redman's eyes, such teaching was terribly destructive. People were encouraged to think that all their sins were suddenly carried away, and such a powerful fantasy would prevent them from the necessary hard work of driving out the inwardly concealed desire of intending to commit sin in the future. If they held on to Christ with only the hand of faith, their other hand of love would still be clinging to sin. Although they might at one time have been afflicted with a tortured conscience because of the fear of Hell, if the Spirit of grace had not inspired their will to hate sin and avoid wickedness, the necessary intrinsic change had not happened, and such people did not yet have the righteousness that was in Christ Jesus.[59] And as for the standard protestant argument that love was the fruit of faith because trust in eternal salvation engendered love for the Saviour, Redman countered that such a notion was both unscriptural and illogical, for love and faith were both equally fruits of the Spirit. To separate faith from all other gifts of the Spirit so that faith alone was present in justification was to fail to grasp the sheer abundance of grace and thus to insult it.[60] Therefore, only in one sense could justification by faith be considered scriptural, if one meant that justification came through trusting solely in Christ, excluding thereby every prideful notion of a person's own worthiness.[61]

Since human choice was so central to salvation in Redman's scheme, and human nature was so feeble, the human will had to be kept fit for

---

[59] 'Quicunque itaque amore atque affectu ad peccatum respiciunt, etsi metu Gehennae aut tormento conscientiae ad tempus afflicti, misericordiam in Christo se quaerere simulent, et fide sua quam ipsi sibi forte somnio fingunt, peccata omnia repente absorberi sibi persuadeant, quandiu tamen peccatum vnquam in posterum committendi propositum non excussum atque abietum intus in corde latet, seipsos misere seducunt et de iustificatione frustra gloriantur. Nam cuique non est indita dilectio per spiritum gratiae, odium autem peccati et sceleris detestatio etiam inspirata, hic quod de iustitia quae est in Christo Iesu superbiat nihil habet': *ibid.*, 11.

[60] '[H]anc opinionem nulla possit scripturae authoritate aut ratione confirmare ... Non ergo sola fides per se caeteris donis exclusis arborem illam Euangelicam facit, sed gratia cuius amplitudinem qui vna tantum fide comprehendunt, nimis in arctum gratiae largitatem constringunt, quippe quae non tantum fidem sed etiam spem, et charitatem parit. Quare vnum hoc tantum fidei donum efferre, caeteris abiectis est gratiae contumeliam inferre': *ibid.*, 13–14.

[61] 'Sententia haec, sola fides iustificat, potest intelligi vera esse, si fidem pro fiducia sumas, et per sola excludas nihil aliud quam omnem aliam fidem siue fiduciam praeter illam quae in Christum est, hoc est omnem superbam opinionem propriae dignitatis': *ibid.*, 38.

the task. This was the role of good works. Because they exercised the will in choosing good, works protected the grace of justification given in baptism and made a Christian's eternal salvation more secure. The justified who through careless indolence did not persevere in doing good works would gradually find that their faith grew weak and their love withered. Eventually they would choose to sin, lose their justification, and once again be under the dominion of the Devil.[62] Nevertheless, should justification be lost, grace equally worked through human efforts to prepare the will to hold on to Christ once again. The spirit of fear in penance humbled sinners, opening the way to the throne of grace,[63] while good works done with the help of that grace made faith more lively, hope more certain, love more ardent until at last penitents were made one Spirit with God. Protestants like Cranmer might argue that since a person must be justified before he can do works pleasing to God, works before justification had no benefit. Redman, however, responded that such reasoning made as much sense as saying that a body must be healthy before one can exercise, therefore exercise could not help make the body healthy.[64] In fact, scripture made perfectly plain that penance came before justification, for in the order of salvation God's grace turned the human will first towards penance and then to faith joined with love.[65] Therefore,

---

[62] 'Primum, iustificationem quam sumus gratuita Dei misericordia nullis praecedentibus operibus adepti [bona opera], tuentur et conservant. Sunt enim opera bona interna atque externa, fidei fructus eiusque exercitium, quae si per negligentiam ac socordiam non proferantur, fides ipsa paulatim euanescit, charitas extinguitur, amittitur iustificatio, et peccatum iterum nobis dominatur. Esto quod semel iustificati sumus et filii Dei, curandum tamen vt vocationem et electionem nostram firmam faciamus': *ibid.*, 20; 'Hostes fortes ac potentes nobis insidiantur ... Nos ipsi ex nobis fragiles infirmi': *ibid.*, 22.

[63] '[P]oenitentia primum et spiritus timoris ... corda terreat ... [N]ec sine poenitentia ad thronum gratiae aditum patere ... Participes ergo Euangelii et sanitatis esse non possumus, nisi pauperes et contriti atque humiliati efficiamur per penitentiam': *ibid.*, 3–4.

[64] 'Iustos quidem fieri oportet antequam iuste operemur, ac propterea bona opera ad iustitiam nihil conducere: perinde acsi dicas, oportet sanum esse priusquam corpus exerceas, ergo exercitatio ad sanitatem nihil prodest. Bona opera fidem viuaciorem, solidiorem et firmiorem reddunt, spem meliorem et certiorem indies pariunt, charitatem alacriorem et ardentiorem efficiunt, ac magis nos Deo appropinquare faciunt et illi firmius adhaerere vt vnus tandem cum eo spiritus efficiamur. Quomodo ergo sunt omnino a iustificatione aliena?': *ibid.*, 29.

[65] 'Poenitentia primo loco et a Ioanne et ipso Christo praedicatur, deinde regnum caelorum, ex quo ordine manifestum est vt posterius consequaris, prius esse necessarium': *ibid.*, 3–4; 'Poenitentia itaque in iustificatione semper primam partem et locum obtinet': *ibid.*, 6; 'Deus ex sola gratia voluntatem nostram praeueniens et praeparans per poenitentiam et fidem viuam id est charitati coniunctam, iustificationem in nobis efficiat': *ibid.*, 16.

doing penance and confessing sins were the necessary beginning for gaining justification.[66]

Yet Redman's epitaph in the Abbey noted that his first name 'John' was derived from the Hebrew word for grace, and throughout his theological career he was no less concerned to emphasize salvation *sola gratia* than protestants like Cranmer.[67] Although Redman insisted on works having a role in justification, he asserted a double defence against the taint of Pelagianism. As we have seen, *De Iustificatione* consistently emphasized the utter necessity of God's grace for the human will to choose to do good. In addition, however, Redman denied that the worthiness of such grace-produced works of penance was the *direct* cause of the remission of sin. Yet to do so, he had to turn to the same sort of scholastic distinctions employed by Fisher in his description of the extra-sacramental way of pardon. According to Redman, penance was not the efficient cause of the remission of sin, but rather a *sine qua non* which preceded justification and was required for it, although human penitence could never fully merit forgiveness.[68] Consequently, God, in his immense mercy, not because of any preceding merits of the penitents, but solely because of his excessive love for humanity even when people were dead in sin, freely chose to give the gift of salvation to those who had humbled themselves through penance.[69] Although Redman never used the technical scholastic term *meritum de congruo*, that in essence was what he was teaching.[70] In short, for Redman

---

[66] 'Cum igitur poenitentiam agere oporteat et peccata confiteri ad iustificationem obtinendam ... Non erit omnino absurdum poenitentiam asserere initium iustificationis, et causam quandam remissionis peccatorum': *ibid.*, 8–9.

[67] 'Hic sita Redmanni sunt ossa (o Candide lector) / Gratia praenomen cui dedit et merito. / Namque Hebraeorum Iohannis gratia vox est / Christi Redmanno quae data larga fuit: / Gratia Christi illum variis ornauit et auxit / Doctrinae et clari dotibus ingenii': Camden, *Reges*, sig. [I4]r.

[68] 'Non praecipuam quidem illam causam aut efficientem aut cui res quam petimus ex operis nostri dignitate debeatur, sed causam vt vocant sine qua non, et quiddam praecedens ac requisitum, et medium quoddam necessarium, quod nisi adhibeatur, res ipsa quam ambimus non perficitur': Redman, *De Iustificatione*, 9.

[69] '[I]ntelligendum est Deum quos iustificare instituit, vbi illorum animos per poenitentiam humiliatos viderit, eorum animos rursum erigere, vt de remissione peccatorum bonam spem per Christum qui est propitiatio pro peccatis totius mundi, et pro omnibus semetipsum dedit redemptionem, hauriant atque concipiant. Hanc veniae spem operatur in cordibus vere poenitentium sola gratia, nec tantum thesaurum vlla praecedentia merita sibi vendicare possunt, sed mera est immensa Dei misericordia, qui propter nimiam charitatem suam qua dilexit nos, cum essemus mortui peccatis conuiuificauit nos Christo, cuius gratia saluati sumus per fidem, non ex nobis, Dei enim donum est, non ex operibus ne quis glorietur': *ibid.*, 9–10.

[70] See A.E. McGrath, *Iustitia Dei*, (2nd edn, Cambridge 1998), 83–91, 109–19. On the one hand, Redman wanted to acknowledge the utility of grace-aided good works

salvation was *sola gratia* because grace was required at each step in the process: for the good works which prepared for justification, for God's acceptance of the humbled heart which these good works had helped to produce, for the gifts of justifying trust and love which God gave only to those so humbled, and for the increase of these gifts throughout life until the time of judgement.

Thus, Redman used scripture, as supported and supplemented at key points by the Fathers and even the scholastics, to argue for a moderate catholic humanist position on justification which attempted to steer between the Scylla of moral laxity encouraged by some medieval teaching on sacramental penance and the Charybdis of immoral licence commonly attributed to solifidianism. In the end, the king agreed with Redman, despite Cranmer's persistent advocacy for protestant soteriology. For the King's Book settled the question of justification along moderate catholic principles, emphasizing choice, change, and grace. True to Redman's *via media*, the new formulary specifically required true contrition in the penitent for an effective absolution and explicitly rejected justification *sola fide*.[71]

Four years later, the situation in England changed dramatically, as the regime under Edward became increasingly, clearly protestant. The new Book of Homilies (1547) reflected Cranmer's adherence to justification by faith alone, and the new Prayer Book of 1549 no longer presented the mass as a propitiatory sacrifice for the sins of the living and the dead. In 1550 altars were ordered to be torn down and replaced with tables set up in the choir, and iridescent medieval interiors were whitewashed so that scripture verses in black letter could teach a purer faith. In the face of this protestant onslaught Redman served the new regime as best he could.

On 19 April 1547 he was made a member of the commission appointed to settle the notorious divorce case of William Parr,[72] while in December of the same year he provided convocation with his written opinion on the equally contentious issue of priestly celibacy. The

---

before justification: 'Et reuera qui attente aduersariorum doctrinam animaduerterit, hoc iniquitatis mysterium apud ipsos deprehendet, vt nostro studio, diligentiae, conatui nec antequam simus iustificati ... admodum quicquam tribuant': *De Iustificatione*, 43. On the other, he insisted that only works afterwards had condign merit: 'Nam [Paul] nihil aliud intelligit quam nos primum sine vllis praecedentibus, saltem iustitiae operibus, gratis iustificari': *ibid.*, 27. Nevertheless, even just works were so only because of God's acceptance by covenant: 'Non sunt igitur bona opera iustitia solum coram hominibus, sed etiam coram Deo, ex sola tamen acceptatione misericordiae, et pacto gratiae': *ibid.*, 30.

[71] *The King's Book*, ed. T.A. Lacey (Church Historical Soc. 1932), 49, 156.

[72] *CPR 1547–48*, 137, 261.

proposition before convocation was to render 'utterly voide and of none effecte' all canons, laws and customs which prevented priests and those in religious orders from entering into marriage. Expressive of his moderate catholic humanism, Redman declined either to forbid clerical marriage or to forbid any constraints on the practice. Since the requirement for celibacy was not a universal scriptural injunction but only an ecclesiastical canon, Redman agreed that the king and convocation had the authority to remove this 'clogge' so that English priests could marry.[73] Yet he could not bring himself to endorse the complete freedom in matrimonial matters granted to clergy by the proposition. He preferred to follow the ancient practice of strictly interpreting St Paul to mean that a priest could have only one wife in his lifetime.[74] When the time came for Redman to sign the poll sheet, he chose the affirmative side. However, rather than simply penning his signature, he began to write a statement that clearly conveyed his more conservative position. Of course, a one-time provision for clerical marriage was not the proposition in question. In the end, Redman's sentence was left unfinished, his aborted entry stricken from the record, and his vote was not recorded for either side.[75] Instead, he provided a full explanation of his 'abstention' which was then appended to the official proceedings.[76]

Shortly thereafter, around January 1548, Redman was included in a survey of opinions on the eucharist, although his responses, if any, have unfortunately not survived.[77] In September he was also part of a gathering of bishops and doctors often called the 'Windsor Commission' which helped prepare the new Prayer Book.[78] Whatever reservations he may have had in this matter, Redman was evidently able to live with the

---

[73] CCCC, MS 114A, p. [400]. Cf. J. Strype's transcription in *Memorials of the Most Reverend Father in God Thomas Cranmer* (Oxford 1840), 223.

[74] 'I thinke that it standeth well with gods worde that a man which hath been or is but ons maried, being otherwise accordinglie qualefied maie be made a preest ... And graunte that it maie be lefull to suche [preestes] as can not or will not conteine to marie one wife. And if she die, then the said preest to mary no more remayninge still in his ministration': CCCC, MS 114A, p. [400]. For St Paul's instruction, see I Tim. 3:2, Titus 1:6. For the patristic application, see number XVII of the Apostolic Canons, reprinted with commentary in 'The Eighty-Five Canons', *The Rudder*, trans. D. Cummings (Chicago 1957), 28–30.

[75] CCCC, MS 114A, p. [398]. Strype, *Cranmer*, 222–3. A. Gasquet and E. Bishop, *Edward VI and the Book of Common Prayer* (1928), 48.

[76] CCCC, MS 114A, p. [400].

[77] Burnet, *History of the Reformation*, ii, 127; v, 197–217). Gasquet and Bishop, *Edward VI and the BCP*, 54–61.

[78] Gasquet and Bishop, *Ibid.*, 104–14. F. Procter and W.H. Frere, *A New History of the Book of Common Prayer* (1901), 45–7.

eventual result. On 12 April 1549, he was appointed to a commission whose two-fold task was to search out Anabaptist heretics, as well as enforce conformity to the new liturgy which was to come into effect on the following Whitsunday, 9 June.[79] Perhaps it was in this capacity that Redman reportedly affirmed to Tunstall that the new formulary was 'an holy book, and agreeable to the gospel'.[80] On 29 May Redman even subscribed to the Book of Homilies, although he was reported to have done so only after being permitted to understand three troublesome sentences according to his own interpretation.[81] In 1550 the chapel of Redman's own Trinity College conformed to the new liturgical order. They sold off over £140 worth of items from the sacristy, removed the elevated altar, and set up a communion table, probably in the middle of the chapel.[82]

Although he resigned as archdeacon of Stafford in 1547, Redman's flexibility was soon rewarded with more preferment. He remained archdeacon of Taunton, and the following year he was made the rector of Calverton, Buckinghamshire.[83] Despite this mutual accommodation between the king and his chaplain, however, the moral consequences of the many religious changes deeply troubled Redman. Preparing one more plea for his catholic humanist *via media*, he wrote *The Complaint of Grace* to speak his mind about the Edwardine church.

Naturally, Redman reaffirmed the description of justification which he had earlier given to Henry VIII. Grace was the fount of all good and everywhere present because Christ's incarnation had purchased an abundance for the world.[84] Nevertheless, receiving its benefits was still a

---

[79] Rymer, *Foedera*, xv, 181–3 (*CPR 1548–9*, 406). Redman remained on the commission when it was renewed 18 January 1551 with the additional responsibility of suppressing the 'errors of the libertines': Rymer, *Foedera*, xv, 250–2 (*CPR 1549–51*, 347).

[80] According to the report of Bernard Gilpin in J. Strype, *Annals of the Reformation* (Oxford 1824), i, I, 117.

[81] 'Master Doctor Redman this day hathe ben before the visitors [of Cambridge University], and bringing with him an interpretation of iii sentences picked owt of the homelies, and declaring and making protestation that he trusted the said sentences meant none other thing but according to that his interpretation, though the verie wordes straitly taken might seme as he thought, to import an other sence, he was contented to subscribe, and so did': PRO, SP 10/7, no. 23 (*CSPD EdVI*, no. 251). Dixon, *History*, iii, 106.

[82] W.W. Rouse Ball, *Trinity College Cambridge* (1906), 50. For the re-ordering of the altar, see Trinity College, Cambridge, Senior Bursar's Accounts: 1547–63, f. 107v.

[83] Le Neve, *1300–1541*, x, 20. The suggestion that Redman had a further tenure of the Lady Margaret chair in 1549 (Venn, iii, 436) was disproved by Dr Rex in his Cambridge lecture of 1 March 2002.

[84] Redman, *Complaint of Grace* (1609), 2, 84–5.

matter of choice.[85] Those who would permit grace to work in them and exercise its properties would grow towards perfect holiness and rejoice in the inward sight of God.[86] Although grace stayed far away from anyone who claimed to deserve salvation, it brought in worthiness to those who knew themselves destitute and dependent. As earlier, however, grace first had to cast them 'downe in repentance, humilitie of heart, lowlines, and confession' before it could make them strong, valiant and able soldiers under the banner of Christ.[87] In short, for those who would not through the malice of their own will resist, grace softened cold human hearts, making them fruitful unto God and producing many good works.[88]

In Redman's eyes, however, the Edwardine church had failed to choose grace. Although he admitted medieval errors such as the imperial papacy and hypocrisy of the religious orders,[89] Redman harshly castigated his contemporaries as even worse:

> Yee be the cursed generation of *Cham*, which mocked his father, and had his delight in laughing at his fathers nakedness. So is your pleasure and pasttime in the report of such faults as you lay to your forefathers, and your owne you will not see, which be a hundred times worse, ye can raile upon their abuses, their superstitions and Idolatry, and ye your selves be worse then Pagans and Infidels, and cleane fallen from God, and from [grace's] governance.[90]

Edwardines were presumptuous in matters of religion, since '[e]very man thinketh himselfe a doctor, every man disdaineth to learne, except it bee of himselfe'. They might write scripture on their walls, like the Pharisees with their phylacteries, but the Word remained far from their hearts. Preachers made people feel good without requiring them to be good, crying peace, peace, when there was no peace.[91] Now it was taught that 'God careth not for long prayers, but for a good heart, and true faith'. Consequently, time at prayer was shorter, lest the church's liturgy last longer than the sincere devotion of the people, rendering the service a mere ritualistic ceremony. Yet, Redman inquired, how could true piety be stirred up without significant time in prayer?[92] And what

---

[85] *Ibid.*, 2, 74, 87.

[86] *Ibid.*, 86.

[87] *Ibid.*, 88, 90.

[88] *Ibid.*, 91.

[89] For the papacy, see *ibid.*, 57–8. Cf. 'Great was the hypocrisie of Monkes and Fryers in these latter dayes', *ibid.*, 72; 'Great was the hypocrisie of some Monkes and Freers in these latter dayes': *Complaint of Grace* (1556), sig. [G8]v.

[90] Redman, *Complaint of Grace* (1609), 61–2.

[91] *Ibid.*, 71–3.

[92] *Ibid.*, 75–6.

had happened to the other two traditional good works, fasting and almsgiving? Redman noted that 'their names remaine in the Scriptures, but the use of them seemeth to be abolished'. The new sort argued that fasting should not be appointed for specific times, but left up to individuals as they were moved. Yet, rarely was anyone so inclined. Although Redman himself was known for his generosity, he had few imitators: 'Every man is so poore in his owne sight, that he needeth all things which hee may come by'.[93] In fact, in Redman's view avarice had become the chief vice of the era, overthrowing every attempt to return to a wholesome Christian morality. For avarice concentrated humanity's focus on earthly things, and the role of grace was to lift up humanity's eyes to heavenly, spiritual things.[94]

Therefore, the protestants may have claimed to be bringing in a reformation that clearly established salvation by grace. As Redman's title implied, however, grace had nothing to do with the new ecclesiastical regime. According to *The Complaint*, grace had abandoned her efforts to bring the 'generall reformation and redresse of things' for which people waited with 'long frustrate expectation'. Rather, grace had decided to work here and there secretly through individuals until the day might come when its influence would be openly welcomed in the world again.[95] In a bitter assessment that clearly conveyed Redman's own attitude toward the Edwardine church as well as his advocacy for his middle way of catholic humanism, grace passed judgement on the English suitation:

> [I]f they had the spirit which they boast of, and had the scripture in their hearts as in their mouth, and considered the ordering of Christs church from the beginning, and the sentences and mindes of Saints touching the same: they would either amend their sayings and doings, or else grant themselves to be an obstinate perversity.[96]

Redman's Reputation

For Redman, the reformation of the English church was always only to be the necessary means towards a needed amelioration of Christian morals. Consequently, he used his considerable scholarship to ascertain the primitive essentials of the catholic faith and practice in which he was reared, and then he worked with his sovereigns to enshrine his

---

[93] *Ibid.*, 77–9.
[94] *Ibid.*, 80–3, 86.
[95] *Ibid.*, 83–4.
[96] *Ibid.*, 77.

findings in the new English formularies. That he handled this task in such a way as to be regarded by all sides as a man of complete integrity was no mean accomplishment, but not without cost. Since he was prepared to concede points to both catholics and protestants about the nature of authentic Christianity, the question remains, how far did Redman actually traverse in his opinions? The controversy surrounding his last days only made the matter more vexed and urgent, for after his death both catholics and protestants in Tudor England came to claim the respected Redman as one of their own.

On 1 October 1551, lying at Westminster 'deseased in my bodye but hole in mynde', Redman sensed he was unlikely to recover from his lingering illness and so finalized his will. True to his churchmanship, the document was unremarkable, neither overtly traditionalist nor clearly protestant. The preamble was a simple statement of faith which any dying Christian could make: 'myself wholye bodie and soule I putt into the handes of our Savior Jesus in whose mercye I truste to attayne everlasting salvation'. And after asking that his debts be paid and his servants rewarded, Redman committed all the rest of his goods

> to the disposition and ordre of my brother George Redman and Richard Burton my servaunte putting my trust in them that they will doo in all thinges according as they knowe shalbe for my discharge afore god.[97]

What exact mortuary arrangements Redman expected his brother and his servant to do for his 'discharge afore god' is not specifically stated and, therefore, beyond objection by either catholics or protestants in those troubled times.[98]

As Redman grew close to death on 2 November, however, he dispensed with such caution. He openly discussed his views on the contentious religious issues of the day with the head master and under master of Westminster School, Alexander Nowell and Edward Cratford, both of whom the month before had acted as witnesses to his will,[99] as well as two Cambridge colleagues, Richard Wilkes, the master of Christ's College, and John Young, a fellow of Trinity and ardent opponent of Bucer, all in the presence of his own servants. Within two days he was dead,[100] and the battle for interpreting Redman's final

---

[97] PRO, PROB 11/40, f. 21v.

[98] For a discussion of interpreting Tudor wills, see E. Duffy, *The Stripping of the Altars* (1992), 504–523. For references to Redman's house, see *Acts 1543–1609*, nos 11, 26.

[99] PRO, PROB 11/40, f. 21v.

[100] The date of his death is given as 4 November 1551 in a Westminster inscription: Camden, *Reges*, sig. K[1]v (see n. 1 above). Note, however, that material printed in Foxe

words and their implications for his theological legacy began shortly thereafter. According to John Foxe, John Young wrote a letter immediately afterwards to John Cheke describing the conversations.[101] In addition, a list for fourteen articles taken from Redman's answers was drawn up, apparently by Nowell, to which those present during the course of that day were asked to subscribe in the house and presence of the dean.[102] Evidently, both documents made their way to the privy council whereupon extracts were taken from Young's letter and included as an addendum to several of the fourteen articles so as to form a single document.[103] At the same time, William Seres, a printer who kept shop at the Sign of the Hedgehog in St Paul's Churchyard,[104] had heard 'sundrye and dysagreynge' reports of Redman's final views on the current religious controversies. When he came across the unified account in William Cecil's chamber at court, Seres asked permission to publish it, 'perceyuing dayly talke to encrease here vpon'. Cecil agreed, giving him as well a separate letter from Richard Wilkes. He published them both in a slim book entitled *A reporte of Maister Doctor Redmans answeres* at London on 12 December 1551.[105]

suggests 2 November as the actual date. Writing on 3 November, John Young speaks of his grief now that Redman has died and promises to relate what the good doctor spoke on religious controversies 'at the houre of hys death'. According to Richard Wilkes, he and John Young had their theological discussion with Redman on 2 November: Foxe, *Actes and Monuments*, 869, 872.

[101] According to Foxe, he found the original autograph written by Young: *ibid.*, 870–2.

[102] A. Nowell, *A Confutation, as wel of M. Dormans last Boke entituled A Disproufe. &c. as also D. Sander his causes of Transubstantiation* (1567), 12r. The servants who subscribed were Richard Burton, Ellis Lomas, John Wryght and Richard Elithorne: *A reporte of Maister Doctor Redmans answeres, to questions propounded him before his death, concernynge certain poyntes of religion, now beyng with many in controversye* (1551), sigs A3r–[A6]r (reprinted in Foxe, *Actes and Monuments*, 867–8). All are named as Redman's servants in his will: PRO, PROB 11/40, f. 21v. Elithorne served in the Abbey choir in addition to his duties in Redman's household, being a lay vicar in 1544 and deputy minor canon in 1556: WAM 37044, f. 1v; 37709.

[103] Cf. Young's 'addendum' in *Redmans answeres*, sigs [A6]r–[A7]r (reprinted in Foxe, *Actes and Monuments*, 868) and his letter in Foxe, *Actes and Monuments*, 870–4.

[104] According to the colophon of *Redmans answeres* the book was printed by Thomas Raynalde for William Seres. Later Cecil also secured for Seres the sole patent to print all primers: *CPR 1566–72*, 268 (no. 2126). For Seres's support of protestant clergy, see B. Usher, 'Backing protestantism: the London godly, the exchequer and the Foxe circle', in *John Foxe: An Historical Perspective*, ed. D.M. Loades (Aldershot 1999), 133. The printer Thomas Reynold is not to be confused with the Thomas Reynolds who was Redman's fellow canon at Westminster and a witness to his will. The latter was one of only three canons not to be deposed under Mary; for this man see *Acts 1543–1609*, i, p. xli, and no. 33; ii, no. 264 & n. 263; Le Neve, *1541–1857*, vii, 72–82; PRO, PROB 11/40, f. 21v.

[105] *Redmans answeres*, sig. A2.

According to *Redmans answeres*, the good doctor had died a good
protestant. He rejected the papacy as 'a sinke of all evyl'. He denied the
medieval understanding of purgatory as well as the mass as a propitiatory sacrifice for the sins of the dead. He thought transubstantiation
was untenable and dismissed an objective, local presence of Christ's
humanity in the elements as falling into the error of the Caphernites,
i.e., those who thought that Jesus expected his followers to act like
cannibals and eat the actual flesh of his earthly body.[106] Redman did
not believe that works could ever deserve everlasting life and regretted
having fought against justification by faith. Now, however, he embraced that doctrine so long as justifying faith was understood to be a
true and living faith which embraced Christ and did not encourage the
people to sin. In fact, according to Ellis Lomas, Redman's servant, the
good doctor had written in favour of justification *sola fide* to Henry
VIII, but thought that it was not to be taught to the people lest they
neglect good works. Finally, Redman had concluded that the consensus
of the church was a poor standard for doctrine so theologians should
look to scripture instead.[107]

Of course, *Redmans answeres* did not settle the matter. During Mary's
reign, Cuthbert Tunstall published *De Iustificatione* (1555), since he
claimed that Redman intended to do so himself but death had intervened, but no doubt also to make clear exactly what Redman told
Henry VIII about solifidianism.[108] About the same time, the 'papal-
friendly' version of *The Complaint of Grace* was published, plainly
proclaiming Redman's attitude towards the Edwardine church. Nevertheless, John Foxe revived the issue in 1563 by including the text of
Redmans answeres along with a transcript of Young's original letter in
his *Actes and Monuments*. Two years later Thomas Dorman accused
Alexander Nowell of slandering Redman.[109] In 1567 Nowell responded,
giving his account of how the fourteen articles came about, and adding
that while he had heard that John Young accused him of lying, Young
himself had subscribed.[110] While Redman's manuscripts make him a
poor protestant, Nowell had a point. Young never seems to have repudiated in writing what was attributed to him, as John Foxe himself

---

[106] Based on John 6:52, Capernaite (also spelled Capharnaite or Capharnite), the
proper name for an inhabitant of Capernaum, became a standard derogatory term for
one who held an overly-carnal understanding of Christ's presence in the sacramental
elements.

[107] *Redmans answeres*, sigs A3r–[B4]v.

[108] Redman, *De Iustificatione*, sig. A3v.

[109] T. Dorman, *A Disproufe of M. Nowelles Reproufe* (Antwerp 1565), sig. +3.

[110] Nowell, *Confutation of Dorman and Sander*, 11v–13r.

pointed out in 1570.[111] Although Young did spend most of the rest of his life during Elizabeth's reign in prison, his fellow Marian catholic Nicholas Harpsfield did not allow his captivity to prevent him from engaging in polemical composition. Without some evidence of Young's clear repudiation of Foxe's letter, the dispute remains more likely to be one of interpretation rather than of facts, especially since the addendum to the fourteen articles included only selective extracts from Young's letter and not the entire text as printed by Foxe.

Consider Redman's statements about justification. His rejection of works meriting salvation sounds protestant, as does his agreeing with justification *sola fide*, but the devil is in the details. At his death Redman insisted that justifying faith had to be a living faith which embraced Christ.[112] In *De Iustificatione* he clearly wrote that a living faith was a faith joined to charity and that both were needed to hold on to Christ effectually. In both *De Iustificatione* and *The Complaint of Grace*, Redman also insisted that such union with Christ was a matter of individuals choosing to respond to the universal offer of grace, not simply a natural response of the elect to the special gift of grace. Finally, in both *De Iustificatione* and *The Complaint of Grace*, Redman held that justification brought intrinsic worthiness, not merely forensic right-eousness. All three points fundamentally contradicted the standard protestant understanding of solifidianism, hence his clear unease with the Book of Homilies two years before. Nothing in Redman's death-bed description of justification by faith explicitly repudiated these qualifications.

Yet if Redman's dying pronouncement on justification remained essentially compatible with his writings, he still was reported to have expressed regret over the issue. From a scriptural point of view, the weakest point of Redman's argument in *De Iustificatione* was following those scholastics who taught that the penitent needed to dispose himself for sanctifying grace through a rigorous process of actively choosing to co-operate with prevenient grace. Such was the premise that lay behind

---

[111] In a new introductory paragraph for the letter, Foxe noted that he printed the 'Epistle of Doct. Yo[u]ng, as I receiued it written by his owne hand in the *Latine* tongue, the copy which he him selfe hath not, nor can deny to be his owne': *Actes and Monumentes* (1570), 1539.

[112] 'That thys proposition *Sola fides iustificat*, so that *fides* signifye *veram viuam et acquiescentem in Christo fidem id est amplexum Christi*, that is to saye: Onely fayth doeth iustifye, so that fayth do signifye a true lyuely, and a fayth restinge in christe, and embrasing Christ, is a true godly swete and comfortable doctryne: so that it be so taughte, that the people take none occasion of carnal lybertie thereof': *Redmans answeres*, sig. [A5].

Redman's insistence on good works before justification.[113] He also stressed, however, that penitents were never to put their trust in their own efforts but solely in the mercy of God as revealed in Jesus Christ. Perhaps Redman did come to conclude that an emphasis on good works before justification undermined the requisite sense of humble dependency on divine grace.[114] Nevertheless, even if he had in fact adopted a more Augustinian view that denied the human will any decisive role in preparing for justification, his continued insistence on personal faith and love as its necessary basis remained thoroughly traditional. Thus, in the light of his other qualifications, by Luther's standard, Redman had still failed to embrace the chief doctrine of protestantism.

If Redman did not die a protestant, did he die a catholic? Not if that is defined as having allegiance to the papacy. Redman's death-bed description of the see of Rome as 'stayned and polluted' with 'horrible vices' was well in keeping with his views as recorded in *The Complaint of Grace* (1609) and should be regarded as genuine. If, however, his adherence to the catholic faith is to be defined by his eucharistic teaching, the other commonly-accepted standard of the day, the issue is less straightforward. With the advent of the Six Articles, Redman began to study in earnest transubstantiation and defended the doctrine as late as 1546 when he helped to persuade Nicholas Shaxton to subscribe to the act.[115] Two years later Redman affirmed Christ's real presence in the sacrament, both in a sermon he preached before the king on 4 March[116] and concerning his understanding of what was the accepted eucharistic position among the higher clergy at the time of Gardiner's sermon on 29 June.[117] Yet Ascham identified justification as the sole major doctrinal

---

[113] '[Poenitentia] vero quae ad resarciendam a baptismo disruptam innocentiae vestem adhibetur, difficilior, multoque maioris negocii et laboris esse credenda sit': Redman, *De Iustificatione*, 6; 'Bona opera ... nos Deo appropinquare faciunt': *ibid.*, 29.

[114] Redman thought the opposite in *De Iustificatione*: 'Quamuis autem bonam opera tantopere praedicamus, gratiae tamen nihil detrahimus' (p. 44).

[115] According to a letter attributed to Thomas Lever, John Young remembered Redman saying 'that he had for the last twelve years directed all his studies and attention to that subject': *Original Letters relative to the English Reformation*, ed. H. Robinson (Parker Soc. 1846), 151–2; original Latin in *Epistolae Tigurinae* (Parker Soc. 1848), 99. According to Bonner's register, Redman was part of a four-person delegation which convinced Shaxton to subscribe to the Six Articles, including the proposition that after consecration, only the substance of Christ's body remained: Guildhall MS 9531/12, f. 100.

[116] Gardiner reported that in his sermon before the king Redman affirmed 'the true presence of Christ's body and blood was in the sacrament of the altar': Foxe, *Actes and Monuments*, 794. For the date of the sermon *Literary Remains of King Edward VI*, ed. J.G. Nichols (1857), pp. civ–cv.

[117] According to those who deposed Redman for Gardiner's trial, 'at that tyme as farre as he remembereth there was no contention or controversy in that matter [regarding 'the

difference between Redman and his protestant Cambridge colleagues.[118] In fact, realist language did not necessarily mean a real presence position, if one meant by that an objective presence of Christ's humanity as well as his divinity in the elements themselves, and that appears to have been precisely the issue at the heart of the dispute over the eucharistic statements Redman made on his death-bed.

According to two different accounts, John Young understood Redman to have specifically affirmed the key catholic teaching of Christ's real bodily presence in the eucharist, even if Redman was unclear on exactly how that presence should be described. In his own letter as printed by Foxe, Young recorded three key statements by Redman. First, the dying man agreed

> that christ dyd gyue, and offer to faythfull and christian men, hys very reall body, and bloud verely and really vnder the sacramentes of bread and wine ... the maner wherby christ is there present, and ministreth to the faythfull his fleshe, is al together inexplicable: but we must beleue ... and think, that by gods mighty power and holy operation of his spirite, this so notable a mistery was made ... [119]

Secondly, Redman believed that Christians were bound to worship Christ's presence in his holy supper and 'that it was most agreying to pietie and godly religion'. Finally, Redman also thought that the words of institution explained what was given in the Supper: '*This is my bodye*, whereby [Christ] doth evidently and plainly shew what by that gifte they should receive, and howe royall and precious a gyfte he would geve them'.[120] Young also discussed Redman's death-bed statements with Thomas Lever who in turn passed on what he had learned in a letter to Roger Ascham. Lever succinctly summarized Young's understanding of Redman's eucharistic views: 'With respect to the presence, he said (as Yo[u]ng related the conversation), that Christ was really and corporally present in the sacrament'.[121]

Yet no such definite statement was included in *Redmans answeres*. Instead, many of Nowell's articles on the eucharistic presence were clearly designed to suggest the opposite, even though the learned would have realized their basic compatibility with traditional catholic teaching.

---

very presence of christes body in the sacrament'], amongst the prelates or learned men of this realme': Foxe, *Actes and Monuments*, 786, 854.

[118] 'In doctrina etiam de conjugio sacerdotum, et aliis controversiis rectissime in publicis scholis Cantabrigiae sententiam et judicium suum declaravit. De justificatione autem solius fidei, nonnihil a nobis discrepavit': Ascham, *Works*, i, 295.

[119] Foxe, *Actes and Monuments*, 871, 873.

[120] *Ibid.*, 873.

[121] Robinson, *Original Letters*, 152.

According to Article 7, Redman said 'that nothing whych is sene in the sacrament, or perceiued wyth any outwarde stuffe is to be worshypped', a seeming endorsement of the reformed protestant position that Christ was only to be worshipped in Heaven where his human body was now present.[122] Yet, Cranmer himself acknowledged that it was common catholic teaching that 'they worship not the sacraments which they see with their eyes, but that thing which they believe with their faith to be really and corporally in the sacraments'.[123]

Articles 8 and 9 only reinforced the impression that Redman thought Christ's human body was absent from the sacrament, for they quoted him as saying, 'we receaue not christes body *corporaliter, id est crasse,* corporally, that is to say grossely, lyke other meates, and lyke as the Caphernites dyd vnderstand it ... we receaue christes body *sic spiritualiter vt tamen vere,* so spirituallye, that neuerthelesse truely'.[124] Such statements, however, could easily have been thoroughly traditional. When Gardiner and Tunstall wanted to distance themselves from Capharnaism, they, too, stressed the spiritual nature of Christ's risen body and, hence, the spiritual manner of his human presence in the sacrament. They also accepted that the benefits of Christ's body and blood were received spiritually by the faithful, for the scholastics were accustomed to distinguish between a sacramental eating of the true body and blood of Christ which all who communicated received, the unworthy as well as the worthy, and a spiritual feeding on the grace conveyed therein, which only the worthy received.[125] Consequently, according to Cranmer, the

---

[122] *Redmans answeres*, sig. A4v.

[123] *Writings and Disputations of Thomas Cranmer... relative to the Sacrament of the Lord's Supper*, ed. J.E. Cox (Parker Soc. 1844), 229.

[124] *Redmans answeres*, sig. A4v. Likewise Young who had subscribed to both statements in Nowell's account: '[C]hrist dyd distribute hys body so spiritually as truely: not so yet neuerthelesse, that by these and the lyke wordes we mighte conceyue any grosse, or carnall intelligence, suche as the Caphernites ones dreamed of: but that (quod he) we myght labour, and endeauour to expresse by some kinde of tearmes, and wordes hys ineffable maiesty': Foxe, *Actes and Monuments*, 873.

[125] '[W]e receive Christ's flesh glorified incorruptible, very spiritual, and in a spiritual manner delivered unto us'; 'Christ giveth [his body] not in a visible manner, nor such a manner as the Capernaites thought on, nor such a manner as any carnal man can conceive; being also the flesh in the sacrament, given not a common flesh, but a lively, godly, and spiritual flesh': Gardiner in Cox, *Cranmer on the Lord's Supper*, 162, 231. Cf. '[Christ's] body after His resurrection is now a spiritual body ... And in the Sacrament the very spiritual body is given invisibly and spiritually, and is received by the faithful ... But in what way the bread which was common before the consecration becomes (*transiret in*) His body by the ineffable sanctification of the Spirit, the most learned of the ancients thought inscrutable, lest, with the people of Capernaum failing to believe the words of Christ but asking how this should be, they should try to be wise above what is right, transgressing soberness of mind': Cuthbert Tunstall, as quoted in D.

crux of his disagreement with Gardiner on the eucharist was precisely over their conflicting interpretations of *spiritualiter*.[126]

Lastly, according to Article 11, when Redman was asked by Wilkes 'what that was, that was lyfted vp betwene the priestes handes' he answered he thought that Christ 'could nether be lyfte vp nor downe'.[127] While Redman appears once again to have rejected the real presence of Christ's humanity in the consecrated bread, this also need not necessarily have been the case, for the scholastics as well denied that Christ himself was effected by a priest's movements in the eucharist. Both Aquinas and Scotus were careful to distinguish between the special manner of the sacramental presence under the species of bread and wine, and the actual location of his humanity according to its own natural dimensions which was only in Heaven and, thus, untouchable by earthly hands.[128] Equally as important, however, Young remembered Redman making this response as part of his non-controversial answer to the question about worshipping the visible sacrament, not to a query about the nature of its substance, and Wilkes's account agreed.[129] In truth, Young was surely accurate when he described Redman as affirming his belief in the real presence, but admitting its exact means to be a mystery of faith. Years later Young himself was to argue that in doctrinal matters reason had to give way to faith.[130] Little wonder, then, Young accused Nowell of slandering Redman.

Stone, *A History of the Doctrine of the Holy Eucharist* (1909), ii, 170. For the distinction between sacramental and spiritual eating in the eucharist see *ibid.*, i, 320, 331, and Gardiner in Cox, *Cranmer on the Lord's Supper*, 70.

[126] 'And if there be any difference between us two, it is but a little and in this point only: that I say that Christ is but spiritually in the ministration of the sacrament, and you say that he is but after a spiritual manner in the sacrament': Cox, *Cranmer on the Lord's Supper*, 91.

[127] *Redmans answeres*, sig. [A5]r.

[128] Stone, *History of the Eucharist*, i, 330–4, 340–1.

[129] Young: 'Lykewyse being asked whether he would haue the visible sacrament to be worshipped that which we see with oure eyes and is lifted up betwene the priestes handes, aunswered: that nothing which was visible and to be perceiued by the sight of the eye is to be adored or worshipped: nor that Christ would be eleuated into any hygher, or brought downe into any lower place: so that he can neyther be lifted vp hygher nor pulled down lower': Foxe, *Actes and Monuments*, 873. Wilkes: 'Then I asked him what he thought of that whych the priest was wont to lyft vp and show the people betwixt his handes, he sayd: it is the sacrament, then sayd I they were wont to worshyp that which was lifted up, yea saith he: but we must worship christ in heven, Christ is nether lifted vp nor down': *Redmans answeres*, sig. B2r. Cf. Lever: '[Redman] affirmed, that the body of Christ was now incapable of being lifted up or let down by any human hands': Robinson, *Original Letters*, 152.

[130] When asked to enter into disputation with William Fulke, Young angrily retorted, 'Our faith is aboue reason ... Our faith is not to bee prooued by reason': Dom Raymund

Yet, neither Redman nor those gathered around his death-bed were content to leave the manner of Christ's eucharistic presence entirely in the hands of faith. Despite his caveat of its inexplicability, according to the surviving accounts Redman did indeed hazard an explanation, an explanation whose key elements no Henrician traditionalist, Marian catholic or even Lutheran protestant would have recognized. While both Gardiner and Tunstall stressed the spiritual manner of Christ's human presence in the sacrament, they did so only in order to follow the church's traditional explanation of transubstantiation.[131] Yet, according to everyone, Redman denied transubstantiation.[132] He admitted that while he had at one time been fully committed to the doctrine, as he examined its defence by Gabriel Biel and other scholastics, he found many of their arguments wanting. Because of these studies his 'former zeale and opinion, touchying the mayntenance of transubstantiation dyd euery day more and more decrease', especially since Justin, Irenaeus and Tertullian vigorously rejected the same.[133] Therefore, consecration was not restricted to specific prayers over the elements but referred to 'tota actio [namely, 'all the whole thinge done'] in ministering the Sacrament as Christ dyd institute it'.[134] Wilkes added that Redman actually went so far as to state specifically that the bread continued to remain during this process.[135]

Webster, '"Conference" at Wisbech: a glimpse of Bishop Watson and Abbot Feckenham in 1580', *The Downside Review*, 54 (1936), 334.

[131] 'How Christ's body is in circumstance present, no man can define; but that it is truly present, and therefore really present, corporally also, and naturally, with relation to the the truth of the body present, and not to the manner of presence, which is spiritual, exceeding our capacity, and therefore therein without drawing away accidents or adding, we believe simply the truth': Gardiner in Cox, *Cranmer on the Lord's Supper*, 329. Cf. 'These words [of institution] ... clearly declare that the body of Christ, not only figuratively ... but the very real and natural body of Christ, although now spiritual, is under the species of bread ... [Christ's] body after His resurrection is now a spiritual body ... And in the Sacrament the very spiritual body is given invisibly and spiritually, and is received by the faithful': Cuthbert Tunstall, as quoted in Stone, *History of the Eucharist*, ii, 170.

[132] Nowell: *Redmans answeres*, sig. [A5]r. Wilkes: *ibid.*, sig. [B3]r. Young: Foxe, *Actes and Monuments*, 873. Lever: Robinson, *Original Letters*, 151–2.

[133] According to Young: Foxe, *Actes and Monuments*, 873. Likewise, Wilkes (*Redmans answeres*, sig. [B3]r), Lever (Robinson, *Original Letters*, 151–2) and a summary of Young appended to Nowell's articles (*Redmans answeres*, sigs [A6]v–[A7]r).

[134] According to Wilkes, *Redmans answeres*, sig. [B3]v. Likewise, Young (Foxe, *Actes and Monuments*, 873) and an extract from Young appended to Nowell's articles (*Redmans answeres*, sig. [A7]r).

[135] '[W]hat, sayth he: nede we to doubte that bread remayneth. Scripture calleth it bread and certayne good Auctours that be of latter tyme, be of that opinion': *Redmans answeres*, sig. [B3]v.

While such views were appropriate for Lutherans, Redman parted company even with them on their continued commitment to an objective presence of Christ joined to the elements during the sacrament. A standard litmus test for Luther's real presence position was the requirement that both worthy and unworthy communicants received Christ's body (*manducatio indignorum*). Yet Redman asserted that the wicked ate only sacramental bread, not the true body of Christ, because the Lord 'would not gyue his moste pure and holy fleshe to be eaten of such naughty, and impure persones: but would kepe it away from them'.[136] Even Young acknowledged this crucial point, adding the significant detail that Redman himself admitted the serious break with tradition this statement represented: 'And this he sayd is, and euer was his opinion, and belefe concerning the same, although he knewe others to be of a contrary iudgement.'[137] In addition, Wilkes remembered that the good doctor not only rejected the strongly realist description that Christ was present in the elements in 'fleshe, bloud, and bone' but also another standard test for Lutheran orthodoxy, that communicants received the very body of Christ with their mouths (*manducatio oralis*). Although Redman struggled over the latter statement, saying 'I can not tel, it is a harde question', he eventually concluded that both descriptions of Christ's presence were too close to the view of the Caphernites. Consequently, he asserted that communicants received the body and blood of Christ 'in our soule by fayth'.[138] If John Young felt that, whatever the dying man's qualifications, Redman's final position was not unlike that of Erasmus which sought at the very least to agree with catholic doctrine *in genere*,[139] Alexander Nowell and Richard Wilkes decided those qualifications were more significant than any realist language and, hence, presented Redman as more clearly reformed.

In the final analysis, the key to understanding why Redman affirmed both realist language and significant non-realist qualifications lies in his concept of the eucharist as a communion. Fundamentally, Christ instituted the sacrament to promote a holy union between God and his people through their consuming of the elements, for Jesus said, 'Take, eat'.[140]

---

[136] According to Young in Foxe, *Actes and Monuments*, 873. Likewise, Nowell (*Redmans answeres*, sig. A4r), an extract from Young appended to Nowell's articles (*Redmans answeres*, sig. [A6]), and Lever (Robinson, *Original Letters*, 152).

[137] Foxe, *Actes and Monuments*, 873. Likewise, an extract from Young appended to Nowell's articles (*Redmans answeres*, sig. [A6]v).

[138] *Redmans answeres*, sigs B1r–B2r.

[139] J.B. Payne, *Erasmus. His Theology of the Sacraments* (1970), 143–54.

[140] According to Wilkes: *Redmans answeres*, sig. B1r. Both Young (Foxe, *Actes and Monuments*, 873) and Nowell (*Redmans answeres*, sig. A4r) cite the words of institution to show the proper use of the sacrament.

Any other practice was an abuse. Therefore, the sacrament was not to be carried in procession, a custom which Redman said he had openly preached against in Cambridge about 1535.[141] Nor was the sacrament to be offered as a sacrifice for the sins of the living and the dead, although he granted the effectiveness of prayers for the dead.[142] For Redman, 'christ dyd gyue, and offer to faythfull and christian men hys very reall body, and bloud verely and really under the sacraments of bread and wine: in somuch that they which deuoutly come to be pertakers of that holy foode, are by the benefite thereof united, and made one with christe in his flesh, and body'.[143] This was possible because in the holy communion earth and heaven came together,[144] and those who received the sacrament properly experienced a wonderful union (*mira unitio*). As St Paul had taught, they were so joined to Christ as to be flesh of his flesh and bone of his bones which quickened their mortal bodies and souls to everlasting joy.[145]

Although both Wilkes and Young remembered the good doctor as saying that those who enjoyed this union received Christ 'by faith', surely Redman meant once again a faith joined with love. Indeed, Young noted him earlier specifying 'faythfull and christian men', and, of course, to Redman a faithful Christian was one who held on to Christ with the faith formed by love through the indwelling grace of justification.[146] Once seen in the light of this stipulation, Redman's denial of Christ's objective presence in the sacrament is not unlike his earlier rejection of absolution *ex opere operato*. God covenanted to bring about the miracle of the eucharist only for those whom grace had already given the necessary two spiritual hands to receive Christ. Since

---

[141] The Cambridge incident was included in Young's account and appended to Nowell's articles (Foxe, *Actes and Monuments*, 873; *Redmans answeres*, sig. [A6]v) but all four agree that Redman considered the procession of the sacrament to be an abuse: Young (Foxe, *Actes and Monuments*, 873), Nowell (*Redmans answeres*, sig. A4r), Wilkes (*Redmans answeres*, sig. [B2]v), and Lever (Robinson, *Original Letters*, 152).

[142] Redman's statement that prayers for the dead were beneficial was included only in Young (Foxe, *Actes and Monuments*, 873). Nevertheless, the accounts of Young (*ibid.*), Nowell (*Redmans answeres*, sigs A3v–A4r), and Lever (Robinson, *Original Letters*, 151) all agree that Redman rejected the mass as a propitiation for the sins of the dead.

[143] According to Young in Foxe, *Actes and Monuments*, 873.

[144] *Ibid.*

[145] Although this language of *mira unitio* and 'bone of his bones' is found only in Wilkes's account, he remembered Redman stressing its importance: 'he was moch in this point': *Redmans answeres*, sigs B1r–B2r. The scriptural description is based on Ephesians 5:28–32 and Genesis 2:23–4. Irenaeus, one of the ancient authorities Redman said influenced his eucharistic doctrine, used similar language in *Adversus Haereses*, v, 2, 3.

[146] Wilkes: *Redmans answeres*, sig. B1v. Young: Foxe, *Actes and Monuments*, 873.

their flesh had been made truly holy through the spiritual gifts of justification, the faithful alone were worthy and able to be united by the Spirit's mystical power to the true and holy flesh of Christ in the eucharist.

Redman had already spoken of this sort of invisible, heavenly communion in *The Complaint of Grace*. Reflecting his Erasmian emphasis on the spiritual over the temporal, he wrote that the work of grace was to shift people's minds away from focusing on the vain things of this transitory world towards God, so that they might gain an accurate understanding of spiritual things and 'inwardly rejoyce in the sight of God'.[147] Since praying lifted up the mind to God, this activity was the special means to keep and increase grace. Redman specifically connected eucharistic grace to the prayerful pursuit of the invisible, spiritual world when he wrote in this context that 'the most solemne prayers' were those 'at the holy communion in the congregation'.[148] Since the purpose of communion was to grant faithful participants this inner spiritual union, he objected to anything that focused too much attention on the merely visible aspects of the sacrament.

Nevertheless, Young was not simply deceiving himself when he left his interview with Redman convinced that the dying man held to some form of presence associated with the eucharistic elements themselves. Indeed, so strong was the connection between the sign and what it signified in Redman's mind that he had to hesitate before deciding to deny that the faithful received the very body of Christ with the mouth and into the body. Evidently, Redman wanted to maintain as close a connection as was possible for the bread and wine with Christ's real body and blood, while still making this relationship dependent on the individual faithfulness of the recipient instead of the inherent power of the sacramental rite. In short, Redman seems to have continued to hold to the catholic teaching on the elements as the instrumental means for conveying Christ's presence and power to the bodies and souls of those able to receive, even if he reinterpreted the manner by which this happened. As a result, in a very real, but supernatural sense, the dying man could say that the true body of Christ was present *in the faithful use* of the eucharistic elements.

Yet by making the miracle of the eucharist dependent on the grace at work in the individual, Redman left behind catholic orthodoxy, even as his understanding of grace's work within the individual did not.

---

[147] Redman, *Complaint of Grace* (1609), 86–8.

[148] *Ibid.*, 75. Cf. 'These were beside the most solemne prayers, whiche were at the holye Communions': *Complaint of Grace* (1556), sig. H3r. For Erasmus on this point see Payne, *Erasmus*, 133.

Therefore, his eucharistic position would have indeed sounded more akin to those protestants who sought a middle way between the real presence position of Luther and Zwingli's memorialism. They, too, argued that the sacraments were effectual signs which actually conferred what they represented to the faithful.[149] Such was Cranmer's final view as well, and Lever reported Redman's endorsement of the archbishop's eucharistic writings against Gardiner.[150] Nevertheless, Redman's description seems closer to Bucer than Cranmer. For Bucer was a symbolic instrumentalist who taught that the sacrament brought about an inner union with Christ when the Spirit entered the communicant's heart by means of the bread and wine. Cranmer, however, was more of a symbolic parallelist, arguing that at the same time as the elements were received the Spirit entered directly into the heart.[151]

In fact, the statements on holy communion attributed to Redman by Wilkes and Young have striking similarities to those made by Bucer while regius professor of divinity in Cambridge. According to Bucer, since Christ in his humanity was unquestionably located in heaven, his presence on earth could only be apprehended by spiritual, not earthly, means.[152] Consequently, as Irenaeus taught, the eucharist consisted of two realities, the physical, earthly signs of bread and wine, and the spiritual, heavenly communion in the Lord which had 'to be laid hold of by faith alone' and which was 'not to be entangled in any concep-

---

[149] See *Oxford Encyclopedia of the Reformation*, ed. H.J. Hillerbrand (Oxford 1996), ii, 76–8.

[150] 'He added, moreover, that it was an excellent book which the most reverend archbishop of Canterbury had lately written upon the eucharist, and he recommended Yo[u]ng to read it with much attention': Robinson, *Original Letters*, 152. Cranmer's *Answer* to Gardiner was published by late September 1551: MacCulloch, *Cranmer*, 487.

[151] For an important study on the divergent views concerning the eucharist in the reformed tradition, see B.A. Gerrish, 'Sign and reality: the Lord's Supper in the reformed confessions' in *The Old Protestantism and the New. Essays on the Reformation Heritage* (Edinburgh 1982), 118–30. For Cranmer's symbolic parallelism, consider the following statement: 'And yet in the Lord's supper, rightly used, is Christ's body exhibited indeed spiritually, and so really, if you take really to signify only a spiritual and not a corporal and carnal exhibition. But this real and spiritual exhibition is to the receivers of the sacrament, and not to the bread and wine': Cox, *Cranmer on the Lord's Supper*, 123.

[152] '[W]hy should we not say [Christ] is present when he dwells in us and stands in our midst? ... For the presence of Christ in this world ... is not one of place, or sense, or reason, or earth, but of spirit, of faith, and of heaven, in so far as we are conveyed thither by faith and placed together with Christ, and apprehend and embrace him in his heavenly majesty ... Therefore, let the teachable be taught that no presence of Christ is enjoyed in the eucharist unless it is rightly observed, and then only a presence both apprehended and retained by faith alone': *Common Places of Martin Bucer*, ed. D.F. Wright (Courtenay Library of Reformation Classics, iv, 1972), 390–1.

tions drawn from this world'.[153] Although remaining distinct, these two realities were linked by divine convenant in a sacramental union that rendered the bread and wine not bare signs, but 'presenting signs' (*signa exhibitiva*).[154] Therefore, Christ imparted his body and blood to those who physically partook of these instrumental elements with true living faith, receiving 'in a spiritual manner the strengthening and increase' of 'that communion whereby they are members of Christ, flesh of his flesh and bone of his bones, to the end that they may become more perfectly his members'.[155] That these two Cambridge theologians had much in common in their approach to the eucharist was surely a consequence of their mutual commitment to the Fathers and to furthering personal holiness. As Redman himself said at Bucer's funeral, he was satisfied with the Strasbourg reformer on many things.[156]

Thus, in the end Redman died too catholic on the chief article of protestant belief but too protestant on the chief articles of catholic belief. Yet this most unlikely inverted equipose arose because of his more fundamental commitment to the early church and its emphasis on good living as a sign of knowing God. If Redman feared that predestinarian solifidianism permitted moral lassitude, he became equally convinced that emphasizing the visible aspect of Christ's presence in the eucharist distracted participants away from their need for an inward sight of God which strengthened their will to serve him. Like his epitaph for Bucer, Redman sought verity more than victory, and considered himself, the church and the world a winner if godliness triumphed more

---

[153] *Ibid.*, 397–8; Cf. '[Christ] has left this world and been borne up to heaven; he is therefore not to be sought in this world in any worldly manner but just as he offers himself, abiding in the heavens, to be perceived not by the senses or reason but by faith': *ibid.*, 391; 'Certainly, faith embraces and enjoys the presence of the whole Christ, God and man': *ibid.*, 393; 'The words "carnally" and "naturally" I will never allow, because they imply reception by the senses': *ibid.*, 394.

[154] 'But if I am asked about the use here of the bread and wine, my reply is that they are presenting signs whereby the Lord presents and imparts himself as bread from heaven ... in exactly the same way ... as he conferred healing of body and mind on many by the touch of his hand ... If I am asked what conjunction can possibly exist between the glorified body of Christ in heaven – and at a particular place in heaven, and perishable bread confined to earth and to a discernible position, I give the answer, "The same as exists between regeneration and being dipped in water, and between the Holy Spirit and the breath of Christ's mouth." It is, I maintain, the conjunction of a covenant': *ibid.*, 395–6. For a discussion of Bucer's teaching on this 'sacramental union' see *ibid.*, 35–6. For 'presenting signs' see *ibid.*, 60 n. 68, 398.

[155] *Ibid.*, 396.

[156] '[G]audere se dicebat, quod in multis sibi a Bucero quum viueret, esset satisfactum': Bucer, *Scripta Anglicana*, 880.

because of better doctrine made more faithful to the primitive church. As a result, John Redman was content to leave this life as he had lived it, gently ambling in the middle ways of God.

CHAPTER THREE

The Sanctuary

David Loades

As has recently been pointed out in a more general context, sanctuary was a social and cultural, as well as a legal institution.[1] It had two quite distinct points of origin. On the one hand was the sanctity of consecrated ground, and more particularly the holiness of relics and the shrines of particular saints. On the other was the jurisdictional franchise or liberty, in which the king had waived his rights in favour of the franchise holder. What might be termed 'ordinary sanctuary' was based entirely upon the former. The claimant was supposed to have committed, or to have been suspected of committing, an offence which placed his (or her) life in jeopardy. The protection lasted for 40 days, at the end of which time the fugitive had either to surrender to the king's officers, or to abjure the realm. There were many minor variations in different places, including elaborate precautions to ensure that sworn abjurers did actually leave the country, but the substance was everywhere the same. Every church, or other piece of consecrated ground was a sanctuary in that sense, and what it offered was not immunity from prosecution so much as a 'cooling off' period. It was not the law which was frustrated, but the lynch mob. Jurisdictional franchises offered no such guaranteed immunity, however limited, but on the other hand they were not restricted in the same way. Any person could move permanently into a liberty, with the permission of the lord, and an offender so doing would have to be extradited to stand trial outside the franchise for any offence committed there. On the other hand, any offence committed within the franchise would have to be tried in the lord's court, and lords varied greatly in their enthusiasm for pursuing criminals.[2] A major religious house like Westminster Abbey partook of both natures, and its custody of the shrine of St Edward gave it a spiritual status enjoyed by only some half dozen other houses in England.

---

[1] A.G. Rosser, 'Sanctuary and social negotiation in medieval England', in *The Cloister and the World. Essays in Medieval History in Honour of Barbara Harvey*, ed. J. Blair and B. Golding (Oxford 1996), 57–79.

[2] The marcher lordships of Wales were notorious as refuges for the lawless because of the laxity (and complexity) of their administration: T.B. Pugh, *The Marcher Lordships of South Wales, 1415–1536* (Cardiff 1963).

Church sanctuaries were matters of custom rather than law, but they had also developed at a time when the line between the two was hazy. Consequently they suffered from problems of definition. It was usually clear enough where the consecrated ground began and ended, but there were frequently disputes over the circumstances in which a suspect might claim protection. The commonest uncertainties were over debt and fraud, which in theory were not covered, but in practice were very often tolerated by the neighbouring communities, which acted as the arbiters in the absence of any more clearly defined authority.[3] The line between crime and misfortune was a fine one in financial transactions, and the longer this kind of tolerance was practised, the firmer the custom became. Ultimately all ordinary sanctuaries depended upon the willingness of the community to respect them. In theory forcing a sanctuary was sacrilege, and carried heavy ecclesiastical penalties, but in practice if a whole community conspired to breach the immunity, there was little that could be done, and nothing in time to help the victim. This seldom happened, because the forty-day rule was normally sufficient to ensure that the law was not flouted or evaded with impunity. Such sanctuaries were relatively uncontroversial, and remained in place until the whole religious culture of England changed in the late-sixteenth century. By 1600 respect for sacred *loci* had waned, and respect for due process of law had increased. Also the law had come to recognize the distinction between murder and justifiable homicide, which removed one of the strongest arguments in favour of sanctuary.[4] In 1624, by the statute of 21 James I c. 28, all such privileges were abolished, but in this respect custom was stronger than law, and some refuges lingered on into the eighteenth century.

The sanctuary of a major ecclesiastical institution was, however, a quite different matter. The occupants of the refuge were under the jurisdiction of the house (abbot, prior or dean), and the forty-day rule did not apply. Stringent safeguards were supposed to be applied to those seeking admission, and to the activities in which they could indulge while there, but in practice many of the sanctuary men became long term residents, even conducting their businesses there, and the possibility of them evading the consequences of their offences indefinitely was therefore real. For this reason serious concern about the desirability of such refuges had been expressed in parliament as early as 1378, when it was eventually decided that the advantages of having some protection against miscarriages of justice outweighed the dangers

---

[3] Rosser, 'Sanctuary and social negotiation', 68–70.

[4] *Ibid.*, 66.

of abuse.[5] It is also very doubtful whether any secular law made at that time could have abolished a privilege which rested upon the protection of a greatly revered saint as well (supposedly) as upon an ancient royal grant. Westminster was not only one of the greatest sanctuaries in England, it was also by far the most sensitively placed. Political fugitives naturally sought it, as the dowager queen Elizabeth and her younger son had done in 1483, and although the legal justification for their action might be challenged, the power of the saint was not.[6] Moreover, the possibility that a fragile regime might be challenged from such a base could not be ignored. On 5 July 1487, immediately after his defeat of Lambert Simnel, Henry VII wrote to Innocent VIII:

> Shortly after we had marched an army against our enemies and rebels a report, erroneous and forged, was circulated in London and Westminster ... that we had been put to flight and our whole army dispersed. When this was heard some of those who, by reason of their crimes, enjoy the privileges and immunities of Westminster, being of opinion that after the commission of any nefarious crime soever they could have the free privilege of returning to that sanctuary (as we wrote more at large to your Holiness for the reform of enormities of this sort), took up arms for the purpose of plundering the houses of those whom they knew to be in the field with us, and mustered in a body for the commission of crime.[7]

Henry had already broken a sanctuary at Culham in Oxfordshire in order to extract his enemy Humphrey Stafford, but it was not in his interest to confront the church more generally on the issue, and neither he nor Innocent eventually did anything about the alleged abuses at Westminster. However, the matter had been raised, and it was not

---

[5] 2 Ric. II st. 2 c. 3. *Rotuli Parliamentorum*, iii, 37, 50–1. The discussions in the parliament of that year appear to have provoked a monk of Westminster (probably William de Sudbury) to write a substantial treatise in defence of the abbey's privileges, which now survives at Longleat as MS 38 in the marquess of Bath's collection: Rosser, 'Sanctuary and social negotiation', 71 & n. 51.

[6] Elizabeth was persuaded to emerge. The quasi-legal argument alleged by Shakespeare (*Richard III*, act 3 scene 2) that neither the queen nor her son could claim sanctuary, having committed no offence, appears not to have been used at the time. It was taken by Shakespeare from More's 'History of King Richard III': *The Complete Works of St Thomas More*, ii, ed. R.S. Sylvester (New Haven 1963), 32–3. The contemporary Dominic Mancini attributed to Richard of Gloucester the rather different argument that the sanctuary at Westminster had been founded 'as a place of refuge, not of detention' (*'ad refugium non ad carcerem ... sit institutum'*): *The Usurpation of Richard the Third*, ed. C.A.J. Armstrong (2nd edn, Oxford 1969), 88–9. Neither argument (if it was actually used) was particularly relevant to the circumstances of the queen and her son. The issue is discussed in detail by R.G. Davies, 'The church and the wars of the roses', in *The Wars of the Roses*, ed. A.J. Pollard (1995), 152–3.

[7] *CSP Ven.* i, 164 (no. 519).

difficult to insist that anyone who used the refuge of sanctuary as a base for the commission of further crimes should forfeit the privilege. Because of his generally good relations with the church, and perhaps as a result of the Stafford case, after 1486 the king was also able to assert successfully that only sanctuaries showing specific charters of privilege (of which Westminster was one) should be allowed to protect traitors.[8]

At the beginning of Henry VIII's reign, the ancient privileges of St Peter's abbey, although not unquestioned, remained intact. The sanctuary was also a sizeable precinct, containing many tenements, gardens and workshops, which could provide accommodation for scores of residents. Exactly how it was defined is not clear. According to one modern study, it corresponded with the abbey precinct itself, which would have been logical;[9] but a different interpretation makes it considerably larger, including Thieving Lane, the Almonry, and the houses on the south side of Tothill Street, as well as the area known as Strutton Ground, and other properties extending as far as the modern Horseferry Road.[10] If that was the case, it may have corresponded with what was (or was thought to have been) the original abbey estate. However it was defined, its boundaries were well established by the early sixteenth century, and it constituted an area large enough for a substantial community. Henry VII's concern about its possible use as a base for hostile action against the crown was not altogether fanciful. However, when the serious attacks began, it was not for that reason. Henry VIII became interested in sanctuary when his relations with the church in general were in crisis, and he was beginning to look on all ecclesiastical immunities with a jaundiced eye. He was also well aware that Westminster returned the abbot a substantial profit of about £100 a year in rentals.[11] By no means all the tenants were 'sanctuary men' in the proper sense of having taken the sanctuary oath to escape the conse-

---

[8] The arrest of the Staffords led to the judgement in king's bench that sanctuary was not pleadable in cases of treason: *Les Reportes des Cases* (1679), 1 Hen. VII, Trinity, pl. 1. Cf. D.A. Luckett, 'Patronage, violence and revolt in the reign of Henry VII', in *Crown, Government and People in the Fifteenth Century*, ed. R.E. Archer (Stroud 1995), 151. The chartered sanctuaries remained privileged because they were liberties: I.D. Thornley, 'The destruction of sanctuary', in *Tudor Studies*, ed. R.W. Seton-Watson (1924), 199.

[9] M.B. Honeybourne, 'The sanctuary boundaries and environs of Westminster Abbey and the college of St. Martin-le-Grand', *JBAA*, 2nd ser. xxxviii (1932–3), 316–33.

[10] N.H. MacMichael, 'Sanctuary at Westminster', *Westminster Abbey Occasional Paper*, no. 27 (1971), 9–14. No sources are given for these statements. According to Stanley, Thieving Lane was so called not because thieves dwelt there, but because they were conveyed that way to the Gatehouse prison, without having to enter the precinct: *Historical Memorials*, 347.

[11] Rosser, *Medieval Westminster*, 67–9, 84–6.

quences of specific crimes, but they were all protected by the jurisdiction of the monk-archdeacon from being answerable to neighbouring civic powers. The description of the sanctuary as an 'enterprise zone' and a 'tax haven', which gave its inhabitants large opportunities for profit and the avoidance of civic obligations, is not inappropriate.[12] The king's first step was a small one, and sensible enough. In 1529 it was decreed by statute that any sanctuary man abjuring the realm should be branded on the thumb, thus (in theory at least) ensuring that he did not evade his sworn undertaking, and remain in England.[13] This did not affect the privilege itself, but merely laid down a rule for its administration. Nevertheless it constituted an encroachment by parliament into an area which it had hitherto avoided. In the following year, as the king's desire to establish a firmer control over the comings and goings of his subjects became more apparent, the whole option of abjuration was abolished, and confinement within a chartered sanctuary was substituted.[14] Whether this was intended literally, or should be seen as a coded warning to discourage potential sanctuary seekers, is not clear. About 1,000 people a year were seeking sanctuary of some kind throughout the country, and the chartered refuges could quickly have become overcrowded, but as far as we know, that did not happen. In 1532 the registered sanctuary men at Westminster numbered 49.[15] Ironically, when John Skelton, who himself lived in the precinct, had wished to throw mud at Cardinal Wolsey about ten years earlier, he had accused him, among other things, of being a breaker of sanctuaries. By 1532 the king would hardly have regarded such a sin as heinous.

The first major breach with custom soon followed. The treason acts of 1534 and 1535, following the break with Rome, not only made it treason to call the king a heretic or schismatic, they also removed treason altogether from the list of offences for which sanctuary could be claimed.[16] Over the next year the attack gathered momentum. In February 1536 Thomas Cromwell reminded himself to establish 'limitation of an order for sanctuaries', at the same time as he was planning the statute for the termination of franchises which became law later in the year. In spite of its sweeping implications, that act did not, in the event, touch ecclesiastical sanctuaries. It terminated all temporal franchises, and made the king's writ run uniformly throughout the land. It also put

---

[12] *Ibid.*, 155–8.

[13] 21 Hen. VIII c. 2 (*SR*, iii, 284).

[14] 22 Hen. VIII c. 14 (*SR*, iii, 332–4). By this act also any sanctuary man committing a further offence forfeited his immunity.

[15] *LP*, v, 1124 (25 June 1532).

[16] 26 Hen. VIII c. 13; 27 Hen. VIII c. 2 (*SR*, iii, 508–9, 532).

an end to the autonomy of the bishopric of Durham, but the sanctuary of holy places remained, and the immunities of St Peter were untouched.[17] It seems clear that further restrictions were intended, probably by Cromwell, because in March 1536 a certain Thomas Dorset, sending the metropolitan news to his rural friend in Plymouth, reported 'Sanctuary is not to be allowed for debt, murder or felony, either at St. Martin's, St. Katharine's, or elsewhere.' But for the time being no steps were taken to realize that intention.[18] It was not until April 1538 that a royal proclamation removed the right of sanctuary for the somewhat esoteric offence of causing death by 'sudden foins with swords', although it seems that by that time opinion in and around London was becoming thoroughly confused about who qualified. A certain Steven Claybroke, arrested for murder, supposed he could have no sanctuary in an ordinary church, but believed that he could have claimed that right had he reached Westminster.[19]

When the monastery surrendered in 1540, all the attendant rights of jurisdiction were implicitly assumed by the king. The shrine of St Edward had already been dismantled, but since the body was not removed the sanctity of the *locus* remained. It was hardly intact, because a saint who could not protect his own shrine from desecration was bound to lose credibility, but the reason for the existence of the sanctuary was unaffected. When the property which constituted the precinct of the refuge was transferred to the newly erected dean and chapter in the same year, the sanctuary itself, and presumably its existing occupants, were transferred with it. Thomas Cromwell's determination to be rid of sanctuaries seems to have persisted until his own fall in the summer of 1540, but he did not live to accomplish his intention, and when the issue was finally addressed by statute the result was rather less radical than he might have wished. Although the preamble to 32 Henry VIII c. 12 spoke of 'certaine lycentiouse privileges and other liberties heretofore grauntid to divers places and territories within this realme commonly callid Sanctuaries' the scheme which was then legislated fell far short of abolition.[20] What the statute did remove were so-called 'chartered' privileges, of the

---

[17] 27 Hen. VIII c. 12 (*SR*, iii, 555–8). Some aspects of Cromwell's campaign against sanctuary were examined by Sir Geoffrey Elton in *Policy and Police* (Cambridge 1972), 288–90. He twice extracted murderers from Westminster, in 1533 and 1539. In the latter case all the accused pleaded the privilege of the sanctuary, and were told by the attorney-general that their plea was insufficient in law.

[18] *LP*, x, 462. By this time the conflict between the privilege of sanctuary and the common law had become clear, but Cromwell had so far relied upon the courts.

[19] *TRP*, i, 263 (no. 179). *LP*, x, 763. It is likely that Claybroke's view was prompted by Cromwell's measures.

[20] 32 Hen. VIII c. 12 (*SR*, iii, 756–8; quotation from p. 756).

kind which Westminster derived from the supposed grant of St Edward. Ordinary church sanctuaries remained, but the range of offences for which refuge could be sought was drastically reduced. Murder, rape, burglary, robbery, arson and sacrilege were all exempted, leaving only a handful of felonies still covered by the protection. Debt was not mentioned, because in theory it had never been protected, but one result of this change in the law was that local custom ensured that ecclesiastical sanctuaries became increasingly occupied by those who could not satisfy their creditors. Westminster was one of the very few places which had the specific right to protect debtors, dating from the reign of Richard II.[21]

The chartered sanctuaries were replaced by eight 'sanctuary towns', and although it was not specifically stated in the act, the intention seems to have been to give those towns the same kind of status and privileges, except that the number of refugees was limited to 20 in each location. The major difference was that these refuges depended for their existence upon the act itself, which was much more vulnerable to repeal than an ancient grant. One of these sanctuary towns was Westminster, and since there is no evidence for the creation of any new sanctuary outside the precinct, it must be assumed that the statute was deemed to have validated and continued the existing arrangement.[22] In 1541 the council wrote to the commissioners who had been appointed to delimit such new sanctuaries 'as myght be convenient for xx[ty.] sanctuary men, and lest noysum and incommodious for the sayd townes', instructing them to report so that the king could make a final determination by letters patent, but neither report nor patent survive.[23] In the previous session of parliament, in what was effectively a tidying-up operation, the jurisdictional rights which had depended upon the dissolved and surrendered monasteries were specifically vested in the crown, and control was conveyed to the court of augmentations.[24] Sanctuary, however, was excepted, presumably because this was thought to depend upon the consecrated use of the premises rather than the franchise itself. Most former monastic properties were, of course, deconsecrated and

---

[21] Rosser, *Medieval Westminster*, 218–19.

[22] The evidence linking the new sanctuary town to the existing Abbey is purely circumstantial. Virtually nothing is known about the operation of the sanctuary towns. A statute of 1541 (33 Hen. VIII c. 15: *SR*, iii, 850–1) removed the sanctuary originally decreed for Manchester to Chester, and on 30 May 1542 the same refuge was further relocated by proclamation to Stafford: *TRP*, i, 311–13 (no. 212). After 1558 there are no further references.

[23] *Proceedings and Ordinances of the Privy Council of England*, ed. N.H. Nicolas (Record Commission, 1834–7), vii, 133–5 (quotation from p. 135).

[24] 32 Hen. VIII c. 20 (*SR*, iii, 770–3).

used for secular purposes. The majority of those which remained as churches became ordinary sanctuaries; but Westminster as a sanctuary town was in a unique position, and it seems likely that St Peter's was as unaffected by this act as it had been by the franchise act.

Isobel Thornley believed that this situation was 'implicitly abolished' by the first treasons act of Edward VI, but the wording of that statute can bear no such interpretation.[25] Henry VIII's treason legislation was repealed, returning the definition of that crime to the basic act of Edward III. The privilege of sanctuary was returned to its 1509 definition, with the exception of murder, burglary and robbery. Nothing was said about the existence or location of the refuges themselves, and no attempt was made to repeal the statute of 1540. The practical effect of this act was therefore to restore sanctuary for rape, arson and sacrilege, and to allow the sanctuary towns to give refuge to traitors, although it is doubtful whether that was intended. Edward VI subsequently resurrected some of his father's treasons, but that did not affect the position of the remaining sanctuaries. Neither did Mary's two acts of repeal touch either the act of 1540, or Edward's treason legislation.[26] The most significant effect of Edward's reign in this connexion probably came through the protestant emphasis upon 'desanctification'. The protestant impact was limited outside the official establishment, and the removal of altars and images from churches was widely unpopular, but the iconoclastic programme was very thoroughly implemented, and certainly persuaded some people that there was nothing particularly sacred about an ecclesiastical building or precinct, and certainly nothing which should extend protection to an offender against the king's laws.

Whatever the exact nature of the Westminster sanctuary as it functioned under the dean and chapter, it was unaffected by the dissolution of the new diocese in 1550, as St Peter's simply became a second cathedral for the diocese of London, with the same properties and privileges. However, in 1556 the whole situation was changed by the re-erection of the monastery. The cathedral establishment created in 1540 was dissolved, and the church, with all its attendant properties, was handed over on 10 November to Abbot Feckenham and his colleagues, who were also granted the necessary corporate status.[27] On 18 November the monks solemnly took possession of their new premises, with much processing and liturgical demonstration.[28] Nothing had so far been said about privi-

---

[25] 1 Edw. VI c. 12 (*SR*, iv, I, 20). Thornley, 'Destruction of sanctuary', in *Tudor Studies*, 204.

[26] 1 Mar. st. 2 c. 2; 1 & 2 Ph. & Mar. c. 8 (*SR*, iv, I, 202, 246–54).

[27] *CPR 1555–7*, 348–54.

[28] *The Diary of Henry Machyn*, ed. J.G. Nichols (Camden Soc. xlii, 1848), 118–19.

leges or jurisdiction, but on St Nicholas's day, 6 December, the monks again solemnly processed and 'before [them] went all the santuary men with crosse keys upon their garments, and after whent iij for murder'.

It seems highly unlikely that this population could have been assembled in less than three weeks, and the obvious conclusion is that most of them had been there before the abbey was restored.[29] In showing them off in this manner, Feckenham was making a point, but his later claim that the sanctuary had altogether disappeared during the wicked days of heresy and schism appears to have been an exercise in selective amnesia. The Chapter Act Book not only records the admission to sanctuary of Canon Edward Keble on 19 September 1553, but in the same month also notes that the chapter clerk's fees included 13s 4d for every person so privileged.[30] By that time Mary was already on the throne, but the country was still in schism, and the queen's accession had not, in itself, made any difference to the cathedral establishment. This was not the only matter over which there was some calculated confusion. In law the foundation of 1556 was a new creation, not the re-erection of the institution which had surrendered in 1540,[31] so if it were to enjoy any privileges and exemptions, they would have to be granted afresh. Feckenham acted from the start as though he was in full possession of the pre-reformation franchise, but it would appear that this was only granted retrospectively in September 1557, when the abbot as he later recalled, was given:

a charter of the Queenes Majestie wherein are graunted to me by generall woordes all liberties priviledges and fraunchises in as large and ample manner as my predecessors Abbots of that place had and enjoyed [them].[32]

---

[29] *Ibid.*, 121. The three murderers were named, and were clearly protected in spite of the king's bench ruling of 1539 and the statute of 1540. The whole story is riddled with inconsistencies of this kind. One of the 'men' was John Elles, a Westminster schoolboy who had killed a market stallholder in what was virtually an accident, but for which he had been convicted: LMA, Acc. 591/1. WAM 65905–13 (with photocopy and correspondence). I am indebted to Dr Knighton for this reference.

[30] *Acts 1543–1609*, nos 140, 183.

[31] All the old foundations had been canonically extinguished by Paul IV's bull *Praeclara charissimi* of 21 June 1555. This was a part of the bargain which had secured the reconciliation of England six months earlier. See C.S. Knighton, 'Westminster Abbey restored', in *Marian Catholicism*, ed. E. Duffy and D.M. Loades (forthcoming).

[32] Bodl. MS Rawlinson D. 68, f. 5v. An imperfect text of this document was printed in the 1st (1868) edn of Stanley's *Historical Memorials*, but was omitted in the final (1882) edn, the one normally cited in the present volume. The grant referred to has not been found either in the patent rolls or in the Abbey muniments. The same grant was also cited, but not quoted, in a letter from Feckenham to the Abbey tenants and officials at Steventon, Berks., also c. 1557: WAM 7344.

The timing of this grant may well have been significant, because problems had been accumulating. In October 1556 two prisoners had broken
out of Bury gaol and taken refuge at Westminster. The council sent the
solicitor-general (William Cordell) into the sanctuary to examine them,
but with what result is not recorded.[33] Then in July 1557 a certain
Edward Vaughan escaped from the Tower and sought the same sanctuary. The council debated the matter, and decided to ask Feckenham
himself to examine the fugitive. They gave an undertaking that if he
confessed, he would be allowed to remain in his refuge, but 'if he leave
any thing undeclared that may afterwardes be tryed against hym, the
Sanctuarye shall then serve hym nether for the same nor any of the
rest.'[34] Someone clearly had second thoughts, because the entry was
deleted from the register. It is possible that Feckenham declined to
participate in what he would have seen as an improper practice, but
also possible that the right of the council to lay down such rules was
challenged. A few days later, on 28 July, they tried again. This time the
abbot was instructed to hand Vaughan over, so that he could be examined with a view to establishing his right to sanctuary: 'signifieng unto
the said Abbot that the same Vaughan after his examinacion so taken
shalbe restored againe to the Sanctuarye, if it shalbe his right so to be,
requiring him neverthelesse to kepe the matter secrete to himself'.[35]
Whether Feckenham co-operated in this renewed attempt, we do not
know, as there is no record of Vaughan's examination, and he was still
in the sanctuary the following January. Probably the abbot stood on his
ecclesiastical dignity, being confident of the support of both the queen
and the cardinal, and the council, whose prime concern was security
and law enforcement was rebuffed. Whatever the sequence of events, it
must have been clear to Feckenham at the end of July that the position
of his sanctuary needed to be clarified and reaffirmed if problems of this
kind were not to recur.

In the following month he came under renewed pressure. On 6 August he was instructed that if one John Poole 'detected to have byn one
of those that committed the late robberies in London' should turn up at
Westminster, he was to commit him to close prison, irrespective of the
fact that robbery was undoubtedly privileged.[36] It was at this point that
Feckenham sought and obtained a fresh grant. The council, however,
was not satisfied. On 12 December he was further ordered to submit a

---

[33] *APC*, vi, 12.

[34] *Ibid.*, 128.

[35] *Ibid.*, 135. At the same time the constable of the Tower was instructed to receive
Vaughan at the abbot's hands.

[36] *Ibid.*, 144.

list of all his sanctuary men (and women) 'with a note of the severall causes for whiche they [tooke] the same', and on 14th the goods of one John Chapman 'remayning in the Sanctuarie' were ordered to be seized and inventoried.[37] Whatever privileges Feckenham believed that he had received, they were even more roughly handled in January 1558. On 27th of that month it was ordered that sixteen named prisoners were to be surrendered to Sir Henry Bedingfield, the captain of the guard. Some were then transferred to the Tower and some to King's Bench.[38] Whether all of these were sanctuary men or, some of them, occupants of the abbot's prison, the Gatehouse, is not clear. In either case his franchise jurisdiction was overridden. The subsequent fate of most of them is not known, and they may have been returned to the abbot when the nature of their offences had been ascertained. However, four of them were coiners, who seem to have committed their crimes very recently, probably in December 1557. Coining was treason, and the legal question was whether the abbot's privileges covered that offence or not. Treason had not been exempted from that clause in Edward VI's statute which had returned rights of sanctuary to the 1509 position, but it is not certain that sanctuary was in question. If Feckenham's patent really granted him all the privileges of the old abbey, then treason was included either way; similarly if he was deemed to hold the rights of a sanctuary town set up under the Henrician act. But if Westminster was no more than an ordinary church, or if the abbot's franchise had not been fully restored, the queen's officers were perfectly entitled to remove coiners for trial. In this case the four offenders were duly tried and condemned in the Hilary Term, 1558, although all were subsequently pardoned.[39] The abbot had been put on his mettle, and seems to have protested at the highest level. The council was unrepentant, but perhaps also somewhat embarrassed, and attempted to resolve the whole issue by referring it to parliament. A bill 'touching sanctuaries' was read twice in the Commons, and committed on 2 February. A summary of its content is provided by a record of the subsequent investigation:

> a bill concerning sanctuaries; declaringe howe by lawes alredie passed in the xxxijth yeare of Henrie the viijth there remained indeede ... no sanctuaries other then churches, churchyards &c. and those as in olde time it hath been used to serve in such cases as theie did serve but for xltie daies and the offender afterwards to abjure; but for that such abjuration could neither be made into the

---

[37] *Ibid.*, 215, 216.

[38] *Ibid.*, 251–2.

[39] The coining offences were allegedly committed between 29 October and 7 December 1557: *CPR 1555–7*, 379–80; *1558–60*, 62.

> parts beyond the seas, the same being forbidden by statute, nor
> unto any sanctuarie within the realme where none was indeed,
> thoughe at Westminster by usurpation and permission it had late
> ben used.[40]

The bill then went on to decree the abolition of all sanctuaries other
than churches, and the removal of all mention of abjuration. It seems
unlikely that this was an official measure, and was probably a private
initiative used as a pretext to get the situation clarified. The brief report
is interesting in a number of ways, assuming that it is accurate. The
drafters either did not remember, or chose to ignore, the fact that
sanctuary towns had been established, and that abjuration had already
been replaced by refuge in a permanent sanctuary. The committee,
however, chaired by Sir William Petre, was well aware of these defects,
and was probably aware also of Feckenham's recent charter, although it
seems not to have been common knowledge. It was agreed 'for as much
as it mighte be that the Abbot of Westminster had some newe graunte
from the Prince since the making of that statute of Kinge Henrie the
viij[th], wereby his sanctuarie mighte have bin created anewe' that
Feckenham should be summoned to defend his privilege.[41]

He appeared the next day, without counsel, pleading the shortness of
the notice, and bearing, not Mary's recent grant but copies of St Edward's
charter and its confirmation by the pope. His oration, of which a record
has survived, was stronger on emotion than it was on law. Starting with
King Lucius, the alleged founder of both the church and the sanctuary,
he claimed that his church had enjoyed for over 1,400 years the right to
pardon every offence whatsoever. The privilege had not been quite
continuous, having been briefly interrupted both by the pagan Saxons
and the Danes, but had been re-established by St Edward, who had
conferred its existing charter with the words 'this charter shall remain
in force as long as the Christian faith endures'. That had been univer-
sally accepted and unchallenged:

> till the time of the late schisme, then when all faithe, when all
> truthe of religion, when all that unitie that containeth all the
> churche of Christe, when all feare and dread of Christian name
> ceased amongst us, then ceased the freedome of sanctuarie, and so
> remained untill the happie time of our moste gratious Kinge and
> Queene, Phillippe and Marye. Theie restored the faithe to us and
> us to the unitie of Christes Churche. Theie have revived the feare
> and dread of Christian name in England. Theie have revived the
> freedome of sanctuarye at Westminster.[42]

---

[40] Bodl. MS Rawlinson D. 68, f. 1.

[41] *Ibid.*

[42] *Ibid.*, f. 3v.

He concluded on a more practical note by alleging (but not producing) his recent royal grant. The committee may, or may not, have been impressed by his passion; some of them, at least, would have known that his memory of recent events was seriously defective, however laudable his enthusiasm for the faith. Feckenham was told to come back with his legal advisers, which he duly did on 12 February, supported by the distinguished lawyers Edmund Plowden and John Story. Unfortunately we do not know what transpired on that occasion, but Plowden was a lawyer of great skill and reputation, and he seems to have convinced the parliament that it would be unwise to pick a quarrel with the crown by legislating so specifically against the queen's recently expressed intention. The bill 'touching sanctuaries' disappeared, but that did not necessarily mean that either the parliament or the council were happy to have the abbot's sanctified refuge on their doorstep. Even Thomas More, whose loyalty to the old faith could hardly be questioned, had expressed himself in unflattering terms about its occupants:

> Nowe vnthriftes ryote and runne in Dette, vppon the boldenesse of these places: yea and ryche menne runne thither with poore mennes goodes, there they builde, there thei spende and bidde their creditours gooe whistle them. Mens wyues runne thither with theyr housebandes plate, and saye, thei dare not abyde with theyr housbandes for beatinge. Theues bryng thyther theyr stollen goodes, and there lyue thereon. There deuise thei newe roberies, nightlye they steale out, they robbe and reue, and kyll, and come in again as though those places gaue them not onely a safe garde for the harme they haue done, but a licence also to dooe more.[43]

Whatever the abbot may have liked to think, it was not only heretics and schismatics who were sceptical about these tough old privileges. Mary, as was her wont, had respected her conscience rather than the advice of her council in restoring the Westminster sanctuary to its former glory.

When she died, it was soon clear that the days of such glory were numbered. If even her conservative councillors had been inclined to regard the sanctuary as a nuisance and an obstruction to the lawful conduct of their business, it was not to be expected that Elizabeth's servants would be more respectful. The abbey was dissolved by statute in the first year of the new reign, and its property transferred on 21 May 1560 to the restored collegiate church. This grant included all the

---

[43] *Complete Works of More*, ii, 31 left (English text), from 'The History of King Richard III'. More was writing 'in character' as the duke of Buckingham, so we cannot be certain that this opinion was also his own; on the other hand there is no hint of disclaimer.

tenements 'within the late sanctuary' at Westminster and all liberties, except sanctuary, 'in the site of the late college of St. Martin le Grand'.[44] In spite of the implications of this wording, the sanctuary was not abolished. There is very little evidence as to how it functioned in the early days of the new establishment, but a degree of continuity can be deduced from the career of James Wynnyngton, who had been a servant of John Feckenham while the latter was dean of St Paul's. When Feckenham became abbot of Westminster, Wynnyngton moved with him. At the erection of the abbey in 1556 there was designated a searcher of the sanctuary. This office does not seem to have existed before, and what duties it carried is not clear.[45] Wynnyngton and another were jointly granted a patent of the searchership in August 1558, with an annual fee of £6 13s 4d. An under-searcher was appointed in the following October. Wynnyngton seems to have been dispossessed when the abbey was dissolved, but was reinstated by the new dean, William Bill, after a long and costly suit.[46] He then held the office on his own until he either resigned or died in 1565/6, when John Whyte was appointed. Searchers continued to be referred to at times thereafter, and the title still exists today.

The legal position was by this time extremely obscure. The charters upon which Feckenham had based his defence related to an institution which no longer existed, and although the statute of 32 Henry VIII had never been repealed, the sanctuary towns seem to have become moribund, and may have simply ceased to exist.[47] The end of the monastery seems to have meant the end of the temporal franchise which, unlike the sanctuary, had not been exercised by the dean and chapter from 1540 to 1556. It was resumed to the crown by the Elizabethan statute of dissolution, and not regranted.[48] It appears also that Westminster no longer

[44] 1 Eliz. I c. 24 (SR, iv, I, 397–400). CPR 1558–60, 397–403 (quotations from pp. 398, 402).

[45] PRO, SP 46/124, ff. 242–242v; 46/162, f. 174. WAM 37713, f. lv. The earlier office was called keeper of the sanctuary; whether the functions were the same is not clear. The oath taken by the sanctuary men, and administered by the keeper/searcher, is printed in Westminster Abbey Charters, 1066–c.1214, ed. E. Mason (London Record Soc. xxv, 1988), 195–6.

[46] WAM Reg. IV, ff. 64v, 89v. PRO, SP 46/162, f. 220 (Wynnyngton to his mother, 12 December [1560]). WAM 33618, f. 1; 33625, f. 3v; 33626, f. 4v. I am indebted to Dr Knighton for these references.

[47] Thornley, 'Destruction of sanctuary', in Tudor Studies 204 & n. 115. Cf. above, pp. 81–2.

[48] It was certainly within the power of the crown to make the grant which Feckenham alleged in 1558, because the franchise jurisdiction resumed by Henry in 1540 had never been reallocated. It remained vested in the court of augmentations until the abolition of that court in 1554, and then presumably in the exchequer until it was (allegedly)

believed it could protect traitors, murderers or robbers, and all the later references to the sanctuary involve debt. It survived for two reasons. One was simply ancient tradition; the rags of sanctity still clung to the great church, and it still housed an important ecclesiastical institution. The other was the financial interest of the dean and chapter. Westminster remained an exempt peculiar, and although this no longer meant that it could protect felons, it could and did provide immunity from many types of civil action, for which it was well worth paying the dean's asking price.[49]

The legal confusion was good news for Edmund Plowden, who was retained by Goodman as he had been by Feckenham, to defend the Abbey's privileges, at the rate of £4 *per annum*.[50] In 1563 and again in 1566 bills were introduced into the House of Commons 'against debtors'. They did not pass, so we do not know exactly what was proposed, but it is likely that a specific statement against sanctuary for debt was included. On the second occasion, as in 1558, the privileges of Westminster were called in question. Archdeacon William Latimer paid 6s 8d for a copy of 'a supplication to the clerk's servant of the parliament house'. Long hours were spent in anxious consultation with Plowden, and John Thomas the dean's servant, spent 4s on boat hire for several trips to visit Speaker Onslow, William Cordell (then master of the rolls) and others 'concerning the sanctuary'.[51] Goodman, presumably influenced by Plowden, apparently used arguments almost identical with those of Feckenham nine years earlier, although without the catholic commentary. Both Lucius and Edward the Confessor were alleged, in spite of the fact that the institution which had allegedly received those grants no longer existed. A civil lawyer, 'Mr Forde', also 'alleged diverse stories and lawes for the same'.[52] Cordell was invited to 'peruse the grants and to certify the force of the law now for sanctuaries'. He was unimpressed by these ancient stories, and the bill was engrossed. Nevertheless it failed on the third reading by 60 votes to 77.[53]

---

regranted to the abbot in 1557. After the second resumption it was no longer alluded to, and was presumably deemed to be extinct.

[49] The desirability of the tenements in the Sanctuary, and the high rents they commanded, was one of the arguments alleged by Dean Goodman in 1566 for its continuance: Widmore, *Westminster Abbey*, 141.

[50] WAM 38370.

[51] G.R. Elton, *The Parliament of England, 1559–1581* (Cambridge 1986), 301, citing *CJ*, i, 73–4, 76, 79. WAM 38407.

[52] Elton, *loc. cit.* 'Mr Forde' was probably Robert Ford, DCL: cf. *CPR 1575–8*, 17 (no. 123).

[53] *CJ*, i, 79.

Unsurprisingly that was not the end of the matter. In the summer of
1567 there was further coming and going about the affairs of one
Walwyn, who appears to have been a sanctuary debtor, and a further
legal opinion cost 10s.[54] In 1569 matters came to a head through the
case of a certain William Whittaker. Whittaker had claimed sanctuary
owing £761, and his creditors obviously thought that he was guilty of
fraudulent deception. Goodman was instructed to produce a list of the
debtors in sanctuary, with the amounts which they claimed to owe, and
that he duly did on 25 May.[55] The list contains 25 names, headed by
William Shorter of London, draper, owing just over £1,400, and including Whittaker. Some of the debts were as little as £50, and virtually
every entry hints at a hard luck story of some kind; 'losses by the sea',
and 'desperate debts', often much larger than the sums owed. On 30
June 1569 the council in star chamber delivered its verdict that:

> In [the judges'] openion the wordes of the letters pattentes and
> grauntes therof made by the Quenes highnes progenitors did not
> extend to priviledge any parson in such cases, beinge to the greate
> prejudice of their subjectes.[56]

Although this is clear enough in respect of the unfortunate Whittaker, it
raises more questions than it answers. What were the letters patent of the
queen's progenitors alleged by Goodman, and what force could they have
had in 1569? Whatever Plowden may have been prepared to argue (and
indeed believe), it is hard to see how the old monastic charters could be
applied to a completely different foundation. That appears to have been
Cordell's opinion, and in any case such charters were not letters patent.
Only the grants of Henry VIII and Mary answer to that description, and
both had been annulled by the dissolution of the receiving institution.

It appears that the status of the Westminster sanctuary after 1559
was more a question of *mentalité* than of law as we would understand it. Ancient custom could still be deemed to have legal force, even
without recent confirmation, provided that no recognized legislation
had ruled against it. There is also doubt about 'such cases'. The judgement could have meant that there should be no sanctuary at all for
debt, or that fraudulent claimants should be excluded. It was probably
the latter that was meant, because at about this time a new oath was
devised for the sanctuary men, against fraud and non-payment. Thereafter any false declaration of assets or liabilities forfeited the refuge.[57]

---

[54] WAM 38689, 38692.

[55] WAM 9594.

[56] WAM 9592. Whittaker was committed to the Fleet.

[57] BL, Lansdowne MS 24, ff. 206–7 (no. 84). This document is printed in full below,
pp. 92–3. The transcript has been provided by Dr Knighton.

By the later years of Elizabeth's reign references to the sanctuary, except as a physical location, are no longer found. That does not mean that the refuge had disappeared, but it had been whittled down to such an extent that it had become innocuous. The 'sanctuary men' proper, if they still existed, were no more than petty debtors, although the other occupants of the precinct continued to enjoy the immunities which protected their enterprises, just as did the theatre owners and brothel keepers who defied the puritanical City authorities from the other liberties in Southwark and Bankside. In the first parliament of James's reign, however, the story was given a strange twist, when it was decreed:

> That so much of all Statutes as concerneth abjured Persons and Sanctuaries, or ordering or governing of Persons abjured or in Sanctuaries, made before the five and thirtieth yeere of the late Queene Elizabeths Reigne, shall ... stand repealed and be voide.[58]

Theoretically, this should have restored the whole situation as it had existed in the early part of Henry VIII's reign, but what the practical significance of that may have been in 1604 is hard to understand. There seems to have been no major revival of medieval sanctuary, and the motives behind the repeal remain obscure. Twenty years later, the legislators changed their minds. Clause vi of 21 James I c. 28 restored all the acts previously repealed, and Clause vii declared that 'no Sanctuarie or Priviledge of Sanctuary shalbe hereafter admitted or allowed in any case'. For all practical purposes that was the end of the story.[59] However, it did not actually legislate the surviving sanctuaries out of existence, it merely declared that no one could take advantage of them. This must be the main reason why the ancient name continued to cling to certain places, Westminster included, and could even be deemed to have some substance, well into the eighteenth century. No law had created sanctuary, and no law could abolish it. The right could be modified by custom, by royal or ecclesiastical decree, or latterly by parliament. So when custom had effectively abandoned the defence, the right could be

---

[58] 1 Jac. I c. 25 (*SR*, iv, II, 1051).

[59] 21 Jac. I c. 28 (*SR*, iv, II, 1237). The afterlife of the English sanctuaries is a monument to the power of custom. Sir Henry Spelman (d. 1641) simply assumed the continuance of the practice, which must have owed something to his personal knowledge: *Glossarium Archaiologicum* (1664), 500. Similarly in 1712 Thomas Staveley (*The History of Churches in England*, 170) discussed it simply to argue the principle that all sanctuaries must be royal creations. By that time no one would have argued in theory that parliament did not have the power to abolish such refuges, but the act of 1624 was strictly interpreted. It had not abolished sanctuaries, but the right of sanctuary, and that was not sufficient to prevent the old refuges from enjoying a lingering and disreputable twilight.

abolished. Today the sanctuary of Westminster is no more than a name plate on a wall, and we are unlikely to see defaulting financiers from the nearby City seeking its protection.

Appendix   Orders for the sanctuary men 1577
BL, Lansdowne MS 24, ff. 206–7

[f. 206] The othe to be geven to all such as shall clayme the sanctuary in Westm'.

1.   Firste that they shall sweare not to crave or clayme the said priveledge or sanctuary to defraude or deceyve any maner of persone therby of his goodes, money, or debtes willinglye, but only for savegarde of theire bodyes, where they are not able presently to paye it.

2.   Item that they shall make a trwe declaration of all suche somme or sommes of money as they do justly owe to any persone or persons with the persons names to whom they are indebted, and what goodes, chattelles, wares, money or debtes they have to satisfye theire credytors with, and also to declare by what means theye are come behynde the hande.

3.   Item wheras they are not able with all they can make presently to paye theyer credytors, that they shall endevor them selves to travell by all means to satisfye them as soone as they can possyblye.

4.   Item that they shall resorte and be present in the collegiat churche bothe at morning and evening prayer to serve God.

5.   Item that theye shall behave them selves honestly and quietly, and to eschewe all suspected houses, unlawfull games, all banketing and ryotus evell companie.

6.   Item that they shall were noe weapone, nor be owt of theyer lodginges before the sonne rysing in the morning nor after the going downe therof at nyght, nor that any of them shall departe owt of the precyncte of the sanctuary without lycence of the dean of Westm' for the tyme being, yf soo he be there present, or of the archedeacon there for the tyme being yf the dean be absente.

7.   Item that they shalbe obedyent to Mr Dean, to the archedeacon, and to other offycers there during theyer abode there.

8.   Item they shall sweare that yf they shall infrynge or breake any of the artycles above mentioned, or shalbe dulye proved to have made an untrwe certyficate touchyng the premisses, that then they shall clayme noe priveledge of sanctuarye, notwithstanding any theyer admission therunto.

[f. 207] Orders after theyer admission.

First the archedeacon doe declare to them what a daynger hit is before God to defraude any man willingly of his goodes, the which is agaynst his lawes which willeth every man to paye, saying *Reddite omnibus*,[1] and also agaynst the lawes of nature which sayeth *hoc faciat alt'* &c., and what a rebuke hit is to any man to clayme sanctuarye and a dyscredyt to his occupying for ever, and doo therfore advyse hym to remember these premisses and to retorne before he be knowen openly.

Then after this knowledg shalbe geven to theyer credytors of them that are in the said sanctuary, or elles yf they come unsent for imedyatly, the said sanctuary men shalbe called before the said dean and archdeacon to heare to theyre demandes, and yf anye of the said credytors cane sertenly prove that the said privelegedymen have brought in with hym money or wares, they shalbe satisfyed therof presentlye.

And yf the credytors doo laye theyer charge that they have [brought *deleted*] more money, debtes and wares then that they will confesse, streyght waye he shalbe comitted to warde for a certen tyme to make hym confesse the trueth of the same yf hyt maye be, and therupon to make an end.

And then yf they can not make hym confesse more then was before confessed, then to travell from tyme to tyme to make them agree. And yf any of them will not be ordered accordingly, then to punishe hym.

And finallie, yf hit be possible for them to bryng in some honest persons to testefye of theyer decaye [*MS broken off*].

Endorsed A note of thothe to be given to such as shall clayme the sanctuary, and orders for their admission. [*Dated in modern pencil*] Nov^{br}. 1577.

---

[1] Romans 13:7 ('*Reddite ergo omnibus debita*').

CHAPTER FOUR

The Musicians of Westminster Abbey, 1540–1640

Stanford Lehmberg

We will never know as much as we would like about the music sung at Westminster Abbey in the sixteenth and seventeenth centuries. No lists of the motets, anthems and canticles which formed part of the daily services survive. It is not even certain what music was performed at great events of state, such as royal funerals and coronations. There is no early catalogue of the choir library. In short, the Abbey, in company with virtually all the ancient cathedrals, possesses disappointingly thin records regarding the music which was such an important part of the liturgy.

In contrast, substantial documentation relates to the musicians who served the Abbey during the first century following the dissolution of the medieval monastery. Financial records give us the names of some choristers and virtually all the singingmen and minor canons. We know what they were paid and in some cases where they lived. The Act Books of the dean and chapter, which begin in 1543, contain frequent references to the singers, organists and masters of the choristers. It is thus possible to track their careers, which sometimes included a lifetime spent in the service of the Abbey. If we cannot say much about the music performed at Westminster Abbey under the Tudors and early Stuarts, we can at least describe the lives of the Abbey musicians.

Financial provision for the choir is included in the several schemes for the foundation of the cathedral in 1540. Both early drafts call for ten choristers, to receive a total of £33 6s 8d a year, and twelve singingmen, whose allocation was raised from £80 in the first version to £96 in the second. The first draft provided for eight minor canons – clergy whose duties included singing in the choir – to be paid £80, but the number was later raised to twelve, each still to receive £10.[1] The two erection books contain the same provisions as the second draft.[2]

---

[1] PRO, E315/24, ff. 5–6, 37–8. Knighton, 'Collegiate foundations', 40. Cf. above, p. 22.

[2] BL, Add. MS 40061, ff. 2–5. WAM 6478, ff. 1–5.

The staff of the secularized Abbey was to include a master of the choristers receiving an annual stipend of £10. He was responsible for housing, feeding and clothing the boys as well as teaching them; he received the money allocated for their expenses. The chanter (this term was used here rather than precentor) was made responsible for 'the ordryng of the quere'; he was to record absences by the priests and lay singers and to fine them a penny for missing matins, the mass or evensong, or ½d for absence from prime or other hours. 'Also that if any of the prestes or syngyngmen go forth of the quere and there tary forth any space without licence than his negligence to be countid an absence although he cum in agayn afore the ende of the service.'[3]

The dean was entitled to nominate all the choristers, although the canons could put forward the names of the boys for the grammar school; this arrangement was confirmed on 7 July 1547.[4] There had earlier (1546) been an attempt to require that the places of the choristers along with those of all the scholars, bellringers and sextons (56 in all) be divided into fourteen portions, of which two were to be in the gift of the dean and one in the hands of each of the twelve canons. The right to nominate minor canons, singingmen, vergers and other officers was likewise shared among the members of the chapter through a system of lots and balls, although one suspects that the influence of the master of the choristers was usually paramount for the musical appointments.[5] Provision for examination of the grammar school candidates was adopted at the 7 July 1547 meeting. Admissions under this procedure are recorded two days later, but at the same time it was decided that the other offices assignable by ballot were to be filled without any further 'common assent or electyon'.[6] Appointments of minor canons, singingmen and choristers are among those recorded in the rear of the Act Book (only) between 1548 and 1556.[7]

The death of Henry VIII and the accession of Edward VI made little difference for the musical establishment. A contemporary account of the procession at Edward's coronation lists some of the music which was sung to the traditional Latin texts, including 'Veni Creator Spiritus'.[8] The introduction of the Book of Common Prayer in 1549 and the consequent proscription of anthems and services with Latin texts did have profound implications for the musical repertoire. There was some

---

[3] *Acts 1543–1609*, no. 14. This order was reiterated under Edward VI: *ibid.*, no. 94.
[4] *Ibid.*, no. 66.
[5] *Ibid.*, no. 50. Knighton, 'Collegiate foundations', 80–2.
[6] *Acts 1543–1609*, no. 69.
[7] *Ibid.*, no. 185.
[8] WAM 51119.

liturgical experimentation at the Abbey: according to Wriothesley's *Chronicle* the ordinary of the mass was sung in English at the opening of parliament in November 1547 and at Henry VII's obit in May 1548. This was in anticipation of the publication of the first Prayer Book. There do not appear to have been trial services prior to the introduction of the more protestant book of 1552 which was first used at St Paul's.[9]

With the accession of Mary in July 1553 Latin liturgies reappeared more rapidly. A solemn Latin mass preceded the opening of Mary's first parliament and new service books, presumably in Latin, were written out for her coronation at a cost of £2. Some members of the choir had evidently kept their old volumes of Latin music, which they now sold back to the Abbey. We know that this was the case with John Wood, who was paid £1 6s 8d for an antiphoner. A total expenditure of £40 for choir books is recorded. Organs were repaired and chalices, bells and vestments were purchased to replace those which had been removed or sold under Edward.[10] The number of choristers had fallen to eight in 1553, but the full ten places were filled by 1556. Five of the twelve minor canonries had also by then come to be held by laymen. One draft of the revived Benedictine establishment of 1556 suggested that the lay choir be continued with eight boys and six men. But the full complement of ten choristers, twelve lay vicars and twelve minor canons (five still laymen) was subsequently provided.

Quarrels, perhaps motivated by differences of opinion about religious matters, appear to have troubled the Abbey in the 1550s. An entry in the Act Book for 6 August 1551 records that John Marckant was discharged from his place as a singingman because he had 'usyd hym selfe byseley raylyngly and sedytyously by castyng of bylles agaynst Scorsse and slanderyng of Roche'.[11] This was later crossed out, but in January 1556 it was decreed that if any of the petty canons, schoolmasters, or any other clerks above the age of 18 called another person enjoying commons a 'foole, knave or any other contumelius or slanderus worde' he should be fined a shilling for each offence, and it was noted that one 'Sir Edmund Hamonde pryste dyd breake John Wodes heade, beinge one of the clarkes, with a pote'. The dean had Edmund confined

---

[9] *A Chronicle of England during the reigns of the Tudors, from A.D. 1485 to 1559, by Charles Wriothesley, Windsor Herald,* ed. W.D. Hamilton (Camden Soc. new ser. xi, xx, 1875–7), i, 187, ii, 2. Knighton, 'Collegiate foundations', 126–7. P.G. le Huray, *Music and the Reformation in England, 1549–1660* (1967), 9–10.

[10] WAM 37634 (coronation); 37437 (Wood); 37727, f. 2v (books) and *passim.* Knighton, 'Collegiate foundations', 151–2.

[11] WAM 33604, f. 3v; 37709, 37713, 37716, 37717; Knighton, 'Collegiate foundations', 151, 163. The lay choir presumably served the Lady Chapel.

in the Gatehouse for three days and ordered him to pay Wode 40s 'for the healinge of his heade'.[12]

The monastic establishment remained for eight months after Mary's death. Elizabeth's coronation was celebrated according to the old rite, although the litany was sung in English and the epistle and gospel read in both Latin and the vernacular. The opening of Elizabeth's first parliament was the occasion for the monastic procession which the queen rebuffed with the famous words 'Away with those torches, for we see very well'.[13] During the last year of Mary's life the choir had again become depleted, with only eight men and five boys at the time of her death, but the first draft treasurer's account for Elizabeth's reign (1560/1) records payments to the full complement of twelve singingmen and ten choristers, still receiving £8 and 66s 8d a year respectively.[14] The Marian entries in the Act Book end on 24 September 1556 and the Elizabethan record begins on 5 July 1560.[15] One of the earliest Elizabethan entries mandates a monthly communion, at which all the priests and almsmen were to receive the sacrament, weekly sermons, preached by the canons, and a regular Saturday 'quire chapitor' at which 'all the quire shall appere for redresse of faultes in the weeke before committed'.[16]

In fact the Act Book for Elizabeth's reign contains virtually no references to faults of choir members at the Abbey. This is interesting because it contrasts with the situation at many of the cathedrals.[17] An order of 23 May 1603 does, however, suggest that there had been problems because the minor canons and singingmen were accustomed to taking authorized days of absence at their own convenience rather than according to a set rota, with the result that sometimes all the voices in one part were absent at once. They were ordered to follow a fixed course 'as the use is in Paulis and other churches; on whiche dayes only they shall have power to be from churche, and otherways to be put in the booke of perditions'.[18]

As early as the 1540s it was recognized that the stipends of singingmen and minor canons (£8 a year for the singingmen, £10 for the minor canons) were inadequate, and they were regularly supplemented by

---

[12] *Acts 1543–1609*, nos 92 (repeated as no. 115), 176.

[13] *CSP Ven.* vii, no. 15 (p. 23). It has been suggested that Elizabeth was principally concerned to walk up the nave escorted by her chapel choir singing the English litany: W.P. Haugaard, *Elizabeth and the English Reformation* (Cambridge 1968), 82.

[14] WAM 37931, ff. 2, 2v.

[15] *Acts 1543–1609*, nos 182, 188. The intervening monastic chapter had no use for the Act Book.

[16] *Acts 1543–1609*, no. 189.

[17] See Lehmberg, *Reformation of Cathedrals*, 218–23.

[18] *Acts 1543–1609*, no. 524.

'rewards' of 40s a year, thus producing salaries of £10 and £12 a year, paid quarterly.[19] These stipends and rewards remained unchanged until the time of the Civil War.[20] Sometimes there were additional payments. In 1545/6 £14 11s 6d was divided among the 'sondry Singingmen servinge ther the same yere'.[21] Under Mary a dividend 'for the voyde stalles' was paid to the minor canons and singers.[22]

During the early seventeenth century the chapter tried to help the singingmen by assigning part of the fines collected for the renewal of leases to them. In December 1606, for instance, the eighteen singingmen received 10s each from the lease of the parsonage of St Martin-in-the-Fields. In 1619 a lease in Leicestershire was granted at a rent of £4 14s and twenty muttons, plus 40s for the singers.[23] In 1626 the duke of Buckingham made an entry fine worth £100 a year for lands in Gloucestershire and Worcestershire; of this £40 was to be paid in quarterly instalments to the minor canons and singingmen, and also to the organist if he did not have a singingman's place. Twenty pounds was allocated for the better apparel and diet of the choristers.[24] Four years later £40 from the revenues of estates in Lincolnshire was assigned to the choir.[25] Half of a gift of £10 made by one Mary Ferrand of Mitcham in 1632 was given to the 'poore singingmen of the churche'.[26] Small gifts might also be given on special occasions; each singingman, for instance, received a shilling on Guy Fawkes Day in 1610.[27] On rare occasions a special contribution might be given to an aged singingman; in 1641/2 40s was presented to Daniel Taylor 'in respect of his age'.[28]

The act for 2 and 3 May 1608 notes that 'in regard of the greatnes of extraordinary expenses this yeare, it is agreed that the household shalbe dissolved the weeke after the election [of scholars at Westminster School] for twoe monthes'. There were still problems in December, when it was decided to reduce expenses and forego some weekly suppers.[29] In Janu-

---

[19] WAM 37064, f. 4 records payments in 1545/6.

[20] WAM 33692, ff. 1v–2 (1642/3); 33693, ff. 1v–2 (1643/4, the last account before the Interregnum).

[21] WAM 37060, f. 5.

[22] WAM 37658, f. 1.

[23] *Acts 1543–1609*, no. 539. WAM Chapter Act Book II, f. 26v (*Acts 1609–42*, no. 34).

[24] WAM Chapter Act Book II, f. 41 (*Acts 1609–42*, no. 53). See also below, p. 249.

[25] WAM 33685, f. 3v.

[26] WAM Chapter Act Book II, f. 52v (*Acts 1609–42*, no. 63).

[27] WAM 33664, f. 5v. MS says '1611' but the account is for the year from Michaelmas 1610.

[28] WAM 33690, 33691, f. 6.

[29] *Acts 1543–1609*, nos 543, 544.

ary 1632 it was said that 'the colledg at this present is destitute of meanes to keepe commons together according as they have done heretofore', so communal dinners were discontinued altogether. Most of the canons, minor canons and singingmen were married and took meals in their own homes, so they may not have cared greatly, but they were not compensated for the loss. The choristers, as well as the scholars and the poor, were to be provided for 'according to the usuall proportion of their allowances'.[30] By 1638 even the choristers were allowed commons only on certain festivals – All Saints, Christmas and the three holy days following, Ascension Day, Whit Sunday, Election Sunday and the day following, and St Peter's Day.[31]

Analysis of the financial records of the Abbey makes it possible to determine the length of service by the singingmen and minor canons. The careers of 148 lay vicars and 65 canons have been tracked in this way.[32]

What is perhaps a surprising number of lay singers remained at Westminster Abbey for only one or two years. Almost half the singingmen fall into this category: 41 are recorded only in a single year, 28 more for only two years. It appears obvious that these singers either proved unsatisfactory or found conditions at the Abbey insufficiently appealing to warrant a longer stay. Numbers of those employed for three years or more are much smaller and are summarized in the table overleaf.

The singingman with the longest tenure was James Hooper, who served from 1601 until 1644. James was a son of the more famous Edmund Hooper, who was master of the choristers at the Abbey and organist of the chapel royal from 1604 until 1621.[33] The family may have included Gabriel Hooper, who sang at Westminster in 1620/1, and William Hooper, listed in 1643/4. It is possible that James had earlier been a chorister; if so, his time at the Abbey may have equalled half a century. Thomas Askewe, about whom nothing else is known, served

---

[30] WAM Chapter Act Book II, f. 53 (*Acts 1609–42*, no. 65). The minor canons, some of whom were married, had been allowed to opt out of Commons since the time of Edward VI: *Acts 1543–1609*, no. 89.

[31] WAM Chapter Act Book II, fol. 68v-69 (*Acts 1609–42*, no. 89).

[32] This analysis is based on examination of all surviving treasurers' accounts from 1542 to 1663 – it was thought desirable to continue the search into the Restoration era in order to see how many of the men appointed before 1640 returned to office after the Interregnum.

[33] *The New Grove Dictionary of Music and Musicians*, ed. S. Sadie (2nd edn 2001), xi, 694–5. le Huray, *Music and the Reformation*, 66 and *passim*. H.C. de Lafontaine, *The King's Musick* (repr. New York 1973), 44, 58.

Length of Service, Singingmen

Years	Number of Men	Years	Number of Men
3	9	17	3
4	7	18	3
5	5	19	4
6	3	20	3
7	3	24	2
8	2	25	1
9	4	26	2
10	3	27	1
11	2	29	1
12	5	30	1
13	6	38	1
14	2	40	1
15	1	42	1
16	2	43	1

Sources: WAM 33603–4; 33622–97, documents in series 37039 x 37985 and others

42 years, from 1555 to 1597. He was listed as a minor canon in 1560 but does not appear to have been in orders and reverted to his earlier status as a singingman the following year. Christopher Brickett, a choirman from 1549 until his death on Ascension Day 1596, had been a chorister in the old monastic Lady Chapel and then attended Westminster School.[34] Thomas Roo (or Rowe or Rowse) may have sung from 1542 to 1580, but since there is a gap in his service it is possible that we are dealing with two men with similar names. Others who are recorded as having sung for 25 years or more are Richard Prynce, Robert Willis, Henry Northedge, William Heather and Thomas Hassard. Heather became a gentleman of the chapel royal in 1615 and headed the list of the chapel in 1625; Hassard (or Hazard) is also listed as a musician to Charles I in 1625.[35]

A number of singingmen must have been brought up as choristers at the Abbey. Since the treasurers' accounts generally do not name the boys it is impossible to compile a full list, but the accounts of the chapel

---

[34] Knighton, 'Collegiate foundations', 349. Lehmberg, *Reformation of Cathedrals*, 208.

[35] Lafontaine, *King's Musick*, 52, 58, 59. Heather, *alias* Heyther, DMus, founded a music lectureship at Oxford in 1627 and the present chair bears his name: *New Grove*, xi, 477.

royal do list the choristers of Westminster who sang at the funeral of James I in 1625 so we know that both John Harding and James Trie, appointed singingmen in 1638, had earlier sung as trebles.[36]

The record for minor canons is similar. Twenty-one men are recorded as serving for a single year, seventeen for only two. The remaining numbers are as follows.

Length of Service, Minor Canons

Years	Number of Men	Years	Number of Men
3	2	13	1
4	7	14	1
6	2	16	1
7	1	19	1
8	1	20	1
9	2	24	1
11	1	26	3
12	1	28	1

Nothing more is known about the longest-serving minor canon, Edward Nelham, who held office for 28 years, from 1616 until 1644. Two of the men who remained at the Abbey for 26 years served as precentor: William Punter, 1570–96, and his successor Matthew Holmes, 1596–1622. Between them they must have assured continuity for more than half a century. A third man who served for 26 years was Thomas Gooding or Goodwin; he is listed as a singingman from 1595 to 1608 and then as a minor canon until his illness and death in 1621/2. Gooding's career points up the fact that the Abbey, like many of the cathedrals, found it difficult to attract minor canons who were ordained priests and possessed adequate voices as well, so these positions were often held by laymen, some of whom had been singingmen previously. Since the minor canons received higher stipends the promotion must have been welcome. A few examples of this practice may be noted. Daniel Taylor, a little-known composer, appears as a singingman from 1618 to 1627 and then a minor canon until 1638, but when it became possible to employ proper minor canons he reverted to his original status for the remaining years before his retirement or death in 1643. George Greene was a singingman from 1598 to 1604, then a minor canon until 1617. Similarly, John Searle served a year as a choirman before being appointed a minor canon in 1594. He held this post for a decade.

---

[36] Lafontaine, *King's Musick*, 59.

Occasionally the records specify that a layman was occupying the place of a minor canon; this was the case with Edmund Dalton in 1572/3.[37] Despite this practice void stalls sometimes existed. Several are recorded in 1569/70 and 1570/1.[38]

Very few members of the choir during this period were notable composers or performers. Much the best known of the singingmen was Adrian Batten, who served at the Abbey from 1614 to 1626. Batten had been born in Salisbury in 1591 and was possibly a chorister at Winchester. Two of his sons were baptized at the Abbey, in 1616 and 1621, but both died in the plague of 1625. In 1626 Batten moved to St Paul's, where he sang until 1635. He died in 1637. While at Westminster Batten was occasionally paid for 'pricking' or copying music, including services by Weelkes, Tallis and Tomkins. Batten's own services and anthems must have been sung as well.[39] John Farmer, John Parsons and Simon Stubbes, all singingmen under Elizabeth or James I, have left a few compositions, but these are rarely performed and cannot match Batten's works.

Some members of the Abbey choir also sang in the chapel royal. These included John Amery, Francis Willoughby and William Lawrence, all listed as members of the chapel who were granted mourning livery for the funeral of Queen Elizabeth; Edward Piers, Edmund Hooper, George Greene and Peter Hopkins, listed as 'gentlemen of the chapel extraordinary' on the same occasion; John Clarke, a chorister at Westminster in 1603, then a tenor in the chapel royal and at the Abbey; Anthony Kirkbie, Ezechiel Wade, William Heather, John Frost senior and Thomas Day, members of both choirs during the reign of James I; and Richard Saundey, Matthew Pownall, Thomas Laughton, Ralph Amner, George Woodson junior, Thomas Pearce senior and John Croker, whose service dated from the time of Charles I. It is unusual for us to know what part the choirmen sang, but the chapel royal records do tell us that Saundey and Laughton were countertenors, Amner and Pearce basses.[40]

---

[37] WAM 33633, f. 2v.

[38] WAM 33630, ff. 10v, 11; 33631, f. 3.

[39] New Grove, ii, 910–11. WAM 33679, f. 5v ('Paied to Mr Batten for pricking Mr Weekes his service and Mr Talles his Magnificat and Nunc Dimittis and alsoe Mr Tomkins service – xxx s.'): le Huray, Music and the Reformation, 409–10 (listing modern editions of Batten's music).

[40] Amner may have been a brother of the composer John Amner. John was organist of Ely Cathedral, while Ralph is known to have been a lay clerk at Ely and Windsor and a gentleman of the chapel royal as well as at the Abbey. He served at Westminster only one quarter, in 1608/9.

Several of the masters of the choristers were men of distinction. During the sixteenth century they usually served as organist as well, although the financial records do not give them that title. The earliest masters are shadowy figures. The erection book preserved among the Abbey muniments lists William Green as the incumbent master of the choristers.[41] He may have held a similar post in the monastic foundation. From March 1543 Robert Foxe was named as Green's successor. In the following January the Chapter Act Book records that he 'shall have the whole governing of the chorustars, to teache them, to provide for meate and drinke, and to se them clenly and honestly apparalled in all thinges, and he to have ther whole stipend', that is the £33 6s 8d allocated for the boys. The chapter also agreed that Foxe should have the house 'over the gate going into the allmery [Almonry] for hymself and the said chorustars rent free, he repairing it sufficiently before Ester next cummyng'. Since the house was 'in grett ruyn' he was given 40s to help meet the cost of repairs.[42] He may have continued to serve under Edward VI but was probably succeeded in 1546/7 by Thomas Heath, a lay vicar, who served as master during the earlier years of Mary's reign.[43] Another obscure figure, Robert Lamkyn, was master of the choristers in the Marian monastery. He continued to be employed as a singingman, but not in a higher capacity, under Elizabeth.[44]

John Taylor was the first Elizabethan master of the choristers, serving from Michaelmas 1559.[45] Evidently Taylor was well thought of, for in June 1569 the dean and chapter entered a testimonial for him in their Act Book, adding that he should give them half a year's notice before leaving his office. In September the chapter had to make temporary arrangements, appointing a singingman to provide for the boys in the absence of a master. Taylor's name is crossed out in the treasurer's account for 1570 and that of Robert White is written in.[46] Edmund

---

[41] WAM 6748, f. 4. Cf. W. Shaw, *The Succession of Organists* (Oxford 1991), 326.

[42] WAM 37045, ff. 5v, 8 (Green paid to Lady Day 1543, Foxe for the Midsummer quarter following); *Acts 1543–1609*, no. 12. In 1545 it was arranged that he should live in the Almonry itself: *ibid.*, no. 49. Cf. Shaw, *Succession of Organists*, 326–7 (misinterpreting WAM 37045).

[43] WAM 6478, f. 4; 33604, f. 4v; 37709, f. 1 v; 37713. Shaw, *Succession of Organists*, 327. I. Payne, *The Provision and Practice of Sacred Music at Cambridge Colleges and selected Cathedrals, c. 1547–c. 1646* (1993), 26–7, 233.

[44] WAM 33198E, m. 7; 37931, f. 3v. Knighton, 'Collegiate foundations', 353. Shaw, *Succession of Organists*, 327.

[45] WAM 33198G, m. 7. Knighton, 'Collegiate foundations', 354.

[46] *Acts 1543–1609*, nos 246 (& n. 191), 248 (& n. 207). WAM 33629, f. 4v. He moved to Salisbury as master of the choristers: Knighton, 'Collegiate foundations', 354–5. Shaw, *Succession of Organists*, 259 (but on p. 327 perpetuating faulty assumption that the Westminster Taylor died there in 1569). *New Grove*, xxiv, 929–30.

Galley was evidently the singingman who bridged the gap between Taylor and White, while Mistress Peryn (presumably widow of a former minor canon named Alexander Perryn) was charged briefly with boarding the boys.[47]

Robert White is an interesting figure. Probably born about 1530 or shortly thereafter, he received the MusB from Cambridge before succeeding Christopher Tye (whose daughter he married) as organist of Ely in 1561. He may have served briefly at Chester as well, but about the end of 1568 he moved to London. He continued as master of the choristers at the Abbey until his death, of the plague, in 1574.[48] He composed a substantial amount of Latin music, including two settings of the Lamentations of Jeremiah. The circumstances under which these fine works were composed are problematic. Some may have been written during the reign of Mary Tudor, while White was still quite young. Others probably date from Elizabeth's years. These could not lawfully have been sung at the Abbey, but it is possible that they were composed for the chapel royal: the queen herself understood Latin perfectly well and appears to have blessed its use there. White is not known to have been attached formally to the chapel, but he may still have provided music for its use.[49] Only five of his English anthems have survived, but some of these are substantial works for five voices.[50] It is only reasonable to suppose that the Abbey choir achieved a high level of excellence under his leadership.

White was followed by Henry Leeve, who had been a singingman since 1571. Leeve was master of the choristers for more than a decade, 1574–85, but has left us no compositions and little information about his life.

Edmund Hooper, whose long stay as master of the choristers spanned the years from 1586 until his death in 1621, was another major figure cast in White's mould. Born in Devon about 1553, he is said to have been a chorister at Exeter. By 1582 he was a member of the Abbey choir; his will contains a reference to his having been at the Abbey for 38 years. He also served in the chapel royal, as an extraordinary singer at Elizabeth's funeral and as a gentleman of the chapel beginning in 1612. A few years later he was named organist of the chapel royal,

---

[47] WAM 33630, ff. 10v, 16.

[48] The Abbey made a payment to Robert Hawkes, the administrator of White's estate, in 1575/6: WAM 33636, f. 5.

[49] See H. Benham, *Latin Church Music in England c. 1460–1575* (1977), 212–16. *New Grove*, xxvii, 341–2. Notes by Peter Phillips included with the recording 'Robert White, Tudor Church Music' by the Tallis Scholars (Gimell CDGIM 030, 1995).

[50] See le Huray, *Music and the Reformation*, 189–90.

serving jointly with Orlando Gibbons. He appears to have been the first person actually designated as organist of the Abbey: he was granted the office by a patent of 1606 and named for life in 1616. Possibly because he was busy elsewhere, he was charged with neglecting his duties at Westminster, with the result that there were 'many disorders in the choristers' in 1603.[51] There was also some complaint that he had not disbursed certain payments due to the minor canons and singingmen, and the dean, Lancelot Andrewes, ordered him to answer their demands. During the years after 1606 John Gibbs received the money set aside for the choristers and was responsible for their care. Evidently Gibbs (and later John Parsons) was in fact master of the choristers and Hooper solely the organist. Hooper was buried in the cloisters of the Abbey, as was his wife Margaret following her death in 1652. As we have seen, their son James served the Abbey as a singingman for many years.

During his lifetime Edmund Hooper was noted as a composer. He wrote five services, including an elaborate verse setting of the evening canticles, eight full anthems and ten verse anthems. We know that he was paid 10s in 1598/9 'for writinge and pricking in eighte partes one whole service'; since the same account records that he was paid for cornets, sackbuts 'upon the Queenes daye' and strings for the viols it may well be that these instruments accompanied that music. There is also his receipt dated 1586 for 10s to his predecessor Leeve for a treble viol, 'without the which I could not use the resydue', for viol strings and 44 sheets of paper for pricking 'songes' for the choir.[52] Hooper's works deserve to be better known, for they display colourful voice writing and effective contrapuntal passages. A number of his anthems do include accompaniments for viols. These compositions may have been performed in the chapel royal as well as the Abbey, and they may also have been sung in the occasional concerts which we know to have taken place in the Jerusalem Chamber during the early seventeenth century. As in the case of White we can reasonably speculate that the music at Westminster was of high quality under Hooper (although he may not have worked effectively with the choristers) and that his works were appreciated both at court and at the Abbey. Certainly the dean and chapter referred to his 'good and faithefull service' in 1616, when they granted him an annuity of £14 and a tenement in Little Almonry, 'contayninge fower rometh, vizt a hall and a kytchen belowe upon the grounde, and two rometh or chambers directly over the same, together

---

[51] *Acts 1543–1609*, no. 529.
[52] WAM 33653, f. 4; 40079.

with a litle yearde or backsyde ... and a privie or widdraught over the common sewer there'.[53]

After Hooper's death in 1621 the office of organist and master of the choristers was granted to John Parsons; it was his to hold for life, because of the dean's appreciation of his 'good and falthfull service', perhaps a reference to his work as organist of St Margaret's, Westminster, since 1616. He was to serve as White and Hooper had done and to receive the usual annuity of £14; he was to live in the tenement in the Almonry 'usuaille heretofore held and enjoyed by the maister of the choristers for the tyme beinge'. Additional annuities and revenues from St Margaret's and St Martin-in-the-Fields were given him as a dividend, and he was to be paid £36 13s 4d for 'teachinge and fyndinge' the choristers, plus a bushel and a half of wheat each week and a new gown for each chorister yearly. Parsons composed a few works for the church, possibly including a service that was sung at the funeral of Charles II; he died in 1623 and like Hooper was buried in the Abbey cloisters.[54]

Parsons's successor, Thomas Day, held office from 1624 to 1632. As early as 1612 he was one of the musicians serving Prince Charles, and he continued as a gentleman of the chapel royal during Charles I's reign. Day probably died during the Interregnum; the records of the chapel refer to him as being dead by March 1661.[55] Orlando Gibbons is listed as master of the choristers, alongside Day, in 1623/4 and 1624/5. In fact Gibbons probably served as organist and Day as master of the choristers, the two offices being separated as they had been under Edmund Hooper. Gibbons died prematurely while awaiting the arrival of Henrietta Maria at Canterbury.[56] The employment of Day and Gibbons at both the Abbey and the chapel royal suggests that King Charles may have wished to bring the two musical establishments into a closer relationship with each other.

The last of the organists of our period was Richard Portman, whose employment was first recorded for the year ending at Michaelmas 1627. Portman is thought to have been named a gentleman of the chapel royal in September 1638 on the death of John Tomkins, who had been one of the organists there, although his name does not appear in the financial

---

[53] WAM 9835, 9836. *Acts 1543–1609*, no. 538. WAM Chapter Act Book II, ff. 3v, 9v, 13, 18v (*Acts 1609–42*, nos 6, 14, 17, 23). Shaw, *Succession of Organists*, 328–9.

[54] WAM Chapter Act Book II, f. 30v (*Acts 1609–42*, no. 38). WAM 9837. Shaw, *Succession of Organists*, 329–30. *New Grove*, xix, 161.

[55] Lafontaine, *King's Musick*, 50–117 *passim*. 118 (vacancy by 9 November 1660), 130 (deceased by 30 March 1661). Cf. Shaw, *Succession of Organists*, 330.

[56] WAM 33681, f. 2; 33682, f. 34v. Shaw, *Succession of Organists*, 6–7. E.H. Fellowes, *Orlando Gibbons and his Family* (1951). *New Grove*, ix, 832–6.

records of the chapel.[57] During the earlier years of Portman's service at the Abbey the treasurer seems to have been confused about the division of labours between Portman and the masters of the choristers, James Trie (1637–8) and Walter Porter (1639–44).[58] Portman is finally listed definitively as organist in 1638, and in January 1641 the chapter acts clarified the financial arrangements:

> Whereas there was a difference betweene the organist and the master of the coristers about a stipend of ten poundes per annum to whether of them it should be paid, and it appeerd to us that the organist hath bene in possession of the said stipend for many yeeres together, but that the right was and is in the master of the choristers. It is therfore thought fitt and orderd by the deane and chapter, that in respect of both theire interests and paines, that the said ten poundes shall be continued to the organist, and that ten poundes more shall be paid by the tresurer to the master of the choristers yeerely. Item it is agreed that the choristers gownes shall be made at the charge of the college.[59]

During the Interregnum Portman lost his office; we know that he had trouble paying his rent and was threatened with imprisonment. He may have eked out an existence by teaching the organ and virginal; John Playford listed him as an 'instructor' in *A Musicall Banquet* (1651). Some manuscript notes by Anthony Wood, preserved in the Bodleian, refer to Portman as 'a little obliging man, a sober religious man'.[60] He left no musical compositions but may have been the author of a devotional tract, *The Souls Life: Pious Meditations for Devout Christians*, first published in 1645 and again in 1661.[61]

Music by the composers who served the Abbey, as well as others, was frequently copied for the use of the choir. The financial records are replete with payments for 'pricking' anthems, services and an occasional organ book. Psalters were purchased, as were books of special prayers for deliverance from the Spanish Armada ('in the tyme of

---

[57] Shaw, *Succession of Organists*, 330–1. Lafontaine, *King's Musick*, 101 and index.

[58] We know little about Trie and Porter except that both had been choristers and singingmen at the Abbey. Porter was a tenor at the chapel royal: Lafontaine, *King's Musick*, 53–84 *passim*.

[59] WAM Chapter Act Book II, f. 77 (*Acts 1609–42*, no. 101).

[60] WAM 65899; Bodl. MS Wood D. 19 (4), f. 103v; he is further said to have been 'bred up' under Orlando Gibbons and 'then travel'd into France with Dr John Williams, Deane of Westminster, by whose favour he became org. of Westm.'. The trip with Williams is not known otherwise and seems most unlikely; possibly it confused Williams with his notional successor as dean, Richard Steward, who was at the exiled Stuart court in France. The story is repeated in Shaw, *Succession of Organists*, 331, and in *New Grove*, xx, 190.

[61] Wing (2nd edn), 3001A, 3001B, 3002.

daunger') and for the coronation of James I, the celebration of his accession on 24 March, and the anniversary of the Gunpowder Plot. A cupboard for song books was built in the choir in 1610/11; locks and hinges were added to it three years later.[62]

Many of the musicians lived in the close or the Almonry, directly west of the Abbey. The muniments contain many of their leases, and occasional references to house repairs and other matters. A collector's roll for 1548 mentions rents paid by several singingmen, including Thomas Roo, Richard Elyot, William Beche and Thomas Heather, for tenements within the close. The rent for these varied from 10s to 20s a year. Three choirmen had houses in the Almonry, for which they paid 20s, while Roger Empson, another singingman, lived on its northern border in Tothill Street.[63] In 1549 Richard Elyot agreed that a canon, Edward Keble, should have his house, on condition that Keble paid for the repairs that Elyot had made.[64] Homes in Lady Margaret's Rents occupied by the singingmen were repaired at the expense of the dean and chapter in 1599, on condition that in the future the occupants would bear the cost of maintenance themselves.[65] It appears that a conscious effort to house all the singingmen was made in the seventeenth century; in 1631 a tenement and back yard in the Almonry was purchased and assigned to Thomas Day, 'so as all the 16 singingmen ar now by the care and charges of the Deane and chapter provided of houses'.[66]

A number of the Abbey accounts record payments to the organ-makers who cared for the instruments at Westminster. From 1547 until his death in 1571 John Howe was custodian of the organ; his stipend seems to have varied from 3s to £8 a year, presumably depending on the amount of work he performed.[67] Howe was the best-known organ-maker of the period. His father, also named John, had established a workshop in London, 'at the sign of the Organ Pype' in Walbrook, early in the sixteenth century. Several undated bills submitted by Howe survive. One of them itemizes his work:

> [For mending the little organ in Henry VII's new chapel:] for the letherynge of the bellous and for takinge out of the pypes, and

---

[62] WAM 33644, f. 4v (Armada); 33656, f. 4v (coronation); 33664, f. 4v (cupboard); 33669, f. 6v (locks).

[63] WAM 37172. Several tenements in the close and Almonry are said to be vacant or 'in utter decaye'.

[64] Acts 1543–1609, no. 95.

[65] Ibid., no. 509.

[66] WAM Chapter Act Book II, f. 51 (Acts 1609–42, no. 62).

[67] WAM 33603, f. 5; 33618, f. 1; 33622, f. 4v; 33628, f. 3v,. 33629, f. 4v; 33631, f. 4; 37112, f. 5; 37978, f. 9v.

newe sowderynge and scowdnge of them, And tuneynge of them, in all x s.

Item for mendinge of the greate woodden orgaynes in the lofte over the greate quere in the bodye of the churche, firste for foure skynnes of lether, ij paire of garnettes, glewe, nayles and scoringe. And makinge cleane the pypes, and sowderinge and scowrynge of leadyn pypes, and makinge viij newe pypes, with cooles and other thinges, somme xx s.

Three further statements list similar expenses, including wire for springs for the keys, candles, and workmanship 'for my selfe [and] my partner for iij dayes, and my man for ij dayes'.[68] During the reign of Mary several of the Abbey accounts list payments to William Howe; it is not clear if this was an error or if William was a son or brother and assistant of John's, possibly the partner to whom John referred.[69] Occasionally other men were employed as well: in 1567/8 Henry Langforth received 16s 1d 'pro emendacione magnorum organorum' and some anonymous men who came 'ad faciendum organorum' were paid 3s 4d.[70]

After Howe's death a number of different men cared for the organs. A man named Pryce is mentioned in the accounts for 1569/70.[71] In 1571/2 Robert Browgh, who is not otherwise known, was paid 40s 'for mending the myddle organs'.[72] In 1576/7 Henry Leeve, the master of the choristers, was given 6s 8d for having repaired the organs for the past three years.[73] Leeve was still being paid for taking care of them in 1584/5, Edmund Hooper in 1585/6.[74] Hooper received 50s for mending the organ bellows in 1602/3, plus 2s 3d for four pair of hinges for the bellows.[75] One George Pendleton was paid 10s for moving and tuning the instrument used at the funeral of James I's daughter Sophia in 1606 as well as 40s for ordinary mending and tuning.[76]

Thomas Dallam, the greatest organ-builder of the early seventeenth century, appears in the Abbey records beginning in 1606/7, when he and Pendleton were paid jointly. His retaining fee was 40s a year, paid 10s quarterly. Dallam alone received the 40s in 1607/8; in 1608/9 he

---

[68] WAM 37421 (Henry VII); 37422 (wire); 38241 (workmanship); WAM 37397 is a bond for payment 28 Sept. 1553. Garnets were hinges.

[69] WAM 33604, f. 5; 37551, f. 5. Lehmberg, *Reformation of Cathedrals*, 216. *New Grove*, xi, 768. C. Clutton and A. Niland, *The British Organ* (1963), 50.

[70] WAM 33627, f. 5.

[71] WAM 33630, f. 16.

[72] WAM 33632, f. 4v.

[73] WAM 33637, f. 5.

[74] WAM 33642, f. 5v; 33643, f. 7.

[75] WAM 33656, f. 4v.

[76] WAM 33659, ff. 4v, 5.

was allowed an additional 10s for mending 'two greate pypes', and again in 1618/19 he charged 10s for making a new pipe and repairing four others. After Thomas Dallam's death in 1630 his son Robert served the Abbey; in 1632 he was responsible for 'removing the little organ from King Henrie the vijth chapple into the quire', work for which he was paid 51s. This may be the 'new organ' for which Mary Ferrand of Mitcham, whose gift to the choir has already been noted, donated £5: she wished to 'guild a pipe uppon the said organ and her name to be sett uppon it'.[77] The last reference to Robert Dallam dates from 1643.[78] Sometimes the organist signs Dallam's bills – Edmund Hooper did so in 1608.[79] For some reason another organ-maker, John Burward, was brought in by Orlando Gibbons in the summer of 1625. Gibbons commended Burward's work and added, 'I know this bill to be very resonable for I have aledy cut him off ten shillings, therfore I pray dispatche him for he hath delt honestly with the church'.[80]

In addition to organs, several other instruments were used for services at the Abbey. The practice seems to have become common late in Elizabeth's reign. Edmund Hooper's music for viols has already been noted and is reflected in the accounts, which also mention the use of two cornets on 9 November 1599 and three cornets on the queen's accession day, 17 November.[81] Viols were certainly played on the school election day in 1600 and 1601, and very likely in other years as well.[82] In 1602/3 Hooper was paid 5s for mending the viols and 2s 6d 'for fetchinge of other violles from Mr Knevetts', probably a sign that instruments occasionally had to be borrowed.[83] He was also reimbursed for mending wind instruments and carrying them 'diverse tymes to the College'.[84] Cornets and viols are mentioned in 1604/5 and 1605/6.[85] Sackbuts appear in 1619, when they were probably played, together with cornets, at the

---

[77] WAM 33660, f. 5 (Dallam and Pendleton); 33661, f. 5 (Dallam alone); 33662, f. 5 (great pipe); 33676, f. 6 (new pipe); 33687, f. 10 (Henry VII); WAM Chapter Act Book II, f. 52v (Acts 1609–42, no. 63).

[78] WAM 33692, f. 5. Cf. Clutton and Niland, British Organ, 53–54; New Grove, vi, 853; S.E. Lehmberg, Cathedrals under Siege. Cathedrals in English Society, 1600–1700 (Exeter 1996), 181.

[79] WAM 41266.

[80] WAM 53317.

[81] WAM 33654, f. 4.

[82] WAM 33655, ff. 4, 4v.

[83] WAM 33656, f. 4. 'Mr Knevet' is probably the courtier Sir Thomas Knyvet; cf. below, p. 204.

[84] WAM 33656, f. 4.

[85] WAM 33658, ff. 3v, 4; 33659, f. 4.

funeral of Queen Anne, and they are recorded in virtually every account from that year until the Interregnum.[86] It is often recognized that strings and wind instruments were employed in the chapel royal, but we now know that they were used during the earlier seventeenth century at Westminster Abbey as well, especially on festive occasions.

It is pleasant to note that members of the Abbey choir participated in festivities which were an important part of the liturgical year. A number of celebrations are mentioned in the accounts for the Tudor period, but they become more common under the Stuarts. In 1544 12s 11d was spent for wine during the midsummer quarter alone; one might think that this is communion wine, especially since there is a reference to 20d for 'syngyng brede', but the fact that fifteen gallons and one 'pottell' of malmsey were purchased suggests more general consumption. Similar amounts were consumed later in the year.[87] The following year there were 'dyverse and sonderie dyners and drynkinges' costing nearly £15.[88]

Seventeenth-century accounts regularly mention dinners on special occasions. In 1613/14, for instance, the singingmen and almsmen were given banquets on All Saints, Guy Fawkes Day, the Epiphany and the Annunciation.[89] Other occasions which were often celebrated were Christmas, Candlemas (2 February), Easter, Whitsunday, St Peter's Day (29 June) and James I's accession day (24 March).[90] Nine dinners were held in 1628/9.[91] When it became impossible to continue the dinners in 1644 the singingmen were allocated £5 19s in compensation.[92] Resumption of dinners followed the Restoration; in 1661 nine of them were again held, at a total cost of £13 1s.[93]

Plays at Christmas, involving special music by the choir and instrumentalists as well as acting by the scholars of Westminster School, were usual under James I and Charles I. The normal cost seems to have been around £2.[94] In addition there might be small charges for torches or setting up the stage in the college hall.[95] In 1631/2 a play on All Hallows' Eve is recorded as well.[96]

---

[86] WAM 33675 (f. 6v) x 33692 (f. 5).
[87] WAM 37044, f. 4.
[88] WAM 37060, f. 6.
[89] WAM 33669, f. 6.
[90] Cf. e.g. WAM 33682, f. 43v, for 1624/5 and 1625/6.
[91] WAM 34163, ff. 44–5.
[92] WAM 33693, f. 4.
[93] WAM 33695, f. 4v.
[94] WAM 33659, f. 4, for 1605/6.
[95] WAM 33658, f. 3v; 33683, f. 8.
[96] WAM 33687, f. 10.

A less happy occurrence, the frequent visitation of the plague, also finds a place in the records. In, for example, September 1569 scholars at Westminster School were sent to live with their families or friends until the end of the contagion, an order repeated in June 1570, but it does not appear that choristers were excused or sung services suspended.[97] Books containing special prayers for deliverance from pestilence were bought in 1569/70 and 1592/3.[98] The houses of two singingmen were visited by the epidemic that accompanied James's accession in 1603, and the chapter made small payments towards their relief in 1603/4.[99] Special expenses incurred at this time included more than £6 paid to one Rice Williams 'for watching and warding with munition and shott in the church during the sicknes and the funerals of our late Queene Eliz. and alsoe for chardges at the coronation of our most gracious soveraigne Kinge James'.[100] There was also a payment 'for watchinge the cloister when the infection was feared' in 1629/30, and twenty marks was sent to the town of Cambridge, 'being visited with the sicknes this yeere'.[101] It was probably the plague that caused the cancellation of the Whitsun dinner for the choir in 1609.[102] In 1621/2 an apothecary was paid 11s 8d for physic given to the singer Thomas Gooding in his sickness, but the medicine failed to save his life.[103] Commons were not kept for a time in 1630/1 because of the plague.[104]

During the first century following its transformation into a secular institution Westminster Abbey played a significant role in the musical life of the realm, as it has done ever since. Its place was probably more important then than now because there were so few other opportunities for professional musicians to find employment or for lay persons to hear fine music performed.[105] Although the Abbey could not claim the

---

[97] *Acts 1543–1609*, nos 248, 252.

[98] WAM 33630, f. 16; 33647, f. 4v.

[99] WAM 33657, f. 3v.

[100] WAM 33658, f. 4.

[101] WAM 33685, ff. 9v, 10.

[102] WAM 33662, f. 5v.

[103] WAM 33679, f. 5v.

[104] WAM 33686, f. 11.

[105] Public concerts were instituted shortly after the Restoration, principally (in 1672) by John Banister, a violinist in the king's musick, followed from 1678 by Thomas Britton, 'the musical small coal man', who converted a warehouse into a hall: J. Harley, *Music in Purcell's London* (1968), 135–51. *New Grove*, ii, 659 (Banister); iii, 308 (Britton). Prior to that time the cathedrals and institutions like the Abbey offered virtually the only music performed by professionals accessible to ordinary people who did not have access to the court or the homes of the aristocracy: see W.L. Woodfill, *Musicians in English Society from Elizabeth to Charles I* (Princeton 1953).

services of Byrd and Tallis, as the chapel royal did, and was served by Orlando Gibbons only briefly, it did offer employment to several composers of distinguished church music. Generations of choristers passed through the choir; even if they did not find a career as musicians they received a musical education and their lives were surely enriched by the experience. Although many of the singingmen moved in and out of the choir rapidly, others spent a lifetime in the service of the Abbey and probably found their work and the companionship of like-minded people rewarding. Their days were enlivened by the seasonal celebrations of the church, both in liturgy and in feasting. If the finest flourishing of music at Westminster lay ahead, in the era of Purcell and Handel, the years from 1540 to 1640 provided a solid foundation for the future.

CHAPTER FIVE

The Coronations of Edward VI, Mary I, and Elizabeth I, and the Transformation of the Tudor Monarchy

Dale Hoak *

Between February 1547 and January 1559 three English sovereigns were crowned in Westminster Abbey, and none was an adult male. This fact alone rendered the rapid succession of Henry VIII's children – Edward VI, a minor, and his unmarried half-sisters, Mary I and Elizabeth I – unique in the annals of English monarchy.[1] In retrospect one can see that the coronations of all three marked an extraordinary 'moment' in the history of the Tudor polity, one that fatefully linked the course of the Reformation to that of the royal succession. Edward's premature death and the duke of Northumberland's botched attempt to bar Mary from the throne in 1553 marked only the *first* phase of a succession crisis, a crisis exacerbated by Mary's demise without issue (17 November 1558) and Elizabeth's decision not to marry. Mary's catholicism and Edward's and Elizabeth's protestantism, as much as the religious inclinations of the men in their parliaments, underscored the historic significance of the outcome of this crisis; reformers and traditionalists alike might well ask whom God had chosen to nurture the faith of His true followers. Because at the moment of accession all three monarchs fell heir to the revolutionary headship of the church created by their father – the royal supremacy of the crown imperial that was established in law in 1533–4 – their coronation oaths, like the terms of their anointing, had to be changed to accommodate the changed rela-

---

* The author wishes to thank the editors most heartily for their many kindnesses in the preparation of this essay, Richard Mortimer for his patient support throughout and Charles Knighton for his assistance in helping me clarify various matters, especially the ones cited in notes 102–4.

[1] Only once before had three sovereigns come to the throne more quickly, but of course all were adult males: Harold Harefoot in 1037, Harthacnut in 1040, and Edward the Confessor in 1042.

tion of the crown to that church, to English law, and to the English people.

The full implications of successive changes in the Tudor coronation oath were perhaps only made manifest in the religio-political maelstrom of Civil War. At his trial for treason in 1644, the archbishop of Canterbury, William Laud, denied that he had altered Charles I's coronation oath in such a way as to enhance the royal prerogative at the expense of parliamentary statute; whatever changes had been made, he said, were those of Edward VI or Elizabeth I.[2] This important testimony, overlooked by historians of the Tudor constitution, allows us to reconstruct part of the lost text of Elizabeth I's coronation oath. As will be seen, her oath, like that of her brother, was meant to expedite and advance a radical Reformation, and it is no accident that the authors of Elizabeth's oath took inspiration from the zealous evangelicals who had staged Edward's coronation. By modifying Edward's oath in 1547, those men had knowingly altered the relations of king and parliament, with profound implications for both royal policy-making and government. What were those changes and what significance did they hold for the development of English 'imperial' monarchy in an age of Reformation?

The Reformation transformed the dignity of English kings, and that transformation also found expression in the coronation pageants of 1547, 1553, and 1559. The tableaux of the pageants and the verses specially commissioned for them have been studied for their literary and dramatic content, as allegorical aspects of courtly spectacle and display.[3] Although such display 'was an inseparable feature of Renaissance kingship', the idiom used to convey royal charisma in fact owed little to the poetical conceits of the pageants. It derived instead, as Malcolm Smuts has shown, from a fusion of traditional elements of two very different types of secular ritual, royal progresses and London civic processions.[4] To this should be added an aspect of a royalist artistic tradition that was central to the development of Tudor charisma – the iconography of 'imperial' kingship.

A coronation put the king's majesty on public display. The chief symbol of that majesty was the great crown of England, one styled

---

[2] Cf. *The Manner of the Coronation of King Charles I*, ed. C. Wordsworth (1892), pp. xliii, xlvii–xlviii, 19, 88–90; P.E. Schramm, *A History of the English Coronation*, trans. L.G. Wickham Legg (Oxford 1937), 218–19.

[3] Witness especially S. Anglo, *Spectacle, Pageantry and Early Tudor Policy* (Oxford 1969; 2nd edn 1997).

[4] R.M. Smuts, 'Public ceremony and royal charisma: the English royal entry in London, 1485–1642', in *The First Modern Society. Essays in English History in Honour of Lawrence Stone*, ed. A.L. Beier, D.N. Cannadine, and J.M. Rosenheim (Cambridge 1989), 67–8.

'imperial' ever since Henry V had exchanged the open royal circlet of the Middle Ages for an arched, or closed, diadem. Henry VI, Edward IV, and Richard III successively advanced the symbolism of the crown imperial. Henry VII so magnified that symbolism after 1489 that he can be said to have invented something new, a veritable cult of sacred 'imperial' kingship.[5] Henry VIII absorbed the artistic programme of this cult most fully, making powerful use of its 'imperial' iconography in a variety of media, beginning with his own coronation.[6] His later assertion of an 'imperial' jurisdiction, the one spelled out legally in 1533–4, drew direct inspiration from this century-old tradition of royal iconography. The coming of protestantism under Edward VI profoundly influenced the development of this tradition, as evangelicals at court invested the symbolism of the crown imperial with new meaning. Although the new iconography of protestant imperial kingship first appeared in Edward VI's coronation pageants, it was given much fuller and more elaborate display in the pageants staged for Elizabeth in 1559. The recent preoccupation with the allegorical aspects of those pageants has obscured the designers' and script-writers' most visible theme, that of the Tudors' 'imperial' legacy. In fact in both 1547 and 1559 the 'imperial' iconography of the tableaux was linked inextricably to the rituals of oath-taking, anointing, and crowning. Moreover, so far from merely foreshadowing the 'imperial' symbolism of the coronation rite, the imagery of the Elizabethan pageants in particular formed part of a new political discourse, a protestant discourse of the commonweal that aimed to modify both the theory and practice of imperial monarchy. This discourse, generated during the protectorate of the duke of Somerset, 1547–9, and fatefully influenced by the experience of Mary's rule, 1553–8, was reshaped in response to Elizabeth's accession.

The first part of the following essay considers the form and nature of the mid-Tudor coronations. By examining the oaths of Edward VI and Elizabeth I and the iconography of the pageants of 1547 and 1559, the second part examines how religious reformists sought to use those coronations to advance their vision of a needed Reformation.

---

[5] For all of this, see my essay, 'The iconography of the crown imperial', in *Tudor Political Culture*, ed. D.E. Hoak (Cambridge 1995), 54–103.

[6] *Ibid.*, pp. 77–8. Loach, 'Ceremonial', 54.

I

A history of monarchy is inconceivable without a history of the coronation ceremony, for the rite itself, although symbolic, is virtually
synonymous with kingship. A religious spectacle of the greatest splendour, the act of crowning constituted the most important event in a
sovereign's life, for it made a king what he was: it consecrated him to
the duties of rulership and vested him with the full power and authority
of his office. If the moment of anointing marked the apex of the coronation service, the rituals of oath-taking and investiture of the king with
his regalia, culminating in the actual crowning, constituted visible, if
symbolic, reaffirmations of the central ideals of kingship. Sir John
Fortescue's epigrammatic formulation of those ideals – 'Lo! To fight
and to judge are the office of a king'[7] – neatly summarized the solemn
obligations that medieval kings promised to uphold. Despite significant
changes, the oaths of 1547, 1553, and 1559 projected the same ideals;
Edward, Mary, and Elizabeth swore to defend their subjects, maintain
peace, and administer justice throughout their realms. At the coronation, four swords, three 'naked' and one sheathed in a scabbard,
symbolized the scope of those promises; each was borne prominently in
procession by a noble office-holder. An observer at Edward VI's coronation, possibly a herald, explained the symbolism of the four swords
which were carried with their blades bare. Two 'had sharpe poyntes';
they represented 'the kinges justice both unto his clergye and temporaltye,
and the other ... had a rebatid poynt and it is callid curtana, signyfying
the kinges mercy toward all his subiects'.[8] The fourth sword, 'the Sworde
in the Scabarde', was the one with which the king was finally girded. It
signified the monarch's God-given temporal power. The terrible power
symbolized by this regal sword bore a nearly numinous reality for the
observer; his remarks provide rare evidence of conventional perceptions
of the awesomeness of kingly might:

> The which [sword] some supposith doth signifie the kinges titill of
> the defendor of the fayth, how be it another saith it should signifie
> that as the kinges majestie is mercyfull and full of clemencye eyther
> to his commons or forans [foreigners] as longe as ther be no cause
> of them to be mynystred to the contrarye but that the sword the
> which signifith [sic] his Regall, may be kepte full in the scabarde so
> contrary wyse uppon contrary occasion admynystred his highnes

---

[7] Quoted in *The Coronation of Richard III. The extant Documents*, ed. A.F. Sutton
and P.W. Hammond (Gloucester 1983), 2, citing Fortescue's *De Natura* (II, viii) in his
Complete Works, ed. Lord Clermont, 122.

[8] BL, Add. MS 9069, f. 30, and the nearly identical passage in Add. MS 71009, f. 53.
On these two MSS see below, n. 45.

> may and ought of dutye by the very word of god to draw forth his
> sworde out of the scarbarde and to correcte the offendours within
> this his Realme or without, and therefore it is written the king
> bearith not the sword in vayne.[9]

As symbolic drama, the medieval ceremony reached the height of its
development in England at the end of the fifteenth century. The extant
documentation for the coronation of Richard III, for example, shows
just how magnificent the symbolism of anointing and crowning had
become.[10] As pageantry, the mid-Tudor coronations were no less spectacular, though evangelical sensibilities transformed the meaning of
both Edward VI's and Elizabeth's anointing, not to mention the celebrated question of the elevation of the host at Elizabeth's coronation
mass.

The majestic splendour of the Tudor coronation is perhaps best remembered in the words of those awed by the sound of it: the Mantuan
envoy, Il Schifanoya, said that with 'the organs, fifes, trumpets, and
drums playing', and 'all the bells in London ringing' at Elizabeth I's
arrival in the Abbey, 'it seemed as if the world were come to an end'.[11]
The sight and sound of singing clergy in procession were no less memorable to one who witnessed Edward VI's service. When the king with
'his trayne marchid forwarde out of Westm[inster] halle dore vnto the
mount', or great coronation stage in the Abbey, three crosses were
borne before him, one for the chapel royal, the other for the archbishop
of Canterbury, and:

> the Thrid was for the Colledge at Westm', and after theme folowid
> all the nowmbre of singing men Both of the chapell and the Colledge
> by copells, who all the way from the halle dore vnto the said place
> did contynually sing diuerse anthyns and respondes, and then next
> after them folowid all the Canons of Westm' with the dean of the
> same and the Subdean of the kinges chapell, all them having very
> ryche Copes.[12]

If the Reformation inevitably drained the ceremonies of 1547 and
1559 of the sacral power of the medieval rite, the essential plan of each
service, like that of Mary's in 1553, none the less followed the tradi-

---

[9] BL, Add. MS 9069, ff. 30v–31v. Cf. the slightly fuller version of this passage in Add.
MS 71009, f. 53. The observer's concern that such awful power might have to be used
against the king's enemies suggests perhaps an evangelical temperament.

[10] Sutton and Hammond, *Coronation of Richard III*. I have followed here the editors'
very useful introduction (pp. 1–12), containing references to relevant recent scholarship
on the subject of the medieval ceremony.

[11] Il Schifanoya to the Castellan of Mantua, 23 January 1559: *CSP Ven.* vii, 17 (no.
10).

[12] BL, Add. MS 9069, ff. 27v–28. Cf. the similar description in Add. MS 71009, f. 52v.

tional Latin *ordo*, fundamentally unchanged since the composition of the *Liber Regalis* of *c.* 1375.[13] The *Liber Regalis* regulated a unique type of private religious service, one whose participants essentially represented a medieval king's affinity. The participants included members of the officiating clergy (the two archbishops, bishops, and, after the dissolution of the monasteries, the dean and chapter of Westminster); lay peers and knights holding offices of state and in the royal household; and others, such as the barons of the cinque ports, to whom by tradition the *Liber Regalis* assigned ceremonial roles. In 1553, for example, four of the barons carried Queen Mary's canopy, a rich pall of cloth of gold held aloft, as the *Liber* prescribed, on four silver staves topped with silver bells.[14] In matters of protocol, the *Liber Regalis* was thus both explicit and comprehensive, stipulating everything from the text of the liturgical prayers to be used to the manner in which a queen consort should wear her hair – loose and 'decently let down on her shoulders',[15] a style that Mary and Elizabeth, the first queens regnant, followed to the letter. The formula of the *Liber Regalis* was amplified in an even more detailed set of instructions first used for the coronation of Richard III; known as the 'Little Device', it covered not only the coronation proper, but also the events of the day before. The 'Little Device' was revised for the coronation of Henry VII, and that schedule, which Henry VIII followed in 1509, provided with variations a model for ordering the coronations of Edward VI, Mary, and Elizabeth.[16]

The events and ceremonies described in the *Liber Regalis* and the 'Little Device' represented only part of the coronation; the full proceedings fell into four stages spread over at least four days.[17] The first stage

---

[13] The fourth and final recension of the liturgy, the so-called 'Litlington ordo', otherwise known as *Liber Regalis* (WA MS 38), was probably made about 1375–7 by Abbot Litlington of Westminster. On the various recensions and Litlington's changes see Schramm, *English Coronation*, 170–1, 211–12; H.G. Richardson, 'The coronation in medieval England', *Traditio*, xvi (1960), 111–75. The text of the *Liber* is given in L.G. Wickham Legg, *English Coronation Records* (Westminster 1901), 81–130.

[14] College of Arms MS I. 18, f. 122. The canopy was of baldekin, or cloth of gold: J.R. Planché, *Regal Records. A Chronicle of the Queens Regnant of England* (1838), 14–15.

[15] Wickham Legg, *English Coronation Records*, 128.

[16] An early sixteenth-century copy of the 'Little Device' of Richard III (BL, Add. MS 18669) is printed in Sutton and Hammond, *Coronation of Richard III*, 213–27. The 'Little Device' of Henry VII (BL, Egerton MS 985), the extant copy of which dates from early in Henry VIII's reign, is printed in Wickham Legg, *English Coronation Records*, 220–39; another copy, in the collections of the duke of Rutland, was published in *Rutland Papers. Original Documents illustrative of the courts and times of Henry VII and Henry VIII*, ed. W. Jerdan (Camden Soc. xxi, 1842), 1–24.

[17] A.L. Rowse, 'The coronation of Queen Elizabeth I', *History Today*, iii, no. 5 (May 1953), 301.

occurred when the monarch took possession of the Tower, a move signalling the crown's control of London. This was a military necessity in the summer of 1553, as Princess Mary enforced her claim to the throne only in armed rebellion against Jane Grey, whose councillors had occupied the Tower in Jane's name following Edward VI's death. At the Tower on the eve of the coronation the monarch also created knights of the bath in an elaborate, symbolic ceremony of shaving, bathing, prayer, and feasting that dated from 1399.[18] The second stage commenced after that ceremony, typically on a Saturday, when, as the 'Little Device' stipulated, the royal entourage rode out from the Tower in grand procession, winding its way through 'the open streetes of London into Chepe, from thence to fleetestreete, and so directly forth vnto the kinges great hall in his pallaice at Westminster'.[19] The third stage, always fixed on a Sunday, witnessed the rituals of crowning and enthronement in the Abbey. The fourth stage, a great state banquet in Westminster Hall, followed immediately upon the conclusion of the coronation service. Other festivities – jousts and tourneys, revels, plays and interludes – were scheduled during the remainder of the week, sometimes spilling over into the next.

Preparations for these events began literally at the moment of the monarch's accession, a process well illustrated in the first of Queen Elizabeth's surviving state papers, a memorandum penned by her secretary, Sir William Cecil, on the very day of Mary's decease (17 November 1558). Among twelve matters of immediate concern was Cecil's reminder to have Elizabeth name 'Commissionars for the Coronation'.[20] The commissioners' task, typically described in a memorandum of their appointment, was to sit as a court 'for the receavinge, allowinge and disallowinge of claymes for services to be donne at the said Coronation' and the subsequent banquet.[21] Edward's six commissioners, named in a proclamation of 4 February 1547, sat as a court of claims at Whitehall on 7 February.[22] Queen Mary, who acceded in July 1553, announced by

---

[18] Loach, 'Ceremonial', 48.

[19] Wickham Legg, *English Coronation Records*, 223.

[20] PRO, SP 12/1, no. 2 (f. 3) (*CSPD 1547–80*, 115). Strype's printed version of this list, from a copy among the Cotton MSS, varies slightly from Cecil's holograph. It includes the phrase 'and the day' immediately following the item cited here: J. Strype, *Annals of the Reformation* (Oxford 1824), i, I, 7.

[21] BL, Harleian MS 6064, f. 4*.

[22] *TRP*, i, 383 (no. 277). The commissioners were Lord Wriothesley, lord chancellor, the earl of Shrewsbury, the earl of Essex, Viscount Lisle, lord admiral, Sir Richard Lister, chief justice of king's bench, and Sir Edward Montague, chief justice of common pleas. Wriothesley, Lisle, and Montague were privy councillors.

proclamation on 1 September that her commissioners would sit in Star Chamber on 4 September to hear suitors' claims.[23] The earliest evidence for the appointment of Elizabeth's five commissioners is found not in a proclamation – she issued none for that purpose – but in another of Cecil's papers, 'Articles concerninge the Quenes Majesties Coronation', composed sometime before 18 December 1558.[24]

The record of claims allowed or denied by such commissioners reveals the important social and material function of Tudor ceremonial. It has been said that coronations were intended not only to impress onlookers and foreign dignitaries, but to accommodate the reciprocal interests of ruler and ruled. The king wished to bind his greatest subjects to him; by rendering service at his coronation, his subjects sought to gain recognition of their honour and preferment. But in claiming roles at a coronation, nobility, gentry, clergy, and office-holders were asserting more than their own status or their family's prestige. They were also seeking material gain in the form of fees paid or rewards given, and this motive, as much as their understandable desire to be associated with 'the mystical attributes of monarchy', enabled the crown to distribute largess to a very wide circle of courtiers and officials.[25] As hereditary chief butler at Edward's coronation banquet, the earl of Arundel was allowed to keep not only the best gold or silver cup placed before the king but also all of the undrunk wine in the hogsheads, pipes, and other vessels left in the cellars at Westminster after the dinner, together with all of the cups and pots there not of precious metal. As panterer at the feast, Viscount Lisle was given the king's finely-chased salt cellar. For their part in the service at the Abbey, the officers of Westminster were rewarded with 100 breads and 88 gallons of wine and the sextons were given the king's resplendent outer clothing and all of the costly carpets specially made for the occasion. Other noble claimants sought to assist the king ceremonially – the duke of Somerset to carry his crown, the duke of Suffolk, his orb, and the marquess of Dorset, his sceptre. The claims of more humble suitors are intriguing.

---

[23] *Ibid.*, ii, 11 (no. 393) The commissioners, all of them privy councillors, were the earl of Bath, Lord Rich, Lord Paget, and Sir Richard Morgan, chief justice of common pleas.

[24] BL, Harleian MS 6064, ff. 4*–5*, a contemporary memorandum undoubtedly deriving from Cecil's office. A copy was made on 25 January 1636 by William Le Neve, Clarenceux king of arms: PRO SP 12/1, no. 51 (ff. 110–110v) (*CSPD 1547–80*, 118). Cf. C.G. Bayne, 'The coronation of Queen Elizabeth', *EHR*, xxii (1907), 651. The commissioners named in the memorandum were the earl of Shrewsbury, Lord Lumley, Lord North, Sir Richard Sackville, and Sir James Dyer; the commission as issued on 18 December also included Robert Catlyn, justice of common pleas: *CPR 1558–60*, 71.

[25] Loach, 'Ceremonial', 44–5, 46–8.

Robert Puttenham, seeking 'to drive out the harlots within the king's house', was denied appointment as Edward VI's 'marshall of the whores'. Nicholas Leghe, moved perhaps by family pride and antiquarian interest, hoped to make for the king's tasting at the banquet 'a Messe' of pottage called *degeront*. The commissioners, fearing Edward's indigestion or worse, ordered Leghe to surrender the recipe to the king's cook, Brickhed, for actual preparation.[26]

Even as the commissioners sat, planning for the coronation went forward rapidly, as it was necessary to co-ordinate the activities of numerous officials at court, the Abbey, and in the City. Streets were to be swept clean and gravelled along the route of the procession, and in many places, wooden rails built to hold back the crowds. Pageants were to be written, and for staging the tableaux, scaffolds and scenery were to be put up in those very streets. At the Abbey a great stepped stage, or 'Siege Royal', with trapdoors and special enclosures was to be built, the altar made ready, banners were to be hung, and in 1553, special 'coles' purchased 'for the p[er]fumyng of Mary's crowns'.[27] At court, schedules for masks, interludes, and tourneys were to be set, not to mention arrangements for the grand procession, crowning, and banquet. The planning at court must have been hurried and intense in 1547, as Edward's coronation took place on 20 February, only twenty-three days after his accession. A herald later remembered that Edward's councillors kept to the council chamber in the Tower every day after their arrival there on 31 January 'for thexpedycon of hys hyghnes Coronacon'.[28]

The forementioned 'Articles' show that as the queen's secretary, Cecil assumed the responsibility of co-ordinating these activities in late November and early December 1558 in such a way as to accommodate, where necessary, Elizabeth's personal interest or role. Since the heralds marshalled the rite, Cecil needed first 'an abstracte from Garter [King of Arms] of the ceremonyes to be done by her highnes ... And to understand the cowrse of the ceremonyes', including 'the Procession and Order thereof'. Of particular concern to Elizabeth – one can almost hear her dictating the questions to Cecil beforehand – were the central elements of a service whose forms, when last administered to Mary, bore for some the stamp of superstition: ' ... the maner

---

[26] PRO, SP 10/1, no. 7 (*CSPD EdVI*, no. 7). S.J. Loach, *Edward VI* (1999), 31. Loach identified Leghe as an esquire of the body at Henry VIII's funeral: *ibid.*, 31 n. 9.

[27] The sum of 6d was spent 'for dyverse penyworthe of coles for the perfumyng of the quenes graces crownes and on the coronacyon day kopyng in fyre for the sencers': WAM 37413, f. 1v.

[28] Society of Antiquaries MS 123, f. 1.

of thanoyntment to be knowen by her Majestie'. Elizabeth was also curious to know if her crowns and coronation ring would actually fit her: ' ... the crowne the circlett and rynge to be broughte that her highnes maye assaie the same'.[29] Some of the 'Articles' were reminders of needed royal action: ' ... the Quenes Majesties plesure to be knowen concerninge the knightes of the bathe'. Others addressed material or financial considerations: preparations were to be made 'for the maske at nighte the daye of the Coronation', and in the Abbey, construction of 'the stages and other carpenters workes [was] to be sett in hand'. Since numerous officials were to be clothed in splendour at Elizabeth's expense, warrants would be needed 'for provision of skarlett and reddes' from the royal wardrobe and the purchase of fine cloth from London merchants. For financial oversight and general accounting, one of the commissioners, a privy councillor who was also an under-treasurer of the exchequer, Sir Richard Sackville, was appointed 'to take the charge of the whole Coronation'.[30]

Because Sackville recorded *all* of the goods and services for which the commissioners ultimately authorized payments, including especially the 'delyverie' of fine fabrics 'for the furnyture of the Coronation', his account book constitutes a veritable catalogue of the material culture of Elizabeth's crowning.[31] What catches the eye immediately is the magnificence of the materials purchased as much as the distinctive nature or staggering cost of the orders placed. 'Silkes' in six colours and multi-hued satins and cloths of silver 'boughte of William Chelsham, mercer', came to £3,942 0s 9d.[32] Forty fine crimson velvet-covered saddles were

---

[29] BL, Harleian MS 6064, ff. 4*v, 5. Among the wardrobe and household accounts for January 1559 is a vellum-covered paper book of eight folios headed, at the top of the first blank folio, 'Coronation'. Included in it is a list of regalia 'To be prepared owte of the jewelhouse' for Elizabeth's coronation: 'The Sceptre   The Rodde   The Balle   Three Crownes   A Ringe   A paier of Bracellettes   St Edwardes Spurres   St Edwardes Staffe': PRO E 101/429/3, f. 4v. The crowns etc. referred to here were described very exactly in the inventory made in 1649 when parliament ordered the destruction of the regalia at Westminster: Society of Antiquaries MS 108, ff. 14–17, printed in Wickham Legg, *English Coronation Records*, 272–4. On the regalia and ornaments generally see W.H. St John Hope, 'The King's coronation ornaments', *The Ancestor*, no. 1 (April 1902), 127–59, and no. 2 (July 1902), 63–81; Sutton and Hammond, *Coronation of Richard III*, 228–44. On the Tudors' great crown of state, the 'Imperiall Crowne of massy gold' that was probably refashioned for Henry VIII in the 1520s and with which Edward VI, Mary I, and Elizabeth I were crowned, see especially the discussion and references in Hoak, 'Iconography of the crown imperial', pp. 86–7, where the crown is pictured (pl. 16).

[30] BL, Harleian MS 6064, ff. 4*v, 5.

[31] PRO, LC 2/4(3).

[32] *Ibid.*, f. 4.

ordered 'ffor Ladies and Gent[lemen]' of the court at a cost of £983 17s 8d, the second largest sum recorded by Sackville.[33] Twenty-nine lengths of special 'bleue clothe' were stitched together to make up a great runner, or carpet, nearly a third of a mile long for the queen to walk upon 'from the marble chair in Westm' hall unto the Quere dore in Westm' Churche' and thence up to her throne on the 'sege Royall', or specially-constructed stage.[34] For covering the 'Sege Royall and the mounte with Steppes goinge uppe to Saincte Edwardes Chaire in the myddest of the same', John Grene and seven workmen used 40,000 special finishing nails, including 8,000 of silver gilt, to attach gold-striped crimson satin coverings, the trimmings for which required 20,000 great hooks and 6,000 'crochettes' for the red ribbons and lace of golden silk.[35] Grene also upholstered St Edward's chair 'ffor the Quenes maiestie to Sitt in whan she is Crowned'. With the assistance of Mary Wilkinson, who affixed to it an elaborate fringe of gold lace, Grene used two sorts of exquisite cloth of gold, one bordered with crimson velvet and the other raised with red velvet, garnishing the whole with 2,000 gilt-headed nails.[36] Workmanship, of course, was always of the highest quality, often requiring an artist's specialized talent: the queen's sergeant painter, Richard Lizarde, created seventeen 'Banners for Trumpettes' of purple, blue, and red damask with fringes, tassles, and buttons of red silk and gold lace, each bearing the queen's arms in 'golde and oyle'.[37]

Calculating the whole cost of a coronation remains elusive. Cecil's 'Articles' of November–December 1558 earmarked £4,000 for immediate use, 'to be distributed as the commissioners shall thinke mete',[38] but that was less than half the total of about £8,800 recorded in Sackville's book,[39] and in any case the payments there covered only 'furnyture' of the type described above, chiefly for the coronation procession and service. It is likely that the Crown spent at least that much more on banquets, tourneys, maskings, etc. If so, Elizabeth's total outlay probably ran close to £20,000, that is just over 10% of her expected first year's ordinary revenue. It was said that in 1553 Queen Mary had been obliged to borrow £20,000 for her coron-

---

[33] Ibid., f. 19.

[34] Thomas Ackworth was paid £145 for these 'xxix peeces of Blewe Clothe conteynynge xxiiij yards a Peece', or 696 yards altogether: ibid., f. 11v.

[35] Ibid., f. 10.

[36] Ibid., f. 10v. Grene was paid £119 9s 6d for materials and labour.

[37] Ibid., f. 12. The materials, including 154 buttons of gold and silk, cost £264 10s 6d. Lizarde received £76 10s for making the banners.

[38] BL, Harleian MS 6064, f. 4*v.

[39] No total is given; £8,800 is my rough calculation.

ation.[40] But the Crown's expenditure was only a fraction of the whole cost of the festivities. Although Elizabeth I lent the City a number of costumes and props,[41] the citizens of London bore the considerable expense of staging the pageants and decorating the processional route with 'fyne payntynge and Riche clothes of arras, syluer, and golde'. To keep track of their charges, the City appointed 'surveyors of the pageauntes', but the surveyors' account books, which also tallied the wages of those involved, are missing.[42] The Londoners' final outlay was certainly great enough to prompt a City official to bring it to Elizabeth's attention – not once, but twice in the course of her procession.[43] Exactly how the mayor and aldermen covered their expenses is not known; perhaps they resorted to something like the device used in February 1547: there 'was levied amongest the citizens of London for

[40] Neville Williams calculated that in 1559 the court expended nearly £16,742, not including the cost of the banquet: 'The coronation of Queen Elizabeth I', *Quarterly Review*, ccxci (1953), 401. The amount that Mary I borrowed was provided by Richard Garnett in a note to his translation of the 1554 Spanish edition of *Coronatione de la serenissime Reina Maria d'Inghilteria* (Rome 1553), a translation Garnett attached to his translation and edition of *The Accession of Queen Mary: being the contemporary narrative of Antonio de Guaras, a Spanish merchant resident in London* (1892), 139, 119. The unknown Italian author of the original tract advanced no proof in support of the belief 'that more than a hundred thousand ducats were disbursed in this coronation at her Majesty's expense'; *ibid.*, p. 123.

[41] Among the Loseley MSS at the Folger Shakespeare Library is a list of such items that Sir Thomas Cawarden, master of the revels, delivered to John Elyott, mercer, on 13 January 1559: Folger MS L. b. 109, printed in D.M. Bergeron, 'Elizabeth's coronation entry (1559): new manuscript evidence', *English Literary Renaissance*, viii, 1 (1978), 5. John Guy has pointed out, however, that the loan of such props 'is not proof of the queen's supervision of the pageants or of her endorsement of the view of monarchy which they propagated': 'Elizabeth I: the queen and politics', *The Shakespearean International Yearbook*, 2: *Where are we now in Shakespearean studies?*, ed. W.R. Elton and J.M. Mucciolo (Aldershot 2002), 200 n. 74. My thanks to Professor Guy for sharing with me the typescript of his article in advance of publication.

[42] The quotations are from the City's manuscript Repertory Books, 14, ff. 97, 115, as cited in R.C. Strong, *The Tudor and Stuart Monarchy: Pageantry, Painting, Iconography*, ii, *Elizabethan* (Woodbridge 1995), 36–7 & n. 18.

[43] As Elizabeth 'went down toward fletebridge ... ' the unnamed official 'noted the citie's charge, that there was no cost spared. Her grace answered that she did well consider the same, and that it should be remembered.' Later, 'in Cheapeside ... When the citie's charge ... was mentioned unto her grace [again], she sayd it shoulde not be forgotton', in: *The Quene's Majestie's passage through the citie of London to westminster the daye before her coronacion*, a pamphlet by Richard Mulcaster which was commissioned by the City authorities and first published in London on 23 January 1559 by Richard Tottel (*STC* 7591), repr. ed. J.M. Osborn (New Haven 1960). I have used the reprint in *Elizabethan Backgrounds. Historical Documents of the Age of Elizabeth I*, ed. A.F. Kinney (Hamden, Conn. 1975), 15–39; the quotations here appear on pp. 31 and 37 respectively.

the Kinges coronation a benevolence after the manner of a xvth and a half'.[44]

As already noted, Cecil's 'Articles' show how direct was his and the queen's involvement in preparing for the coronation, and by how much he necessarily relied on the heralds for ordering virtually every one of the queen's ceremonial steps. For the coronations of Edward VI and Mary I we are fortunate to possess heralds' and others' eye-witness accounts of almost all aspects of the festivities, from the monarch's possession of the Tower to the closing tournaments. Some of these sources are cited or used here for the first time.[45] Although

---

[44] Wriothesley, *Chronicle*, i, 182.

[45] For Edward VI's coronation, the earliest and fullest of the extant manuscript versions is the second item in a volume in the library of the Society of Antiquaries, a group of forty folios discussed by Sydney Anglo: 'The coronation of Edward VI and Society of Antiquaries manuscript 123', *Antiquaries Journal*, lxxviii (1998), 452–7. There are two similar versions in the College of Arms, in MS I. 7 and MS I. 18, the former, transcribed (but not always accurately) in Nichols, *Literary Remains*, i, pp. cclxxviii–cccv, being the fair copy of the latter. BL, Egerton MS 3026, also a contemporary fair copy, is a running synthesis and fusion of both. BL, Add. MS 9069 is a small ($3\frac{1}{2} \times 5\frac{1}{2}$ inches) volume of extracts bearing a date of 1570 (on f. 2). It contains material copied from now-lost originals, which cannot be found elsewhere, including a herald's eye-witness account of Edward VI's procession from the Tower to Westminster on 19 February 1547 (ff. 17–22v) and 'The trew order of the Coronacion ... ' the next day (ff. 23–43). A nearly identical account is BL, Add. MS 71009, a volume of 114 folios, described in a type-script calendar in the Manuscripts Reading Room as 'a copy, in several hands, of a collection of material concerning the organisation of the royal household', gathered in the 1550s by John Norris, gentleman usher of the chamber after c. 1536, 'from his own and other peoples' knowledge'; ff. 51–2 cover the procession from the Tower to West-minster, ff. 52–6 the coronation and banquet. The material here and in Add. MS 9069 were apparently copied from the same source, the version in Add. MS 71009 being slightly fuller. Both provide details not found in any other account. A copy of another brief, independent contemporary account, a copy said to have been in the hand of Thomas Cranmer, was itself copied by one J. Cary; Cary's extract, originally in a collection of MSS in Ely Cathedral, was published in E.C. Ratcliff, *The English Corona-tion Service* (1936), pp. 111–15. Cary's copy may well have been taken from CCCC, MS 105, pp. 235–40, which is certainly in a mid-Tudor hand. I wish to thank Professor Diarmaid MacCulloch for his kindness in giving me a copy of these pages. For Mary I's coronation, none of the extant heralds' accounts has been published. In the College of Arms, MS I. 7, fos. 65–73, constitute a fair copy, probably in an early-Elizabethan hand, of the eye-witness's rough version in MS I. 18, ff. 116–132. The latter draft contains words and phrases omitted in MS I. 7. Society of Antiquaries MS 123, item 3, is a group of ten folios setting out the order for Queen Mary's procession from the Tower and her coronation the following day. It is clearly a herald's schedule, with spaces left blank for the insertion of the names of officers who were to perform the tasks mentioned. PRO SP 11/1, no. 15 (*CSPDM*, no. 20) and the narrative in Planché, *Regal Records*, 1–32, draw heavily on the College of Arms MSS, though some of Planché's references are to volumes there which have since been assigned different call numbers. BL, Harleian MS 6166, ff.

similarly full documentation has not survived for Elizabeth's coronation – the three extant first-hand descriptions are of limited use[46] –
there does exist a series of invaluable pen-and-ink drawings that a
herald produced as a guide for ordering the queen's procession and
the events that were to take place in the Abbey and Westminster Hall,
including a floor-plan of the arrangements for her crowning, together
with explanatory notes.[47] And for the pageants of 1559 and Elizabeth's reaction to them, we have Richard Mulcaster's unique description
of *The Quene's Majestie's passage through the citie of London to
westminster the daye before her coronacion*, which is said to have
created 'a new literary genre' of reportage.[48] Taken together, these
materials allow us to reconstruct, if only in outline, the essential
elements of the mid-Tudor ceremonies.

When Strype, no admirer of Mary I, described the preparations leading up to Mary's coronation on 1 October 1553, he said that everyone

---

67–8, is an eighteenth-century copy of 'The Order of the Knights of the Bath at the
Coronation of Queene Mary', printed with slight differences in J. Anstis, *Observations
Introductory to an Historical Essay, upon the Knighthood of the Bath* (1725), Collection
of Authorities, no. LXVIII (pp. 53–6).

[46] Of the three, one by an unknown English spectator now exists only in Anthony
Anthony's copy in Bodl. MS Ashmole 863. PRO SP 15/9, no. 9 (ff. 17–19) (*CSPD
Addenda 1547–65*, 486) is a transcription of Anthony's copy. A second, fragmentary
account, probably by a herald, is College of Arms MS W. Y., f. 198a. It is a copy dating
from the early seventeenth century. The third, by Il Schifanoya, the Mantuan envoy, is
given in *CSP Ven.* vii, 11–19 (no. 10). All three are printed and discussed in Bayne,
'Coronation of Queen Elizabeth,' 650–73. See G. Lockhart Ross, 'Il Schifanoya's account of the coronation of Queen Elizabeth', *EHR*, xxiii (1908), 533–4, for a corrected
translation of a crucial passage in the Mantuan's description.

[47] BL, Egerton MS 3320, a book of twenty-four large paper folios, gives the order for
those in procession ahead of the queen on ff. 15–20v. It is tempting to think that these
drawings were produced for Cecil and the queen, in response to the secretary's request,
quoted above, that Garter king of arms supply him with an 'abstract' of the proceedings,
including especially the order of the procession. 'Mr Secretarye Cecill' (f. 16v) is only
one of three persons actually named in the herald's diagrammatic list of officers, clergy,
and courtiers making up the procession in front of the queen's litter. For a brief description of the provenance of this manuscript, together with reproductions of the sketches
and transcriptions of the accompanying notes, see A.J. Collins, 'The ordering of the
coronation of Elizabeth I: drawings and descriptions from a contemporary official manuscript', *Illustrated London News*, ccxxii, no. 5954 (30 May 1953), 880–3. A.L. Rowse
briefly narrated what one sees on these folios in 'Coronation of Queen Elizabeth I', 305–
7.

[48] D.R. Starkey, *Elizabeth. The Struggle for the Throne* (2000), 270. For a discussion
of the pamphlet and its problematical relationship to actual events, see J.M. Richards,
'Love and a female monarch: the case of Elizabeth Tudor', *JBS*, xxxviii, 2 (1999), 143–
52. The pamphlet itself is not evidence of the queen's prior approval of the pageants and
scripts that Mulcaster described: Guy, 'Elizabeth I: the queen and politics', n. 74.

involved, including the mayor and aldermen, had resolved to make her ceremonies 'very splendid and glorious'.[49] Regarding the public festivities, he also might have said loud and musically boisterous, for the signal announcing the sovereign's arrival in London was traditionally a volcanic booming of ordnance, followed by the almost continuous music-making of costumed singers and players. On Thursday, 28 September 1553, Mary departed St James's Palace with her entourage, and after dinner there made her way through the park to Westminster where, from the privy stairs, she boarded her barge for the approach by water to the Tower. We may imagine her embarking in much the same way that Il Schifanoya recounted Elizabeth's departure from Whitehall on another Thursday, 12 January 1559:

> The necessary ships, galleys, brigantines, &c., were prepared as sumptuously as possible to accompany her Majesty and her Court thither by the Thames, which reminded me of Ascension Day at Venice, when the Signory go to espouse the sea ... her Majesty, accompanied by many knights, barons, ladies, and by the whole Court ... embarked in her barge, which was covered with its usual tapestries, both externally and internally, and was towed by a long galley rowed by 40 men in their shirts, with a band of music, as usual when the Queen goes by water.[50]

In 1553 the mayor and aldermen of London met Mary en route on the Thames to the sound of trumpets, in boats festooned with banners and flying streamers, and as the colourful flotilla of royal and civic vessels approached the Tower, a great volley of shots rang out from the guns within. In a little ceremony before the watergate at the Tower the queen thanked the City officials for the pains they had taken in arranging this salute, all to the sound of more trumpets and singers and musicians playing regals and shawms and the pounding of cannon, which continued, said a herald, well after her highness had landed.[51] We hear nothing about music when Edward entered the Tower on horseback from Enfield on 31 January 1547, though there must have been trumpets at least. An eye-witness was more interested in the young king's predictably excited response to the thunder of the artillery: the nine-year-old thought the blasts quite wonderful.[52]

---

[49] J. Strype, *Ecclesiastical Memorials* (Oxford 1822), iii, I, 51.

[50] *CSP Ven.* vii. 11–12 (no. 10).

[51] Planché, *Regal Records*, 3. College of Arms MS I. 18, f. 117. The regal was a portable organ, the shawm an oboe-like instrument.

[52] The herald said that 'there was greate shotte of ordyaunce in all places there abowtes aswell owt of the Towre as they [*sic*] shyppes lyinge there abowtes wherine hys grace hadde greate felycytye': Society of Antiquaries MS 123, f. 1.

The Tower was also the setting for a symbolic chivalric ritual of the
deepest religious meaning. On the night of her arrival Mary gave order
to fifteen men of reputedly 'ancient blood' to present themselves on the
morrow, Friday the 29th, to be 'bathed and Shreven according to thold
Vsage of England' and then dubbed knights of the bath.[53] The ceremony began with a feast where each of them by tradition bore a dish
to the queen. During 'all the Banquett tyme the Sackebutts, and viols
did play.'[54] At about six o'clock attendants led the initiates to the bath
chamber where all were shaved except a few whom the queen had
excused. Putting off their clothes, they each donned 'a linnen breche'
and, after having their feet washed, ' ... satt in the Bath all naked' until
four of the queen's officers, led by the earl of Arundel, the lord
chamberlain, read them their oath.[55] At four in the morning, 'being
sounded up with the Minstrells', they were escorted to mass. After this
'the Bathing Tubbes were taken away' and they were led back to bed.[56]
At eleven the next morning they rode off to Westminster Hall in gor-
geous array, wearing red taffeta surcoats and mantles adorned with
great lace collars of white silk and gold knobbing, and fine gloves with
lace ties. Dismounting at the Hall door, they strode into the queen's
presence chamber in double file where, on a signal from the lord chamberlain, they made 'three Courtesyes' before Mary, who sat beneath her
cloth of estate. After kneeling, each in turn kissed both knees of the lord
chamberlain who was himself kneeling, facing them, beside the queen.[57]
At Arundel's commandment, they put on ceremonial spurs which had
been given them, and holding their gloves between their hands, still
kneeling, they raised their hands over their heads so that Arundel, who
held a great sword, might dub them. He 'did girde ittabout' them, and
laying his hand on the shoulder of each, said, 'here be trew knight'.
With this the knights rose, and after curtseying again, were led into the
Tower chapel where they surrendered their personal swords to several
priests. Leaving the chapel, they gathered round a table covered with a
white cloth for the last symbolic act of the ceremony, a traditional
speech by, of all people, the queen's cook. Waving a great dressing knife
before them he said, 'Sir Knight, see thou bee a true knight ... [and]
perform thine oathe, or else', he said with mock emphasis, 'I will strike

---

[53] College of Arms MS I. 18, f. 116.

[54] BL, Harleian MS 6166, f. 67v.

[55] Besides Arundel, the officers were Sir Edward Hastings, master of the horse, Sir
William Petre, principal secretary, and Sir Thomas Wharton, master of the henchmen,
whom the author said represented the queen: *ibid.*

[56] *Ibid.*

[57] *Ibid.*, f. 68. College of Arms MS I. 18, f. 116.

thee off by these spurs', whereupon the cook claimed their spurs and 8s 6d as his fee in warning that they should never offend against the order of knighthood. After another banquet of three courses they exchanged their brilliant red surcoats etc. for the apparel they would wear in the queen's procession the next day – hooded violet gowns trimmed with white miniver and points, or ties, of white silk on the shoulder, each hood 'like a Master of Arts Hoode'.[58]

On the Saturday before a coronation, to the sound of more cannon-fire – the 'peale of gonnes' in 1547 was so 'teryble and a fereful' that it 'causidde many of the howses in London to shake'[59] – the monarch left the Tower for Westminster in a great cavalcade of officers and noblemen and knights and foreign dignitaries – more than 500 on horseback, according to the French ambassador who witnessed the spectacle in 1553, and upwards of perhaps a thousand in 1559, if we are to believe Il Schifanoya, who was himself riding in Elizabeth's procession.[60] The purpose of this procession was to introduce a new king to his subjects, to enable onlookers actually to see his face and person. But amidst hundreds of gloriously arrayed horsemen, how was he to be distinguished? The 'Little Device' solved this practical problem by requiring the king to appear in a uniquely resplendent way, dressed in white cloth of gold and riding bare-headed on a richly trapped courser – even the royal saddle was covered in gold cloth – under a golden canopy borne on glittering gilt staves by four gorgeously apparelled knights.[61] Thus for his procession through London on 19 February 1547 Edward VI dressed to rule in blinding white and silver and gold from head to toe: he wore 'a riche gown of clothe of silver all over embrodered with damaske gold' and matching doublet, boots, belt, and cap of white velvet, all worked with filigrees of 'Venyce silver' in which were set intricately patterned knots of diamonds, rubies, and pearls. He set out from the courtyard of the Tower 'walking a lytell before his canapy, because the people might the better see his grace', but later, as he grew tired, he rode under the canopy, which was borne by six mounted knights in bright surcoats of scarlet and blue, the boy-king's small white figure set off like a precious ornament against his charger's caparison of pearl- and gold-studded

---

[58] BL, Harleian MS 6166, f. 68. For the ritual as it was performed in 1483 see Sutton and Hammond, *Coronation of Richard III*, 28–30, who reconstruct it from fifteenth-century sources.

[59] BL, Add. MS 9069, ff. 17v–18.

[60] Planché, *Regal Records*, 4, citing the report of Noailles in 1553. *CSP Ven.* vii, 12 (no. 120) for Schifanoya's observation.

[61] Wickham Legg, *English Coronation Records*, 222.

crimson satin.[62] This picture has come down to us in the words of a
herald who marched in the procession. Another participant, Sir Anthony
Browne, one of Edward's privy councillors and the master of the
king's horse, was riding at Edward's side that day. Before his death in
1548 Browne commissioned a mural at Cowdray House, his residence
in Sussex, showing this very procession in panoramic view, winding its
way from the Tower to the precincts of Westminster, the king clearly
visible on horseback under his fringed canopy. Cowdray House burned
down in 1793, but a copy of the mural survives in a large drawing of
1785 now in the possession of the Society of Antiquaries of London.
As such, it preserves a unique visual record of a Tudor procession.[63]

Edward's stunningly jewelled appearance reminds us that the rituals
of the coronation offered a monarch the first and greatest opportunity
for public display of royal magnificence. Jewelry and the richest imaginable cloth – the most costly then being woven in Europe – conveyed
the magnificence of royal wealth immediately: this was jewelry of gold
and silver and cloth of a sort that only kings and queens could wear.
The first sight of Elizabeth's glinting entourage when it left the Tower
on 14 January 1559 caused Il Schifanoya to catch his breath: ' ... the
whole Court so sparkled with jewels and gold collars that they cleared
the air'. The colour-co-ordinated reds and metallic threads of the costumes and coverings provided brilliant settings for the gems: even the
fabrics on that snowy, overcast day touched off a blaze of crimson,
gold, and silver. Exquisite cloth of gold 'of the richest sorte, the ground
golde and [the] tisshewe silver and gold', covered the queen's gold- and
silver-fringed chariot. The coverings for the horses' headstalls, collars,
and reins were of resplendent gold cloth and silver silk; even the cours-
ers' 'Slophouses' dripped of cloth of gold. The gold-striped crimson
satin coverings and linings of the 'iij Chariottes Wherin the Ladies of
honoure did ride' were studded with the heads of 24,000 gilt nails. The
ladies themselves, like velvet-draped dolls, sat on huge 'hassockes' of
crimson damask. The queen's ten footmen – Il Schifanoya was so taken
with the sight of them he called them 'a multitude' – were brilliantly
attired in cloaks, coats, doublets, and hose of yellow cloth of gold and
crimson velvet, their crimson jerkins flashing with silver-spangled em-
broidery. And 'Her Majesty was dressed in a royal robe of very rich

---

[62] This is a transcription of College of Arms MS I. 7, printed in Nichols, *Literary
Remains*, p. cclxxx. See also H. Chapman, *The Last Tudor King. A Study of Edward VI*
(1961), 88.

[63] The drawing, 75.4 × 152.2 cm, by Samuel Hieronymous Grimm, is discussed and
reproduced in C. Lloyd and S. Thurley, *Henry VIII. Images of a Tudor King* (1990), 45,
52–6, pl. 39.

cloth of gold, with a double-raised stiff pile, and on her head over a coif of cloth of gold ... [was] a plain gold crown ... covered with jewels.' It made, said Il Schifanoya, 'a superb show'.[64] Later, when Sir John Hayward recalled this spectacle, he echoed Il Schifanoya's remark, saying 'that in pompous ceremonies a secret of government doth much consist, for that the people are naturally both taken and held with exteriour shewes.'[65]

The royal procession was one sort of show, the City's pageants and musicians and players and tableaux another. Thousands of spectators, including some from 'all partes of the realm', it was said in 1553,[66] came to gawk at theatrical battlements, arches, and fabricated 'mounts'; mechanical angels, giants, and low-flying clouds; and at the conduits, wonderful wine-spewing fountains fed by hydraulic devices. The scene along the processional route was at times circus-like, the unceasing noise of the crowd drowning out actors' speeches. No matter if the staging of the tableaux was tawdry and the devices crude, onlookers found the gimmickry a fascinating spectacle. At Mary's coronation, the resident Florentine merchants devised the most popular crowd-pleaser, an ingenious green angel with hinged arms strung up at the highest point above Gracechurch Street between four gigantic 'pictures' surmounting 'three thorow fares or gates' below. When a 'Trumpeter who stood secretly in the Pageant did sound his Trumpe, the Angel did put

---

[64] PRO, LC 2/4(3), ff. 13, 14, for the queen's litter. Seventeen yards of cloth of gold coverings, together with the yellow and silver silk and satin used for the linings, fringes, tassles, etc. cost £377 18s 2d: *ibid.*, f. 14v. For the three chariots: *ibid.*, ff. 16, 17, 18. The total cost of outfitting the three chariots came to £481 17s 6d, including £30 to Anthony Silver, wheelwright, 'ffor Timbre and Workemanshipp'; *ibid.*, f. 18. Outfitting the footmen cost £350 13s 0d, including £58 18s 8d for 136oz of silver spangles; *ibid.*, ff. 25, 26. For Schifanoya's description see *CSP Ven.* vii, 12 (no. 10). The 'robe' he referred to was the one worn by Mary I in her procession; 'ffor translaytynge', or refashioning it for Elizabeth, Walter Fish, the queen's tailor, and William Jordan, her skinner, were advanced £42 17s 6d for material and labour. The costume actually consisted of a mantle, surcoat, and kirtle of cloth of gold 'tisshewed with gold and siluer ... the kirtle ffurred with powdred ermyne aboute the skyrtes, the rest lyned with white sarscinett, the kirtle being hole afore with a highe coller and laced on both sides with sleves with amelettes hookes and eys of siluer and gilt': LC 2/4(3), f. 5. The so-called 'Coronation' portrait of Elizabeth I, a panel painted about 1600 by an unknown artist from a lost original executed in 1559, portrays this very dress: J. Arnold, 'The "Coronation" portrait of Elizabeth I', *Burlington Magazine*, cxx (1978), 727–38; *idem, Queen Elizabeth's Wardrobe Unlock'd* (Leeds 1988), 52–5.

[65] *Annals of the first four years of the Reign of Queen Elizabeth, by Sir John Hayward, Knt. D.C.L.*, ed. J. Bruce (Camden Soc. vii, 1840), 15.

[66] *A Breuiat Chronicle* (1554: STC 9970.5), sig. Oii: ' ... suche a multitude of people resorted out of all partes of the realme, to see the same [coronation of Mary I], that the lyke haue not bene seen tofore'.

his trumpe to his mouth, as though it had bin the same that had sounded, to the great maruelling of many ignorant persons.'[67] The 'pictures' of such tableaux often bore Latin inscriptions, but the Latin, like that of the spoken verses, was of course lost on the ignorant. Literate commoners could at least gaze upon oversized 'tables', or tablets, bearing translations, and since in January 1559 the scenery of the pageants was left up for viewing three days afterwards, spectators could come back 'to wander through the the streets and drink in the protestant propaganda' of the sign-boards.[68]

Professional acrobats also offered dare-devil diversions at certain points along the processional route. In 1547 the City paid an Aragonese tumbler to rig a rope as thick as a ship's cable from the 'vppermoste part of the stonne worke' of the steeple of St Paul's to an anchor in the garden of the dean's house. When Edward's party reached St Gregory's Church in St Paul's churchyard, the acrobat 'cam slyding down' head-first on his chest, arms and legs outstretched, 'so swyftly as he had byne a birde'. 'And', marvelled the observer, 'he [was] not hurte'.[69] Someone else nearby explained why: he 'fell uppon a fetherbed and a mattrasse to save hym selfe from the dawnger of the ground'.[70] The acrobat got up, kissed Edward's foot, 'and after certain words to his highnes', walked up the rope again to a point 'over the midst of the said churchyard' where he began 'tumbling and casting hymself from one legg to another'. The king and 'peres and nobles' about him were so delighted by this performance – they stayed 'a good space of time', laughing 'right hartely' – that when the tumbler 'came downe again', Edward commanded that he be given 'a Reward'.[71] At Mary's coronation 'Peter a Dutchman' scaled the weathercock on the steeple of St Paul's, and standing on one foot, shook his other foot while waving a 15 foot streamer in his hand, 'to the great mervayle and wondering of all ...

[67] J. Stow, *Annales* (1631), 616. In Edward VI's pageants, 'besides monstruous persons, strange figures' and many excellent speeches, there 'was usid moche melodye aswell with trompettes and shalmes as with singing of songes and plaing with the same oon the regals': BL, Add. MS 71009, f. 52.

[68] R.C. Strong, 'The 1559 entry pageants of Elizabeth I', in his *Pageantry, Painting and Iconography*, ii, 50. The 'ij tables' accompanying the Florentines' pageant in 1553 were 'clothe of sillver' hangings, 'the one table in Latten, and the other in Inglyshe myter, gratefyeng': Nichols, *Chron. Jane and Mary*, 29.

[69] BL, Add. MS 9069, f. 22v.

[70] Society of Antiquaries MS 123, f. 24.

[71] *Ibid*. Nichols, *Literary Remains*, i, p. ccxc. *The Chronicle of Fabian, whiche he nameth the Concordaunce of Histories, newly perused and continued from the Beginnyng of King Henry the Seventh to thende of Queene Mary* (1559: STC 10664), 535. Robert Fabyan, an alderman of London, died in 1513. This part of his Chronicle was added by Robert Recorde. See also Anglo, *Spectacle*, 292–3.

[who] behelde him, because yt was thought a mattyer impossyble'. He had set up torches and eight more big streamers on scaffolds just above and beneath the cross on the steeple, and would have set the torches on fire before his act, but the 'Torches ... could not burne, the Winde was so great'. For the Dutchman's 'costs and paines, and all his stuffe', the City paid him £16 13s 4d, in part because his act advertised the sponsorship of the mayor and aldermen, his streamers 'having the red crosse and the sworde [of] the arms of the cyty of London' on them.[72] The sensational aspect of such entertainment was also olfactory: the children singing 'salutacions' to Queen Mary as she passed by a pageant in St Paul's churchyard held burning tapers which gave off the 'most swete perfumes'.[73]

The City's part in all of this reminds us that an English coronation entry was at once royal progress and civic procession bringing together two very different groups, one representing the wealth of London's mercantile élite, the other the traditions of the court and England's great landed families. The ceremonial fusion of aristocratic courtiers and London magistrates was meant to show that bonds of loyalty to the sovereign transcended social or official status. This fusion appears to have been a distinctive feature of English coronation processions (and royal entries generally), in contrast to French practice, for example, where Parisian city officials confronted the king ceremonially, retaining their separate, corporate identity.[74] By bringing different status groups into a unified whole under the Crown, the procession enabled both ruler and ruled to act out the reciprocal nature of those unifying bonds of loyalty. In 1559 Elizabeth had prepared herself well for the symbolic moment in the procession when by tradition the monarch acknowledged the obedience of London's most powerful 'citizeins'. The moment came 'by appointment' at 'the upper ende of Cheape' when the recorder of the City, on behalf of the mayor, aldermen, and 'comminaltie', presented her with a richly wrought purse containing a thousand marks in gold as a gesture of the City's 'gladnes and good wille' towards her. Elizabeth's reply – that not only would she be 'your good ladie and quene' but also 'for the safetie and quietnes of you all, I will not spare, if nede be to spend my blood' – struck a powerful, responsive chord, for who in the audience was not remembering the burnings of another queen, only a year before? A 'mervaylous showte and rejoysing' went up in the crowd.[75]

[72] Stow, *Annales*, 617. Nichols, *Chron. Jane and Mary*, 30.

[73] Nichols, *Chron. Jane and Mary*, 30.

[74] Smuts, 'Public ceremony and royal charisma', 73.

[75] *The Quene's Majestie's passage*, 26–7.

Such expressions of reciprocal loyalty comprehended 'the people' as well as the mercantile élite – a remarkable, indeed innovative, aspect of the procession of January 1559. Elizabeth I was the first English monarch to exploit the theatrical, psychological possibilities such moments afforded an untested, uncrowned ruler. She did so as perhaps only an actress could, by empowering 'the people' with her words, gestures, and facial expressions. Thus at Fenchurch, where she received the City's first formal greeting – a child's recitation of praise in admiring, doggerel verse – she 'thanked most hartely both the citie for this her gentle receiving … *and also the peple for confirming the same* [my italics]'. Elizabeth's genius was 'not only [to] shew her … love toward the people in general, but also privately', to particular individuals along the route, in unrehearsed stops. From her open chariot she singled out 'baser personages' in the crowd, allowed them to speak directly to her, and accepted their supplications and gifts.[76] If not quite the first royal walkabout, here was a new-style monarchy.

Like her manner of engaging humble bystanders, Elizabeth's reaction to the City's pageants was also memorable, for by stopping to reply to the script-writers' themes, themes articulated in both actors' speeches and 'pictured' texts, Elizabeth 'turned the procession into a conversation' between the queen and her people, something Richard Mulcaster, the 'reporter' who also helped script the pageants, realized was unprecedented.[77] Mulcaster had been associated with the men who composed Edward VI's coronation pageants, the first pageants of their kind to render advice to the king on a matter of national policy: in one of them the figure of 'Trewth' embodied the hopes of the English 'nation' for the furtherance of Henry VIII's Reformation.[78] Elizabeth's pageants not only drew upon that theme, they enhanced it and emphatically advanced it, and in so doing, broke with the past in another way. Coronation entries had traditionally offered praise to the king or exhorted him to behave well towards his subjects. The pageants presented to Elizabeth did this and more: the extraordinary degree to which they specifically sought to advise her on the right course of action in religion

---

[76] 'How many nosegaies did her grace receive at poore women's handes? How oftimes staied she her chariot, when she saw any simple body offer to speake to her grace?': *ibid.*, 38.

[77] Starkey, *Elizabeth*, 270. Starkey does not identify Mulcaster as either the author of *The Quene's Majestie's passage* or one of the script-writers of the pageants.

[78] As King Edward passed by the pageant at the Great Conduit in Fleet Street, a child representing Truth saluted him with words to the effect that Henry VIII had freed Truth, which in England had for a long time been suppressed by 'hethen rites and detestable idolatrye': Nichols, *Literary Remains*, i, p. ccxci.

was without parallel.[79] It remains to be seen how Edward's coronation not only pointed in that direction, but also provided a model for changing the nature and practice of Tudor kingship. Several aspects of the coronation rite will serve to introduce this topic.

II

Outwardly the coronations of Edward, Mary, and Elizabeth followed the formulae of the *Liber Regalis* and 'Little Device', the fundamentals of their services remaining unchanged: the presentation of the sovereign to the people, the oath-taking and anointing, the vesting of the monarch with the ornaments (sword, bracelets, mantle, ring, sceptre, etc.), the crowning itself, always to a great fanfare of trumpets and, finally, a solemn high mass. What differences there were in the mid-Tudor ceremonies reflected the personal preferences of Mary and Elizabeth or, in 1547, the need to modify a protocol written for an adult sovereign. Citing the king's 'tendre age', Edward's privy councillors cut the 'tedious length' of 'the old observaunces' from eleven or twelve hours to about seven, including time for the banquet. At the opening ceremony of recognition, where the *Liber* had the king standing beside St Edward's chair and simply turning to face the sides of the stage, four gentlemen ushers carried King Edward in a 'litill cheyre' to the four corners of the dais so that he could be seen as Cranmer presented him to the people.[80] The council also shifted the ceremony of investing the king with his spurs from before Edward's crowning to just afterwards; at the appropriate moment, the earl of Rutland 'kneled downe ... & gave his Grace the spurres' but, following the council's order, immediately took them off so again so that they would not 'encombre' the boy.[81] Finally, because 'tyme would not serve' for the nobility and clergy to do homage individually to the king, Protector Somerset 'declared their homage in generall unto his Majesty'.[82] Mary's chief concern was not with the traditional *ordo*, which she followed to the letter, but with the oil that Cranmer, the schismatic, had used to anoint her brother. Needing properly consecrated chrism for her anointing, she procured from the bishop of Arras, Antoine Perrenot de

---

[79] Anglo, *Spectacle*, 357–8.

[80] *APC*, ii, 29. Chapman, *Last Tudor King*, 91. Nichols, *Literary Remains*, i, p. ccxciv. BL, Add. MS 9069, f. 34v.

[81] CCCC, MS 105, p. 239, printed in Ratcliff, *English Coronation Service*, 115. *APC*, ii, 32.

[82] Nichols, *Literary Remains*, i, p. ccxcvi.

Granvelle, three phials of acceptable unction.[83] The same oil was used in 1559; Elizabeth, ever fastidious, reportedly thought the cream 'was grease and smelt ill'.[84] Did she also think that its use reeked of super-stition? Perhaps she remembered what the reform-minded Edwardine, John Coke, had written in 1550 about the 'holy oyle' used in the French coronation ceremony, that it was nothing but Spanish olive oil, 'very good for salettes'.[85]

Elizabeth's real interest lay in the form of the mass that was to follow the ritual of crowning, for her personal religious convictions would not allow her publicly to accept certain aspects of the traditional Latin service. But what were her convictions? Roger Bowers has shown how, when she was fifteen years old, her chaplain, Edmund Allen, converted her finally and formally to the theology and liturgy set out officially in the Order of Communion of 1548 and the Prayer Book of 1549. Except for its provision for communion in both kinds, the Order of 1548 was technically still in force at the time of her coronation in January 1559. Bowers's close analysis of the conduct of Elizabeth's coronation mass reveals that the queen modified the conventional Latin service in three crucial respects. First, the epistle and gospel were read in English. Secondly, following the Latin consecration, the celebrant, George Carew, dean of her chapel, did not elevate the host, offering Elizabeth a ver-nacular ritual of preparation prior to her reception of the eucharist. Thirdly, 'and in plain contravention of law, she received in both kinds.' However, this act, which was known only to Carew, remained hidden

---

[83] She obtained the holy oil from Granvelle through the offices of Simon Renard, the Imperial ambassador in London. On 9 September 1553 Renard and his colleagues in London wrote to Emperor Charles V: 'The Queen entertains a scruple that the holy chrisms prepared in England may not be such as they ought because of the ecclesiastical censures upon the country; and desiring that her coronation may be in every way regular, she has sent us a request to write to the Bishop of Arras to send her some of the holy oil from over there for their anointing, as secretly and expeditiously as possible, so that it may reach her in time for the ... ceremony': *CSP Span.* xi, 220. On 13 September at Mons the Bishop reported to Renard: 'I am sending you the three holy oils the Queen asked for, which are those that I usually carry about with me': *ibid.*, 231. I am grateful to Dr Knighton for bringing these entries to my attention.

[84] Quoted in Starkey, *Elizabeth*, 272. On the anointing ceremony and oil see Schramm, *English Coronation*, 137–9; J.W. McKenna, 'The coronation oil of the Yorkist kings', *EHR*, lxxxii (1967), pp. 102–4; Sutton and Hammond, *Coronation of Richard III*, 7–10.

[85] *Le Débat des Hérauts D'Armes de France et d'Angleterre suivi de The Debate between the Heralds of England and France by John Coke*, ed. L. Pannier and P. Meyer (Société des Anciens Textes Français [xxi], Paris 1877), 64. The full statement is: 'Lykewyse for theyr holy oyle, it is great supersticion to gyve credyte to it, or to any suche fayned thynges invented by Sathan to blynde the symple people. Theyr oyle is oyle olyve whiche was brought out of Espayne, very good for salettes.'

from view, as she communicated in secret within a 'traverse', or temporary curtained enclosure in the sacrarium (sanctuary).[86]

Elizabeth I's coronation service has attracted attention because it was thought to have anticipated her settlement of religion. But discussions of the nature of that service have never been connected to the iconography and themes of her pageants or to the one context that might have been deemed relevant to the crowning of a protestant queen – the coronation of her brother, England's first protestant imperial sovereign. And what of the oath that Elizabeth swore, surely a matter of concern to the queen and to those like Cecil who had witnessed Edward's coronation? In fact, the history of the making of the oaths of Edward VI and Elizabeth I suggests that the coronations of 1547 and 1559 should be understood as two phases of a single historical problem or issue. Mary I's coronation is central to this issue, for the constitutionally troubling questions associated with a queen's unwed status did not arise *de novo* at Elizabeth's accession: they were first raised at Mary's accession in 1553.[87] But if we look at this problem rightly, we shall see that the issue was not primarily one of female rule. The circumstances of a royal minority created this problem: how were evangelicals in King Edward's council and parliaments to square their demands for a godly Reformation with the young king's supreme headship of the church? The experience of Mary's rule only made this question more insistent for them at Elizabeth's accession. In order to appreciate how they used the ceremonies of Elizabeth's coronation to force this issue, we need to examine some key elements of their thinking.

Thematically, the threads connecting the coronations of 1547 and 1559 first appeared in the writings of two Marian exiles, John Aylmer, the future bishop of London, and John Hales, a royal office-holder and former MP. Aylmer's Cambridge connexions in the early 1540s had given him an entrée to the circle of scholarly evangelicals patronized by Queen Catherine Parr, a link that helps explain his appointment as Jane Grey's tutor and, at the court of Edward VI, his opportunity to form at first hand an estimation of Princess Elizabeth's character.[88] In exile at

---

[86] R.D. Bowers, 'The Chapel Royal, the first Edwardian Prayer Book, and Elizabeth's settlement of religion, 1559', *HJ*, xliii, 2 (2000), 320–8, especially p. 327, where Bowers cites the relevant literature of this famous controversy. Bowers follows the general lines of William P. Haugaard's argument, 'The coronation of Elizabeth I', *JEH*, xix, 2 (1968), 161–70, which corrected earlier readings of what happened. One recent biographer ignores Haugaard on this point, and by relying solely on Bayne's interpretation of 1907, falls needlessly into error: Starkey, *Elizabeth*, 274.

[87] J.M. Richards, 'Mary Tudor as "Sole Quene"? Gendering Tudor monarchy', *HJ*, xl, 4 (1997), 895–924.

[88] J. Strype, *Historical Collections of the Life and Acts of the Right Reverend Father in*

Strasbourg Aylmer composed *An Harborowe for faithfull and trewe subiectes*, a tract published in London in April 1559 in answer to Knox's *Blast* of 1558 against queenship. *An Harborowe* is more than a defence of female government. It is the first work to associate Elizabeth's rule with the traditional role of the Virgin Mary as a 'Second Eve', making Aylmer an unacknowledged architect of the 'cult' of Elizabeth I.[89] It also projects a powerful view of parliament's unique function in the governance of England. While this aspect of Aylmer's thought has not gone unnoticed,[90] it has never been connected to his new iconography of protestant queenship. This connection is vital to Aylmer's argument, for his notion of how an unmarried woman should govern a protestant polity is inseparably tied to his understanding of parliament's historic role in the creation of that polity under Edward VI. Hales, a clerk of the hanaper after 1545, sat in Edward VI's first parliament. From the end of April 1551 he was attached to King Edward's embassy to the emperor, doubling as a personal agent for Cecil, who was then the king's secretary of state.[91] Hales returned to England by 3 January 1559 and addressed an 'Oration' to Elizabeth on the occasion of her coronation, a manuscript 'delivered to Her Majesty by a certain Nobleman', according to John Foxe, who later printed it.[92] In his 'Oration', Hales set out a view of the relations of crown and parliament very similar to what Aylmer advanced in *An Harborowe*.

Although nothing has so far been found to connect Aylmer and Hales in exile, they were the first to project for Elizabeth a proper model of

---

God, John Aylmer, Lord Bp. Of London in the Reign of Queen Elizabeth (Oxford 1821), 2–3, 196–7. S.E. James, *Kateryn Parr. The making of a Queen* (Aldershot 1999), 138–42. On Aylmer's Cambridge ties see W.S. Hudson, *The Cambridge Connection and the Elizabethan Settlement of 1559* (Durham N.C. 1980).

[89] D.E. Hoak, 'A Tudor Deborah? The coronation of Elizabeth I, parliament, and the problem of female rule', in *John Foxe and his World*, ed. C. Highley and J.N. King (Aldershot 2002), 73–88. H. Hackett, *Virgin Mother, Maiden Queen. Elizabeth I and the Cult of the Virgin* (New York 1995), 38–71.

[90] See A.N. McLaren, *Political Culture in the Reign of Elizabeth I. Queen and Commonwealth 1558–1585* (Cambridge 1999). *Idem*, 'Delineating the Elizabethan body politic: Knox, Aylmer, and the definition of counsel 1558–88', *History of Political Thought*, xvii, 2 (1996), 224–52. P.-A. Lee, 'A bodye politique to governe: Aylmer, Knox, and the debate on Queenship', *The Historian*, lii, 2 (1990), 242–61.

[91] G.T. Peck, 'John Hales and the Puritans during the Marian exile', *Church History*, x (1941), 159–77. During Mary's reign Hales's residence at Frankfurt is first recorded in September 1555. For his official biography and career in parliament, see the entry in *Hist. Parl. 1509–58*, ii. 276–7.

[92] The 'Oration' is BL, Harleian MS 419, ff. 143–8, first printed in the 1576 edition of Foxe, *Actes and Monuments*, 2005–7. Victoria de la Torre very kindly provided me with a photocopy of the manuscript; my thanks also to Tom Freeman for the printed reference.

queenly behaviour, the biblical figure of Deborah. The Deborah of the book of Judges (chapters 4 and 5) – at once wife, judge, prophetess, and mother – put to flight Israel's foes, bringing forty years of peace to her people. Aylmer and Hales anglicized this Deborah, transforming her into a parliamentary queen, a ruling magistrate who not only seeks and accepts the guidance of her parliament and council in the making of law, but acknowledges their superior counsel and authority. Aylmer reminded Elizabeth why a queen, like any male sovereign, must rely on parliament: 'For it is not she that ruleth, but the lawes'. This was Aylmer's chief piece of advice to Elizabeth at her accession, and he hammered it home: '*she* maketh no statutes or lawes, but the honerable court of Parliament' [my italics]. The monarch, he said, 'can ordein nothing without' parliament.[93] When Hales applied this test to Queen Mary he found her rule disastrously wanting. The problem was that she had refused to accept the superior authority of parliament. Worse were her threats and violence, her intimidation of voters and expulsion of freely elected members from the House of Commons. This and procedural irregularities in the calling of her parliaments – the omission from the writs of summons of the title and style of 'supreme hed of the churche of England', which title and style by a statute made in Henry VIII's reign was to be 'united and annexed for ever to the Imperiall crown of the Realm' – had rendered her acts of parliament null and void.[94] After Mary's cruel 'Tyrannye' Hales rejoiced that God had chosen Elizabeth 'to be our Debora' in order that England, 'our naturall mother England ... the most godly nacion of the earth', be 'clensed, made hoole, and then kept in good order'.[95]

The similarity and coincidence of Aylmer's and Hales's views of a queenly Deborah's role *vis-à-vis* parliament is remarkable, as the identical figure of a Tudor parliamentary Deborah appeared in one of the tableaux of Elizabeth's coronation pageants, a tableau in Fleet Street designed by Richard Grafton and scripted by Richard Mulcaster. The scenery of the tableau evoked the hill country of Ephraim, complete with an artificial palm tree shading 'Deborah', an actress who sat enthroned, anachronistically 'apparelled in parliament robes, with a sceptre in her hand, as a Quene', surrounded by two representatives from each of the three parliamentary estates: nobility, clergy, and commonalty. Mulcaster's gloss left no doubt about how Queen Elizabeth

---

[93] J. Aylmer, *An Harborowe for faithfull and trewe subiectes* (Strasbourg 1559: STC 1005), sigs H3v and H3r, respectively. I have used the facsimile edition (Amsterdam and New York 1972).

[94] BL, Harleian MS 419, ff. 145v–146. The statute is 26 Hen. VIII c. 1.

[95] *Ibid.*, ff. 147v, 144.

was meant to interpret the scene: 'The ground of this last pageant was, that ... she might be put in remembrance to consult for the worthie government of her people ... that it behoveth both men and women so ruling to use advise of good counsell.'[96]

The City had given Grafton responsibility for devising the themes of all of the pageants that Elizabeth saw en route to her coronation in the Abbey.[97] The Deborah of his and Mulcaster's invention embodied two powerfully congruent themes of recent English history and political culture, themes clearly articulated in other coronation tableaux – Tudor royal imperialism and godly Reformation. From her father and brother Elizabeth had inherited the mantle of imperial kingship; the iconography of Henry's crown imperial was a visually prominent aspect of Grafton's pageantry, just as it had been in Edward's coronation pageants. In 1547, for example, an enormous replica of Edward VI's 'crowne imperyall of golde' topped a 'sumptuous founteyne' at the Great Conduit in Cheapside. Farther on, at the Little Conduit, great banners and streamers framed a specially constructed tower which had been cut away to reveal the figure of 'an auncyent man setting in a chere ... representing the state of Kynge Edward the Confessor' wearing, anachronistically, 'a crowne imperiall upon his hede'. The image of Edward the Confessor enthroned in imperial majesty carried a double meaning, as his reputed holiness and canonization (1161) had rendered him officially the patron saint, as it were, of later kings of England, all of whom at their coronations were first crowned with St Edward's crown before being crowned with the imperial state crown. More to the point, however, was a pageant in 1547 that borrowed both mechanics and themes from a tableau originally constructed in 1533 for Anne Boleyn's coronation. In 1533 Anne's heraldic falcon had flown out of an ingenious 'cloud' of white sarsenet into a bed of Tudor roses where it was crowned by an angel bearing an imperial diadem. Verses accompanying the scene announced that by angelic agency God had conferred imperial authority on Anne and Henry's issue by her. Cloud, bird, and roses were recycled for King Edward's viewing in February 1547; as there had been a passing of queens in the meantime, beasts and symbols were added or changed to fit the dynastic facts of Edward's parentage. Thus Anne's falcon became the phoenix of Edward's mother, Jane Seymour.

---

[96] *The Quene's Majestie's passage*, 32–3. As noted above (nn. 41, 48) there is no evidence that Elizabeth I accepted the view of the monarchy which the pageants projected.

[97] For the roles of Mulcaster and Grafton see Anglo, *Spectacle*, 346 & nn. 3, 4; Bergeron, 'Elizabeth's coronation entry', 3–8; R. DeMolen, 'Richard Mulcaster and Elizabethan Pageantry', *Studies in English Literature*, xiv (1974), 209–21.

The silk-fringed cloud, 'powdered with sterres and bemes of golde', was re-rigged so as to enable the phoenix to make a clean landing on a scaffold hung with cloth of gold. Awaiting the phoenix there in a bed of roses was Henry VIII in the form of an old lion. By an extraordinary confusion of biological functions, the lion, simply by 'moveing his head sundry tymes', made 'semblance of amyty unto the bird ... between the which familiarity as it seemed there came forth a young Lyon that had a crowne imperiall brought from heaven above, as by ij angelles, wich they sett upon his head. Then the old Lyon and Phenix vanished away, leaving the young Lyon, being crowned, alone.' In some rather tawdry verse, the young lion was also likened to the warrior Urson, 'an emperour's son of excellent majestye'.[98]

Nicholas Udall helped write the scripts for Anne Boleyn's tableau; Udall helped train Richard Mulcaster in this craft. Mulcaster, as already noted, was connected to those who staged Edward VI's pageants. Although the figure of 'Trewth' in those pageants looked 'forward' to King Edward's wise rule, a rule mercifully guided by the 'God of Truth', nothing in the 'imperial' iconography of Edward's coronation tableaux was linked specifically to a godly Reformation of the type that evangelicals anticipated in early 1547. Nor was that iconography connected to the sort of parliamentary advice and counsel that Mulcaster's and Grafton's imperial 'Deborah' was supposed to follow in 1559. Here is where the evangelicals of 1559 transformed the meaning of the royal supremacy of the crown imperial. Visually, Elizabeth's 'imperial' pedigree was announced in the first tableau in Gracechurch Street where the City had erected artificial battlements connected by three ascending

---

[98] On St Edward's crown and Anne Boleyn's tableau of 1533 see Hoak, 'Iconography of the crown imperial', 59 and 54 respectively, where the relevant sources are also cited. The contemporary description of Edward VI's pageants is in Nichols, *Literary Remains*, i, pp. cclxxxiii, cclxxxvi, cclxxxviii. The most substantial of Edward's pageants had been written by John Lydgate in 1432 to celebrate Henry VI's return from France. The Edwardine organizers, having little time, simply recycled Lydgate's verse and prose as adapted by Robert Fabyan and published in 1542. However, Urson's speech, with its oblique reference to Edward VI's 'imperial' descent, was added in 1547; Anglo, *Spectacle*, 283–6. The point of using Henry VI's originally quite elaborate pageants was not to associate Edward VI with the undeniable popularity of Henry VI as a royal saint – Cranmer used Edward's coronation to launch a vehement attack on the 'idolatry' of such saint-worship – but to remind alert viewers that on his return from his coronation at Notre Dame, the fifteenth-century child-king had also claimed through his father an empire that included a French domain. Another addition to the 1547 pageants was a reference to Henry VIII's taking of Boulogne, with the result that when Edward 'to manhood doth sprynge, he shalbe streight of iiij realmes the Kynge': Nichols, *Literary Remains*, i, p. ccxc. For Henry VI's French coronation and reception on returning to England see B.P. Wolffe, *Henry VI* (1981), 60–4.

stages, the whole garnished with wreaths of symbolic red and white roses. The figures on the stages dramatized what the roses signified, 'The uniting of the two houses of Lancaster and Yorke'. On the lowest stage in a single royal throne sat a crowned Henry VII in a huge red rose and Elizabeth of York in a white; branches from the two were united at the second stage in the figures of Henry VIII and Anne Boleyn, and from them one branch produced at the third, topmost stage a representation of Elizabeth I herself, 'crowned and apparelled as the other princes were', that is, as Mulcaster explained it in his pamphlet, 'crowned with a crown imperiall' like 'the valiant and noble prynce king Henrie the eight'.[99] For Elizabeth, the historic meaning of that imperial legacy, as Grafton himself later averred, was the 'coniunction and coupling together of our Soueraigne Lady with the Gospell and veritie of Goddes holy woorde, for the peaceable gouernement of all her good subiects'.[100] Here was the aim of True Religion in a godly polity. The Deborah of Grafton's tableau, however, was obviously not the embodiment of *Henrician* imperial behaviour, for Elizabeth's role as an imperial Deborah – her authority to wield the powers of the royal supremacy – would be subject to limitation in parliament: the godly men of parliament would guide an imperial queen's reformation of religion.

Grafton's view of the place of parliament in the 'empire' that was England was part of a new protestant discourse of the commonweal. The parliamentary Deborahs of Aylmer's *Harborowe* and Hales's 'Oration' were quite deliberately drawn from this discourse, I think, for it is a discourse that connected all three, Grafton, Hales, and Aylmer, to the originator, Sir Thomas Smith. In *De Republica Anglorum* Smith asserted that 'The most high and absolute power' – indeed the very 'force and power' – 'of … England, is in the Parliament.'[101] This well-known remark, although first penned about 1562–5, reflects Smith's memory of the extraordinary parliamentary political realities of King Edward's minority, especially the promise of a godly parliamentary *imperium* during the protectorate of the duke of Somerset. It was then that Smith generated his new discourse of the protestant commonwealth. Jonathan McMahon has argued that Smith's views in *De Republica Anglorum* on the relations of crown and parliament can been traced back to Smith's

---

[99] *The Quene's Majestie's passage,* 18–19.

[100] *Graftons Abridgement of the Chronicles of Englande, newely corrected and augmented, to thys present yere of our Lord. 1572* (1572: STC 12152), f. 195. In 1559 one of the captions of the pageant in Cornhill proclaimed that '*The seat of worthie governance*' rested on a foundation of '*Pure religion*': *The Quene's Majestie's passage,* 22.

[101] Sir Thomas Smith, *De Republica Anglorum,* ed. M. Dewar (Cambridge 1982), 78.

work as head of a team of specialists appointed by Somerset in 1548 to gather evidence justifying a union of the crowns of England and Scotland.[102] Other members of the group included Richard Grafton and William Cecil.

Smith almost certainly helped compose one of the tracts that grew out of the committee's efforts, *An Epitome of the title that the kynges Majestie of Englande, hath to the souereignitie of Scotland*, published by Grafton in 1548.[103] The author (or authors) of *An Epitome* en-

---

[102] Jonathan McMahon, 'The humanism of Sir Thomas Smith' (College of William and Mary MA dissertation 1999), especially ch. 1, 'De Republica Britannica'. McMahon summarized his thesis in 'Sir Thomas Smith and the discourse of the protestant commonwealth: or, putting the politics back into *De Republica Anglorum*', a paper presented at an international colloquium on John Foxe at The Ohio State University, Columbus, Ohio, 1 May 1999.

On 18 October 1548 the French ambassador, Odet de Selve, reported to Henri II: 'cejourd'huy le docteur Semeith second secretaire d'estat du roy d'Angleterre avec VI ou VII aultres ont commence de se reduyre et retrouver ensemble pour faire la recherche des tiltres et enseignementz concernantz les droictz que ce roy pretend au royaulme d'Ecosse': *Correspondance Politique de Odet de Selve Ambassadeur de France en Angleterre, 1546–1549*, ed. G. Lefèvre-Pontalis (Paris 1888), 461. And who were the others? Sir John Mason, clerk of the parliaments, was one, for on 11 October 1548 the privy council had authorized payment of £20 from the exchequer to him 'and others for theyr peynes in serching registres for recordes of mattiers of Scotland': *APC*, ii, 225. Cuthbert Tunstall, bishop of Durham, was another, for on 3 October 1548 the council had charged him to search the archives of the palatinate to the same end: M. Merriman, *The Rough Wooings. Mary Queen of Scots 1542–1551* (East Linton 2000), 62, 266, 287. Cecil retained extracts and abstracts of all such records searched: HMC, *Salisbury MSS*, i, 56. There exists a fair-copy MS book of precedents culled from the notes collected by Mason bearing date 1549: BL, Add. MS 6128. Merriman (p. 288 n. 46) cites other related MSS.

[103] *STC* 3196, printed in abridged form in *The Complaynt of Scotlande*, ed. J.A.H. Murray (Early English Text Soc., extra ser. xvii, 1872), 247–56. Error and confusion reign over the authorship of this tract. In a dedicatory preface, the author styled himself 'Nicholas Bodrugan otherwise Adams'. He was in fact Adams *alias* Bodrugan, a lawyer from Dartmouth who sat in the parliament of 1547: *Hist. Parl. 1509–58*, i, 294–5. Nothing has so far been found to connect Adams to the research team appointed by Somerset in 1548, or to Somerset's circle of advisers then, or to the ideas advanced in *An Epitome of the title that the kynges Majestie of Englande hath to the sovereignitie of Scotland*, published by Grafton (1548). Mary Dewar was the source of the suggestion that Smith 'had something to do with' writing *An Epitome*, but her suggestion was based on her misreading of an attribution credited to Thomas Martin, the eighteenth-century antiquary. Martin had ascribed to Smith not the *Epitome*, but *An Epistle ... to vnitie & peace* (*STC* 22268, repr. in Murray, *Complaynt*, 237–46), a unionist tract ostensibly written by Somerset, which Grafton also published in 1548: Dewar, *Sir Thomas Smith. A Tudor Intellectual in Office* (1964), 48 & n. 1. C.H. and T. Cooper, *Athenae Cantabrigienses* (Cambridge 1858–61), i, 373. R.A. Mason thought it probable that Somerset's Scottish adviser, James Henrisoun, contributed to this *Epistle*: 'Scotching the Brut: politics, history and national myth in sixteenth-century Britain', in *Scotland and England 1286–1815*, ed. Mason (Edinburgh 1987), 80 n. 40. Henrisoun was himself the

visioned a protestant empire of England and Scotland, 'thempire of Greate Briteigne', a new polity subject in practice not to an imperial king – here the author abandoned Henry VIII's asssertion of an 'imperial' jurisdiction over church and realm – but to parliament and the church of England. Only protestantism could preserve such an empire, one in which a king followed the godly counsel of men in parliament. Indeed, the most striking feature of Smith's argument, if we may credit it to him, was that a protestant empire of an imperial king of Great Britain ought to be governed by the parliament of England.[104] It has been said

---

author of a tract dedicated to Somerset and published by Grafton in 1547, *An Exhortacion to the Scottes to conforme themselfes to the honorable, Expedient, & Godly Union betweene the two Realmes of Englande & Scotlande* (STC 12857, repr. in Murray, *Complaynt*, 207–36. McMahon ('Humanism of Sir Thomas Smith', 23) has argued persuasively that, thematically 'the *Epitome* was a continuation of the *Exhortacion*'. The point is that Henrisoun's *Exhortacion* of 1547 and the *Epistle* and *Epitome* of 1548 were part of Somerset's carefully orchestrated campaign of unionist propaganda, and must be read as such. For the best discussion of these and other tracts in this context see Merriman, *Rough Wooings*, 10–20, 265–91. Given Henrisoun's close contacts with Smith, Grafton, and Cecil, I think it likely that Henrisoun was also a member of the shadowy research team of 1548; on Henrisoun's career see Merriman, 'James Henrisoun and "Great Britain": British union and the Scottish commonweal', in Mason, *Scotland and England*, 85–112. Was Smith the ghost-writer of the *Epistle* and/or the *Epitome*? Dewar's error aside, it remains likely that Smith helped shape the *Epitome*; like Cecil, he was heavily involved in Somerset's Scottish campaign in the autumn of 1547, accompanying Somerset as far as York where illness detained him. Perhaps the *Epitome* itself provides the best evidence of Smith's hand, for as McMahon observed ('Humanism of Sir Thomas Smith', 28) the author's extraordinary command of a wide range of classical and contemporary historical sources can only be explained by his access to a very well-stocked library. Smith's library counted 406 volumes, including 104 works of history in Greek, Latin, French, English, and Italian. For the titles see Strype, *Smith*, 274–81.

[104] Although he argued for the union of England and Scotland, the author accepted the superiority of 'this realme now called Englande the onely supreme seat of thempire of great Briteigne': *Epitome*, sig. 'A Vv' (Murray, *Complaynt*, 250). On 6 September 1547 a Londoner, John Mardeley, in an unpublished poem imagined 'one whole kingdome callede great breataigne', the first such usage in the 1540s: Merriman, 'Henrisoun', 94–5. The first printed reference to 'great Britayn' appeared in February 1548 in the *Epistle*, and in the course of that year the phrase gained wider currency in English court circles, the author of the *Epitome* employing it more than twenty times: *ibid.*, 95. On the concept and language of 'Great Britain' in the Anglo-Scottish context of the 1540s see Merriman, *Rough Wooings*, 18–20, 262–4, 265–91; Mason, 'Scotching the Brut', 66–71 (in *Scotland and England 1286–1815*); *idem*, 'The Scottish Reformation and the origins of Anglo-British imperialism', in *Scots and Britons. Scottish political thought and the Union of 1603*, ed. Mason (Cambridge 1994), 161–86; D. Armitage, 'Making the empire British: Scotland in the Atlantic world 1542–1707', *Past & Present*, no. 155 (May 1997), 39–40; *idem*, 'Literature and empire', in *The Oxford History of the British Empire*, i, *The Origins of Empire. British Overseas Enterprise to the Close of the Seventeenth Century*, ed. N. Canny (Oxford 1998), 113–14; *idem*, *The Ideological Origins of the British Empire* (Cambridge 2000), 24–48. Although the *Epitome* drew

that 'the royal supremacy became a Trojan horse for protestantism' under Edward VI.[105] One might add that from Smith's point of view it was a supremacy to be exercised by authority of parliament.[106]

If revolutions are measured in terms of their lasting legacy, the reign of Edward VI ushered in perhaps the one true revolution in sixteenth-century English society, the coming of protestantism. Diarmaid MacCulloch has recently shown how Thomas Cranmer and a small, closely knit band of like-minded evangelicals at court engineered the Edwardine Reformation with the greatest fervency and determination: they planned it from the start, knowing they had the young king's full, enthusiastic support.[107] Edward VI was crowned on 20 February 1547 in a rite that was rewritten almost certainly by Thomas Cranmer to fit the unprecedented advent of a protestant supremacy. No historian of Edward's reign or Reformation has discussed the significance of Cranmer's revisions of the young king's coronation. The principle underlying Cranmer's revisions was announced on 31 January 1547 in an extraordinary royal proclamation, the first known proclamation in England to deal with the royal succession. Under his own signature (the sign manual) and in his own name the nine-year-old king was made to declare that he had come to the throne 'fully invested and established in the crown imperial of this realm', the implication being that no further legal action was required for recognition or confirmation of his authority. With one stroke of the pen, the council had rendered the traditional coronation ceremony an empty form.[108] It was a signal of things to come. There would be a coronation, but one that brought the old rite into conformity with the crown's new imperial jurisdiction, for as the council itself said in a secret memorandum, 'many poinctes' of the 'old observaunces and

---

upon an existing vocabulary of *British* unity, the author's vision of the *parliamentary* basis of a British imperial monarchy was unprecedented: McMahon, 'Humanism of Sir Thomas Smith', 25–7, 29.

[105] J. Guy, 'Tudor Monarchy and its critiques', in *The Tudor Monarchy*, ed. Guy (1997), 96.

[106] McMahon has rightly pointed out that in this sense, the origins of Patrick Collinson's 'monarchical republic' are to be found not in Queen Elizabeth's reign but in the early years of Edward VI's: McMahon, 'Humanism of Sir Thomas Smith', 30. Anne McLaren thought that Smith's views on monarchy in *De Republica Anglorum* were influenced by his career in Edward's reign, but she traced those views back to a different, more limited context in 1549, and does not mention Smith's involvement in Somerset's Scottish cause or his crucial research team of 1548, and the ideas to be found in the unionist literature of 1547 and 1548: 'Reading Sir Thomas Smith's *De Republica Anglorum* as protestant apologetic', *HJ*, xlii, 4 (1999), 911–18.

[107] D.N.J. MacCulloch, *Tudor Church Militant: Edward VI and the Protestant Reformation* (1999).

[108] *TRP*, i, 381 (no. 275). Schramm, *English Coronation*, 97.

ceremonies ... were ... by the lawes of the realme att this present ... nat allowable'.[109]

One of those laws was the act of supremacy of 1534, and to bring Edward's coronation into conformity with it Cranmer changed the words that he himself would speak in presenting the king to his people. In the traditional formula a king had been 'elect chosen and required ... by all three estates' of the realm 'to take vpon him ... the Crowne [and] royall dignitie of Englande.'[110] Cranmer deleted all of this, saying instead that the 'lawes of God and man' had already made Edward heir 'to the Royal Dignitie and Crowne Imperiall',[111] thus echoing what the earlier proclamation had asserted. Edward was king of England and supreme head of the church by divine, not human agency. At the coronation itself, in an unprecedented address prior to the anointing, Cranmer reasserted this point by explaining how Edward's supremacy had forever diminished the meaning of a royal coronation. Although 'The solemn Rites of Coronation have their Ends and Utility', kings 'be God's Anointed, not in respect of the Oil which the Bishop useth, but in consideration of their Power, which is Ordained ... [and] Of their Persons, which are elected by God.' Turning to Edward he said, 'Your Majesty is God's Vicegerent, and Christ's Vicar within your own Dominions'.[112] Cranmer wanted those present, many of whom would sit in Edward's parliaments, to understand this point in practice. He did so by another deft alteration of the words spoken at his presentation of the king to the three estates. By changing the traditional '*Syrs*' of the address – that is the 'sirs' present – to the word '*serve*', Cranmer transformed an otherwise innocuous question, whether those assembled would give their 'willes and assentes' to Edward's coronation,[113] into a demanding new reminder that they *must* 'serve' King Edward, 'as by your dwetyes of allegeance ye be bownde to do'.[114]

With this Cranmer had prepared the ground for fundamental changes in the coronation oath. The oath that kings of England had sworn since the fourteenth century set out five requests that the officiating prelate

---

[109] From a minute of the council's proceedings of 13 February 1547 at the Tower: *APC*, ii, 29.

[110] From the 'Little Device' for the coronation of Henry VII, in Wickham Legg, *English Coronation Records*, 228–9.

[111] *APC*, ii, 30.

[112] J. Strype, *Cranmer*, i, 205–7. Despite questions that have been raised about the pedigree of the text of Cranmer's address – Strype's copy is the earliest known version – its authenticity seems beyond doubt: this is Diarmaid MacCulloch's conclusion in *Cranmer*, 364 n. 2. Another printing of the speech is in Cox, *Letters of Cranmer*, 126–7.

[113] From the 'Little Device': Wickham Legg, *English Coronation Records*, 229.

[114] *APC*, ii, 30. Schramm, *English Coronation*, 176.

was to make on behalf of the king's subjects. The king was asked to (1) confirm laws and liberties that kings before him had granted to the English people; (2) do the same in respect of the liberties of the clergy; (3) promise peace and concord to clergy, church, and people; (4) be just and merciful in all his doings; (5) and observe 'such lawes as ... shalbe chosen by your people'.[115] Cranmer condensed the first of these in such a way that all reference to what constituted laws and liberties vanished: it was left to the crown to decide *what* in future should be recognized as law and liberty. Peace and concord, moreover, were now promised only to church and people, not the clergy, and the second question, touching the king's protection of the clergy's liberties and privileges, was deleted entirely. With this, the gates were opened wide to royal Reformation, and to confirm that legally, the fifth point was rewritten in such a way as to *reverse* its traditional meaning: henceforth it was the people, not the king, who were to consent to new laws.[116]

The speech that Cranmer delivered at Edward's coronation explained these revisions. This speech, or address, is one of the important documents of the Edwardine Reformation, as it limited still further the meaning of the coronation oath. Recalling Pope Paul III's threatened deposition of Henry VIII on the grounds that, contrary to his coronation oath, Henry had fallen into heresy, Cranmer rejected as inherently impossible the notion that the supreme head could so violate such an oath. He argued that as the king's temporal and spiritual authority derived from God, the promises in the coronation oath did not touch such authority: the oath was to be understood as a bulwark of the supremacy, not terms by which kings could be held accountable.[117]

Cranmer's revisions of the coronation oath suggest that he and Somerset intended to proceed to the reformation of the church by royal prerogative. We now know, thanks to the discovery of one of Paget's confidential memoranda to Somerset, that that was in fact originally their plan.[118] Grounding Edward's Refomation on statute proved the preferable course legally and politically, and the result was momentous, as the Edwardine Reformation, which was accomplished by statute and not the royal prerogative, changed forever the form of law itself: acts of

---

[115] From the text of Henry VII's oath, as given in the 'Little Device': Wickham Legg, *English Coronation Records*, 230.

[116] Schramm, *English Coronation*, 217.

[117] Strype, *Cranmer*, i, 205–6. Schramm, *English Coronation*, 217–18. Cranmer referred to Pope Paul III as 'late Bishop of Rome', when in fact Paul III died in 1549.

[118] Paget to Somerset, 25 December 1548: Northamptonshire Record Office, Fitzwilliam (Milton) MS C.21, quoted in D.E. Hoak, *The King's Council in the Reign of Edward VI* (Cambridge 1976), 175–6.

parliament were no longer merely declaratory statements or definitions of the law as it was thought to exist, but new laws in their own right. The effect was to remove all limitation on the scope and authority of statute.[119] Of course this had also been true of Henry VIII's laws after 1533, but unlike the later Henrician statutes, the legislation creating a new protestant polity in the reign of Edward VI was not the work or will of a king; it was generated by parliament under the direction of Cranmer and the dukes of Somerset and Northumberland. The example of what parliament did in this case powerfully shaped the thinking of men like Aylmer, Hales, Smith, Grafton, and Cecil. They had seen how Edward's council and parliaments had taken over the royal supremacy, had used it not as an imperial king might have done, but had made it subordinate in practice to the will of parliament. What Cranmer and a small group of evangelical councillors had done in the name of a child's supremacy might be repeated in 1559 under the authority of an unwed, inexperienced female sovereign – or so men like Grafton, Aylmer and Cecil thought. The key was to crown Elizabeth I in the same way that Edward VI had been crowned; to present Elizabeth to her people in the way Cranmer had presented Edward to his lords and commons; to reassert, in the queen's coronation oath, a royal supremacy that would allow her godly advisers to complete the aborted Reformation of Edward's reign, a Reformation that some of them, such as Cecil, had actually helped script under the duke of Northumberland.

Much therefore turned on the form of Elizabeth's coronation, especially the form of her oath. We know that during the first days of her reign the coronation oath was very much on her mind and Cecil's. She asked about it at sometime prior to 18 December 1558, because the 'Articles concerninge the Quenes Majesties coronation' among Cecil's papers include the reminder: 'a copie of the othe that her Majestie shall take to be sene and perused by her highnes'. Cecil knew that the copy he needed could be found in 'the bokes [which] remayne withe the abbott of Westm''.[120] Just which version or versions of the oath Elizabeth 'perused' remains unknown. It is unlikely that Cecil or Elizabeth would have countenanced using the oath sworn by Mary I. Mary certainly did not use Cranmer's revised text of 1547; although the text of Mary's oath has not survived, we know that her 'integrity' demanded that the coronation oath be specially changed for her: presumably this was the oath that her brother had sworn.[121] The only certainty is that when Elizabeth's coronation service actually began on Sunday, 16 January

---

[119] P.H. Williams, *The Later Tudors. England 1547–1603* (Oxford 1995), 136.
[120] BL Harleian MS 6064, f. 4*v.
[121] Schramm, *English Coronation*, 218.

1559, a copy of the oath to be used was not in the hands of Owen Oglethorpe, bishop of Carlisle, the prelate who was to adminster it. Cecil had it, and in one of the most extraordinary scenes imaginable, at the appropriate moment in the ceremony he emerged from the side of the coronation stage and 'delivered' to Oglethorpe, who was standing before the seated queen, 'a Booke' containing the text of the questions that were to be put to her.[122] A.L. Rowse quipped that this was 'the most symbolic move in the whole show'.[123]

Symbolic indeed. Can there be any doubt that Cecil had had a hand in recasting Elizabeth's coronation oath? The text of that oath has never come to light. Laud's testimony in 1644, however, allows us to deduce its essentials. It was, I believe, substantially the oath that Cranmer wrote for Edward VI in 1547, with one addition. We know that Charles I used James I's oath, an oath that restored the pre-Reformation formula that the king was to observe existing laws. But James's oath also contained a phrase nowhere to be found in *any* surviving text, a phrase that Laud attributed to either Edward VI or Elizabeth I. Since the words Laud referred to in James's oath were not used in 1547, they can only have been added in 1559. These were novel words to the effect that in respect of the law, the sovereign was to act 'according to the Laws of God, [and] the true profession of the Gospel established in this Kingdom',[124] language which can only reflect a protestant sensibility, the legacy of Edward's reign. If I am correct, Cecil was, if not the author of this addition, at least the one responsible for its insertion.

The tableaux that Grafton conceived for Elizabeth I projected a vision of a polity also founded on 'the true profession of the Gospel'. This was the vision of Aylmer, Hales, and Cecil. Like Smith, all three had come to believe that such a polity should be governed as a parliamentary monarchy. Hales and Cecil had both sat in Edward VI's revolutionary parliaments. Within a few years of Elizabeth's coronation Cecil was to devise a government for England in the event of the queen's sudden

---

[122] From the text of an Englishman's eye-witness account, PRO, SP 15/9, no. 9 (f. 18v), and Bayne, 'Coronation of Queen Elizabeth', 667–8. See especially Bayne's n. 74 (p. 667), and n. 77 (p. 668). Starkey (*Elizabeth*, 272–3) speculated that the 'Booke' Cecil handed to Oglethorpe was not the oath but the queen's pardon, but this cannot be so, as the pardon was read out after the oath-taking, anointing, and crowning. Although the Englishman's account is confused in places, he gets the order of the ceremony right: he has Cecil delivering the 'Booke' before the anointing and crowning just at the point where the oath would have been administered.

[123] Rowse, 'Coronation of Queen Elizabeth I', 309.

[124] Quoted in Schramm, *English Coronation*, 218–19.

demise without issue.[125] His scheme for a conciliar/parliamentary inter-regnum in the early 1560s looks less fanciful against the background of the way in which Edward VI's coronation had allowed the king's council and the parliament of England to assume the crown's imperial jurisdiction over the church. Did Cecil think that in 1559, at Elizabeth's coronation, history could be made to repeat itself? For some of Cecil's contemporaries, the coronations of Edward VI and Elizabeth I constituted the greatest moments in Christian church history, and they were prepared to act upon their convictions. The history of those coronations shows that in doing so, they forced the political culture of Tudor monarchy into a new mould.

---

[125] For Cecil's scheme, see S. Alford, *The Early Elizabethan Polity: William Cecil and the British Succession Crisis, 1558–1569* (Cambridge 1998), 109–19, 225–8.

CHAPTER SIX

'Under the shadowe of the Church'? The Abbey and the town of Westminster 1530–1640

J.F. Merritt

Like so many religious institutions, Westminster Abbey witnessed a decisive shift in its fortunes in the sixteenth century as its organization, religious functions and interior decoration all changed profoundly. But the century that followed the Reformation also saw the transformation of the town of Westminster, in which the medieval Abbey had played such an important role. The town of Westminster had never been part of the city of London and the area of its post-Reformation parishes – St Margaret, St Martin-in-the-Fields and St Clement Danes – was set to change radically from the 1530s onwards.[1] The new prominence of the royal court in the locality, the expansion of London as a metropolis, and the enormous changes in the population and social structure of Westminster's parishes could not help but have a major impact on the development and character of the Abbey, and the experience of its dean and chapter. It is this transformation of the Abbey's environs, and the determined efforts of the collegiate church to maintain its secular powers and influence in the developing town of Westminster, which will be the focus of this article.

As well as their obvious impact on the religious life of Westminster, the dissolution of the abbey and the other religious changes ushered in by the Reformation struck at the roots of urban government in the town. This was particularly the case since local authority in Westminster was tied to religious structures, in the shape of the monastery of St Peter's and the powerful lay fraternities of the adjacent St Margaret's parish. The medieval abbot, for example, had hitherto played a significant role in the government of the unincorporated town of Westminster. Although medieval Westminster was effectively a city in an economic and social sense, the abbey had presided over a manorial system of

---

[1] The pre-Reformation parish of St Mary-le-Strand was abolished during the reign of Edward VI and its civil functions assigned to the adjacent parish of St Clement Danes: R. Somerville, *The Savoy: manor, hospital, chapel* (1960), 48–9.

government more usually associated with rural communities, and the abbey's dissolution immediately raised problems of local government. It is true that the vill of Westminster had had its own traditions of purely informal self-government operating at the parish level, in the shape of its religious fraternities. It was through the more informal activities of these parish fraternities that townsmen had responded to many of the social and economic problems of the later Middle Ages. But here too, Reformation changes undermined channels of authority within the town as lay fraternities, like monasteries, were ultimately dissolved.[2]

The very physical and social environment in which the abbey functioned also witnessed profound changes during the early sixteenth century. The first of these was the building of the great royal palace of Whitehall. From the late 1520s, with the destruction by fire of the old Westminster Palace, Henry VIII set about creating a new palace for himself in the heart of the old vill of Westminster.[3] Here was no mere re-siting of a royal palace, but a determined attempt by the crown to make this quarter of the town the centre of a new type of princely court. The main thoroughfare of the town, King Street, was redeveloped and partially absorbed by the new palace. At the same time, the crown secured substantial tracts of undeveloped land to the north and west of Whitehall, which became royal parkland. This property, which included Hyde Park and St James's Park, secured the water supply for Whitehall Palace as well as extending the royal hunting grounds. The crown was able to obtain this land primarily through a series of 'exchanges' with various religious institutions, with the holdings of Westminster Abbey forming the most significant part.[4] Henry VIII as Renaissance prince and builder was already transforming the locality, then, even before the dissolution. In addition, the building of Whitehall Palace marked the beginning of a more assertive and interventionist role for the crown right on the doorstep of the Abbey.

The presence of the palace of Whitehall in the heart of the town of Westminster undoubtedly hastened the remarkable social and economic transformation of the area in the Elizabethan and early Stuart period.

---

[2] Rosser, *Medieval Westminster*, 35–41. *Idem*, 'The essence of medieval urban communities: the vill of Westminster, 1200–1540', *TRHS*, 5th ser. xxxiv (1984), 91–112, repr. in *The Medieval Town. A Reader in English Urban History (1200–1450)*, ed. R. Holt and Rosser (1990), 216–37. J.F. Merritt, 'Religion, government and society in early modern Westminster, 1525–1625' (London PhD dissertation 1992), 18–19, 24–6, 33, 41–6, 48–9, 64–95, 102–5.

[3] S. Thurley, *The Royal Palaces of Tudor England* (1993), 39, 51, 54–5, 58–60, 68.

[4] A.G. Rosser and S. Thurley, 'Whitehall Palace and King Street, Westminster: the urban cost of princely magnificence', *London Topographical Record*, xxvi (1990), 57–77.

The century following the Reformation would witness the large-scale gentrification of much of the area, culminating in the opening of the luxury shopping arcade of Britain's Bourse, the new development of Covent Garden and the creation of the pleasure gardens and other amenities to support and supply the fashionable society of the burgeoning 'West End'.[5]

The long-term impact of these upheavals on the Abbey's role within the town has never been properly analysed. What the Abbey's continuing role should be in this transformed urban landscape was far from clear. Would the new dean and chapter retain the authority that the abbey had previously exercised over the town? Or would the monarch's heavy-handed intervention in the locality mark the end of medieval patterns of government and the creation of a new jurisdiction around the royal court, kept tightly under royal control? Or was it possible that a new city would emerge and take strength from the very suppression of the monastery, with an invigorated corporate, civic identity to rival that of London?

I

After the traumatic royal intrusions of Henry VIII's reign, the crown did not in fact seek to intervene as decisively in the area again. Despite occasional concern over disorder or plague in the area, which might elicit privy council intervention or royal proclamations, the crown showed little desire to intrude directly into the day-to-day running of the town. Nevertheless, the creation of the new post of high steward of Westminster – a position generally held by the monarch's chief minister or favourite – gave the crown the chance to exercise an indirect but no less significant control over the area. It is the role of the high steward in Westminster, and the nature of his links with the dean and chapter, which therefore require careful investigation.

The creation of the office of high steward was an important innovation in the post-Reformation town. Its real significance lay in the extension of royal authority that the office introduced into this important area surrounding the court – an area where the abbot had formerly stood as the chief local notable. The first high steward for Westminster seems to have been Sir Anthony Denny, a trusted member of Henry VIII's privy cham-

---

[5] L. Stone, 'The residential development of the West End of London in the seventeenth century', in *After the Reformation*, ed. B. Malament (Manchester 1980), 167–214. J.F. Merritt, *The Social World of Early Modern Westminster. Abbey, Court and Community, 1525–1640* (forthcoming), chs 5–6.

ber and strong protestant, who was appointed in 1545. Denny retained this position until his death in September 1549, but no one appears to have succeeded him in the office until 1561, although in the Edwardine period the Seymours exerted an important unofficial influence in the area.[6] From 1561 onwards, however, Westminster's high stewards were prominent court figures. Particularly striking is the fifty-year period when William Cecil, Lord Burghley, and then his son Robert Cecil, earl of Salisbury, held the high stewardship in succession. Obviously such men provided a direct link with the monarch and it is easy to see how this arrangement might have suited the dean and chapter.

It is difficult to determine whether deans actually had much choice in the selection of high stewards. Officially the high steward was appointed by the Westminster dean and chapter, which formally issued letters patent.[7] Certainly the dean and chapter liked to emphasize in formal records that the high steward was merely their appointee, and to talk elsewhere in lofty tones of 'the Deane or his Steward' or 'the Deane and Chapter and their Steward'.[8] Nevertheless, it is clear that the crown wielded a major influence over this appointment and that the dean and chapter was very open to influence. In practice the dean and chapter may well have been happy simply to accept suggestions put forward by the crown when making appointments. It is also important to remember that the position of dean was itself a crown appointment.[9] Certainly

---

[6] *Acts 1543–1609*, no. 32. *Hist. Parl. 1509–58*, i, 144. For the Seymours see *Acts 1543–1609*, nos 63–4, 76, 106.

[7] The principle of appointment is asserted in WAM 6557. The patents, as of other offices granted by the dean and chapter, are generally registered, e.g. WAM Reg. XII, ff. 53v–54 (Rochester's patent 1612). The duke of Buckingham's patent (1618) also happens to survive in its original form: WAM 9886. The sharing of power was implicitly recognized in the structure of the court of burgesses, which was presided over by the dean and the high steward's deputy.

[8] WAM 6561, p. 7; 9886.

[9] W.H. Manchée, *The Westminster City Fathers (the Burgess Court of Westminster) 1585–1901* (1924), 6. Influence potentially worked in more than one direction, whatever the formal technicalities of an appointment, and certainly contemporaries thought that high stewards might affect the choice of deans. On 19 June 1601, only two days after the death of Dean Goodman, the earl of Pembroke wrote to Sir Robert Cecil 'in the behalfe of Dr. Montegue to be Deane of Westminster' (as the letter is endorsed): Bodl. MS Ashmole 1729, no. 92 (ff. 173–174v). Since Pembroke refers to 'my cousin ... that I think will be a sutor', this must have been James Montague rather than Richard Montagu (as the catalogue suggests). Hacket probably exaggerates when he says that the deanery 'had ever been confer'd by the nomination of him that was Steward of the College and City of Westminster': *Scrin. Res.* i. 44. Nevertheless, while the power of nomination was not intrinsic to the office of high steward, the high steward was often a sufficiently influential political figure to play a role in the appointment, as Hacket himself implies by reproducing (*ibid.*) Williams's suit to Buckingham for the post.

the Elizabethan dean and chapter was susceptible to pressure. When Robert Cecil received his patent for the office of high steward in 1598, he had no qualms in sending it back to the Abbey with the brisk instruction that they should remove a clause requiring the dean and chapter's approbation of his deputies – a measure which they promptly approved.[10] It is striking that in 1628, when the dean failed to secure royal approval in advance for his choice of high steward, the real lines of authority were swiftly revealed. Charles I recognized that the dean and chapter had the authority to make the appointment, but made it crystal clear that he expected them to follow his own instructions without question.[11]

It should be noted that the experience of Westminster differs from other towns where the post of high steward was created in the mid-sixteenth century. In most towns, the initiative for choosing high stewards – and for including the office in corporate charters – seems to have come from the town itself. Given the virtual absence of a central executive for the town, however, this was not the case in Westminster. The new office of high steward, if anything, made it easier for the crown to intervene directly in Westminster affairs, even if he might potentially act as a mediator between townspeople and the crown.[12]

During the period of Cecil ascendancy, high stewards soon became an important force in local society, exercising substantial amounts of patronage. Unlike so many high stewards in other parts of the country, William Cecil established a permanent residence in the place where he held office, in the shape of Burghley House, a great aristocratic palace in the Strand, in the parish of St Clement Danes. His son Robert was born in Westminster, and himself built a fine town house in St Martin's parish, where he also developed a substantial urban estate. He would later describe the particular attachment that he felt towards the locality,

---

[10] *Acts 1543–1609*, nos 498 (4 Dec. 1598), 500 (30 Jan. 1599). In 1612 John Chamberlain claimed that the 'bayliwicke' of Westminster was reputedly worth £500 a year: *The Letters of John Chamberlain*, ed. N.E. McClure (American Philosophical Soc. Memoirs, xii, Philadelphia 1939), i, 351.

[11] PRO, SP 16/114, nos 45, 50; 16/117, nos 2, 22 (*CSPD 1628–9*, 276, 277, 327, 330–1). Dean Williams's offering of the high stewardship to the earl of Holland without properly consulting the king may have been partly prompted by his mistaken belief that the office of high steward only dated from the 1585 act for the good government of the city (27 Eliz. I c. 31; *SR*, iv, I, 763–4).

[12] On the office of the high stewardship and its history, see V. Hodges, 'The electoral influence of the aristocracy 1604–1641 (Columbia PhD dissertation 1977), 202–13. In Westminster, as elsewhere, the terms 'steward' and 'high steward' do not always seem to have been used consistently in contemporary documents, and the two offices may not always have been filled simultaneously.

'having been bred and born within these poor liberties of Westminster', doubtless recognizing its importance as a local power base.[13] As high stewards, Cecil patronage is most evident if we turn to what were new avenues of patronage, such as the choice of Westminster's members of parliament. The right to return members to parliament had only been granted in 1540, and by the Elizabethan period this political patronage was exercised largely via the combined efforts of the crown and the Cecil family. It can sometimes be difficult to disentangle crown influence from Cecil family influence, given the key position of the family at the heart of government, and it may well be that contemporaries did not always make this distinction. Elsewhere in the country, other high stewards nominated at least one of a town's parliamentary representatives, especially in those cases where the high steward had helped the town to gain a parliamentary seat in the first place.[14] This had not, of course, been the case in Westminster, but the Cecils were nevertheless able to wield substantial electoral and other patronage. Robert Cecil even gained his first parliamentary experience by sitting for Westminster in 1584 and 1586. Most commonly, MPs for Westminster were either Cecil family relations (such as Richard Cecil, Lord Burghley's grandson and William Cooke, a Cecil cousin) or officials in the exchequer and court of wards – departments most directly connected with Lord Burghley.[15] It should still be emphasized, however, that although these government bureaucrats would have been promoted by the Cecil interest, they were generally local residents who continued to live in the area even after serving in parliament.[16]

---

[13] J. Diprose, *Some Account of the Parish of St Clement Danes* (1868), i, 146 (on Burghley House). HMC, *Salisbury MSS*, xx, 213.

[14] J.E. Neale, *The Elizabethan House of Commons* (1949), 210, 234–7.

[15] Richard Hodges (1559), William Staunton (1571), John Dodington and John Osborne (1572), and Peter Osborne (1588/9) were all exchequer officials, although only Peter Osborne, the lord treasurer's remembrancer, held a position of any great importance. Similarly, both Robert Nowell (1563) and Thomas Wilbraham (1572) were both attorneys in the court of wards when elected for Westminster.

[16] This discussion is based on *Hist. Parl. 1509–58* and *1558–1603*, and the identification of these men in parish records, especially parish rate books. Both Peter Osborne and his son John were related to the Cecils through their Cooke relations. The only man who does not fit easily into this pattern is the courtier Sir Thomas Knyvet, of Escrick, Yorkshire, and in his case the Cecil influence must account for his first election in 1584. Thereafter, Knyvet sat for Westminster in every parliament but one from 1584 until he was elevated to the peerage in 1607. The frequency with which he represented Westminster, combined with his positions as JP for Middlesex (1583) and subsequently Westminster (1619) and keeper of the palaces of Westminster (from 1581) and Whitehall (by 1585) should easily have accorded him the status of a loyal notable: *Hist. Parl. 1558–1603*, ii, 423–4. I would like to thank Dr Andrew Thrush of the History of Parliament for

The patronage networks of the Cecils were not merely restricted to the town's members of parliament. The pervasiveness of Cecil influence in Westminster was partly linked to the way in which it operated on a number of different social and political levels. On the parish level, for example, many prominent members of St Martin's parish and vestry had reason to consider the Cecil family as their patrons, often enjoying crown employment by the royal office of works – an important force in the parish – as well as periodic employment by the Cecils. Indeed Cecil-sponsored building work at Britain's Bourse, Salisbury House and Hatfield House involved many of the master craftsmen who were the principal parishioners of St Martin's. Other, more gentlemanly members of St Martin's vestry could also fairly be described as clients of the Cecils.[17]

Given the major role performed by high stewards such as the Cecils, where did the Abbey fit into the equation? On the face of it, one would assume a diminution of the dean's powers. For all the new importance of Cecil patronage from at least 1561 onwards, however, it is important to recognize that the dean of Westminster still remained a powerful figure in the locality and, as we shall see, retained many of the powers which the abbots had formerly enjoyed. The dean and the Cecils were certainly not involved in any sort of competition, and Gabriel Goodman, who remained in Westminster for over forty years as its dean (1561–1601), was actually a friend and chaplain of Lord Burghley's. Goodman seems very much to have been Burghley's man and in the locality the particular interests of each man appear to have harmonized quite naturally. In addition, their spheres of influence were also complementary rather than conflicting.[18] Within the town, the influence of the Cecils was most evident in the parish of St Martin's, whereas the dean and chapter's influence still remained particularly strong in the parish of St Margaret's, the old 'vill' of Westminster.[19] Within the Abbey itself, though, Burghley normally seems to have assumed that Goodman would support his exercise of patronage. In 1586, Lord Burghley felt able to write to one of his own secretaries, simply informing him that he desired the appointment of Richard Webster, a fellow of St John's

---

allowing me to consult an updated biography of Knyvet, which provides more accurate dates for these offices.

[17] See Merritt, *Social World*, ch. 4.

[18] I discuss Goodman's religious views and the significance of his lengthy tenure as dean in more detail in 'The cradle of Laudianism? Westminster Abbey 1558–1630' *JEH*, lii (2001), 623–46.

[19] For the distinction between the manor and 'vill' of Westminster, see Rosser, *Medieval Westminster*, 14–15, 226–30.

Cambridge, to the prebendal stall currently vacant by the recent death of Thomas Wagstaff.[20]

In practice, then, the Abbey enjoyed mostly amicable relations with high stewards. Under Robert Cecil the almost symbiotic relationship continued. In the early years of James I's reign, Cecil patronage continued to operate on many levels within Westminster which blurred the character of institutional relationships.[21] Robert Cecil, as we have seen, succeeded his father as high steward in 1598, and he clearly kept close tabs on the locality, albeit mostly through the use of intermediaries, and his surviving papers reflect concerns over plague, public order, residential development and ecclesiastical patronage. Although Dean Goodman had died in 1601, the dean appointed in 1605, Richard Neile, was yet another former Cecil chaplain. A more politically prominent figure than Goodman, Richard Neile held the influential position of clerk of the closet, but he could actually boast that he was Westminster born and bred, and had even attended Westminster School.[22] In these early years of the reign, Cecil patronage also continued to determine Westminster's parliamentary representation, with two members of the Cecil inner circle being returned during Salisbury's remaining years – Sir Walter Cope in 1604 and Sir Julius Caesar in 1610.

The death of Salisbury in 1612, however, was a watershed in Westminster's history and led to substantial changes in the network of influence that had developed in the town over the space of some fifty years. Thereafter, both deans and high stewards were more deeply immersed in the labyrinthine politics of the court, while their shorter tenure in office may have undermined their influence on the parish level. It is particularly striking that after Goodman's death, every subsequent dean of Westminster before the Civil War went on to become a bishop, while deans Richard Neile, George Montaigne and John Williams ultimately rose to be archbishops of York. In each case, we are dealing with what might be termed courtier clerics – men who moved easily at court, keen to please the monarch and with one eye on further preferment.

The new high steward after Salisbury's death was the royal favourite Robert Carr, later earl of Somerset. If the handsome Carr's appointment reflected his growing influence with the king, it also illustrated the way

[20] *CSPD 1581–90*, 367.

[21] See J.F. Merritt, 'The Cecils and Westminster 1558–1612: the development of an urban power base', in *Patronage, Culture and Power. The Early Cecils*, ed. P. Croft, *Studies in British Art*, 8 (2002), 231–46, and Merritt, *Social World*, ch. 4.

[22] Merritt, 'Cecils and Westminster'. A.W. Foster, 'A biography of Archbishop Neile (1562–1640)' (Oxford DPhil dissertation 1978), and below, pp. 183–206.

in which the Cecil patronage was carved up among the many who aspired to Salisbury's old positions.[23] As dean of Westminster, George Montaigne was already in place when Carr received his patent as high steward, but thereafter Montaigne continued to ally himself closely with both Carr and the powerful Howard family which supported the young favourite. Montaigne even preached a sermon at the controversial wedding of Carr (now earl of Somerset) to that notorious divorcée, Frances Howard.[24]

But how did such court manoeuvring affect Westminster? On the level of town government, this generally meant that town officers appointed by successive deans were increasingly men associated with the mercurial fortunes of court favourites rather than those with more long-standing local ties. Carr's appointment, for example, was accompanied by two other new appointments. Walter James became bailiff and escheator of Westminster, while Samuel Baker received a patent for the offices of coroner and clerk of the market. Neither man was a notable local figure, and both seem to have been nominated by the high steward. It is significant that when the dean and chapter ratified the nominations they specifically limited the term of office to 'the naturall life of Robert vicunt Rochester'.[25] At least in theory, such offices had previously been considered life appointments. Carr had little time to establish himself in Westminster, however, and the city's MPs during his ascendancy were not specifically associated with him.[26] Carr's lack of a town house in Westminster – he lodged at court in the Cockpit – further emphasizes his relatively shallow links with the locality and certainly contrasts with the impressive houses maintained by Burghley and Salisbury.[27]

With the scandal of the Overbury murder and Carr's subsequent fall from power, a new favourite emerged at court, and rapidly assumed Carr's Westminster offices. George Villiers, later duke of Buckingham, received his patent as high steward of Westminster on 8 December 1618. As in the case of Carr, new officers were appointed at the same

---

[23] Appointed 5 December 1612: WAM Chapter Act Book II, f. 10 (*Acts 1609–42*, no. 14).

[24] *DNB* (Montaigne). For the sermon see *Letters of Chamberlain*, i, 496.

[25] WAM Chapter Act Book II, f. 10.

[26] T. Moir, *The Addled Parliament of 1614* (Oxford 1958), 189. These were Edmund Doubleday and Sir Humphrey May; at this time the latter was only known as a groom of the privy chamber.

[27] *Survey of London*, XIV, *St Margaret Westminster*, iii (1921), 46. Carr had also become keeper of Whitehall Palace in 1611. Although an earlier keeper had lived at the Cockpit, Sir Thomas Knyvet, Carr's predecessor, normally seems to have stayed in his King Street house in St Margaret's: *ibid.* Cf. e.g. WCA, E149 (1599–1608), *passim*.

time, but once again only for the duration of the new high steward's life. In addition, Buckingham moved men in and out of these offices several times in a matter of years. In making these local appointments it would appear that neither Carr nor Buckingham sought to cultivate local patronage networks. Of course the long years of Cecil influence meant that local links and Cecil links had gradually come to seem much the same thing, but none of Salisbury's successors served long enough for this to happen even if they had been canny enough to encourage such a development. If town officials changed more rapidly in the post-Cecil period, this was also matched by greater contention over parliamentary elections. Certainly, the duke of Buckingham could not count upon the smooth running of elections. In fact, nearly every single parliamentary election in Westminster during the 1620s was contested.[28]

II

Much of our discussion thus far has focused on the workings of patron-age and how the dean and chapter were connected to the world of the court. But how significant a role did the dean and the Abbey play within the burgeoning town? Here it is important to remember that whatever ties of patronage bound dean to patron, the deans of West-minster continued to wield a surprising amount of influence within the town in their own right and ultimately retained many of the powers which the abbots had formerly enjoyed.

To begin with, deans of Westminster adopted a highly visible role in the town as local magistrates. It should be emphasized that this role was not merely honorific. Instead, it was an important means by which deans involved themselves in the affairs of the town. It also brought the dean into more direct contact with the consequences of the town's enormous expansion, which was fuelled largely by poor immigrants from the country. Historians often think of the growth of parishes such as St Martin-in-the-Fields as part of the development of the West End, but this fashionable development, while undoubtedly important, repre-sented only one facet of the town's overall growth. The spread of shoddy new housing, increase in disease, grinding poverty and petty crime all accompanied this suburban expansion. The control of unregulated build-ing, attempts to control disease and the punishment of crime were all part of the duties exercised by the two judicial bodies upon which deans of Westminster sat. The first of these, the court of burgesses, was

---

[28] Merritt, *Social World*, ch. 3.

essentially a revamped version of the abbot's manorial court with an emphasis upon the regulation of nuisance and the punishment of immoral behaviour – such as scolding and fornication – and was purely a local affair. In addition, however, deans of Westminster served as justices of the peace for the county of Middlesex. As Middlesex JPs, this involved them in the exercise of substantial powers of summary justice. Deans had the power, for example, to bind men over to keep the peace or to appear before the sessions, and as a member of the Middlesex bench the dean also approved the accounts of parochial expenditure on the poor of the Westminster parishes.[29] It was also as JP that deans occasionally co-operated with the adjacent city of London in the pursuit of criminals and 'sturdy' beggars. During Elizabeth's reign, for example, Dean Goodman personally co-ordinated joint searches for undesirable elements with Recorder Fleetwood.[30] Such powers could be sweeping and highly invasive. The theft of numerous pewter vessels stamped with the arms of the collegiate church in the 1610s prompted Dean George Montaigne to order a 'diligent and privie search' to be made of all houses within the liberty 'as also truynckes, cobberds and chestes of any suspected persons whatsoever', including the seizure of stolen property, with those suspected to be brought before him in his capacity of justice of the peace.[31] It is striking that when a new Westminster sessions authority was established in 1618 (presumably in response to increasing demands placed upon magistrates throughout the county of Middlesex), deans continued to serve as justices, although it must be said that Dean John Williams, who also held the powerful office of lord keeper, was, not surprisingly, a far less active magistrate than his predecessors had been. Westminster deans were not the only clerics to serve as magistrates in the area. A few canons of Westminster, such as Gabriel Grant and Roger Bates, also served as JPs in the town – further evidence of the continuing clerical role in the secular government of the Westminster parishes.[32]

As we have seen, individual members of the Abbey establishment played a role as local magistrates, where in effect they implemented the social policy of the day. As severe figures of authority and punishment they provided one face of the Abbey. At the same time, however, the dean and chapter took care to uphold the Abbey as an important institution with communal obligations of charity towards the locality. The public charity of the Abbey obviously evoked the tradition of

---

[29] E.g. WCA, E149 (1599–1600), f. 26v; E151 (1618–19), f. 57.
[30] *Queen Elizabeth and Her Times*, ed. T. Wright (1838), ii, 19, 165, 186.
[31] LMA, WJ/SR (NS) 1A/4.
[32] LMA, WJ/SR (NS) 2/146, 16/29.

monastic charity which had been seen within the town, although from the fourteenth century the charity of the monks was becoming increasingly of only token value and even in the earlier period it was easily eclipsed by the spectacular doles distributed by the royal household under monarchs such as Edward I.[33] The charity of the post-Reformation Abbey was potentially outshone even more in a town where the poor were now helped via rates and charity collected and distributed by the town's parishes. Nevertheless, the impressive ritual of weekly doles – bread and beef distributed to the poor within the Abbey itself – attracted the notice of foreign visitors.[34] The value of the 'College Alms' as it was called, varied, but was usually said to be sufficient to provide forty 'messes' every Sunday. In 1614, for example, £34 13s 4d supplied forty dishes of meat, forty loaves and forty pence in cash every week to lucky recipients.[35] Dean Goodman also supplemented these amounts with a further £9 9s 8d in bread at Christmas and Easter, from his own personal income.[36] In addition, deans of Westminster gave charity to the various parishes of Westminster on an occasional basis particularly during times of plague, when such sums helped to support a limited system of quarantine. Less obviously, the dean and chapter helped to subsidize the poor by assigning a portion of its income. For example, Dean Tounson handed over to St Margaret's overseers of the poor the fees he received from parishioners for issuing licences to eat meat in Lent.[37] Similarly when St Margaret's parishioners were fined for breaking the Sabbath (keeping shops open during the time of divine service, for example) these fines were passed over from the collegiate church as charity to benefit St Margaret's poor.[38] Such sums, it must be admitted, were token given the scale of poverty in the town as well as being an undoubted reflection of the weak financial position of the collegiate church. Nevertheless, even in the late medieval period, the poor of the town had depended heavily on the organized charity of lay people, particularly through their efforts as members of lay fraternities, and in this sense the eclipse of the

---

[33] Rosser, *Medieval Westminster*, 295–300. Cf. M.C. Prestwich, *Edward I* (2nd edn 1997), 112.

[34] E.g. WCA, E144 (1566), n.f.; E145 (1572–3), n.f.; (1578–9), n.f. *The Journals of Two Travellers in Elizabethan and Early Stuart England*, ed. P. Razell (1995), 41.

[35] WCA, E150 (1614–15), n.f.

[36] ECA, E147 (1594–5), n.f.

[37] E.g. WCA, E147 (1593–4), f. 8v; E151 (1618–19), ff. 37–8. Carpenter, *House of Kings*, 150.

[38] WCA, E149 (1599–1600), f. 12. For the dimensions of poverty in Westminster see Merritt, 'Religion, government and society', 273–8, 287–8, 284–8, 301–2, 303–6, 316 and Merritt, *Social World*, ch. 8.

Abbey's charity by the parishes was an extension of pre-Reformation developments.[39]

One of the most striking characteristics of early modern Westminster, in comparison with the capital as a whole, was the unusually powerful role played by its parishes, a phenomenon which partly resulted from the virtual absence of town government. Unlike the city of London, there was no lord mayor, body of aldermen or common council, so parish vestries assumed a great deal of power.[40] Given these circumstances, how did the Abbey relate to Westminster's three parishes of St Clement Danes, St Martin-in-the-Fields and St Margaret's? Although the presence of the Abbey within the town was doubtless considered a defining feature of the area, the collegiate church dominated the parish of St Margaret's far more than it did the increasingly fashionable St Martin's parish or St Clement's parish, located in the legal quarter of the capital. That being said, a number of canons of the collegiate church also became vicars of St Clement Danes, a fact probably connected with Cecil control of the living. More generally, it is clear that Westminster canons became local incumbents, rather than local incumbents gaining prebendal stalls.[41] In these circumstances it might be thought that a local living was a mere sinecure, but this seems not to have been the case. At St Clement's, the vicars were involved in the parish to the extent of serving as JPs, while their duty to preach in the parish church may have been seen not simply as a requirement of the position but also as a means to further preferment, given the presence of well-born parishioners, many with legal connections. At the neighbouring parish of St Martin's, where the living was a crown appointment, only one Westminster canon became incumbent. This was Thomas Montford, who served as vicar from 1602 until his death in 1633. Once again, it is clear that Montford was an active force in the parish. He was also a frequent preacher who more than once defended parochial privilege in matters which included St Martin's right to choose its own lecturer against the patronage of local peers or the crown.[42] Were these clerics taken to be 'Abbey' men by their parishioners? Probably not, since most had several important sources of patronage and often sought other advancement.[43] Indeed, their role as incumbents may have been more

---

[39] Rosser, *Medieval Westminster*, 221–4.

[40] Merritt, *Social World*, ch. 4.

[41] For the religious complexion of the Westminster parishes and their incumbents see *ibid.*, ch. 9.

[42] Merritt, 'Religion, government and society', 334–6, 348–9.

[43] Montford, for example, was also a prebendary of St Paul's, while Webster owed both his Westminster stall and his living at St Clement's to Cecil influence: Le Neve,

important to the Abbey as a means of linking the chapter more firmly to those local notables who lived beyond the immediate vicinity of the collegiate church. Certainly Montford, who was an exceptionally long-serving and active canon at the Abbey as well as a local incumbent, formed an important point of contact between the Abbey and the fashionable parish of St Martin's for some three decades.

By contrast, the close relationship between the parish of St Margaret's and the Abbey stretched back to the medieval period and remained surprisingly unaffected by the Reformation. Originally St Margaret's medieval parishioners had actually worshipped in the Abbey church, and even after the erection of a church dedicated to St Margaret, the Abbey continued to influence the life of the parish. Although lay frater-nities ensured the vibrancy of parochial life at St Margaret's, monks from the Abbey had helped to officiate at holy days, while St Margaret's had occasionally borrowed plate and other items to help celebrate feast days.[44] After the Reformation, these informal links survived but it was the formal ecclesiastical link between Abbey and parish that is most striking. The dean and chapter appointed a curate for St Margaret's, generally a rather undistinguished non-graduate until 1622, with the appointment of Dr Isaac Bargrave. This contrasted with the better qualified men who served at St Martin's and St Clement's. While the latter parishes fell within the jurisdiction of the bishop of London, St Margaret's was also unusual in coming under the ecclesiastical jurisdic-tion of the dean and chapter. Every year one of the canons was selected to serve as archdeacon of Westminster, which made him responsible for imposing conformity within St Margaret's parish. This could be impor-tant, as for example in 1562, when Archdeacon William Latimer seems to have overseen the removal of 'superstitious' church goods at St Margaret's and to have secured the removal of two newly elected church-wardens (presumably for their conservative views).[45] The ecclesiastical jurisdiction exercised by the Abbey also meant that it proved wills within a peculiar court of Westminster (which applied almost exclu-sively to parishioners of St Margaret's), while it also operated a church court, broadly similar to a bishop's consistory court, although we know virtually nothing of how active it really was.[46]

The secular and ecclesiastical powers exercised by the dean and chap-ter stemmed from the fact that St Margaret's parish had originally

1541–1857, i, 36. CSPD 1581–90, 367. Novum Repertorium Ecclesiasticum Parochiale Londinense, ed. G. Hennessy (1898), 127.

[44] Rosser, Medieval Westminster, 251–2.

[45] Hennessy, Novum Repertorium, 294. WCA, E4 (1561–2). WAM 38126.

[46] WCA, Peculiar Court of Westminster, will registers (named volumes). Fragments of

formed the old 'vill' of Westminster. This long-standing connection was also reflected in the fact that the dean and chapter remained the major landowner in the parish, and the leases that it granted gave it substantial powers of patronage. The simple presence of the collegiate church as a large religious institution meant that it could offer lucrative employment to those who provisioned and repaired it and to those who formed part of its administrative staff, while its authority in the vill meant that it also controlled the appointment of minor local office-holders.[47] As a result, many of those who acted as parish officials at St Margaret's possessed some link to the Abbey and this was especially true of members of St Margaret's vestry. Nevertheless, the parish was never a mere dependency of the Abbey, perpetually quiescent and unquestioning. Many prominent parishioners were wealthy brewers, butchers, victuallers, innkeepers and minor government officials – the main groups that had thrived in the town since medieval times and which held a sense of their own importance. They might benefit from close connections with the Abbey, but they did not necessarily define themselves in relation to it.[48] Other members of St Margaret's vestry such as William Ireland and William Man – who were important parochial figures – served the Abbey more directly. The case of William Man, who seems to have started life in the timber business, illustrates this point most forcefully. Man's public career in the town saw him as one of the lynch-pins of parish government. From 1590 he served successively as an overseer of the poor, a churchwarden, a vestryman and by 1610, as a member of the court of burgesses (a body where St Margaret's men figured very prominently). At the same time, Man also seems to have earned positions of increasing trust within the collegiate church, beginning in 1598 with that of joint surveyor of works and joint receiver for the rents of Westminster and Knightsbridge.[49] Man also built up a remarkable portfolio of no fewer than 31 different tenements located within St Margaret's parish and leased to him by the collegiate church – a feat presumably made possible by his privileged links to the Abbey.[50] He obviously commanded the trust of the Abbey establishment and, as we shall see, he was also elected to sit as a member of parliament for Westminster in 1621, with the dean's explicit backing. Most striking of all, however, was the fact that when Man died in 1635, we find that his house was serving as a virtual repository

---

pre-Civil War church court material survive in WAM A1/1 and A2/2.

[47] Merritt, 'Religion, government and society', 201–5.

[48] Merritt, *Social World*, chs 3, 4.

[49] *Acts 1543–1609*, no. 491. He was appointed jointly with Roger Man.

[50] Merritt, 'Religion, government and society', 202. *Acts 1543–1609*, no. 504.

for some of the most important documents and records pertaining to the collegiate church (including twelve registrar's books, three books of calendars of registers, all old counterparts of leases belonging to the Abbey and a book 'of the Chapter Actes from 1542 to the yeare 1606') – presumably a reflection of a career culminating in his appointment as registrar to the dean and chapter.[51] Nevertheless, throughout this time of Abbey preferment, Man continued as an active vestryman at St Margaret's and in 1618, when he became a justice of the peace for Westminster, he seems to have done so in his capacity as a St Margaret's man, dealing especially with his own parish.[52]

These powers of patronage, particularly in the old 'vill' of Westminster, and the role played by a close friend and ally of the Abbey, like Man, are vividly illustrated by the controversy surrounding a disputed Westminster parliamentary election in 1621. It is worth examining this episode in greater detail for the light it sheds on the Abbey's wider relations with the town and also the role that deans might play in elections. In December 1620, complications followed the election of Sir Edward Villiers and Edmund Doubleday as MPs for Westminster. Doubleday, the local man, died only days after being elected.[53] Complaints then arose over the manner in which the dean of Westminster, John Williams, arranged for a successor to be elected. This resulted in parishioners from St Martin-in-the-Fields, St Clement Danes and St Mary-le-Strand contesting the election of the new MP, William Man. Their petition to the committee of privileges furnishes most of the evidence for what took place.[54]

According to the petitioners, the dean chose a new day for the election of another member which 'he appointed and nominated to be Mr Manne … upon the former precept but noe publique notice thereof gyven'. Apparently, so eager was the dean to promote his candidate that only 'private notice' was given the night before to 'every particular house in the parishe of St Margaret'; this after private 'conference' at the Abbey. Nevertheless, rumour of the election spread from parishioners of St Margaret's to some of their friends dwelling in the other Westminster parishes.[55] The men of these other parishes managed to

---

[51] WAM 9589; Reg. XIII, f. 226 (I am grateful to Dr Andrew Thrush for this reference).

[52] PRO, C 181/2, f. 331 (I am grateful to Dr Andrew Thrush for this reference). LMA, WJ/SR (NS), 16/29.

[53] Doubleday was buried 26 December 1620: *Memorials of St Margaret's Church, Westminster*, ed. A.M. Burke (1914), 519.

[54] Guildford Museum Muniment Room, Loseley MS 1989. I would like to thank Alan Davidson, formerly of the History of Parliament, who allowed me to consult a photocopy of this document from the papers of Sir George More.

[55] *Ibid.*

organize themselves quickly. They went to Westminster Hall at the appointed time and made choice of Edward Forsett, who was a vestry-man of St Martin's, as well as a Middlesex JP. But the petitioners found that the dean was intent on returning Man, a St Margaret's vestryman and as they described him, 'collector of his [the dean's] rentes and one that receyveth fee and wages from the Collegiate Church'. The petition-ers described how, on the day of the election, Man entered Westminster Hall in the company of the bailiff of Westminster, and 'a grete multi-tude of others (whereof some were gentlemen of worth) but the greatest part were serving men, Apprentices, women, children, watermen [and] Porters'. With this support, Man was returned 'notwithstandinge that they were admonished that a verie great number of them who cried for Mr Manne were children and other people ... who had no voice'.[56]

Undoubtedly this account is highly coloured, but the emphatic desire to cast the dean as the villain of the piece is very notable. The document also illustrates the extent to which St Margaret's parish was seen to represent the core of the dean's local support and Man taken to encap-sulate the incestuous links between Abbey and parish. In later years, Dean Williams claimed that one of Westminster's MPs was normally chosen by the 'town' and that this was a decision that the dean merely rubber-stamped. But the term 'town' is ambiguous here, since Williams seems to use it to refer to the parish of St Margaret's – that is, the old 'vill'. If anything, this disputed election reflects the extent to which the old 'vill' of Westminster still played a central role in the politics of the locality. This may have been appropriate during the medieval period, when the more populous vill constituted the economic heart of West-minster and its properties formed a significant proportion of the Abbey's revenues. By the seventeenth century, however, the vill no longer tow-ered over the other Westminster parishes as it had done previously. Indeed, the petition objecting to William Man's election specifically emphasized that these other Westminster parishes – St Martin-in-the-

---

[56] *Ibid.* Although Sir Arthur Ingram and Robert (later Sir Robert) Pye supported Man's election, Sir Edward Wardour, who appears to have been present, objected to it, particularly on the grounds that many people who voted were not eligible to do so. Wardour also noted that Dean Williams 'refused to number them by the Poll': *CJ*, i, 528–9. Pye was a client of Buckingham's: G.E. Aylmer, *The King's Servants. The Civil Service of Charles I, 1625–1642* (1961), 311–13. R. Lockyer, *Buckingham. The Life and Politi-cal Career of George Villiers, first Duke of Buckingham, 1592–1628* (1981), 121 and *passim*. Ingram's connexion with Westminster remains unclear, although surprisingly his name appears on the indenture for the 1620 election: WAM 9629. Wardour was a Westminster resident, while his father, Chidiock Wardour, had been a prominent St Martin's vestryman under Elizabeth: WCA, F2001. The bailiff of Westminster was William Jeve.

Fields, St Clement Danes and St Mary-le-Strand – now formed 'the greatest part' of Westminster as a whole.[57]

III

The grievances expressed in 1621 gave eloquent testimony to the growing dissatisfaction at the Abbey's continuing role in the government of the town, and the degree to which the expanding town felt itself to be unrepresented. Traditionally, historians assumed that a fatal blow was dealt to the power of the Abbey in the area with the creation in 1585 of what was called the 'court of burgesses', which was to oversee law and order in the area. The court of burgesses was born partly out of strong pressure for more stringent regulation of law and order in the area in the wake of a host of escalating social problems in Westminster, many of which were associated with massive immigration into the area. Although it is tempting to characterize Westminster in this period in terms of the rise of a fashionable and courtly West End, it is important to remember that so much of the area's expansion came from the poorest sectors of society. Fears of crime, disease and social disorder dogged Westminster – and as a consequence Whitehall itself – so that there was an obvious case for creating more systematic regulation. The creation of the court of burgesses has attracted much attention over the years, not least from Westminster's modern governors. In 1985, Westminster City Council celebrated what it claimed was the 400th anniversary of its creation, apparently dating itself back to the 1585 act which established the court of burgesses. Most commentators, following the eighteenth-century historian William Maitland, have maintained that the 1585 act marks the point at which 'arbitrary' clerical rule in Westminster was replaced by the more representative government of the laity.[58] The reality, however, was far different. The act ultimately established what was little more than a remodelling of the old abbot's court, even if it did try to provide a more effective structure for its activities.[59] If anything,

---

[57] Rosser, *Medieval Westminster*, 43–5, 52–4. Guildford Museum, Loseley MS 1989.

[58] W. Maitland, *The History and Survey of London from its Foundations to the Present Time* (2nd edn 1756), ii, 1348.

[59] For example, the court of burgesses could not tax its residents or own or administer property, and had no law-making role: it functioned almost exclusively as a means of enforcing the orders set down in the 1585 Ordinances. These orders were mostly concerned with the old manorial offences and market regulation, although the court of burgesses did increasingly become involved in the prosecution of inmates and masterless men and women, and attempts to regulate building. The twelve chief burgesses were essentially the twelve chief pledges of the manorial court under another name, although

the act actually enabled the dean to regain some of the secular powers that former abbots had lost to the laity, including the appointment of townsmen to what now went under the name of the court of burgesses. So firm was the retrenchment of clerical power in Westminster government, in fact, that John Williams singled it out for particular attention during the debate on the bill for church reform in parliament in 1641. Arguing against the restriction of clerical involvement in secular government, Williams noted the potentially devastating impact such a bill would have in Westminster: 'if some Salve or Plaister shall not be applied to Westminster in this Point, all that Government and Corporation is at an end'.[60]

It would be wrong, however, to conclude from the weaknesses of the court of burgesses that the Abbey's powers over local government continued undiminished and unchallenged throughout the century following the Reformation. Nothing could be further from the truth. The protests of 1621 reveal the degree of resentment that the dean's secular powers aroused among some of the townspeople of Westminster. During the medieval period, the relations between townspeople and Abbey had in fact been far more harmonious than was often the case elsewhere. The upheavals of the Reformation, though, left the jurisdictional boundaries between the town and the dean and chapter ill-defined. This in itself did not bring about an inevitable clash of interests. There is also little evidence that Westminster inhabitants specifically attacked the secular powers of the dean and chapter as part of a principled objection to clerical authority within towns (in contrast to the palatinate of Durham, where arguments over clerical authority spilled over into more general complaints in parliament concerning clerical justices of the peace).[61]

---

the dean's right to appoint them represented a regaining of powers of appointment that had been lost by the abbot: cf. Rosser, *Medieval Westminster*, 234. Merritt, 'Religion, government and society', 102–54.

[60] Hacket, *Scrin. Res.* ii, 175.

[61] For Durham see A.W. Foster, 'The clerical estate revitalised', in *The Early Stuart Church, 1603–1642*, ed. K.C. Fincham (1993), 157–8. There are difficulties in comparing Westminster with other English towns. Cathedral cities necessarily had bishops, as well as deans and chapters, and served as administrative centres in a way that the collegiate church of Westminster did not. Cf. M.C. Cross, 'Conflict and confrontation: the York dean and chapter and the corporation in the 1630s', in Marcombe and Knighton, *Close Encounters*, 62–71; C. Estabrook, 'In the mist of ceremony: cathedral and community in seventeenth-century Wells', in *Political culture and cultural politics in early modern England*, ed. S. Amussen and M. Kishlansky (Manchester 1995), 133–61; R.A. Houlbrooke, and I. Atherton and V. Morgan, in Atherton *et al.*, *Norwich Cathedral*, 507–39, 540–75.

Nevertheless, the problems associated with the urban expansion of Westminster drew attention to certain anomalies in its government, anomalies that were ultimately linked to the continuing secular powers of the collegiate church. A fundamental problem was that those men who struggled to govern Westminster's expanding parishes did not have access to a whole panoply of powers that were provided elsewhere in the country by the structures of an established town government. Although the crown had granted Westminster the right to call itself a city in 1540,[62] this was a city that had no right to legislate, and no power of taxation to fund its own courts. It was also a city without its own income, and therefore with no money to pay an independent bureaucracy. These facts help to explain what was a long and drawn-out campaign to replace weak manorial government with a more powerful corporate structure, and in the process to wrest power away from the Abbey.

As we have seen, the 1585 act essentially ensured the continuation of clerical authority in the city. But this was not necessarily the original purpose of the bill. In fact, the triumph of the dean and chapter was only achieved through a highly effective rearguard action to defend itself against a major threat to its authority. The most recent published account of the act notes that the bill went through a great many amendments in both Lords and Commons, but entirely misses the point that much of the controversial nature of the bill arose from its origins in local conflicts between the townspeople and the dean and chapter.[63] Indeed, the early Stuart dean and chapter complained directly that at the time of the 1585 act 'the Townsmen of Westminster endeavoured ... to have a Corporacion and to exempt themselves out of the Jurisdicion of the deane and Chapter'.[64]

The bill seems to have been initiated by substantial townsmen of Westminster, especially those of St Margaret's. Amazingly, for a very long time the dean and chapter remained completely ignorant of the bill, which passed the House of Commons without their knowledge, and it was only amended at a late date.[65] It is also clear that the original bill represented a far graver assault on the secular powers of the dean and chapter than was the case with the final act. The legal advice that the chapter sought on the impact of the proposed legislation makes it

---

[62] *LP*, xvi, 379(30).

[63] D. Dean, *Law-making and Society in Late Elizabethan England* (Cambridge 1996), 254–5. The omission is all the more surprising given Dean's emphasis throughout his book on the importance of parliamentary lobbying.

[64] WAM 6561, p. 6.

[65] *Acts 1543–1609*, no. 376.

clear that their rights ran the risk of being seriously infringed.[66] For example, the bill would have effectively abolished Westminster's right of sanctuary, so that the Close and the Sanctuary would have been subject to all aspects of the legislation.[67] It is more than likely that these compromises with the Abbey were only agreed to because the act was explicitly presented as a temporary measure (and regularly required renewal). Indeed, an account of the debate in parliament over the bill makes it clear that it was intended to be a temporary measure 'to make tryall', which would be 'easly repelled' if it was unsatisfactory.[68]

It is clear, then, that there was a strong desire in 1585 among many of the townspeople for a more centralized and lay-dominated government for Westminster, with more independence for the burgesses, and the shadow at least of a proper incorporated governmental structure. Even if the 1585 act still left the dean in a prominent position, it is important to recognize that hopes of substantial change still remained, and in this context the degree to which the court of burgesses imitated the terminology and practices of London government is of significance. The reality of administration followed medieval, manorial structures, and differed substantially from the centralized and judicial functions of London's government.[69] Nevertheless, for those people eager for a stronger government on London's model, the imitation of London's structures and terminology was not a matter of mere irony, but rather gave symbolic expression to their aspirations. This new court of burgesses may have been under the dean's control, but it still nursed a potential civic identity.

The ambiguity of Westminster's position and the extent of local ambitions resurfaced again in 1601, when a coat of arms was granted to the

---

[66] These survive as 'Mr Vales notes and Rem[em]braunces for some amendment of the bill for the good government for Westminster': PRO, SP 12/177, no. 27 (CSPD 1581–90, 233). Dean (Law-making, 254 n. 162) notes that Vale's opinions on the bill were 'mostly unfavourable'; but it seems likely that Vale was the attorney employed by the dean and chapter, at the prompting of the Lords. In 1587, Vale received a patent for 'court keeping' and at the same time was made receiver-general jointly with George Burden: Acts 1543–1609, no. 403.

[67] Sanctuary had nearly been abolished during Mary's reign, when only a dramatic speech in Parliament by Abbot Feckenham had saved the Abbey's rights. Dean Goodman had also defended sanctuary during the 1560s: Westlake, Westminster Abbey, ii 426–7, 429, and above, pp. 82–91. The right of sanctuary was also a recurrent issue in the City of London: I. Archer, The Pursuit of Stability (Cambridge, 1991), 299–302.

[68] BL, Lansdowne MS 43, f. 178. Proceedings in the Parliaments of Elizabeth I, ed. T.E. Hartley (Leicester 1981–95), ii, 60, 72, 98, 102.

[69] Merritt, 'Religion, government and society', 117–21. F. Foster, The Politics of Stability. A Portrait of the Rulers of Elizabethan London (1977), 13, 27–8, 37. C.N.L. Brooke, London 800–1216. The Shaping of a City (1975), 166, 169. Archer, Pursuit of Stability, 83.

city of Westminster. The text of the grant is interesting partly for the very lack of reference to the dean and chapter, despite the fact that the arms incorporated elements of their own coat. The grant of arms also shows that even if Westminster lacked a proper civic government, its burgesses were clearly determined to acquire as many of the symbolic trappings of incorporation as possible.[70]

Such symbols of civic prestige clearly haunted at least certain Westminster officials. A striking example of a nascent civic spirit is detectable in the extraordinary will left by Morris Pickering, an original member of the 1585 court of burgesses, and one of those to whom the grant of arms was addressed. Pickering's 1603 will reads like a single-handed attempt to manufacture a set of traditions and corporate identity for Westminster which would loosely parallel the experience of London's élite citizenry. Pickering left money for civic plate, for civic feasts and for a sumptuous burial cloth with the city arms to be used only by members of the court of burgesses. Cautiously, however, Pickering stipulated that this sum was only to be paid out 'if the Acte nowe Enacted for the good government of the said cittie of Westminster or any other hereafter to be made to like effect, shall contynewe in force'.[71]

The campaign for incorporation came within a whisker of its objective only a few years later in 1607, when a draft proposal for the incorporation of the town actually gained royal approval. This proposed incorporation was justified by its supporters as enabling the better government of the town, the better relief of poor inhabitants, and 'for avoyding of oppression'. Again, the dean and chapter seem to have been crucial in their opposition to the scheme, and the margins of the surviving draft charter are annotated with their objections.[72]

---

[70] Manchée, *Westminster*, 209–10 (see n. 9 above).

[71] WCA, Peculiar Court of Westminster, 482 Elsam. Manchée, *Westminster*, 209–10. The Pickering cup is described and illustrated *ibid.*, 250–2. Pickering made many other bequests to individual burgesses, Westminster canons, and servants of the dean and chapter. It should be emphasized that his attempt to generate a civic spirit among the burgesses was not intended to be hostile to the Abbey. Pickering had been verger of the Abbey since 1572, had served as keeper of the Gatehouse Prison 1557–90, and had also leased property from the Abbey: *Acts 1543–1609*, nos 396, 413, 415, 517 n. 107. His will acknowledged a lifetime of service by bequeathing a silver basin and ewer to the dean and chapter, and providing 40s with which the servants of Westminster school were to make themselves a dinner on the day of his funeral. Pickering was also a beneficiary of the 1601 will of the canon, and head master of Westminster School, Dr Edward Grant. On Pickering's career see more generally Merritt, 'Religion, government and society', pp. 121–3, 203–4.

[72] These objections are collected together in WAM 6587, but this is now badly torn and incomplete. An apparently accurate copy was made in the 1630s (WAM 6561, pp. 5–7) and this is the text I have used.

The proposed charter seems to embody a systematic attempt to re-move the powers successfully preserved by the dean and chapter in the 1585 act and to create instead an institution run by and for the towns-people. The chief burgesses were to be elected by the townsmen, and not (as the 1585 act had required) by the dean or high steward – nor were the latter to be parties to the making and establishing of laws and ordinances. A further section urged the creation of a 'Court of Record and Cognizance of all pleas in Westminster', thereby taking away the court baron of the dean and chapter.[73] Another related document speci-fies that the intention behind the bill was explicitly to imitate the structures of government in the city of London. Even the selection of Westminster's MPs was to be taken in hand by the new corporation, with the stipulation that they be chosen from among the principal burgesses. This document twice punctiliously insists that the high stew-ard should be chosen or appointed 'by the Deane of Westminster and his sucessors as Tyme out of mynde he hath Bene ... And as they by Auncient Charters have Acthoritie so to Appoint', but this represents a rather token sop to the concerns of the dean and chapter, as the pro-posed incorporation left the high steward with no real function in the locality.[74]

In their arguments against the scheme, the dean and chapter pro-tested that the petition for incorporation came from 'a populer faccion of the meanest sort of the inhabitants of Westminster' who wished to enjoy 'diverse liberties and privileges' which the dean and chapter had always exercised. The proposal and its presented rationale were 'verie scandelous to the deane and Prebends, and their Officers, and verie preiudiciall to the said Collegiate Church'. Taking their stand on the fact that they had continually exercised authority in the town since the Reformation, the dean and chapter protested that any complaints about the nature of that government constituted a personal attack and must be justified. It was 'a great imputacion to them and their Officers' that the government should be altered 'by reason of their misgovernment, want of charitie, and oppression, before they be convicted of such Crimes, and the Cause be heard'. If there were indeed 'anie defect' in

[73] *Ibid.* These various provisions are typical of borough incorporations; see M. Weinbaum, *British Borough Charters* (1943); S. Bond and N. Evans, 'The process of granting charters to English boroughs, 1547–1649', *EHR*, xci (1976), 104–5; R. Tittler, *The Reformation and the Towns in England. Politics and Political Culture, c. 1540–1640* (Oxford 1998), 87–96, 161–76, 188–95, 345–6.

[74] WAM 6557. The document appears to be a précis in English of the contents of the proposed incorporation. It is dated 'temp. Eliz.' in the WAM description slip, but references throughout the document to the king imply that it must date from the early Stuart period.

the dean and chapter or their officers they desired that it be made known, stressing that 'they are willing to be reformed and to submit themselves unto anie censure'. For the proposed charter itself, the dean and chapter pointed out every single provision that represented a diminution of the authority that the 1585 act had preserved, and particularly urged the 1585 proviso that nothing contained in the act should be prejudicial to the dean and chapter or their successors. The jurisdiction and privileges that would be given to the townsmen, it was warned, 'must of necessitie be occasion of continuall broyles' between the townsmen and officers of the dean and chapter for their several jurisdictions 'as is daylie apparant, betwene the Universities and the Townes wherin they are seated'.[75]

Yet once again the Westminster dean and chapter succeeded in blocking this 1607 draft charter for incorporation, in the same way that they had managed to water down the 1585 act. Although the proposal for incorporation progressed as far as receiving royal approval, it was ultimately blocked.[76] There are a number of possible reasons for their lack of success. Even if the chapter exaggerated in claiming that the draft was merely the work of 'a popular faccion' of the meanest sort, it is still quite possible that the townsmen were themselves split, and that some of the more prominent burgesses from St Margaret's were more supportive of the Abbey's interests. These were presumably 'the chiffest persons of the Towne' who, the dean and chapter reported, both disclaimed the work of the 'faction' and signed a certificate to the attorney-general dissociating themselves from the proposed incorporation.[77] It may also have been the case that the current dean, Richard Neile – a Cecil protégé – ultimately enjoyed the support of Robert Cecil, whose own authority as high steward might potentially have been threatened by the new corporation.[78] There is certainly evidence that the dean and chapter seem to have petitioned Salisbury directly, presenting the proposed incorporation in the worst possible light.[79] Clearly

---

[75] WAM 6561, pp. 5, 6.

[76] LPL, Shrewsbury Papers, MS 709, f. 149.

[77] WAM 6586, ff. 2, 16 (marginal notes). The fact that the Hatfield paper cited below (n. 79) describes a petition drawn up 'without the consent of the Dean *and burgesses*' (my italics) further implies that at least the majority of the burgesses were among the 'chiffest persons' who wrote to the attorney-general.

[78] One may also assume that the city of London would have been firmly opposed to the creation of such a rival jurisdiction.

[79] Among the Hatfield MSS is an undated paper entitled 'A brief of such privileges and grants as is desired to be granted from the King unto the meanest sort of people in Westminster without the consent of the Dean and burgesses': Cecil Papers, 109/86. This is essentially a summary of the points in WAM 6561, pp. 5–7. The calendar

the proposed incorporation must have had powerful backers to inter-
cede for it if it gained the king's assent and it is possible that Sir Thomas
Knyvet – an influential courtier and MP at the time of the first attempted incorporation in 1585 – was involved. But it seems most likely
that the opposition of Robert Cecil and the dean proved overwhelming.

The dean and chapter still thus hung on with remarkable resilience to
much of the control of daily government in the locality, which still had
a distinctly medieval, manorial air. Despite the enormous increase in
population, wealth, prestige and also of social problems that beset the
locality, the crown's close links with Westminster's deans and high
stewards meant that in the last resort it was usually prepared to listen
sympathetically to the complaints over threats to the Abbey's status that
full-scale reform generally involved. For the next twenty-five years, the
cause of incorporation appears to have been dead.

IV

A century after the convulsions of the 1530s, then, the Abbey authorities had still managed to preserve much of their role in the area, despite
the building of Whitehall Palace, the Reformation, and the social, economic and demographic transformation of the surrounding city of
Westminster. It was in the 1630s that all these different features came
together once more in a manner which illustrates both the complexity
of Westminster society and government, and the continuing influence of
the Abbey.

Like the 1580s, the 1630s represented a time when the need to
control the forces of disorder in the area around Whitehall was again
proving to be a source of royal concern. For the first time since Henry
VIII, the crown seems to have contemplated a significant reorganiza-
tion of the area. Charles I was not a ruler short of grandiose ideas for
the transformation of the capital. There were plans, at least, for the
rebuilding of Whitehall Palace, and an attempt to tighten up building
regulations, and Charles seems to have intervened decisively in the
development of Covent Garden.[80] Nevertheless, many of his plans never

---

(HMC, *Salisbury MSS*, xxii, 289–90) dates the Hatfield MS tentatively to 1636, but it
seems more logical to assume that it is a debating paper presented to the first earl in
1607; the second earl would have had less reason to be involved in the later push for
incorporation, in the 1630s, since Philip, earl of Pembroke, was then high steward of
Westminster.

[80] R.M. Smuts, 'The court and its neighbourhood: royal policy and urban growth in
the early Stuart West End', *JBS*, xxx (1991), 117–49. Merritt, *Social World*, ch. 6.

went beyond the drawing board (and arguably were unlikely ever to do so) – there is little indication that Charles was prepared to pursue them aggressively against the enormous political, social and legal opposition which they would have provoked. The general impression that one gains is of a revived sense of the need to control the area around Whitehall in the face of the dramatic increase of population along with the poverty, crime, traffic problems and air pollution that accompanied it, rather than a grand programme of sustained reform of the area.

One obvious way of resolving the problem was to strengthen the existing government of the area, and this obviously raised issues of concern for the Abbey. The ultimate result, as is well known, was the so-called 'New Incorporation of the Suburbs', which was established by Charles's government. As Professor Pearl has shown, 'the origins and purposes of the incorporation were mainly economic and social', with little attempt to erect a new form of political government for the area.[81] Nevertheless, previous accounts of this 'New Incorporation' have not realized that this limited form of economic incorporation was only implemented after the failure of a different campaign for a separate political incorporation of the city of Westminster, and after prolonged pressure from the Abbey to protect its interests against the proposed 'New Incorporation'.

The proposed incorporation of Westminster, which was apparently submitted in 1633, is an intriguing project.[82] Unlike the efforts of 1585 and 1607, it seems to have been drawn up with the active, even enthusiastic, co-operation of the dean. According to Dean Williams's later testimony, this was proposed to him by some of the inhabitants of Westminster 'for the better reiglinge of their Inmates and imployinge of their poore'.[83] The proposal seems to represent what would ultimately be a cautious extension of the 1585 act. Rather than a new corporation, this would take the form of what was described as 'a Charter Supplemental' to the previous act. A new, perpetual town government would be created; it would be 'a full and perfect Corporacon', licensed to purchase and receive lands to the value of at least £200 per annum for the public use of the corporation. It would have the power to admit freemen or members of the liberty or corporation and 'to exclude all others that intrude upon them to overcharge and impoverish their whole liberties, and to overthrow the good orders there established'. It

---

[81] V.L. Pearl, *London and the Outbreak of the Puritan Revolution* (Oxford 1961), 33–7. D. Johnson, *Southwark and the City* (Oxford 1969), 314–16.

[82] The proposal, with comments by Dean Williams, survives in a contemporary copy: WAM 6561, pp. 1–4, for which see below, p. 179 and n. 87.

[83] WAM 25095, f. 4.

would have its own commission of the peace[84] with two chief burgesses, for whom a certain amount of civic pageantry would be provided. In addition, 'for the better and more ornament for their persons and respect for their places' the burgesses would have two sergeants or mace-bearers 'carrying little Maces before them when they walke abroad', while a common seal would also be provided.

While some of the trappings of civic identity would therefore be provided, in comparison with the neighbouring city of London, for example, this was nevertheless a rather lame, clerical form of incorporation which largely preserved the powers of the dean and chapter. The new corporation would be comprised of the dean and chapter, the high steward, bailiff, twelve burgesses and twelve assistants – in other words, precisely the personnel of the old court of Burgesses. The dean would appoint all the officers of the corporation, including the recorder, coroner and clerk of the market. No mention was made of the election of the burgesses, but since the proposal was merely for letters patent supplemental to the 1585 act, they were presumably still to be selected by the dean. Many of the principal features of the 1607 incorporation were therefore absent: no chamberlain, no high bailiffs, no change in the selection of town officials, no court of record, no power to make apprentices, no new markets or gaol. The reality of this proposed corporation was made starkly evident in the final sentence of the proposal, which claimed that the inhabitants did not want the extra expense of a new corporation but instead 'with more advantage doe desire to shelter themselves under the shadowe of the Church and their highe Steward for the time'. Such wording was clearly calculated to procure the dean's assent, and heightens the suspicion that this proposed incorporation was the work of those Westminster notables who had always enjoyed a close working relationship with the Abbey.

It is easy to see why Dean Williams was happy to endorse this proposed corporation 'under the shadowe of the Church', and to recommend its submission to the king through the lord chamberlain (the earl of Pembroke and Montgomery, who also conveniently doubled as Westminster's high steward).[85] The rationale behind the timing of this petition is also clear: the previous year had seen a series of exchanges between the privy council and the city of London over the need to deal

---

[84] Westminster came under the jurisdiction of the Middlesex justices of the peace, although a separate subdivision for Westminster had been established in 1618.

[85] PRO, SP 16/342, no. 44 (*CSPD 1636–7*, 315). As Williams was urging the presentation of the petition in 1633, it seems reasonable to assign this undated petition to 1633 rather than 1636 as suggested in the calendar.

with disorders in the suburbs, and the privy council had specifically proposed that 'part of the suburbs' should be incorporated within the city of London, or that a new incorporation of tradesmen and artificers covering all the liberties and outparishes should be created.[86] In the face of this threat, the dean was understandably anxious to pre-empt the absorption of Westminster within a larger incorporation by seeking separate corporate status for Westminster, but under the strict control of the Abbey. Dean Williams (who was also the bishop of Lincoln) would soon after be charged by a group of his political enemies among the Westminster canons of having plotted a treaty with the townspeople. According to this highly-coloured tale, Williams had acted without consulting the chapter, partly, it was alleged, in order to form a corporation which would undermine the authority and reputation of the Abbey. On this charge, at least, there is no reason to doubt Williams's innocence, and the justice of his claim that by the proposed scheme the royalties and liberties of the church were left 'full and compleat, in the hands of the Church'.[87]

Nothing seems to have come of this proposed corporation 'under the shadowe of the Church'.[88] In 1636, what historians of London have come to know as the 'New Incorporation of the Suburbs' was finally established. But this did not occur without the outraged protests of the dean and chapter, who did all that they could to oppose the scheme. Their protests, formally drawn up against 'the New Intended Corporation of the City of Westminster ... in such forme and manner as is *nowe desired*' also make it clear that, at least as it was first proposed, the 'New Incorporation of the Suburbs' probably aimed at far more wide-ranging powers than those that ultimately emerged.[89] Amid doleful warnings of the dangers of corporations erecting 'popular Governments' whose 'Insolencyes' would later need to be suppressed, the dean and chapter protested that all their privileges and powers of nomination would be 'suppressed and trod underfoot'. It seems clear that the proposed new incorporation made no explicit allowance for the preservation

---

[86] Pearl, *London*, 33. Johnson, *Southwark*, 314–15.

[87] WAM 25095, ff. 3v–4. The contemporary copy of the proposal and of Williams's comments on it (WAM 6561, pp. 1–4) would seem to have been made in pursuit of this charge against Williams in 1635. The copy of the dean and chapter's objections to the 1607 incorporation, which is appended to this document (pp. 5–7) and is described as the reasons 'against a like Corporation formerly projected, viz. Anno 1607', represents a mischievous and unwarranted attempt to equate two entirely different proposed incorporations, presumably the better to support the charge against Williams. For the charges against Williams generally, see below, pp. 211, 252–4.

[88] See further Merritt, *Social World*, ch. 3.

[89] Italics mine. The dean and chapter's protests are recorded in WAM 6559.

of other powers and jurisdictions, except for a clause which specified only that it would not violate any of the liberties and privileges of the city of London.[90] The dean and chapter undoubtedly feared that as a consequence the form of government established in Westminster by the 1585 act would be completely overthrown. Accordingly, they therefore rehearsed many of their objections to the 1607 incorporation, and they sounded a truly apocalyptic note:

> the priviledges granted to the Church by so many Kings and Queenes of England must all bee subverted, the profits of the Church diminished and their Rents delapidated, their officers dishonoured and displaced, and many of them Quite undone, and the Authority of the dean and chapter must bee shut up within the wall of the Church yard, or the Gates of their Cloysters.[91]

The complaints of the dean and chapter may have contributed to the pressure that helped to ensure the rather weak and half-hearted nature of the eventual Incorporation of the Suburbs, which finally stipulated that the jurisdictions and 'formes of government already established' in Westminster as well as the other suburbs were to remain intact, and as were also the 'libertyes, priviledges, imunities' and other rights granted to the dean and chapter 'or lawfully used by them and their high Steward'.[92]

The dean and chapter had sought to exclude Westminster altogether from the 'New Incorporation of the Suburbs',[93] but in the event, Westminster *was* included within the jurisdiction of the New Incorporation. The weakness of the new body and the fact that the governor of the New Incorporation was Peter Heywood, a St Margaret's vestryman and friend of the Abbey, may at least have provided some reassurance. While the new corporation stirred up major opposition from the City of London it does not appear to have had a significant impact on the suburbs themselves, with many reluctant to enroll with the new cor-

---

[90] The dean and chapter drew attention to the fact that, unlike the 1585 act, the bill included no 'salvo' for preserving the 'ancient power and Jurisdicon of the Steward, Marshall and Coroner of his Majestyes Houshold' [i.e. the Marshalsea and palace courts]: WAM 6559, p. 3. This was an astute point to have raised at a time when Charles was concerned with the authority of the new palace court: PRO, SP 16/211 nos 16, 17 (*CSPD 1631–3*, 266).

[91] WAM 6559, p. 3.

[92] WAM 6558. The desire to underline its separate status may also explain why in 1636/7 St Margaret's paid 18s to a goldsmith for cutting a silver seal 'with the Armes of this Towne': WCA, E20 (1636–7), n.f.

[93] WAM 6560. They also claimed that no other part of the suburbs had the power to regulate and order trade and tradesmen as Westminster had, although this is surely an exaggeration.

porations, and the new corporation soon fell into abeyance with the calling of the Long Parliament.[94]

The New Incorporation did little, then, to change Westminster government. The crown had ultimately rejected both a wide-ranging political incorporation of Westminster along with the other suburbs, and also the low-key incorporation of the City of Westminster 'under the shadowe of the Church'. As in the past, the crown had preferred to block the development of a proper corporate government in Westminster. The authority of the dean and chapter was therefore left intact, but the fundamental weakness of town government in Westminster remained.

What has emerged from the foregoing account is a picture of an Abbey that was most emphatically not an inward-looking institution which stood loftily apart from its surroundings; nor was it merely a dining society for clerics with more important jobs elsewhere. On the contrary, the collegiate church continued to play an important, sometimes decisive, role in the socially complex local society which was emerging. The creation of Whitehall Palace and the growth of aristocratic society in the area had greatly expanded the crown's role and interest both in the area surrounding the Abbey and in the town more generally, but the crown had not ultimately sought to change or undermine the local power of the collegiate church. Instead it favoured a more pragmatic approach which avoided major administrative innovation or the creation of powerful new institutions. But the Abbey had played its own part in frustrating attempts by local townspeople to put Westminster's government on a more coherent civic footing. In this sense, at least, the Abbey's greatest influence on the area was essentially a negative one. It is a role that is not to be underestimated: its determined opposition to attempted incorporations has played a significant role in affecting the development of the suburbs, and occupies an important place in the history of the metropolis itself. Historians working on the capital in this period, particularly its western suburbs, have understandably been attracted to the growth of the West End, or to the social problems of suburban sprawl, as subjects of study, and as a result have often written as if the Abbey had ceased to exist. But the Abbey must remain in the foreground of any study of the area. Its social and economic power may have been gradually eclipsed by the emergence of new social forces – the rising parishes, the emergent West End, and its accompanying fashionable

---

[94] For the details and fortunes of the new incorporation, see *CSPD 1635–6*, pp. 359–60; Bodl. MS Bankes 12/46 (a draft of the terms of incorporation from which a bill was to be prepared for the king's signature); *SRP*, ii, 234; Pearl, *London*, 34–5; Johnson, *Southwark*, 314–16.

society of wealthy aristocrats. But while it was no longer the dominant, hegemonic force in the locality, the Abbey's central position, jurisdictional powers, and resources of land and housing meant that it was still an important player in the complex and multi-layered society that was developing outside its doors.

CHAPTER SEVEN

Richard Neile, Dean of Westminster 1605–1610: Home-grown talent makes its mark

Andrew Foster*

On 5 November 1605, an inauspicious date for catholic conspirators in the area, Richard Neile was installed dean of Westminster. He was the first native of the city of Westminster to become dean, and he had attended Westminster School thanks to the generosity of Dean Goodman, backed by the Cecil family, who later took him into their household.[1] Archbishop Bancroft probably had a hand in sponsoring the appointment, but the formal recommendation to the crown was made by Robert Cecil, first earl of Salisbury, in his role as high steward of Westminster. Westminster was a royal peculiar and the post of dean entailed extensive duties: direction of the affairs of the collegiate church; a leading part in state ceremonies; oversight of the already famous school; and finally, certain judicial functions within the city of Westminster. It also gave control of extensive estates, not to mention noteworthy ecclesiastical patronage. The dean's basic income in respect of these responsibilities was £232 10s *per annum*.[2] This was actually no mean sum when one considers that it was worth more than some bishoprics – a fact which was taken into account when Neile was allowed to keep

* I would like to thank Charles Knighton and Richard Mortimer for their encouragement, advice and patience while this piece was being written. Kenneth Fincham made perceptive comments as ever, and I was fortunate to be able to present a version of this essay at the seminar which he runs with Nicholas Tyacke, Susan Hardman More and Michael Questier at the Institute of Historical Research; I regret that I have not been able to make more of valuable suggestions made on that occasion in an article of this length. Pauline Croft offered timely thoughts on the Cecil family, while my wife Julia has kept me on task. The work owes much to research carried out some years ago, augmented more recently.

[1] For early acknowledgement of the significance of Neile's appointment to Westminster see J. Le Neve, *The Lives and Characters ... of all the Protestant Bishops of the Church of England* (1720), i, II, 140; T. Fuller, *The History of the Worthies of England* (1662), 241.

[2] WAM 33659, f. 2. This figure is exclusive of dividends from sealing fees, entry fines and other casualties.

the deanery *in commendam* to supplement the income of the see of Rochester in 1608.[3] It is a sign that Neile was already in good favour at court in 1605 that he was allowed to keep all his current livings, except that of the vicarage of Cheshunt, on his appointment to Westminster. This meant that he retained lucrative posts in Bedfordshire and Sussex, all of which he neglected shamelessly in favour of London posts which still included his mastership of the Savoy, only given up on his appointment to Rochester in 1608.[4]

The aim of this essay is to provide a modern account of Neile's work as dean of Westminster. Much is now known of his career as bishop of no less than six dioceses in his lifetime, a career which culminated in his work as archbishop of York between 1632 and 1640. A great patron of a group of theologians known as 'Arminians', which included William Laud, John Buckeridge, John Cosin, Thomas Jackson and Francis White, Neile's service to the church was such that earlier phases of his career get neglected in favour of the admittedly significant work of the 1620s and '30s.[5] Yet it is important to look at his work as dean of Westminster because this post saw not only a local boy made good, but also witnessed the development of policies and practical administrative strategies which came to characterize his whole career. To place this in context it will be necessary to say a little more about his humble origins, examine the various ways in which he wished his work at Westminster to be assessed – by reference to his remarkable Dean's Book compiled in 1610 – whilst placing this work in turn within some contextual remarks about the state of the Church of England and life in Westminster under James I.

Richard Neile was the second son of Paul and Sybil Neile, of King Street, Westminster. His father was a tallow-chandler and he was baptized at St Margaret's, Westminster, on 11 March 1562.[6] The whole extended family retained close links with Westminster through-

---

[3] Rochester was technically worth £358 4s 9¾d [below, n. 135]. Neile was permitted to pay £322 7s 3¾d in first fruits and tenths: PRO, SO 3/4, Nov. 1608.

[4] Neile passed Cheshunt to his half-brother Robert Newell in 1605, held Toddington (Beds.) until 1608, likewise the mastership of the Savoy; he gave up the treasurership of Chichester together with the rectory of Eastbourne in 1610; it is not entirely clear when he finally gave up his prebend of Firle, but the next appointment was made in 1624: Le Neve, *1541–1857*, ii, 29.

[5] See my 'Biography of Archbishop Richard Neile (1562–1640)', (Oxford DPhil dissertation 1978); my 'Function of a bishop: the career of Richard Neile, 1562–1640', in O'Day and Heal, *Continuity and Change*, 33–54; and my 'Church policies of the 1630's', in *Conflict in Early Stuart England. Studies in Religion and Politics 1603–1642*, ed. R.P. Cust and A.L. Hughes (1989), 193–223.

[6] Burke, *St Margaret's*, 20.

out their lives. Neile's father died in 1574 and was buried in St Margaret's; his mother remarried there in April 1575, through which union Neile gained a half-brother, Robert Newell, born in 1576.[7] Neile's elder brother William was buried in the Abbey cloisters in June 1623, presumably close by where his first wife Katherine had been buried in 1620.[8] Neile's sister Dorothy, who married William Holmes, was buried with some ceremony at St Martin-in-the-Fields, Westminster, in June 1623, when no less a figure than Neile's rising chaplain, John Cosin, preached the funeral sermon.[9] William Neile provided his brother with a Westminster home long after he had vacated the deanery, something which only became unnecessary when Richard gained the rich see of Durham in 1617, and with it a London palace, Durham House, off the Strand.

Neile was extremely fortunate to be born in Westminster, for it gave him the opportunity to attend Westminster School. There he fell in with illustrious contemporaries including (though he was not formally a pupil) Robert Cecil, younger son and in politics the heir of Lord Burghley. Neile's precise date of entry into the school is unknown, but he undoubtedly benefited from the teaching of the eminent master of that period, Edward Grant. It does not look, however, as if Neile appreciated it at the time, for according to Alexander Leighton, the schoolmaster 'was never off his breech; by which he became so very a Dunce, that untill that hour he could never make a right Latin Theam'.[10] Neile's school-fellow Peter Smart was probably the source of this story, for he was scandalized when Neile apparently cheerfully confessed his weakness at Latin during visitation table-talk at Durham in 1627. Smart, too, had no love for Neile, and claimed that at school he had been 'counted an heavy-handed lubber'.[11] There is probably some truth in these stories, even though they come from partisan sources, for Neile himself is recorded to have once stopped a boy from being beaten on the grounds that it had done him no good.[12] Moreover, it looks as if Neile's whole career hung in the balance in 1580 when, if his mother had taken Mr Grant's advice, 'the best of my fortunes

---

[7] *Ibid.*, 290, 427 & n. 6.

[8] *The Marriage, Baptismal and Burial Registers of the Collegiate Church or Abbey of St. Peter, Westminster*, ed. J.L. Chester (Harleian Soc. x, 1876), 117, 122.

[9] J. Cosin, *Works*, ed. J. Sansom (Oxford 1843–55), i, 24–43.

[10] A. Leighton, *An Epitome or Briefe Discoverie ... of ... many and great Troubles* (1646), 75.

[11] P. Smart, *A Short Treatise of Altars* (Edinburgh 1629), Preface, 3.

[12] S.R. Gardiner, *History of England from the accession of James I to the outbreak of the Civil War, 1603–1642* (1886), vii, 9, cites this story which actually also derives from Leighton.

would have bin to have become some Bookesellers apprentice in Paules Churcheyard'.[13]

What saved Neile's career was the crucially important patronage of the Cecil family, for which Neile was always grateful. He was sponsored to go to St John's College, Cambridge, by Mildred Cecil, Lady Burghley. The Cecil family dominated Westminster local politics as well as the national stage and, as Pauline Croft has done much to reveal, their house off the Strand was a mecca for satellite families, and may well have included favoured local children who attended the school.[14] Having perhaps become a playmate of Robert Cecil, Neile was recommended for a private scholarship to St John's in April 1580 by Dean Goodman, on the grounds that he was 'a poor fatherless child, of good hope to be learned'; the foundation was in Goodman's name, but the money came from Lady Cecil.[15]

Neile seems to have worked fairly diligently at his studies, obtaining his BA in 1584, MA in 1587, BD in 1595, and his DD in 1600.[16] Yet he was clearly no great intellectual, and much of his time in Cambridge seems to have been spent in working as an agent for the Cecils, taking messages back and forth, attending to business affairs relating to Cheshunt and the Cecil residence at Theobalds, and assisting in the education of other members of the family. Neile was not sufficiently distinguished to be considered for a Cambridge fellowship, although between 1595 and 1603 he was apparently short-listed for the masterships of Magdalene, Clare Hall, and finally Corpus.[17] A clerical career seems to have recommended itself to him as his best bet, however, for he was ordained deacon and priest on the same day, 6 July 1589, at Peterborough Cathedral, at the age of 27.[18] Ordination clinched his continued connexion with the Cecil family, for he became one of Lord Burghley's household chaplains, a post he was also to fill for the first earl of Salisbury. In November 1590 he was given the vicarage of Cheshunt in Hertfordshire, which incorporated the Cecil house of Theobalds.[19]

---

[13] WAM, Muniment Book 7 (the Dean's Book), f. 5.

[14] P. Croft, 'The religion of Robert Cecil', *HJ*, xxxiv (1991), 773–96; also, an unpublished conference paper she gave at Westminster School in 1997.

[15] Le Neve, *Lives of the Bishops*, i, II, 137–8. P.M. Handover, *The Second Cecil. The Rise to Power, 1563–1604, of Sir Robert Cecil, later first Earl of Salisbury* (1959), 14 (suggesting that Neile was sponsored for his education as a playmate of Robert Cecil, although this involved some disruption of their companionship).

[16] Venn, iii, 236.

[17] T. Baker, *Hist. St. John's*, ed. J.E.B. Mayor (Cambridge 1869), ii, 609. PRO, SP 12/278, no. 131; 12/287, no. 44 (*CSPD 1598–1601*, 600; *1601–3*, 296).

[18] Venn, iii, 236.

[19] HMC, *Salisbury MSS*, xiii, 436.

Tantalizingly little is known of Neile's religious views while at Cambridge. He seems to have kept aloof from the major religious controversies of the day and stuck to the practical, no-nonsense approach to deep matters of theology which later became his trademark. In 1629, when facing charges of Arminianism and being inclined to popery, he denied that he had ever read more than a few lines of Arminius, claimed that he had once produced barely a sheet of notes for Lord Burghley dismissing the Baro affair, and admitted frankly that he had never resolved some of the burning questions of the day concerning falling from grace.[20] Neile appears to have gravitated towards a moderate group at St John's, becoming friends with people like George Benson, his tutor William Bayley (whose career he later tried to assist at Westminster), and Richard Clayton, whose candidature for the mastership of St John's he supported in 1595 on the grounds that he was 'the only man without exception, most indifferently desired'.[21] If one accepts a letter written much later (in 1612), Neile was certainly not part of Henry Alvey's puritan group at St John's, for he felt that the college had still not 'recovered itself of that prejudice which Alvey's government in Dr Whitaker's time brought upon it'.[22] On taking his DD in 1600 Neile faced the wrath of Dr Overall for sticking lamely to a conservative line on questions of purgatory and confession, but it was probably a wise thing to do in the circumstances of a very troubled year in Cambridge.[23]

As late as 1605 it was said of Neile that he was 'a man of no great note, more then that he is the earle of Salisburies chaplain'.[24] This may be an apt comment on what is known about his religion, yet it underestimates what he had achieved by that date, for he had already been brought to court by the Cecils and gained several important posts. In 1598 he had been given a clutch of sinecures: the rectory of Toddington in Bedfordshire and the treasurership of Chichester Cathedral, to which came attached the rectory of Eastbourne.[25] More important, on the

---

[20] Prior's Kitchen, Durham Hunter MS 67, item 14.

[21] BL, Lansdowne MS 108, f. 17.

[22] SJC Archives, D.105.1.

[23] H.C. Porter, *Reformation and Reaction in Tudor Cambridge* (Cambridge 1958), 398–9. For confirmation of heated controversies in Cambridge see *The Diary of Baron Waldstein. A Traveller in Elizabethan England*, ed. G.W. Gross (1981), 95–9; N.R.N. Tyacke, *Anti-Calvinists. The Rise of English Arminianism, c. 1590–1640* (Oxford 1987), 33–7.

[24] *Letters of Chamberlain*, i, 209 (Chamberlain to Ralph Winwood, 12 October 1605).

[25] Venn, iii, 236. *The Acts of the Dean and Chapter of the Cathedral Church of Chichester, 1545–1642*, ed. W.D. Peckham (Sussex Record Soc. lviii, [1960 for] 1959), 148.

death of Dr William Mount in 1602, Neile took up the useful post of master of the Savoy, which clinched his access to a range of important courtiers who lived there.[26] In July 1603, at the age of 41, he became a royal chaplain, and not only that, but also clerk of the closet, a post he was to occupy for the next 29 years.[27] Worldly success may have come to Neile relatively late in life – and after many years of obscure and faithful service to the Cecil family – but access to James I, with whom he seems to have struck up an instant rapport, transformed the rest of his life and ensured that the deanery of Westminster was not to be the pinnacle of his achievements.

Opinion on Richard Neile is sharply divided – as it was at the time. He is either seen as an effective, loyal defender of the Church of England, who brought great practical skills to bear on the problems of the day.[28] Or he is lambasted as a great enemy of true religion, a man who hated preaching and true worship, a man who was secretly plotting to take the Church of England back towards Rome, a line consistently taken by William Prynne.[29] This dichotomy is picked up in the work of previous historians of Westminster, who have preferred to write about more intellectual deans like Lancelot Andrewes and John Williams. Yet it is also true to say that historians of Westminster were among the first to sing Neile's praises for the very practical achievements of his period of office. Hence, for Richard Widmore, writing in the mid-eighteenth century, Neile was a 'wise and wary man', while more recently A. Tindal Hart waxed lyrical about 'Richard Neile's crowded five years'.[30] Old images are hard to escape, however, for when making an unusually good comparison with the more idolized Andrewes, Dr Hart felt constrained to write that 'Neile may have been a clumsy courtier and a poor scholar, but he was a very much better business-man than Andrewes had ever been.'[31] It is Hart's general assessment, however, that still stands as the best to date, and which serves as the basis upon which this article builds.

Hart realized more than many historians writing in the 1960s that Richard Neile was a significant and worthy figure in the Church of England; and this assessment was based on close analysis of just five years of his career. Of Neile he wrote:

---

[26] PRO, SP 12/286, no. 13. Somerville, *Savoy*, 67.

[27] HMC, *Salisbury MSS*, xv, 199. J.M. Bickersteth and R.W. Dunning, *Clerks of the Closet in the Royal Household* (Stroud 1991), 18–20, 108.

[28] P. Heylyn, *Cyprianus Anglicus: or, the History of the Life and Death of … William … Archbishop of Canterbury*, (1668), 59–60, 459–60.

[29] W. Prynne, *The Antipathie of the English Lordly Prelacie* (1641), i, 222–4.

[30] Widmore, *Westminster Abbey*, 146–8. A. Tindal Hart in Carpenter, *House of Kings*, 144–6.

[31] Hart in Carpenter, *House of Kings*, 144.

> His five years' decanate was in fact crowded with every kind of activity, from building and repair work, and the increasing of revenues, to the refurnishing of the church, the overhaul of the charters and registers, and innumerable acts of charity.[32]

This is a worthy summary of what Neile achieved, but it now requires some elaboration.

One reason why Westminster historians have been quicker than most to appreciate Richard Neile lies with the excellent source materials which have survived at the Abbey, central to which are records commissioned by Neile himself as part of his administrative reforms. The main sources of information on the Abbey in his period come from voluminous inventories and accounts which Neile caused to be drawn up, chief among them being the 'Dean's Book'. This was a memorial book written in 1610 to commemorate Neile's departure from Westminster with an account of his achievements.[33] Perhaps in anticipation of scepticism – and with all the pride of a local boy made good – Neile had the book carefully witnessed by seven canons, who vouched for the veracity of the contents. Yet surviving bills, receipts and separate inventories all seem to tally with this remarkable record. It is interesting to note the sections into which the book falls: building and repair work, increase of revenues, increase of goods and furniture, improvement in the custody of charters and registers, and charitable works. It is apparent that Neile saw his own achievements in very practical terms, utterly typical of the man. It is true that Neile was not a charismatic preacher like Andrewes, not an intellectual like Richard Montague and John Cosin, nor a single-minded leader like his friend William Laud; but Neile was possibly a more practical, pragmatic, efficient church politician than any of these, despite those who laughed at his shortcomings. Moreover, all of those mentioned appreciated this fact, for as Heylyn acknowledged, 'what he wanted in himself, he made good in the choice of his servants, having more able men about him from time to time than any other of that age.'[34]

From the opening chapter meeting held on 3 December 1605, Neile made it clear that he was going to be an active dean. Although Andrewes had apparently taken care of his own house, 'what he does not appear to have done is to have dealt with the grave decay of the Abbey Church'.[35] For Armitage Robinson, writing in 1911, Neile was the first dean to organize any major structural changes or repairs since the

[32] *Ibid.*, 144–5.
[33] WAM Book 7.
[34] Heylyn, *Cyprianus*, 59.
[35] P.A. Welsby, *Lancelot Andrewes, 1552–1626* (1958), 76.

foundation of the collegiate church in 1560.[36] Over the five years that Neile was at Westminster, a total of £1,128 was spent on construction work for the Abbey, the school, and the school extension at Chiswick. The 'necessary repairs' section of the accounts shot to nearly £200 in Neile's first year in office, a staggering figure which was double that spent in the immediately preceding or succeeding years.

During 1606 major extension work was completed upon the dean's lodgings to the value of nearly £200. This included the creation of a study with a 'presse and a great nest of great boxes for writinges and papers' for the new, energetic dean. Work was also carried out on bedrooms and a new parlour – a sure sign that the deanery now had a mistress.[37] One historian of the Abbey feels that these household improvements were carried out because Neile entertained on a lavish scale.[38] This certainly fits Neile's known extrovert nature and later reputation for hospitality when at Durham House. Large-scale building work in the grounds during 1606 certainly provided improved guest facilities, with:

> a large Stable sufficient to receave 14 or 16 Geldinges with a haie loft over yt, a Coachehouse, a Saddlehouse, and a Chamber for the Groomes and coach-man, and a Gate-House neere to the Stable.[39]

Much of this work was paid for by Neile himself or generous donors at court. Lancelot Andrewes was an immediate beneficiary of Neile's hospitality, for he and his servants were put up at the Abbey, at no charge, for just over three months before Andrewes finally found lodgings elsewhere in the capital.[40]

Within the Abbey itself Neile's changes revealed his personal taste for ceremonial, order, and reverence for the sacraments, sentiments which were later to be seen as such hallmarks of those labelled Arminians in the 1620s and '30s. In fact these views were common to a small coterie of friends at the turn of the century – Andrewes, John Overall and John Buckeridge – which also seems to have included Robert Cecil.[41] Much of the discussion at Neile's first chapter meeting concerned the erection of new prebendal stalls to be placed uniformly facing each other down either side of the choir, providing an uncluttered view of the altar.[42] Significantly, Neile donated communion plate worth over £40 to the

---

[36] Robinson, *Abbot's House*, 14.

[37] WAM Book 7, f. lv. Robinson, *Abbot's House*, 59–60, prints most of these entries. For Neile's marriage see below, pp. 203–4.

[38] Hart in Carpenter, *House of Kings*, 145.

[39] WAM Book 7, f. lv.

[40] *Ibid.*, f. 4v.

[41] Tyacke, *Anti-Calvinists*, 29–86. Croft, 'Religion of Robert Cecil', 791–6.

[42] *Acts 1543–1609*, no. 538.

Abbey soon after becoming dean, and work was quickly under way to beautify the high altar, now to be more visible than hitherto.[43] £58 was spent in providing it with 'a large backeffront of cloath of gould and blue vellvett'. Another £22 was spent on 'one other pall of cloth of gould for the communion table for dailie use'.[44] This was largely carried out during 1606, at which time parliament was debating the problems of the church in terms of the catholic threat and the need to provide for an adequate preaching ministry.

It was also in 1606 that work was begun on providing an organ for Henry VII's chapel, in which the singing of anthems now became a daily matter.[45] Neile's career shows a strong interest in church music. He seems to have been instrumental in the provision of at least three organs in his life, at Westminster, Durham and York. In all of his dioceses there is evidence of his interest in choral music, and he must bear some responsibility for the anthems sung at Durham which caused such an uproar when reported to parliament in 1628. In an effort to better attendance and improve the quality of the singing at Westminster, Neile increased the pay of the choir by £18 *per annum*, gained through leasing out the parsonage of St Martin-in-the-Fields. Perhaps just as significantly, he paid for improvements to their diet.[46] Neile may have been encouraged in these efforts when King James expressed his support for 'the singing and organ services in cathedrals' before the convocation held in 1606.[47] While it is probable that Neile drew his inspiration for his work from Lancelot Andrewes, of whom he was certainly in awe, there is no evidence that Andrewes had attempted to carry out liturgical changes on this scale. Andrewes did, however, attempt to gain improvements in choral music in 1603, and he put repairs on a more systematic footing.[48]

Neile's initiative placed a severe strain on the Abbey's financial resources, something taken account of in 1608 when cutbacks were introduced.[49] Attempts were made to increase revenues, but on the whole action was limited to negotiating new leases as and when they lapsed. Over Neile's five years at Westminster the annual revenue was

---

[43] WAM Book 7, f. 3v.

[44] *Ibid.*, f. 3.

[45] *Ibid.*

[46] *Ibid.*, ff. 4v, 5 (for money and food).

[47] *A Constitutional History of the Convocation of the Clergy*, ed. J. Joyce (1855, repr. 1967), 642.

[48] *Acts 1543–1609*, nos 524, 529. Cf. S.E. Lehmberg above, p. 98. See also N.R.N. Tyacke, 'Lancelot Andrewes and the myth of the Anglicanism', in *Conformity and Orthodoxy in the English Church, c. 1560–1660*, ed. P.G. Lake and M. Questier (Woodbridge 2000), 5–33.

[49] *Acts 1543–1609*, no. 544.

raised by approximately £96 *per annum* in this fashion.[50] There was barely enough to keep pace with Neile's demands, and he was forced to turn for support elsewhere. The king himself proved to be a generous patron: prior to the visit to the Abbey by the king of Denmark in autumn 1606, James I donated £66 for repairs to statues of his ancestors buried in the church. It was Neile who presided over the eventual completion of the tomb of Anne of Cleves.[51]

Neile also collaborated with tenants to benefit the Abbey. In the spring of 1609 the tenant at Chiswick agreed to re-site the farmhouse there away from the house used by the Westminster clergy and scholars. This allowed for a degree of modernization, and moved the centre of the farm to a more convenient place in the manor. The crucial point is that it was financed largely by the tenant, with a small financial inducement by Neile. The dean and chapter agreed to pay the tenant £260 over a period of twenty years. Thus, as Neile pointed out in his memorial book, in return for relinquishing a rent increase of £13 *per annum* negotiated in Dean Goodman's time, the college was off-setting work to the value of £866 13s 4d. Both Neile and the tenant emerge with credit from this transaction for taking the long view of investment in the interest of the church.[52]

In 1607 Neile shared with Lord Salisbury the cost of a 'perfect and exact survey' of the manor of Launton in Oxfordshire 'for the settling of the Colledge inheritance there'. Edward Wright was employed to draw up maps to end 'divers controversies and suites', and provide a basis for all future transactions.[53] The very nature of this survey is typical of Neile's business-like approach, as is the fact that the Abbey was not the sole bearer of the costs. As this survey and the work at Chiswick reveal, money was not only spent on the Abbey. No doubt drawing upon his own school days, Neile later noted that:

> at my first being deane I obteined that the Scollers Commons might be mended by a Chapter decree, so that now they have 6[d] meat in a messe at everie meale throughout the weeke, saving fish meales.[54]

Price rises had eroded the amount of food being given to the boys, so this improvement was costly. Over the next five years the dean and chapter paid out nearly £1,300 above what the original foundation

---

[50] WAM Book 7, f. 1.

[51] *Ibid.*, ff. 2v, 3. In the treasurer's account the king's gift is given as £70: WAM 33659, f. 6v. *The Funeral Effigies of Westminster Abbey*, ed. A.E. Harvey and R. Mortimer (Woodbridge 1994), 21–3.

[52] WAM Book 7, f. 2.

[53] *Ibid.*, f. 4. WAM 15218 (Wright to Neile, 24 September 1606).

[54] WAM Book 7, f. 4v.

provided for food.[55] During the same period the cost of providing meals for the dean, canons and all servants also rose considerably. It was not until 1609 that the pupils were eventually charged an increase of 10s per quarter to pay for their improved diet.[56] At about that time the canons themselves were also ordered to take fewer suppers in an effort to cut costs. Neile's care for the college may not have involved intellectual inspiration for the pupils, as it had done under Andrewes, but it certainly led to improvements in their physical well-being.

The fact that Neile did not exude the learning of his illustrious predecessor does not seem to have harmed the school. Numbers increased during the period; between 140 and 160 pupils attended by 1609, and many of these privileged boys went on to become quite famous. In 1606 George Herbert was 'commanded to the care of Dr Neale' and the teaching of Richard Ireland, the head master. Neile showed a commendable interest in the welfare and future of the pupils,[57] such that in 1610 he felt able to write:

> Myselfe have yearlie sent out of this Schoole to the Universitie besides those 6 that have bin elected, whome I have gotten placed in schollerships in other colledges besides Trinitie Colledge and Christ Church, some yeares two, some yeares three, and with some charge to me.[58]

This he did in memory of his own patronage at the hands of Goodman and the Cecils. Dean Goodman had reinforced the special relationship between Westminster, Trinity and Christ Church in 1572; although Neile sponsored pupils to other colleges (probably because of his own background as a town boy), he did not neglect the existing ties which benefited the foundationers. £30 was spent in gaining royal confirmation of the 1572 arrangement when the anniversary of the letters patent then issued came up in July 1607.[59] Moreover, new terms were negotiated for Westminster fellowships at Trinity.[60] One local boy who benefited from Neile's patronage was Samuel Harding, who went up to St John's, Cambridge, in the Easter term of 1607. Neile seems to have been a friend of the family, for it was Samuel's brother Thomas whom he appointed under master of Westminster School in 1610.[61] The school

---

[55] *Ibid.*

[56] WAM 41290.

[57] I. Walton, *The Life of Mr. George Herbert* (1670), 12. For numbers of pupils we have Neile's letter to Salisbury 6 May 1609: HMC, *Salisbury MSS*, xxi, 50.

[58] WAM Book 7, f. 5.

[59] WAM 41258.

[60] WAM Book 7, f. 3v.

[61] *Acts 1609–42*, no. 10 & n. 86. Venn, ii, 302, 303.

must have had quite an influence on its pupils, for it has been calculated that 'far more of the documented cathedral clergy attended Westminster School than any other institution', and this change from the previous dominance of Eton and Winchester came about in the seventeenth century.[62]

Despite rising costs and lack of resources, inventories and surveys for new work were a constant feature of Neile's tenure of office. No sooner had the first major building work begun than Neile called for a complete survey of all movable goods at Westminster; this was at the chapter meeting held in December 1606.[63] This naturally led to new expenditure as deficiencies were unearthed. Neile had realized that the stock of communion plate was inadequate soon after his arrival at Westminster.[64] He even went so far as to draw up a list of defects relating to the crown jewels which were handed over to his safe-keeping by his predecessor Andrewes on 7 December 1605.[65] New silver pots and dishes, carefully stamped with the college coat of arms, were acquired for everyday use. Suitably blazoned service books were also ordered for the choir.[66] The paper-work involved in keeping track of these purchases was rising, and required a trusty and reliable registrar, a post given to Neile's brother William in May 1609.[67]

As late as 1610, when Neile was deeply involved in parliamentary affairs, he was still committed to building projects, including one financed by him and his brother William to construct a porter's lodge at Westminster.[68] Together they spent over £150 rebuilding the lodge, which was considered before 'a meare slovenly dogg hole'.[69] It was only when this work was near completion that William Neile finally vacated Cheshunt parsonage, where he had served as Robert Newell's household steward, a post he later took up on behalf of his more illustrious brother Richard.[70] It was in 1610 that Neile authorized and supervised the spending of large sums of money on St Margaret's, Westminster. At a cost of £120 the sanctuary yard was extended 'for that in regard of the late infection there was not ground sufficient for the buriall of the dead'.[71] He was also still preoccupied with the supply of ornaments and

---

[62] Lehmberg, *Cathedrals under Siege*, 93.

[63] *Acts 1543–1609*, no. 539.

[64] WAM Book 7, f. 3v.

[65] Bodl. MS Ashmole 837, f. 243.

[66] WAM Book 7, ff. 3, 3v.

[67] *Acts 1543–1609*, no. 540 & n. 323.

[68] WAM Book 7, f. 2v.

[69] WAM Reg. X, f. 336.

[70] Prior's Kitchen, Durham, Hunter MS 44, item 17.

[71] WAM Book 7, f. 5v. Neile consecrated the new burial ground on 8 April 1611,

cloth for the communion table. St Margaret's was furnished with altar cloths and cushions to the value of over £33. Even while he was drafting his memorial book on his five years at Westminster, Neile was still spending money on external repairs to both church and school.[72]

It is apparent from one section of the Dean's Book that Neile regarded public charity as one of the prime duties of the dean and chapter. Money was disbursed to 40 poor people of Westminster after service each Sunday, which amounted to the princely sum of £198 6s 8d over five years.[73] Further amounts to the tune of £100 were given on the feasts of Christmas, Easter and Whitsun.[74] In December 1607 the lease of two tenements in Tothill Street were allocated to provide for the poor of St Margaret's parish. By 1610 over £50 had been raised from this source.[75] In his memorial book Neile also recorded that £20 had been spent on emergency relief in 1607, 'being the winter of the great frost'.[76] As always with charity, private initiative was as important as official action. Often the part played by the dean and chapter was simply to endorse the schemes of others, as when Thomas Bellott's plan to use the proceeds of a local market for the poor was approved by the chapter in December 1607.[77]

Plague was frequently a cause of concern in Westminster. During 1608 and 1609 the sum of £35 was spent on the relief of the families of plague victims.[78] Neile's reaction to this outbreak affords an interesting contrast to that of Dean Andrewes, who apparently deserted the area for the relative safety of Chiswick in 1603. Andrewes was strongly criticized for this action by Henoch Clapham, and his modern biographer Paul Welsby has since compared him unfavourably with Thomas Morton, who tended the sick when faced with a similar situation at York.[79] It might have raised Welsby's opinion of Neile had he chosen to make the comparison nearer home. In April 1609 Westminster was

---

when 3s 2d was spent on sweeping the whole churchyard on the morning of the ceremony, and for ringing the bells during it: Churchwardens' accounts 1610–11, printed in H.F. Westlake, *St Margaret's Westminster* (1914), 222. The immediately preceding entry is for 6d on salt 'to destroye the fleas in the Churchwardens pewe'; this has been assumed to refer to the epidemic of the previous year: J.F.D. Shrewsbury, *A History of Bubonic Plague in the British Isles* (Cambridge 1971), 304. I owe these additional details to Charles Knighton.

[72] WAM Book 7, f. 5v.
[73] *Ibid.*, f. 4.
[74] *Ibid.*
[75] *Ibid.*, f. 5.
[76] *Ibid.*, f. 4v.
[77] *Ibid.*, f. 5. *Acts 1543–1609*, no. 541 & n. 346.
[78] WAM Book 7, f. 4v.
[79] Welsby, *Andrewes*, 78.

again caught in a plague outbreak, but Neile remained at the centre of events and was eventually trapped there by the deaths of college staff. Neile merely apologized to Salisbury for his absence from court, and said he was remaining where he was for fear of spreading infection.[80] His close understanding of their plight led him to give generously to the households of plague victims. He did not neglect his duty to the school, however, for the pupils were sent to Chiswick for the summer.[81]

It would be foolish to claim that Neile accomplished all these changes on his own, for he clearly relied heavily on others, and it is a feature of his career that he seems to have been an extraordinary motivator of others, a natural business manager. Established Westminster staff like George Bellott, his receiver-general for the first two years, William Man, the Abbey surveyor, and William Cooke, clerk of the kitchen, seem to have responded well to their new dean, and helped to supply accurate paper-work for the range of initiatives set in train. All were rewarded for their efforts in terms of favourable leases to property or direct payment and promotion. The team was augmented by friends and members of Neile's family. The Holmes family was already represented at Westminster by Matthew Holmes, the precentor. He was soon joined by William Holmes as a bellringer, the man who married Neile's sister Dorothy. Neile's brother William was appointed to several posts at the Abbey: bellringer, keeper of the monuments and college porter, not to mention the critical role of registrar. It was William who, among members of Neile's family, most benefited while Neile himself was at Westminster; yet in the long term the reversionary grant of a canonry which Neile gained for Robert Newell in 1607 was of greater significance.[82] Robert had followed Neile to Cambridge in the 1590s, and thence into the church. His first appointment was as rector of Wormley (Herts.) in 1599, and later he succeeded Neile at Cheshunt (1605). When Neile finally vacated his Chichester treasurership in 1610, it went to Robert Newell.[83] He was one of the most able members of Neile's immediate family, and gained his doctorate of divinity in 1615. This nepotism must be kept firmly in perspective, for it was common for the period, and Neile's family simply took on several posts previously held by members of the families of Lancelot Andrewes and Gabriel Goodman.

Neile could not have carried out his great programme of work without the support of his more immediate colleagues in the chapter. And here it is a tribute to his nature as an assiduous, conscientious bureau-

---

[80] HMC, *Salisbury MSS*, xxi, 46 (Neile to Salisbury, 29 April 1609).

[81] *Ibid.*, 50 (Neile to Salisbury, 6 May 1609).

[82] PRO, SO 3/3, June 1607.

[83] Peckham, *Chichester Chapter Acts 1545–1642*, 188.

crat, that we scarcely have any minutes of meetings which he did not attend. He seems to have been assisted most effectively at chapter meetings by Thomas Montford, BD, who also held the crown living of St Martin-in-the-Fields, Richard Hakluyt, the already famous author and geographer, Edward Buckley, and Christopher Sutton, a greatly admired preacher. Others who provided good support were John Foxe (not the famous martyrologist), who was also a canon of St Paul's, Adrian Saravia, one of a growing band of distinguished foreign theologians who found the Church of England a congenial resting place, and two bishops who were glad to keep a residence in the capital – Thomas Ravis, bishop of Gloucester before he gained London in 1607, and William Barlow, bishop of Rochester from 1605, who was translated to Lincoln in 1608.[84] Unlike the case of so many collegiate bodies then and now, there is no evidence of any great chapter feuds during Neile's tenure as dean, which is perhaps in itself a comment on his leadership qualities and amenable style.

It was at Westminster that Neile started to gain a reputation as a generous and loyal patron of young theologians and scholars. His patronage also reveals that he had moved firmly into the camp of those labelled by Nicholas Tyacke as Arminians *avant la lettre*. Only a few months after his Westminster appointment Neile licensed two sermons by Richard Meredith for publication.[85] Meredith was a fellow royal chaplain, but the relationship may have dated back to a short period when they were at Westminster School together. They were also fellow chaplains of the Cecil household. One of Meredith's published sermons extolled the virtues of prayer, and was deliberately written:

> to diminish and abate the credit, of a certaine new fangled, and over-licentious opinion, which is of late conceived amongst men, to wit, that all the chiefe parts, and points of the christian religion, consisteth in the reading of scriptures, frequenting of Lectures, and hearing of Sermons.[86]

This would certainly have chimed in with Neile's opinions; he once urged a nonconformist minister to exchange a little less preaching for a little more learning.

Neile may well have been instrumental in aiding Meredith's appointment as dean of Wells in November 1607, for he was now very close to

---

[84] *Acts 1543–1609*, i, pp. xlvii–xlviii.

[85] W.W. Greg, *Licensers for the Press, &c. to 1640* (Oxford Bibliographical Soc. Publications, new ser. x, 1962), 71.

[86] R. Meredith, *Two Sermons preached before his Majestie, in his Chappell at Whitehall, the one, the xi. of Februarie, the other the xxv. of the same moneth* (1606, STC 17832), 40.

the king, using his post as clerk of the closet to promote the interests of young, like-minded theologians; he was also acting carefully for Bancroft and Cecil in keeping a close eye on affairs in Cambridge. James I valued Neile's company and practical advice, and publicly rewarded him with £200 in the New Year gift list of March 1608.[87] Yet Neile was definitely not one of those theologians who aided the king in his literary endeavours of this period; if anything, he was asked by Bancroft and Salisbury to try to distract James from such work. When the *Apology for the Oath of Allegiance* was attacked in 1608, Neile wrote to Salisbury that he had told the king that he thought the criticism to be 'a loose, libellous weak discourse, scant worthy his reading, no way worthy his answering, but a just subject for the Bishop of Bath to labour in, he being somewhat unmannerly used by the author in it'.[88] The king would not listen, however, for in October 1608 James Montagu informed Salisbury that Neile was still trying in vain to restrain James from writing.[89]

It is evident that Neile was starting to play a political role in the church even if things did not always go his way. When John Still, the previous bishop of Bath and Wells, had died in February 1608, Neile quickly wrote to Sir Thomas Lake about the promotion possibilities this created. He knew that James Montagu had been nominated to the see as a reward for helping to write the *Apology*; this left the deanery of Worcester vacant. Lake's brother Arthur had been nominated for this post; but, mindful that George Abbot had the powerful backing of the earl of Dunbar, Neile shrewdly suggested that if Lake were wise, 'his brother should attend Abbot's preferment, to get his deanery of Winchester'. For Worcester, Neile hoped that John Buckeridge 'might be so bound to you as to remember him to his Majesty'.[90] Lake ignored this advice, and his brother accepted the deanery of Worcester in April 1608, but this is early evidence of Neile's interest in church politics, and his position vis-à-vis the rising George Abbot well before the latter's promotion to Canterbury.

Neile was now clearly moving in particular circles with Arminians *avant la lettre*. As the story above illustrates, he had become friends with John Buckeridge, a fellow royal chaplain, at that time president of St John's College, Oxford. In later nonconformist circles Buckeridge was referred to as 'Neile's disciple'.[91] It was apparently on Buckeridge's

[87] J. Nichols, *The Progresses, Processions, and Magnificent Festivities of King James the First* (1828), ii, 190.

[88] HMC, *Salisbury MSS*, xx, 226 (Neile to Salisbury, 11 August 1608).

[89] *Ibid.*, 260 (Montagu, Bishop of Bath and Wells, to Salisbury, 24 October 1608).

[90] PRO, SP 14/31, no. 59 (*CSPD 1603–10*, 410; Neile to Lake, 29 February 1608).

[91] Dr Williams's Library, London, RM/J 1644.

advice that Neile first employed William Laud as his personal chaplain in August 1608.[92] This was obviously the start of an important long-term relationship that eventually led to both men occupying the top jobs in the church in the 1630s. It was Neile who arranged for Laud to preach at court in September 1609; a royal chaplaincy followed in 1611.[93] One of Neile's last acts before he left Westminster was to obtain for Laud a reversion to a Westminster canonry.[94] Laud's half-brother William Robinson also seems to have benefited from Neile's patronage, for he followed Neile from Westminster to Lincoln, and ended his career working as Neile's archdeacon of Nottingham.

In the autumn of 1607 Neile intervened in the affairs of Gonville and Caius College, Cambridge. The death of the old master, Dr Thomas Legge, had precipitated an acrimonious election contest. Dr John Gostlin was chosen to succeed Legge, but apparently with rather undue haste and scant regard for the college statutes. The matter was reported to the king at Farnham, and Neile was deputed to investigate on behalf of Lord Salisbury. Neile later reported that the election of Gostlin had been 'a plain conspiracy' and a 'thing long plotted for by them of his faction'.[95] Yet Neile was not entirely guiltless himself, for it seems that George Downham had first been proposed for the post, but he and Samuel Harsnett had worried that 'Puritanism flourisheth enough in Cambridge'.[96] A neutral candidate, William Branthwaite, eventually gained the post, but Neile maintained contact with Gostlin, who finally became master of Caius in 1619.[97]

It is from this period that we have evidence of Neile's strong links with lawyers, both common and civil. In March 1609 he became one of a select band of clerics to be admitted as an honorary member of Gray's Inn – probably on the strength of his Cecil connexions, for this was essentially their 'club'.[98] At Westminster he struck up a good working relationship with his official, Robert Masters, who also served him as co-chancellor of Rochester, and later moved with him to Lichfield.[99] Of greater long-term significance, it was at Westminster that Neile met and

---

[92] Heylyn, *Cyprianus*, 59.

[93] *The Works of William Laud*, ed. W. Scott and J. Bliss (Oxford 1847–60), iii, 134.

[94] PRO, SO 3/5, Nov. 1610.

[95] HMC, *Salisbury MSS*, xix, 204–5 (Neile to Salisbury, 3 August 1607; quotations from p. 204).

[96] Dr Williams's Library, London, RM/I 663(4).

[97] Neile mobilized Gostlin's support in the election of Buckingham as chancellor of Cambridge University in May 1626: CUL, University Archives, Lett.12 (a.2).

[98] *The Register of Admissions to Gray's Inn, 1521–1889*, ed. J. Foster (1889), 121.

[99] B. Levack, *The Civil Lawyers in England, 1603–1641. A Political Study* (1973), 254.

supported the early career of William Easdall, a man who later rose to be his chancellor at York. Easdall acted as Neile's secretary until 1617.[100] Neile cultivated his contacts with common and civil lawyers alike. The attorney-general Sir Henry Hobart was made one of the Abbey's legal counsel in 1609.[101] When a new joint steward was required in May 1610, Sir James Whitelocke won the post 'by the favour and friendship of Doctor Richard Neel'; this in spite of Whitelocke's speeches against impositions in parliament that year.[102]

An intriguing case of patronage relates to the famous scholar Edward Topsell. In September 1606 this man presumed to dedicate *The Historie of Adam* to Neile 'because you love the Church and every divine thing'.[103] Most of this orthodox theological work had been written by Henry Holland, vicar of St Bride's, Fleet Street, a parish in the Abbey's gift. Holland had died in 1603, and Topsell, curate of St Botolph's, Aldersgate (another Westminster living) completed the book. With due deference to his clerical superior, he dedicated the work to Neile, but the short preface reveals little knowledge of the dean. Yet within a year Topsell had produced another work of his own, which he once again dedicated to Neile. It was the comprehensive *Historie of Foure-footed Beastes*, the work for which he is best known. The dedication was longer and more fulsome than before; now Topsell praised Neile as 'a famous preacher', referred to practical matters concerning his wages, and signed off as 'your chaplain'.[104] It is not clear whether this was simply a figure of speech, but Neile does seem to have given Topsell material support: when the lease of St Botolph's was renegotiated in May 1607 Topsell's income was more than doubled.[105] Topsell's next book, *The Historie of Serpents*, was dedicated to Neile in 1608, and there was no talk of poverty now.[106] Sadly, we know nothing more about this relationship. We do not know if Neile was genuinely interested in Topsell's zoological work, or whether he simply patronized him on account of his Westminster connections. This is tantalizing when one remembers that Neile's son Paul became a founder member of the Royal Society, and his grandson became a distinguished mathematician.[107]

[100] *Ibid.*, 227. Foster, 'Neile' (thesis), 62–3.

[101] *Acts 1543–1609*, no. 545.

[102] Liber Famelicus *of Sir James Whitelocke, a Judge of the Court of King's Bench in the reigns of James I and Charles I*, ed. J. Bruce (Camden Soc. lxx, 1858), 19.

[103] H. Holland, *The Historie of Adam* (1606; STC 13587), sig. ¶ 2.

[104] E. Topsell, *The Historie of Foure-Footed Beastes* (1607; STC 24123), sig. [B3].

[105] WAM Book 7, f. 1.

[106] E. Topsell, *The Historie of Serpents; or, the Second Book of Living Creatures* (1608; STC 24124).

[107] Sir Harold Hartley, *The Royal Society. Its Origins and Founders* (1960), 65. DNB,

Neile could exercise influence, but had little real say over the appointment of canons to what was, after all, a royal peculiar. But, as already noted, he does seem to have been able to assist one or two figures like William Laud and his own half-brother Robert Newell in gaining reversions to canonries. During his short tenure of office few of the livings in the Abbey's patronage fell vacant, but here Neile's influence can perhaps be more clearly discerned. A fellow royal chaplain, John Aglionby, principal of St Edmund Hall, Oxford, and one of those who worked on the king's new Bible, was granted the rectory of Islip in May 1608.[108] When he died in 1610 the living went to Newell.[109] When the rectory of South Benfleet fell vacant in May 1609 Neile granted the living to his old Cambridge tutor, William Bayley, having already tried unsuccessfully to give that man Sawbridgeworth in 1606.[110]

Neile was occasionally called upon to conduct special services at the Abbey. The state visit of the king of Denmark has already been noted, and it was probably on that occasion that Neile received a ring which he valued highly when making his will.[111] No doubt Neile conducted the funerals of the Princesses Sophia and Mary in 1606 and 1607.[112] Nor did such special work cease on his departure from Westminster, for it was to Neile that King James turned when he wanted the body of his mother, Mary, queen of Scots, transported from Peterborough Cathedral for reburial with full honours at Westminster in 1612.[113] In the regular round of preaching the dean of Westminster was traditionally given the Good Friday court sermon; thanks to the work of Peter

---

'Neile, William (1637–1670)'. For more on Topsell, a man of 'very little originality', see C.E. Raven, *English Naturalists from Neckham to Ray* (Cambridge 1947), 218–19.

[108] *Acts 1543–1609*, no. 543 & n. 371.

[109] *Acts 1609–1642*, no. 4 & n. 23.

[110] *Acts 1543–1609*, nos 538 & n. 272, 545 & n. 415.

[111] Borthwick Institute of Historical Research, York, Reg. 32, f. 4v. King Christian gave a large number of gifts to the royal household, probably the occasion on which Neile received his treasured ring: John Pory to Sir Robert Cotton, 12 August 1606, reproduced in W.S. Powell, *John Pory, 1572–1636* (Chapel Hill, N.C. 1977), microfiche supp., 7. For the visit to the Abbey see above p. 192.

[112] Stanley, *Historical Memorials*, 156 (where the princesses are wrongly said to have died in the same year, 1607). Cf. *HBC*, 40, and *Burke's Guide to the Royal Family* (1973), 207 (which differ as to the month, though not the day and year, of Princess Mary's death). Princess Sophia's burial cost the dean and chapter £1 6s 4d: WAM 33659, f. 6v.

[113] Prior's Kitchen, Durham, Hunter MS 44, item 17, p. 5. See J. Woodward, *The Theatre of Death. The Ritual Management of Royal Funerals in Renaissance England, 1570–1625* (Woodbridge 1997), 137–40, where it is noted that Neile's dual role as dean of Westminster and clerk of the closet gave him general responsibility for this occasion; reference to 'the Chapel Royal in Westminster Abbey' (p. 139) is erroneous – which extra information I owe to Charles Knighton.

McCullough we can now confirm Neile's own testimony that he preached frequently at court, but we have no evidence that he ever preached at St Paul's (as he also recalls that he regularly did), and none of his sermons survives in print.[114]

As dean of Westminster Neile had many civil responsibilities. Westminster Gatehouse was used as a prison, and on taking office Neile was involved with Lancelot Andrewes in the interrogation of the infamous Fr Henry Garnett over the Gunpowder Plot.[115] Such affairs no doubt increased Neile's regular contact with his patron, Salisbury, to whom the chapter granted a new patent as high steward of Westminster in December 1607.[116] Salisbury had succeeded his father in this post in 1598, and though the renewed appointment was obviously a formality, it confirmed the link between Neile and the Cecils, and entailed a range of contacts on quite mundane matters of local government. On one occasion Neile tactfully informed Cecil that he had given a ruling against a dead body being exhumed in a suspected murder case, bearing in mind the risks of infection.[117] On another occasion certain abuses of justice relating to one Edmond Keene, whose goods had been taken illegally in a debt case, were referred to Neile by Cecil.[118] And it is clear that Neile's tough stance in relation to criminals and nonconformists was already evident when dean, for one sad story records that he suffered the 'heavenly saint' Randall Bate to rot to death in Westminster Gatehouse, despite earnest solicitations from the doctors.[119]

In this approach, as in all things, Neile no doubt had the full support of Salisbury. Neile had worked closely with the famous civil lawyer John Cowell in conducting what amounted to a visitation of Cambridge for Cecil in 1604–5, in support of Bancroft's subscription campaign.[120] Heads as distinguished as Laurence Chaderton of Emmanuel wrote to assure Neile that they had 'begun to reduce our College to the statutes of the University, and to the order of other colleges' in December 1604.[121] Cecil wrote later to congratulate Cowell on making 'our famous university so clear of any inconformity', and Neile was left in

---

[114] P.E. McCullough, *Sermons at Court. Politics and Religion in Elizabethan and Jacobean Preaching* (Cambridge 1998), 148–9.

[115] *The Works of Lancelot Andrewes*, ed. J.P. Wilson and J. Bliss (Oxford 1851–4), ix, 9.

[116] *Acts 1543–1609*, no. 541. For the high stewardship and the Cecils see J.F. Merritt, above, pp. 155–8.

[117] HMC, *Salisbury MSS*, xix, 94–5 (Neile to Salisbury, 14 April 1607).

[118] *Ibid.*, 513.

[119] B. Brook, *The Lives of the Puritans* (1813), ii, 234–5.

[120] Croft, 'Religion of Robert Cecil', 778.

[121] HMC, *Salisbury MSS*, xvi, 381 (Chaderton to Neile, 12 December 1604).

charge of enforcing further orders with the sweetener of presiding over talks to improve the career prospects of the suitably newly reformed Cambridge graduates.[122] In Pauline Croft's opinion, the impressive programme of refurbishment which Neile embarked upon as soon as he became dean 'could not have been carried out without Salisbury's approval'. In her view, Cecil should be seen as one of the critical bonds shared by Arminians *avant la lettre* like Harsnett, Neile, Barlow and Andrewes. Moreover, the new Cecil family chapel built for Hatfield House reveals close similarities to the style of worship being promoted by Neile at Westminster.[123]

Further afield, Neile exercised manorial rights in the name of the Abbey. College lands were scattered throughout England, and Neile seems to have been diligent in visiting manors to hold courts, usually in the summer months, when bishops also tended to hold their visitations. He always added a personal touch to these visits, usually through gifts to his servants and the poor. In 1607 he spent two months touring the western lands and the midlands at a cost of £80, 'of which myself paid of mine own purse £46 and the College £40'.[124] But Neile clearly loved the life in London, and these visits – as indeed his later commitments to Rochester diocese – were never allowed to take up more than a few months of the year. Certainly there is no evidence that he ever visited his more far-flung livings in Chichester diocese during his time as dean of Westminster. It is also possible that some of his trips to the midlands were timed to coincide with royal progresses or to take in visits to Hatfield.

As Neile was the first married dean of Westminster for more than fifty years, it is sad that we know so little about his wife. It is with Neile's arrival at Westminster that we learn that Neile was married, for the Dean's house was altered to make provision for Mrs Neile.[125] She was Dorothy Dacre, daughter of Christopher Dacre and Alice Knyvet of Lanercost, Cumberland. Through the Knyvets she was a cousin of Catherine, Countess of Suffolk, a matter alluded to in material relating to the Essex marriage annulment case of 1613.[126] She thus provides one

---

[122] CUL, MS Mm.1.40, p. 383 (Cranborne, as chancellor, to Cowell, vice-chancellor, n.d. but before May 1605 when Cranborne advanced to earldom of Salisbury).

[123] Croft, 'Religion of Robert Cecil', 792.

[124] WAM Book 7, f. 3v.

[125] See above, p. 190.

[126] *A Complete Collection of State Trials*, ed. W. Cobbett (1809), ii, 806. We have only recently established the name Dacre through an inquisition *post mortem* of her brother Henry, dated 15 January 1624, that refers to an annuity given to her on 28 September 1602, and the fact that she was now the wife of the Bishop of Durham: PRO, C 142/399, no. 148. For this eagle-eyed identification I am indebted to Dr Henry

explanation for the links that Neile developed with the Howard faction on the death of Salisbury in 1612. An uncle, Thomas, first Lord Knyvet became the dean and chapter's tenant at the Peacock, King Street, Westminster by 1610, and so one of Neile's neighbours.[127] These families were obviously friends, for the deaths of Sir Thomas and his wife in 1622 were recorded in William Neile's diary.[128]

We have no evidence whatsoever of the date and venue of the wedding. From the absence of comment in William Neile's diary, it probably took place before that was begun in 1593. That Dorothy Neile played a big part in providing hospitality for Richard's friends and chaplains can be attested to by the acknowledgements she received in a range of wills. John Buckeridge left her a bed. Augustine Lindsell wrote appreciatively of her, and Richard Butler left her a ring.[129] On the Neiles' departure from Westminster in 1610 the chapter promised to bury Neile himself, if he so wished, free of all charges in the Abbey north porch, together with his wife and mother.[130] Richard and Dorothy were also provided with a key and full use of a pew behind the pulpit to guarantee them access to all services during their lives – apparently quite a treasured gift in the overcrowded churches of Westminster.[131] In the event, Richard was buried in York Minster; Dorothy and their only son, Sir Paul Neile (born in 1613), were both buried in St Benet Fink, London – Dorothy in 1647 and Paul in 1686.[132]

Neile might have stayed longer at Westminster had it not been for Bancroft's failing health in 1610. It was first rumoured that he might move to Lichfield when Overton died in April 1609;[133] such rumours surfaced again early in 1610 on the announcement that George Abbot was moving to London.[134] Neile was understandably reluctant to leave the capital, court and the king. He was also being asked to give up a range of livings with a combined income in the excess of the paltry

---

Summerson. It is now tempting to suggest that the annuity was a wedding present, for in 1602 Neile was still a relatively unknown clergyman with few prospects.

[127] *Acts 1543–1609*, no. 533 & n. 244; *1609–42*, no. 5 & n. 47.

[128] Prior's Kitchen, Durham, Hunter MS 44, item 17, p. 13.

[129] Buckeridge: PRO, PROB 11/160, f. 17v; Lindsell: PRO, PROB 11/166, f. 365; Butler: PRO, SP 14/70, no. 66 (*CSPD 1611–18*, 147).

[130] WAM Reg. X, f. 263v. *Acts 1609–42*, no. 5.

[131] WAM Reg. X, f. 328. Cf. J.F. Merritt, 'The social context of the parish church in early modern Westminster', *Urban History Yearbook* (1991), 25–6.

[132] Guildhall MS 4097, f. 132 (burial of the archbishop of York's wife in St Benet Fink, 3 May 1647); MS 4098, p. 24 (burial of Sir Paul Neile there, 9 Feb. 1686).

[133] S. Clarke, *A General Martyrologie* (1660), 61.

[134] See below p. 205. A *congé d'élire* was actually drawn up for the move: HMC, *Salisbury MSS*, xxi, 197.

figure offered by Lichfield and Coventry.[135] Neile does not seem to have seen the move as promotion, and indeed sought compensation if it should ever come about. William Easdall was dispatched to produce a report on the state of the proffered diocese.[136] It was eventually a politically astute move, for what became apparent during 1610 was that Bancroft was dying, and Cecil may have fallen slightly from court favour after failure to deliver the 'Great Contract' in parliament.

At the end of January 1610 John Chamberlain informed Dudley Carleton that 'the bishop of Rochester shold go to Lichfeild, but they say he will not remove unles he may retaine Rochester or Westminster'.[137] In the event this did not occur, but Neile struck a reasonably good bargain in the circumstances. Neile's 'promotion' at the close of 1610 bears all the hallmarks of a last effort by the old Bancroft/Cecil alliance to preserve the power of a group of like-minded clerics in the church in the face of growing opposition and the king's interest in making Abbot the compromise archbishop of Canterbury. When Neile was eventually translated, his friends John Buckeridge and George Montaigne were nominated for Rochester and Westminster respectively. Neile was allowed to pass his Chichester treasurership to Robert Newell, while Buckeridge's promotion paved the way for a controversial – and successful – campaign to gain the election of William Laud as president of St John's College, Oxford, in his stead.[138]

It is a measure of Neile's influence with the king that not only were these factional advances approved, but Neile's financial affairs were also taken into account. On 26 November 1610 Neile was issued with a grant by the dean and chapter of Canterbury, acting clearly on the wishes of the dead archbishop. The grant recognized that the revenues from Lichfield and Coventry were small, and thus ordered:

> that you may retain Southflete Rectory in Rochester diocese and Ferlis prebend and the place of a residentiary in Chichester Cathedral in commendam as long as you hold the Bishopric.

---

[135] Lichfield and Coventry was worth £559 17s 3½d, but Neile eventually paid only £503 17s 6d in first fruits and tenths: PRO, SO 3/5, March 1611. J. Bacon, *Liber Regis* (1786), 850, records the value of Rochester as £358 4s 9½d, which with Westminster rated at £232 10s (exclusive of dividends) would have made a combined income of c. £590 *per annum*.

[136] A survey was carried out by Easdall in June 1610: Lichfield Joint Record Office, CC 124100, 16–17 (a reference I owe to the kindness of Rosemary O'Day).

[137] PRO, SP 14/52, no. 23 (*CSPD 1603–10*, 583; *Letters of Chamberlain*, i, 295–7, quotation from p. 296; Chamberlain to Dudley Carleton, 23 January 1610).

[138] Heylyn, *Cyprianus*, 60–1. For Abbot's appointment in context see K.C. Fincham and P.G. Lake, 'The ecclesiastical policies of James I and Charles I', in Fincham, *Early Stuart Church*, 23–49.

He was further permitted to exchange these livings and acquire others to the value of 200 marks, so long as 'the cure of souls in them is not neglected'.[139] Royal confirmation of this grant appears to have been a formality, and the scale of these concessions was such that Neile was an obvious candidate to choose when the practice of holding livings *in commendam* was exposed to legal discussion in a *cause célèbre* in 1613.[140]

So Neile's tenure as dean of Westminster came to an end just as he was beginning to make a real impact on the Abbey. And not only the Abbey, for Neile's devotion to his city of Westminster was such that he even left his mark on the streets of the area, recording with pride that the chapter paid out over £80 for paving around the school and Abbey precincts, and a similar sum in 1610 for work on Drury Lane and St Martin's Lane.[141] His episcopal career was safely launched, but the fate of the Church of England still hung in the balance with Abbot's appointment as archbishop of Canterbury in 1611. The Westminster experiment provides clear evidence of Neile's ecclesiological preferences, but it was by no means clear in 1611 that these would eventually come to shape views prevailing in the whole Church, as they did in the 1630s. Westminster reveals Neile to be a canny political operator with a sound, practical administrative bent, a man who was prepared to drive policies forward and carry colleagues with him. It also shows just how dependent Neile was upon first, noble patronage, and then the support of the crown. Neile was extremely fortunate in being the first local boy to become dean of Westminster; in turn, it looks as if he more than paid his debts to the local community, Abbey and school.[142]

---

[139] Peckham, *Chichester Chapter Acts 1545–1642*, 217–18.

[140] Bodl. MS Eng. Hist. C. 494.

[141] WAM Book 7, ff. 5–5v.

[142] Since this article was written, Diarmaid MacCulloch has drawn attention to the importance of Westminster as a 'showcase of liturgical and choral excellence': *Tudor Church Militant*, 210–13. He has gone so far as to suggest that we should think of a 'Westminster Movement', an intriguing thought that casts this article in a new light.

CHAPTER EIGHT

Canon Fire: Peter Heylyn at Westminster

Anthony Milton

There can be few Anglican churchmen who have had their monuments in Westminster Abbey deliberately defaced.[1] Peter Heylyn, however, was no ordinary churchman, and both before and after his death he proved himself remarkably adept at making enemies. His historical writings – violent in their attacks on Calvinism and puritanism – stirred up remarkable outrage among some of his readers. Even the proverbially moderate Richard Baxter declared that people like Heylyn 'speak of blood with pleasure, and [are] as thirsty after more or as designing to make Dissenters odious'.[2] Samuel Coleridge could only exclaim: 'Who being a Christian can avoid feeling the worldly harsh unspiritual Spirit of this bitter Factionary! I scarcely know a more unamiable Churchman, as a Writer, than Dr Heylyn.'[3]

Heylyn the historian has always had his outraged detractors, then. But what of the man himself? For all his other activities, Heylyn is linked inextricably with Westminster Abbey. The position of sub-dean was the highest ecclesiastical post he was ever to attain. Nevertheless, from this base, Heylyn was to play a controversial role as a polemicist, justifying the policies of the Personal Rule. In the Abbey itself, he is most notorious for his cat-and-dog squabbles with its dean, John Williams, over the best part of a decade, culminating in a public clash in time of divine service in late 1640. But how should we understand Heylyn's career at Westminster and his feud with Williams? Was this simply a personal clash between two ambitious men? Or did it represent a confrontation between two different styles of churchmanship?

---

[1] *A Survey of the Cities of London and Westminster* (6th edn, 1754), ii, 614. It is here reported that Heylyn's monument 'hath had Violence offered it by rude Hands'.

[2] R. Baxter, *Church-History of the Government of Bishops and Their Councils Abbreviated* (1680), sig. a4r.

[3] Coleridge, *Collected Works*, xii, ed. G. Whalley (Princeton 1984), 1097 (Coleridge's marginalia in Heylyn's *Cyprianus*: I am grateful to Judith Maltby for this reference). For other critiques of Heylyn's works, see e.g. Bodl. MS Add. C. 304b ff. 74–9; J.A.I. Champion, *The Pillars of Priestcraft Shaken* (Cambridge 1992), 73–7.

Was Heylyn simply the pawn of other forces? Or was he manipulating them to serve his own ends? And who in the end emerged as the victor?

For all of the notoriety that he commanded both before and after his death, and his prolific output of printed works (well over thirty items in total, several of which went through numerous editions) Peter Heylyn remains one of the more shadowy figures of the seventeenth century. Despite two rather hagiographical accounts of his life published in the early 1680s, he has never received a full biographical study.[4] Nevertheless, current research suggests that he is a richer, more complex figure than might have been assumed. To begin with, he was not a natural churchman. Born in 1600, Heylyn's writing in his early years was more concerned with geography and poetry rather than divinity. His early contacts were not necessarily among the budding high-church party, and the ideas that he expressed in print gave little hint of Laudian convictions (and indeed in some respects ran counter to them).[5] Nevertheless, by the end of the 1620s he was clearly seeking the patronage of the king, and most particularly that of the rising Bishop Laud. To Laud he sent a report on church matters in the Channel Islands in April 1629, advising urgent intervention by the government.[6] In January of the following year he was sworn a full royal chaplain in ordinary.[7] Just six months later (and one month prior to his first stint as household chaplain) Heylyn pushed himself to Laud's attention once more by preaching an extraordinary sermon at the Oxford Act in which he mounted the first attack on the puritan feoffees for impropriations. It was later noted that a copy of this notorious sermon had been presented to Laud 'in writing bound up in Velome, who thus endorsed it with his own hand *S. Mat. 13.25. Master Peter Heylin*; and reserved it as a monument in his

---

[4] George Vernon, *The Life of the Learned and Reverend Dr. Peter Heylyn* (1682). John Barnard, *Theologo-Historicus, or the True Life of the Most Reverend Divine and Excellent Historian, Peter Heylyn D.D.* (1683). Barnard's work was republished and edited by J.C. Robertson in his edition of Heylyn's *Ecclesia Restaurata* (Cambridge 1849), i, pp. xxix–ccxii. This is the edition that I have used in this article. On the complicated relationship between the Vernon and Barnard biographies, see *ibid.* i, pp. xxi–xxviii.

[5] These claims are documented in my forthcoming biographical study of Heylyn, provisionally entitled *The Voice of Laudianism: the Career and Writings of Peter Heylyn (1600–1662)*.

[6] Printed in Heylyn, *A Survey of the Estate of France* (1656), 281–422.

[7] PRO, LC 5/132, pp. 165, 166. Bodl. MS Rawlinson D.353, f. 93. In 1638 Heylyn's month of waiting shifted to January (LC 5/134, p. 204). Heylyn had been appointed a supernumerary royal chaplain in February 1629, just before his departure with the earl of Danby to the Channel Islands (and therefore conceivably by Danby's means): LC 5/132, p. 87.

study'.[8] Heylyn's alliance with Laud, and his consequent access to the king's patronage, was sealed six months later, when Laud arranged for Heylyn's obsequious *History of St George* – a flattering act of obeisance towards the Order of the Garter – to be presented to Charles I.[9] Heylyn's appointment to a stall in the Abbey later in the same year (1631) was thus a natural step on the patronage ladder for the rising churchman.

But Heylyn's appointment was not simply another living to add to his portfolio, gratifying though it undoubtedly was for him. It was also transparently an attempt to set an unscrupulous opponent in the heart of the dean's powerbase. Dean Williams's relations with the crown had been deteriorating for some years. After being dismissed from his post of lord keeper in 1625 he had been accused of betraying privy council secrets in 1627 and a charge against him had been pending in star chamber since 1628, accompanied by attempts to force him to give up the deanery. The appointment of Heylyn was all the more apt a move on the king's part as Williams (in his capacity as bishop of Lincoln) had only just refused to institute Heylyn to the living of Hemingford Abbots in Huntingdonshire, to which the King had sought to present him.[10]

Heylyn had good qualifications for amassing 'evidence' against those unpopular with the government. He was engaged in a long-running feud with the regius professor of divinity at Oxford, John Prideaux, and would soon play a prominent role in assembling the materials against William Prynne's attack on stage plays and players, *Histriomastix*. Prynne would complain in 1634 of how Heylyn had acted as Laud's agent in maliciously selecting 'scatterd fragments or dimidiated sentences' from the book, 'annexing such horrid, seditious, disloyall, false glosses, applicacions, construccions and inferences ... as none but heads intoxicated with malice, disloyalty, and private revenge could ever fancye'.[11]

Heylyn was, then, a formidable and dangerous opponent for Williams to have in the chapter, and the new canon soon got to work in building a case against the dean, which would help the crown to threaten his tenure of the deanery. Heylyn attended his first chapter meeting on 22 December 1631 yet by July 1632 he was already offering information to

---

[8] W. Prynne, *Canterburies Doome* (1646), 386. The sermon survives in Magdalen College, Oxford, MS 312.

[9] Heylyn, *Memorial of Bishop Waynflete*, ed. J.R. Bloxam (Caxton Soc. 1851), p. xx.

[10] Heylyn, *Ecclesia Restaurata*, i, pp. lxxvii–lxxix. See also Knighton, below, p. 244. The royal mandate for Heylyn's installation as canon of Westminster, dated 4 November 1631, was endorsed by Williams 7 November, authorizing any of the other canons to execute it: WAM 53333 (I am grateful to Dr Knighton for this reference).

[11] Heylyn, *Cyprianus*, 230–1. *Documents relating to the proceedings against William Prynne in 1634 and 1637*, ed. S.R. Gardiner (Camden Soc. new ser. xviii, 1877), 32 (cf. p. 36). For the list of errors accumulated by Heylyn, see *ibid.*, 3–13.

the secretary of state, Sir John Coke, against Williams that he had wheedled out of the civil lawyer Dr William Spicer.[12] This first move against Williams involved a series of remarks that Spicer was alleged to have made in a conversation with Heylyn at his house in Westminster on 22 July 1632. According to Heylyn, Spicer reported a number of remarks delivered in his hearing by Williams during and after dinner at Buckden around the 12th of the same month. Finding Spicer 'somewhat contractable in certaine propositions made unto him' (presumably in business concerning the library), Williams said to Spicer 'with greate scorne and laughter ... that he would crosse him out of the Catalogue of his freinds as the king had crossed him (the saide Bishop) out of the list of his privie Counsell'.[13] Williams was also said to have remarked during the same meal 'that the Lords of the Starre-chamber could leape a statute when they pleased'. Potentially more incriminating, however, were the remarks made afterwards to Spicer by the bishop in private. Williams was alleged to have said:

> that howsoever he had had some troubles in the Courte, and that the king was made against him: yet he had made himselfe so strong, and stood so firmely that he did not care for any of them all. And as for those which had so made the king against him, they had donne the king none of the best offices: for should there come a parliament (which newes, saide he, yf thou hadst brought mee, thou hadst bene a wellcome man indeed) then should such things be called to an account, that both the king and they should have cause to repent of medling with him: or to that effect.

Here were prophetic words indeed, and ones which were not entirely implausible for Williams to have uttered. Heylyn sought to make the most of them. He gave a sworn account of Spicer's alleged words to Secretary Coke on the 26 July, stressing (as he put it) that Williams's reported speech included 'some passages which to mee did seeme to tend to the dishonour of his majestie, and to the preiudice of his affaires, yf time should serve'. 'Which,' Heylyn added sanctimoniously, 'being a sworne servant of his majestie, I doe conceive all other obligations sett aside, that I am bound both by oathe & duetie to make knowne unto him'.

That Heylyn was acting alone, rather than in league with Spicer, is made apparent by the account which Spicer himself was then required to provide. Spicer went out of his way to minimize the damage. He

---

[12] WAM Chapter Act Book II, f. 52v (*Acts 1609–42*, no. 63). PRO, SP 16/221, nos 41, 42 (*CSPD 1631–3*, 391–2).

[13] PRO, SP 16/221, no. 41. Williams was presumably punning here by alluding to the catalogue of the Abbey library to which Spicer had donated books: see Knighton below, pp. 243–4.

admitted that Williams had said that the king had discharged him from the privy council, and that the lords of the star chamber leapt over statutes, but said that Williams had specified that he would call 'Sir John Lambe and others into question' if there were a parliament (with no word of the king). Moreover, where Heylyn had claimed that the speeches were made in a 'scornefull manner', Spicer averred that they 'were spoken in ordinary passage with a great deale of modestye as I then and yet conceived it without any taunting scoffing or repining etc.'[14] Spicer also failed to mention the alleged remarks about a parliament threatening the king when repeating Williams's words in the hearing of another of the canons, Dr Lewis Wemys, on 25 July. Despite prompting by Heylyn, Spicer allegedly 'paused, and answered, that he durst not tell all the passages which were betweene them'.[15]

Spicer's coyness undoubtedly helped to ensure that these charges progressed no further. Nevertheless, Williams was left in little doubt of Heylyn's intentions. Williams had allegedly informed Spicer that he had told him things in private conference which he dared not repeat before Heylyn, 'nor held it safe for him [Spicer] so to doe.'[16] Williams can hardly have been surprised when he was confronted by the canons' articles against him two years later, and can have had no doubts as to their true author. Williams's chaplain and later biographer John Hacket was certainly convinced that Heylyn was behind these charges, 'whom I have heard call'd General Wrangler, the Challenger that undertakes all Modern Writers, of as much ingenuity as Tertullian's Hermogenes, *Maledicere singulis officium bonae conscientiae judicat*'.[17] Certainly, it was Heylyn who provided a Latin translation of the articles, and who was chosen as advocate by the canons at the hearing of the commission into the grievances in February 1636. It was later reported that, after Heylyn had presented his speech concerning the canons' right to sit in the 'great pew', after a long pause Williams made the brief but telling (and indeed prophetic) response: 'If your Lordships will hear that young fellow prate, he will presently persuade you that I am no Dean of Westminster.'[18] While the articles failed, Heylyn was not a loser thereby. Hacket's remark that 'every one of his Adversaries had a Recompence given them, like a Coral to rub their Gums, and make their Teeth come the faster' is not far from the truth.[19] Heylyn's teeth were certainly soon in action again.

---

[14] PRO, SP 16/221, no. 42.

[15] PRO, SP 16/221, no. 41.

[16] *Ibid.*

[17] Hacket, *Scrin. Res.* ii, 91. For Hacket's account of the articles, see *ibid.*, 91–3.

[18] Vernon, *Life of Heylyn*, 80.

[19] Hacket, *Scrin. Res.* ii, 92. For Williams's response see below, pp. 252–4.

The next stage of Heylyn's campaign against Williams (which followed only months after the failure of the articles) involved the adversaries stepping outside the Abbey, and into the arena of a pamphlet controversy. Here, the work which prompted Heylyn's attack was an anonymous letter which Williams had written to the vicar of Grantham in 1627 concerning the position of the altar in his church. Called upon to mediate in a conflict between vicar and alderman over the former's decision to place the communion table at the east end of the chancel (and his threat to build an altar of stone there), Williams stayed up most of the night to produce a letter that proposed a solution. Rather than the communion table being an altar fixed at the east end of the church, Williams resolved that the table should not be called an 'altar', should not stand 'along close by the wall' at any time, and that it should not be fixed in the higher part of the chancel, but (as the canons directed) should at the time of communion be moved to the place where the minister would be most conveniently heard by the congregation (presumably in the body of the church or chancel).[20]

Even if the origins of Williams's 'Letter to the Vicar of Grantham' were particular and pastoral, the 'Letter' soon assumed a more important public role. The growth of the more elaborate ceremonialism of the so-called 'Durham House Group', with their penchant for east-end altars, and the development of the altar policy by the Laudian bishops in the 1630s meant that Williams's 'Letter' was seized upon as providing a detailed defence for those opposing these innovations. The 'Letter' was reportedly discussed in the House of Commons (presumably in the debate in the 1629 session on Bishop Neile's innovations concerning the altar, in which the actions of the vicar of Grantham were mentioned). Allegedly John Prideaux, the anti-Laudian regius professor in Oxford, spoke publicly of the 'Letter' in reverential tones, and it was also fully discussed at the St Gregory's hearing in 1633, where the east-end altar policy was debated in the presence of the king.[21] Its fame resulted in the

---

[20] [J. Williams], *The Holy Table, Name and Thing* (1637), 5–20. I have throughout used the edition (*STC* 25725.6) printed in facsimile in *The Work of Archbishop Williams*, ed. B. Williams (Abingdon 1979).

[21] Williams, *Holy Table*, 5, 58; *Commons Debates for 1629*, ed. W. Notestein and F.H. Relf (Minneapolis 1921), 52 (cf. p. 133). Hacket, *Scrin. Res.* ii, 102. Prideaux's published Act lectures (*Viginti-duae Lectiones de totidem religionis capitibus*: Oxford 1648) do not refer to Williams's 'Letter' directly. Nevertheless, his 1631 lecture 'De Missae Sacrificio' does make a number of points very similar to those made in the 'Letter', especially in the interpretation of Hebrews 13:10 (compare *Lectiones*, i, 252 with Williams, *Holy Table*, 17). Prideaux was quite capable of using these lectures to make implicit attacks on Laudian policy: see A. Milton, *Catholic and Reformed* (Cambridge 1995), 116–17.

rapid spread of manuscript copies, although the 'Letter' itself was not printed.

By 1636 the Laudian altar policy was being implemented throughout the country, and it was clearly considered desirable that the 'Letter' receive an effective refutation.[22] This was a task which almost inevitably fell to Heylyn. Heylyn had just distinguished himself by writing a detailed defence of the government's anti-sabbatarian policy, his *The History of the Sabbath* (dedicated to the king and partly derived from court sermons). In this work Heylyn had shown himself ready to re-write the history of the English church in order to defend government policy.[23] But this was the first time that he had been involved in a full pamphlet debate with another divine. A bizarre form of shadow-boxing was pursued by the two principals. Heylyn published his attack on the 'Letter' – entitled *A Coale from the Altar* – under the motto of 'a judicious and learned Divine' (presumably under instructions). Williams followed suit by publishing his reply – *The Holy Table Name and Thing* – anonymously, claiming to be merely 'a Minister in Lincolnshire' (although the book did bear Williams's imprimatur, in which he declared the book, written by 'some Minister of this Diocese', to be 'most Orthodox in Doctrine, and consonant in Discipline, to the Church of England'). Heylyn finally revealed his own identity in his reply to *The Holy Table* – entitled *Antidotum Lincolniense* – which was published with the full panoply of authorial name and dedication to the king in 1637. Williams never identified his adversary in the *Holy Table*, although he ironically dubbed him 'Dr Coale' and pretended that he was responding to 'D. Coal, a judicious Divine of Q. Maries dayes', thereby mischievously implying that Heylyn was Henry Cole, the zealous Roman Catholic provost of Eton (and canon of Westminster), who had preached before the burning of Thomas Cranmer.[24] Similarly, Heylyn never attacked Williams by name, even claiming of the 'Letter' that 'I am confident it can be none of his who is pretended for the author'.[25]

That being said, it would be naive to suggest, as one recent historian has done, that Heylyn 'really believed this', and was genuinely unaware

---

[22] Hacket also suggested that the 'Letter' was raised by Williams's enemies at this point in order to injure his case in star chamber: *Scrin. Res.* ii, 101. Vernon claims that it was John Towers, dean of Peterborough and canon of Westminster, who engaged Heylyn to answer Williams: *Life of Heylyn*, 89–90. On the timing and nature of the altar policy see K.C. Fincham, 'The restoration of altars in the 1630s', *HJ*, xliv (2001), 919–40.

[23] Heylyn, *The History of the Sabbath* (1636), epistle dedicatory. K. Parker, *The English Sabbath* (1988), 204–6.

[24] MacCulloch, *Cranmer*, 600–1.

[25] Heylyn, *A Coale from the Altar* (3rd impr. 1637), 3.

that Williams was the author of both 'Letter' and tract.[26] The true authorship of the works in the dispute seems to have been a fairly open secret. Heylyn's authorship of the *Coale* was public knowledge by September 1636 (almost a year before he openly acknowledged it in the *Antidotum*) and Williams was commonly said to have avowed his authorship of the 'Letter', while Laud was commenting as early as 5 April 1637 that 'the world says' (and he agreed) that Williams was the author of the *Holy Table*.[27] Both authors also dropped heavy hints that they knew each other's identity.[28] If Heylyn really did think that Williams's work was by the extreme puritan John Cotton, then he was the only person in England who seemed to be under that impression. His readiness to level accusations against Williams on the basis of the least whisper of wrong-doing makes it simply implausible that Heylyn would not have sought to father the 'Letter' and subsequent treatise on Williams. Rather, Heylyn was pursuing other polemical objectives. Ingenuously granting the anonymity of the tract allowed Heylyn to adopt a combative tone not otherwise appropriate for dealing with his ecclesiastical superior. It also permitted him to imply that Williams's views were so extreme that they *must* be those of a separatist. Heylyn could be confident that the public would not assume that Williams was therefore not the author (he was well understood everywhere already to be the author), but that instead they would detect the apparently puritan potential in the position that Williams was adopting.

Adopting this polemical tactic made it possible for Heylyn to father the most unlikely political and religious radicalism on Williams's text. While his *Coale* directly stressed at several points that the author of the

---

[26] Williams, *Work of Williams*, 93 (and comments on 'Text 2' at end [unfoliated]).

[27] John Winthrop's correspondent Robert Ryece reported in a letter of 9 September 1636 that the author of the *Coale* 'is an notable flatterer of the Courte one Dr. Heylyn': *Winthrop Papers*, iii, *1631–1637* (Massachusetts Historical Soc. 1943), 303. See also [W. Prynne], *A Quench-Coale* (1637), 187, 194; Laud, *Works*, vii, 337.

[28] Heylyn's *Coale* (pp. 20–1) digs out examples of the Marian dean of Westminster (Hugh Weston) and one or other of the Marian bishops of Lincoln calling the protestant communion tables 'oyster boords', a sally which Williams clearly understood and complained of (*Holy Table*, 98), to which Heylyn even more plainly replied 'there is (as you have now discovered him) one Bishop of Lincoln and Deane of Westminster, that calls it standing Altar-wise, by the name of Dresser': *Antidotum Lincolniense* (1637), i, 98. At one point (*ibid*. i, 77) Heylyn slips into quoting the text of the 'Letter' against the author of the *Holy Table*, implying that both works were written by the same author. Note also Williams's sneering reference to princes having their powers profaned by 'bunglers ... and Chaplains (to shew how ready they are, at the very first call, to be dealing in matters of State) ... puddling in studies they do not understand': *Holy Table*, 22–3. Heylyn was of course a royal chaplain.

'Letter' belonged to the popular puritan party,[29] the *Antidotum* made the supposed similarity of the works of the author of the *Holy Table* and those of the puritan firebrand Henry Burton its central framing device. Having provided a table at the beginning of the work comparing the two authors, and accused Williams of swapping notes with Burton, Heylyn made constant scornful allusions to 'your deere disciples', 'your brethren', 'your holy brethren', 'the brethren of your partie', and 'your Partizans'.[30] The author was ready to go on the next ship to New England, to join 'your good friend I[ohn] C[otton]'.[31] The *Holy Table* itself had been carefully timed in its publication, 'calculated like a common Almanack ... with an intent that it should generally serve for all the Puritanes of Great Brittain.'[32] Even Williams's reference to bishops as being of apostolical institution was seized on as betraying malicious and radical intent: the failure to describe them as being *iure divino* revealed that Williams had 'a good mind to betray the cause' and was ready with 'your holy brethren' to get rid of bishops.[33] Every attempt was made to link religious radicalism to political radicalism. Williams's description of the *Coale* as a 'licensed libell' was thereby an attack on the lord treasurer and star chamber who were responsible for the licensing process. 'How great a Royalist soever you pretend to be', Heylyn commented, 'you love the King well, but the Puritans better.'[34]

Such comments all served the broader policy of Laud towards his moderate, episcopalian opponents. This could take two different forms. In cases unlike that of Williams, Laud sought to co-opt these figures (even against their will), making them appear to support Laudian policies. For example, in the case of John Prideaux – the regius professor at Oxford and enemy of both Laud and Heylyn – a policy of forced co-option was employed, with Heylyn providing the means (and perhaps the inspiration). An attack made by Prideaux on extreme sabbatarianism at the Oxford Act in 1622 was seized upon and republished in the 1630s by Heylyn with his own preface so that it would seem to speak in favour of the Book of Sports.[35] Where such opponents proved intractable, however, and co-option was not possible, efforts were directed instead towards marginalizing them, and this was the policy adopted

[29] Heylyn, *Coale*, 42, 47–8, 77–8.

[30] Heylyn, *Antidotum*, i, preface, and pp. 41, 42, 86, 99; ii, 8, 11–12, 26, 28.

[31] *Ibid.* i, 3, 16 (cf. ii, 11).

[32] *Ibid.* i, 3.

[33] *Ibid.* ii, 7–8.

[34] *Ibid.* i, 2, 36.

[35] A. Milton, 'Licensing, censorship and religious orthodoxy in early Stuart England', *HJ*, xli (1998), 648.

towards Williams. In Williams's case, the 'Letter' and *Holy Table* were more obviously opposed to royal policy, and Heylyn's efforts were therefore aimed at discrediting the work. Rather than being a work that offered a moderate critique of Laudian policy from the middle-ground of English protestantism (and from a bishop at that), it was crucial that the *Holy Table* be represented as a more radical publication.

In his turn, Williams sought to maintain his claim to the middle-ground by depicting Heylyn himself as an anti-episcopalian radical. The *Coale* was, Williams claimed, 'but a libel against a Bishop', and he systematically threw Heylyn's arguments back at him. Heylyn's championing of the vicar of Grantham's actions against those of the bishop enabled Williams to compare Heylyn with John Cotton and Thomas Cartwright, and to accuse him directly of puritanism. He compared Heylyn's high-handedness to the writings of the presbyterian Cartwright, who 'from his Presse at Coventry, was wont to send abroad much of this stuff in Martin Marprelates dayes.'[36] The vicar of Grantham he shrugged off as being mentally unstable – another example of Williams's determination to use all the stock materials of conformist defenders of the status quo against dangerous radicals.[37] Just as Heylyn had used Williams's anonymity to brand him a radical puritan, so Williams returned the compliment.

Williams's chaplain, John Hacket, was the man who was ultimately caught out in these elaborate games. During a sermon given at his archidiaconal visitation of Bedfordshire in 1637, Hacket seized on the opportunity to condemn the author of the *Coale from the Altar*, 'shewing how the Coale, in a most rancorous sort, and knowing the Author, yet had most despitefully and virulently abused the Bishop; as the Jesuites dealt with K. James his booke, which they pretended not to know in their Answeres.' In suggesting that the 'Letter' had been written by John Cotton, Heylyn had written 'quite against his own conscience'. If a presbyter publicly wrote against an episcopal act and inveighed against it, declared Hacket, he was guilty of puritanism, 'though it come forth cum licentiâ' (thereby repeating Williams's complaint). Hacket concluded in emphatic manner that he knew of a case in France where a man had shot his enemy with an arrow, but had claimed falsely that it was a hunting accident: 'he pretended he tooke him to bee a wolf but he suffred as a murderer.'[38]

---

[36] Williams, *Holy Table*, 58, 70–1, 73–4, 75.

[37] E.g. Williams, *Holy Table*, 8, 59, 78. Cf. A. Walsham, '"Frantick Hacket": prophecy, sorcery, insanity and the Elizabethan puritan movement', *HJ*, xli (1998), 62–4.

[38] LPL, MS 1030, nos 58, 67 (cf. nos 65–6).

It was Hacket, however, who was the one to suffer: he found himself berated for opposing royal policy on the information of a local clergyman, Jasper Fisher. On hearing the sermon, Fisher (who had recently fallen foul of Williams) hastily penned an account of it to another of the bishop's new enemies, John Pocklington (who had himself written against Williams on the altar controversy). Pocklington swiftly informed Laud, and Hacket was eventually driven to make a humble petition to the archbishop.[39] Hacket's treatment provides clear evidence that Heylyn was writing to official orders: an attack on Heylyn's anonymous work was construed as an attack on government policy. Laud himself made a point of attacking the *Holy Table* in his speech at the censure of the puritan 'martyrs' Burton, Bastwick and Prynne. While refraining from identifying the author, Laud stressed that 'in the judgment of many learned men, which have perused this book, the author is clearly conceived to want a great deal of that learning, to which he pretends.' His main concern, though, was to emphasize that Heylyn's detection of the author's radical intentions was correct. 'For my own part, I am fully of opinion', Laud declared, that 'this book was thrust now to the press, both to countenance these libellers [Burton, Bastwick and Prynne] and, asmuch as in him lay, to fire both Church and State.'[40] There could be no clearer official endorsement of the argument of Heylyn's *Antidotum Lincolniense*.[41]

It was ecclesiastical politics, rather than different styles of churchmanship, that drove this debate forward. Williams's own style of piety was certainly not averse to Laudian styles of ceremonialism. Heylyn would later complain that Williams wrote 'both against his science and his conscience' (notably echoing the phrase used by Laud in his speech at the Censure) noting that the communion table stood altarwise in Westminster Abbey itself.[42] The *Holy Table* reported that the vicar of Grantham was ultimately satisfied by the bishop's ruling on the placing of the communion table because he perceived the bishop's position to be 'very indifferent, because he observed (as he said) the Table in his Lordships privat Chappell to be so placed [altarwise at the east end],

---

[39] *Ibid.*, nos 58–9, 65–7. On Williams's clash with Fisher a few months previously, see nos 51, 53.

[40] Laud, *Works*, vi, 63. Hacket complained that Laud made the accusations 'reading out of his Notes', implying that these 'Notes' were provided by Heylyn: *Scrin. Res.* ii, 129.

[41] Laud also approvingly sent a copy of the *Antidotum* to Viscount Wentworth: *Works*, vii, 372.

[42] Heylyn, *Observations on the History of the Reign of King Charles* (1656), 136. Heylyn here adopted the phrase used by Laud at the censure of Burton, Bastwick and Prynne: Laud, *Works*, vi, 63. Cf. Heylyn, *Antidotum*, ii, 25.

and furnished with Plate and Ornaments above any he ever had seen in this Kingdome, the Chappel Royall onely excepted.'[43] Anthony Cade, in a work dedicated to Williams, recalled the dramatic impact that the bishop's chapel at Buckden had made on him, rhapsodizing about 'the windows enriched with costly pictures of Prophets, Apostles and holy Fathers', and the chapel:

> most beautifully furnished with Seats, Windows, Altar, Bibles and other sacred books costly covered, clasped and embossed with silver, and gilt with gold; with Bason, Candlesticks, and other vessels all of bright shining silver; and with stately Organs curiously coloured, gilded and enameled... And the whole service of God therein performed with all possible reverence and devout behaviour of your own person and all the assembly.[44]

Heylyn might hope to use this evidence to convict Williams of hypocrisy and wilful contrariness, of writing 'out of a meer Spirit of Contradiction'.[45] But this was also evidence which, in the 1630s at least, could further strengthen Williams's claim to mainstream legitimacy. Where puritan opponents of Laudianism might seek to discredit Laudian innovations as popish superstition and idolatry, Williams's chosen ground was more legalistic: he denied that it was either legal or appropriate to extend east-end altars beyond private chapels (such as his own) into churches more generally. He was careful, too, to litter his work with approving quotations from the increasingly fashionable Richard Hooker, as well as the respected moderate Calvinist bishop of Durham, Thomas Morton.[46]

Williams particularly took his stance against the Laudian style of episcopal intervention. He seized upon Heylyn's reference to 'the piety of the times' and delivered a stinging attack on the coercive style of current ecclesiastical government, urging 'Moderation, not Domination' with the pithy observation that 'Bishops have ever governed their Clergie by Canon Law, and not by Canon shot'.[47] In dealing with a person as politically astute as Williams, however, it would be dangerous simply to read off a style of churchmanship from this polemical stance. His opposition to the forced imposition of the Laudian 'beauty of holiness' showed a sensitivity to the pastoral problems that such a

---

[43] Williams, *Holy Table*, 12.

[44] A. Cade, *A Sermon Necessarie for these Times* (Cambridge 1639), sig.¶ 2r–v. This is a 1634 visitation sermon, dedicated to Williams. Cade's agenda in this work is not straightforward: I hope to discuss it in more detail elsewhere.

[45] Heylyn, *Examen Historicum* (1659), 277–8.

[46] Williams, *Holy Table*, 105, 109, 118, 122, 130, 139, 155, 156–7, 196, 208, 211, 215 (Morton); 67, 69–70, 74, 85, 114, 176, 218–19 (Hooker).

[47] *Ibid.*, 65–70, 82–6, 112.

policy would engender among evangelical but conformist figures such as the town élite of Grantham. There may well have been an instinctive sympathy on Williams's part for a more pastorally engaged, sensitive approach – it would certainly have appealed to his political pragmatism. Nevertheless, Williams's remarks later in the same chapter concerning the Franciscan priest Sancta Clara make it quite clear that he was not simply seeking to provide sober advice on ecclesiastical tactics which the manuscript distribution of the 'Letter' had forced him to make public. Having primed his readers to be wary of Heylyn's references to the 'Good work now in hand' and the 'speciall inclination of these times, to a peculiar kinde of pietie', Williams slyly commented that 'I should therefore reasonably presume that this *Good work in hand*, is but the second part of Sancta Clara'.[48] Franciscus a Sancta Clara was a Franciscan priest who had in 1634 published a work which sought to propose the means whereby the Church of England's Thirty-Nine Articles could be made compatible with the decrees of the council of Trent.[49] Williams's reference to Sancta Clara here is clear evidence that, as well as chiding the approach adopted by Laud, he was manifestly seeking to question the doctrinal probity of the government, and to imply that the new policies were linked to a broader plan to reconcile the Roman and protestant churches. He may not have tossed around the epithet 'popish' as freely as Prynne or Burton, but his remarks concerning Sancta Clara amounted to very much the same thing.[50]

In this sense, Williams's determination to present himself as a moderate mainstream churchman provided a gloss on what was actually a consciously 'oppositionist' position. He can hardly have been unaware that his opposition to Laud would enable him to position himself favourably in the eyes of the next parliament, whenever that might be called. Williams's reported remarks to Spicer in 1632 make it clear that this was an active consideration of his, and certainly Laud was regularly

---

[48] *Ibid.*, 84–5. See also the reference (p. 71) to 'these judicious Divines that tamper so much in doctrine with Sancta Clara'.

[49] On Christopher Davenport, *alias* Franciscus a Sancta Clara, whose *Deus, Natura, Gratia* appeared in two editions in 1634 and 1635, see J.B. Dockery, *Christopher Davenport* (1960); R.I. Bradley, 'Christopher Davenport and the Thirty-Nine Articles', *Archiv für Reformationsgeschichte*, lii (1961), 205–28; Milton, *Catholic and Reformed*, 239, 250–1.

[50] Williams's claim in his recantation that he had not intended to make people fear that 'there were an intent or preparation to introduce the Romish religion. Or that those that are entrusted and employed therein under your sacred Majesty endeavoured the same' (Williams, *Work of Williams*, 104) needs to be read in the context of his use of Sancta Clara and comments on 'the piety of the times'.

fearful that a parliament might indeed be imminent.[51] It is certainly true that Williams's subsequent prosecution by the government made him a martyr in the eyes of many in the country. His prosecution in star chamber excited national interest. One hostile commentator had reported in October 1635 how 'the eyes of all the kingdom are set upon this cause as the determining cause betwixt Puritans and loyal subjects', with Williams regarded as the champion of the puritans 'and the only man that dare oppose his Majesty's government'. The son of the puritan minister Robert Catlin recalled how the news of Williams's censure in July 1637 was brought to his father on his deathbed. Hearing of this treatment of Williams, 'reputed at that Time a very good Man, whom my Father knew to be a great Freind to the Good ministers in his Diocese and a great enimy to the setting the Tables Altarwise', Robert Catlin exclaimed 'Alas poore England, thou hast now seen thy best daies; I that am 4 score yeares old, and I have in al my time seene no alteration in Religion, nor any foreign Enemy setting foot in England, nor any Ciuil wars, amongst ourselves, do now forsee euil daies a comming.'[52] There was no shortage of venerable divines later reported to have forecast the Civil War, but nevertheless the importance which puritan ministers attached to Williams's trial is doubtless accurate. Public opinion was of course notoriously fickle and easily misled, as revealed in the case of the 'popish' Bishop Godfrey Goodman, who won popular acclaim when he was imprisoned for initially refusing to subscribe to the Laudian canons of 1640, although Laud later claimed that Goodman's objections were only to the anti-catholic aspects of the canons.[53]

Even in a period notorious for the venomous style of its polemic, Heylyn's exchanges with his dean exhibit remarkable reserves of vitriol. The fact that the two antagonists knew each others' identities all too well, and had already built up a substantial amount of personal animosity, surely helps to explain the bitterness of their exchanges. However, this was a battle which was not to be decided by the power of the pen, however poisonous its ink. Williams was apparently preparing a response to Heylyn's *Antidotum* when the star chamber case (appearing in the same month as the publication of the *Antidotum*) led to the seizure of all his books, leaving him unable to mount an effective reply.[54] Heylyn was not involved directly in the final star chamber prosecution of Williams for subornation of perjury, although he was

---

[51] E.g. Laud, *Works*, vii, 502.

[52] LPL, MS 1030, no. 38 (quoted in Williams, *Work of Wiliams*, 47). *The Works of Richard Sibbes*, ed. A. B. Grosart (1862–4), i, pp. cxxxiv–cxl.

[53] G.I. Soden, *Godfrey Goodman, Bishop of Gloucester, 1583–1656* (1953), 299–317.

[54] Hacket, *Scrin. Res.* ii, 109–10.

doubtless an enthusiastic observer. Williams's removal did, however, clear the way for Heylyn to play a more direct role in the running of the Abbey.

Heylyn's appointment as canon treasurer in December 1637 followed directly on the establishment of a new commission into the running of the Abbey.[55] His son-in-law later claimed for him, among the good deeds done for the Abbey in these years, that sections of the roof which were much decayed had been newly timbered, boarded and leaded, and that the arch over the preaching place was newly vaulted and its roof raised to the same height as the rest of the church (at a cost of £434 18s 10d).[56] The listing of these works was a fairly transparent attempt by Heylyn's later supporters to deploy a run of good deeds to rival the improvements made by Williams, although there is no suggestion that any of these improvements were made at Heylyn's own expense, and there is no clear evidence that he was the main promoter of them. Indeed, improvements at the Abbey became yet another battleground for Heylyn and Williams. After Williams's death, Heylyn was anxious to play down the extent of the ex-dean's good works. He attacked Fuller's claims that Williams had spent much on the Abbey church and library, objecting that the charges were met by the Abbey rents rather than by Williams's private purse, and indeed claimed that Williams profited from a reallocation of the Abbey rents.[57] Williams's own biographer, his ex-chaplain John Hacket, protested loudly at these attacks, and provided his own documentation of Williams's expenses on the Abbey from the Chapter Acts. Heylyn, Hacket complained, was 'the Wolf that howls against this Bishop [Williams] both living and dead'.[58]

Heylyn's famous show-down with Williams did not occur until the bishop's triumphant return to power after his release from the Tower in November 1640. With the calling of the Long Parliament Williams was

---

[55] WAM Chapter Act Book II, f. 65 (*Acts 1609–42*, no. 82). Heylyn's accounts as treasurer for the years ending Michaelmas 1638 and 1639 are WAM 33688–9. For some of his earlier account books see WAM 33962, 41800 (for 1634), WAM 41818 (for 1636); his notes on accounts for the years 1637–42 are WAM 34165.

[56] Heylyn, *Ecclesia Restaurata*, i, p. cxii.

[57] Heylyn, *Examen*, 272–3. Heylyn claimed that, on being made lord keeper, Williams had successfully lobbied that for administrative convenience he should receive all the Abbey rents, out of which he would pay the annual stipends of canons, schoolmasters, choirmen and lay officers, along with the scholars' commons, with the result that the remaining amount remained in Williams's own hands, though with his assurance that this would be spent for the good and honour of the Abbey. Heylyn added that he had offered to prove before the commissioners at the 1635 visitation that the surplus remaining in Williams's own hands was larger than the sum he had spent on the Abbey and Library. Cf. below, pp. 243, 252.

[58] Hacket, *Scrin. Res.* ii, 89 (wolf), 92–3 (expenses).

now free to play the role of the pivotal mediator between the crown and its opponents to which he had so often aspired. Fifteen years later, Heylyn could still remark bitterly of how at his release Williams had been feted 'his person looked upon as sacred, his words deemed as Oracles'.[59] Heylyn had a right, not just to be bitter, but also to be fearful. Williams had already indicated to William Spicer back in 1632 that, given the chance, he would not be charitable towards his enemies, and Heylyn was undoubtedly someone that the vengeful dean would have had in his sights.

The most detailed account that we have of the public clash between Heylyn and the newly-released Williams is Heylyn's own, and it therefore needs to be treated with some caution. Heylyn was prompted to write the account some sixteen years later by the accusation that, having trampled on and insulted Williams in the 1630s, Heylyn had gone crawling to Williams in a servile fashion once the bishop was released from the Tower.[60] Nevertheless, the account repays careful study, and when supplemented by other sources provides an intriguing glimpse of Heylyn's state of mind at this crucial stage in his career.

Heylyn claimed that he did not attend on Williams after the dean's release from the Tower, but only saw him at the next chapter meeting, where he 'gave him as few words as might be the common civility of a complement, for his return unto the College'. It was the Sunday following his appearance before the parliamentary committee for the courts of justice that Heylyn was famously confronted by his dean. Preaching in the Abbey, he was interrupted by Williams who knocked on the pulpit with his staff and exclaimed 'No more of that point, no more of that point'. By Heylyn's account, he explained to his auditors that he had virtually finished the present point, but would proceed to the next as he was bid.[61] Williams's intervention would appear to have been prompted by a passage of the sermon in which Heylyn deplored that people no longer harkened to the voice of the church, 'what schism in every corner of this our Church! ... some rather putting all into open tumult, than that they would conform to a lawful government, derived from Christ and his Apostles to these very times.' According to Heylyn's son-in-law (who seems to have had access to his father-in-law's sermon notes) Heylyn then moved on to more tactful generalizations, condemning others 'combining into close and dangerous factions, because some points of speculative divinity are otherwise maintained by some than they would have them'. This led him to a pious denial 'that a difference

---

[59] Heylyn, *Observations*, 217.

[60] Heylyn, *Extraneus Vapulans* (1656), 43, 53–4.

[61] *Ibid.*, 58. Heylyn's full account appears on pp. 58–66.

in a point of judgment must needs draw after it a disjoining of the affections also, and that conclude at last in an open schism. Whereas diversity of opinions, if wisely managed, would rather tend to the discovery of the truth than the disturbance of the Church, and rather whet our industry than excite our passions.' He ended with the lament that, if only 'we' had observed due moderation and not ignored patristic admonitions that people should not be suspended from the communion of the church, 'we had not then so often torn the Church in pieces, nor by our frequent broils offered that injury and inhumanity to our Saviour's body, which was not offered to his garments [by those that crucified him].'[62]

Heylyn's hypocrisy was palpable here. Nevertheless, the fact that Heylyn could openly admonish his hearers 'that we are so affected with our own opinions, that we condemn whosoever shall opine the contrary' also provides a useful reminder of just how widely deployed and easily adopted the language of moderation and irenicism was in this period. It would have been ludicrously foolhardy for Heylyn to have attacked his puritan opponents too directly. Nevertheless, by intervening before Heylyn had provided a more pacificatory gloss on his words, Williams clearly felt that he had finally nailed his opponent. After Heylyn's sermon was over Williams moved swiftly: summoning another canon as witness, he demanded that Heylyn give him a copy of the sermon that he had just preached. Heylyn claimed that he did so, and that he gave Williams 'the whole book of Sermons that he then had with him'. Coming out of the service on the same evening, Williams sent one of his gentlemen to desire the sub-dean (Newell), Dr Thomas Wilson and Heylyn to come to his lodging. Heylyn answered 'in a full Cloyster' that he would not go; he would meet Williams in parliament, the law courts, or the Abbey's public chapter house and answer charges, 'but that he would never shuffle up the business in the Bishops lodging, or take a private satisfaction for a publick Baffle'. Having disrobed, Heylyn then passed the time with his friends Robert Filmer (the theorist of absolutism) and John Towers (the fiercely Laudian bishop of Peterborough) and in their presence the sub-dean came back from Williams returning the book of sermons that Heylyn had delivered to him. Heylyn stoutly refused to accept the book, stating 'that the Book was taken from him in the sight of hundreds, and that he would not otherwise receive it, than either in the same place or a place more publick'. He then (so he claimed) urged Williams to read over all the other sermons and find what he could against him, and 'that as he did not court his

---

[62] Heylyn, *Ecclesia Restaurata*, i, pp. cxxviii–cxxx.

favours, or expect any thing from him, so neither did he fear his frown, or any further mischief which he could do to him, equall to what he had done already; And finally, that he was more ashamed of the poorness of this prostitution, than at the insolencies of the morning'. The sub-dean in response simply threw the book into the room and left.[63]

Heylyn confessed that some people subsequently thought 'that he had carried it with too high a hand'. As relations continued to be frosty, the sub-dean finally met with Heylyn in the Common Orchard and urged him in Williams's name 'to apply himself to the Bishop, as being better able to help or hurt him than any other whatsoever'. After consulting with friends, Heylyn finally waited on Williams on a Saturday evening. Meeting alone in Williams's private gallery and, 'after some previous expostulations on the one side, and honest defences on the other, they came little by little unto better terms, and at the last into that familiarity and freedom of discourse, as seemed to have no token in it of the old displeasures'. This was clearly a ceasefire rather than a real reconcilia-tion – Heylyn explained that he never met Williams again except when he later visited the bishops imprisoned after their presentation of a protestation in December 1641.[64]

What should we make of Heylyn's account? As we have stressed, he was undoubtedly keen to emphasize as much as possible his hostility towards Williams and his refusal to kowtow to him, largely in order to refute the charge of craven hypocrisy. Nevertheless, the account of his behaviour (allowing for overstatement) does seem to fit with what we know of Heylyn's character. He was quite capable of behaving aggres-sively and self-righteously towards his ecclesiastical superiors: in the 1630s even the Laudian Bishop Walter Curll, who was supposedly Heylyn's supporter, had struggled to deal with his junior colleague's peremptory demands over his right to claim trees from the bishop's woods.[65] Heylyn's natural determination to defend his interests would have been reinforced by the fact that he had every reason to be on his guard against Williams, who was quite clearly bent on revenge. Heylyn had already received information that Williams had talked in private with Heylyn's other professed enemy, William Prynne.[66] Moreover, those involved in another publication against Williams's *Holy Table* met an instructive fate. Pocklington was proceeded against for his *Altare Christianum*, which was burnt and the licenser William Bray forced to

---

[63] Heylyn, *Extraneus*, 58–61. Barnard's account of the events differs in some details: Heylyn, *Ecclesia Restaurata*, i, pp. cxxxi–cxxxii.

[64] Heylyn, *Extraneus*, 63–5.

[65] Bodl. MS Rawlinson D. 353, f.100v (Curll to Heylyn, 11 February 1636).

[66] Heylyn, *Extraneus*, 56.

preach a recantation sermon simply for his involvement in the book's publication.[67] The proceedings against Pocklington were particularly savage: the House of Lords directed on 12 February 1641 that he be deprived of all his ecclesiastical livings, disabled from ever holding any place in the church, have his two books to be publicly burnt, and be forbidden from ever coming within the verge of the court again.[68] This judgement, and especially the final point which was so clearly aimed at purging the chapel royal of the influence of a Laudian chaplain, must have made Heylyn – himself a royal chaplain – dread his own fate.

The prosecution of Bray and Pocklington makes it all the more re-markable that Heylyn did not receive the same treatment, despite the fact that he had written two books against Williams on the altar, which had all gone into several editions and were more prominent than that of Pocklington.[69] Both Williams and Prynne had a right to bear personal grudges against Heylyn, and there was plenty of material in his printed sermons, let alone his manuscript sermon book, which could have been used against him. He had already been attacked in the opening week of the Long Parliament, 'his bold Pamphlets' being taken as key evidence for the secret 'worke in hand' (the phrase that Williams had objected to) to 'drawe the Religion to olde Ceremonies'.[70] Alongside all this he had generated enormous popular hostility. He himself remarked that he was 'most despitefully reviled and persecuted with excessive both noise and violence' by members of the public who thronged the doors of the parliamentary committee concerned with investigating Prynne's pros-ecution.[71]

How, then, can we account for Heylyn's remarkable escape, and the astounding self-confidence that he mustered in his dealings with Williams, and the dean's own back-tracking? Two possibilities present themselves. The first would be that Heylyn was energetically working to cut a deal with the parliamentary committee. He was certainly capable of per-forming sudden somersaults of opinion and allegiance, as his early

---

[67] Heylyn, *Examen*, 242–3. *LJ*, iv, 180, 183, 219.

[68] *LJ*, iv, 161.

[69] Pocklington was also proceeded against for his *Sunday No Sabbath*, but Heylyn's *History of the Sabbath* was no less intemperate in its argument, and also went into two editions. Williams's reported exclamation in the committee on religious innovations (sitting in the Jerusalem Chamber) that all books should be publicly burnt that had disputed the morality of the Lord's Day sabbath would undoubtedly have been aimed at Heylyn just as much as Pocklington: Heylyn, *Examen*, 243.

[70] *The Journal of Sir Simonds D'Ewes from the Beginning of the Long Parliament to the Opening of the Trial of the Earl of Strafford*, ed. W. Notestein (New Haven 1923), 6 and n. 30. For Heylyn's awareness of these attacks, see his *Extraneus*, 55.

[71] Heylyn, *Cosmographie* (1652), sig. A3v.

career testifies. His accounts of how the committee of enquiry into the prosecution of Prynne treated him are suggestive. He claimed that:

> though he made his first appearance with all those disadvantages of prejudice and prepossession, which commonly obstruct the way to an equal hearing, yet got he so much ground on them, by his own modest confidence on the one side, and the want of fit proofs on the other, that in the end he was dismissed, not only with cheerfull countenance from them all, but with expression also of esteem and favour from divers of them.

Heylyn also claimed that the violently anti-Laudian John White, who was a member of the Prynne committee (and 'most eagerly bent against' Heylyn 'at his first appearance') and had attended his Abbey sermon, yielded to Heylyn's request to read out Heylyn's account of the sermon to the committee, testified to the truth of Heylyn's account, and thereby won the unanimous support of the Prynne committee for Heylyn's sermon and a condemnation of the behaviour of Williams. This sounds highly implausible, of course, but Heylyn's appeal to the testimony (if it were to be required) of 'not only Mr Prynne himself, but several members of that Committee, who are still alive' is significant.[72] It is also suggestive that Heylyn does not appear in John White's *The First Century of Scandalous, Malignant Priests* (1643), in which the behaviour of so many Laudian divines was upbraided. Moreover, the account of one committee member (Sir Simonds D'Ewes) of the committee's behaviour suggests that Heylyn was being pacificatory. He noted that under cross-examination 'Dr Helin excused all malice' and D'Ewes was reduced to commenting that if only Heylyn 'had proceeded with the spirit of Christian Mansuetude hee might have prevented Mr Prinns punishment'.[73] At the committee's meeting on 23 December Heylyn also felt confident enough to raise the question of whether he was actually being called as a delinquent, or simply as a witness.[74]

Clearly, moreover, the committee was most concerned to incriminate Laud himself, rather than see the blame attached to a minor official such as Heylyn. On 15 December the committee all agreed 'that the now Archbishop of Canterburie had a hand in this prosecution of Mr Prinne as deepelie as Dr Helin'.[75] The notes of John White's committee on the feoffees for impropriations are similarly suggestive in that, while they mention 'Dr Heylin's Act Sermon', they emphasize that it was Laud who procured the crushing of the feoffees, and bragged that he

---

[72] Heylyn, *Extraneus*, 57, 62–3.
[73] D'Ewes, *Journal*, 132.
[74] *Ibid.*, 186.
[75] *Ibid.*, 158–9.

was the man who had set himself against it (a report that could only redound to Heylyn's favour).[76] Whether Heylyn was actively trying to detach himself from Laud is unclear; at least he does not seem to have been dissuading the parliamentary committees from doing this. Later rumours of Heylyn's grovelling before Williams might reflect such attempted repositioning. Heylyn would certainly not have been the only divine seeking to distance himself from the archbishop: Laud's erstwhile vicar-general Sir Nathaniel Brent was to become one of the archbishop's most determined opponents.

This does not provide a complete explanation, however. Things did not proceed as smoothly as Heylyn would have us believe. The Prynne committee *did* find Heylyn guilty as a delinquent, and if his case then disappeared in the committee on religion this was explicable partly by the sheer pace of political events and workload of the committee concerned. If Heylyn had indeed cut a deal, then it is unlikely that he would not have been used more publicly, or that the news would not have circulated more widely. A more likely solution is suggested by Heylyn's anxiety to present himself to the Prynne committee as a mere 'employee' acting under the instructions of the attorney-general in amassing evidence against Prynne. The fact that when Williams was pursuing him for his Westminster sermon Heylyn made a point of sending an account of his sermon to the king is also highly suggestive.[77] It is Heylyn's determination to link his activities very directly to the king which seems the most likely explanation of why his opponents drew back from their engagement. Williams in particular did not want to jeopardize his new relationship with the king. It was later reported that when Williams demanded as part of his reconciliation with Heylyn that the latter should publicly acknowledge his error in publishing the *Antidotum Lincolniense* and have the book called in, Heylyn refused, and maintained 'that he received his Majesty's royal command for the writing and printing of that book'.[78] Heylyn's own account of his actions is conspicuously silent on the subject of the king, but with Laud already in the Tower there was no one else obvious whose support he could invoke.

Events at the end of January 1641 provide further evidence for this interpretation. On 30 January 1641 the Prynne committee finally

---

[76] PRO, SP 16/473, no. 105 (*CSPD 1640–1*, 329–30).

[77] Heylyn, *Extraneus*, 62.

[78] Heylyn, *Ecclesia Restaurata*, i, pp. cxxxiii–cxxxiv. While Barnard does not specifically date this exchange, Vernon (*Life of Heylyn*, 116–17) locates it at the meeting when Heylyn and Williams resolved their differences, described in Heylyn, *Extraneus*, 63–5. Heylyn's own account, as we have seen, makes vague allusions to 'expostulations ... and honest defences' but does not refer specifically to this exchange.

delivered their verdict on Heylyn, finding him 'a delinquent, in having been a promoter and furtherer of the suite against Mr Prinne in the Starre-chamber and having since preached and written in his printed bookes libellouslie against him Dr Bastwicke and Mr. Prynne'.[79] The day before this final judgement (and presumably having advance knowledge of the committee's broadening of the charge to include his later pamphlets) Heylyn wrote an anxious letter to the courtier Endymion Porter. Heylyn was clearly panic-stricken, reflecting that 'it cannot be worse with me, than it is alreadie'. Heylyn's urgent request was for some form of written attestation from the king of his support for Heylyn's actions. He emphasized 'how much it doth concerne the king in honour to iustifie the intimacion of his owne commands' (presumably the royal prompting to write his *Briefe and Moderate Answere* against Burton, which the Prynne committee was now intending to charge him with, and which had been published 'by authoritie' with a dedication to the king). At the same time, Heylyn was anxious to emphasize that 'the Attestation which I now desire … cann no way conduce to the disservice of his Majestie, or the dishonour of his Ministers'.[80] The complete silence of Heylyn and his biographers on this matter in their accounts of Heylyn's actions is all the more telling.

Heylyn's readiness to invoke the king's direct involvement in his activities may have helped to secure lenient treatment, at least temporarily. He could not escape the upheavals of the war, though. He seems to have obtained leave to depart from Westminster in the spring of 1641 after a series of false starts in his prosecution, and he retired to his rectory at Alresford, Hampshire.[81] After avoiding Sir William Waller's attempt to arrest him there late in 1642, Heylyn fled to the royalist stronghold of Oxford, where he spent some time as a political journalist, writing several editions of the royalist newsletter *Mercurius Aulicus*, as well as contributing other works of royalist propaganda.[82] The defeat of the royalist cause saw Heylyn's retirement from public life, but it certainly did not witness his retirement from the world of print. Indeed, Heylyn was one of the most prolific authors active in the 1650s, as he contributed a whole series of polemical works which acrimoniously

---

[79] D'Ewes, *Journal*, 305–6.

[80] PRO, SP 16/476, no. 97 (*CSPD 1640–1*, 440).

[81] Heylyn, *Ecclesia Restaurata*, i, pp. cxxxv–cxxxvii. After signing the chapter minutes for 10 February 1641 (his first signing since Williams's release from the Tower) Heylyn did not sign for meetings between May 1641 and February 1642. He did, however, sign the minutes of a meeting on 25 May 1642 – an apparent visit to the metropolis on which his biographers are silent: WAM Chapter Act Book II, ff. 77v–81 (*Acts 1609–42*, nos 99–109).

[82] PRO, C 5/377/105. Heylyn, *Ecclesia Restaurata*, i, pp. cxxxviii–cxl.

picked over the events of the early Stuart period, as well as working on the series of major historical works that would be published in the 1660s. In the controversial works of the 1650s, Heylyn returned compulsively and irresistibly to his clashes with Williams. He devoted nearly ten pages of his *Examen Historicum* (1659) to a venomous attack on the long-dead dean.[83] Among the extraordinary charges that he levelled, he claimed that Williams had never once attended the chapel in the Tower between July 1637 and November 1640, when he was incarcerated there.[84] Indeed, it was Heylyn's continuing vendetta against Williams that helped to prompt Hacket to compose his famous life of Williams in the late 1650s.

The Restoration finally saw Heylyn restored to his Westminster stall, and appointed sub-dean, which he remained until his death in 1662.[85] In the small time that remained to him at Westminster Abbey, perhaps Heylyn's finest hour was the sermon that he delivered in 1661 on the anniversary of the king's restoration. Alongside his idolizing of the king, Heylyn reflected on the past and delivered some very clear advice and warnings to the government. In a very direct allusion to his earlier clash with Williams, Heylyn defiantly applauded 'the Piety of these times' – twenty-five years had clearly done little to remove the scars of Heylyn's exchange with the former dean.[86] He lauded the attention that had been paid to the restoration of divine service and the bishops, and the splendid readornment of the chapel royal, particularly praising the revival of church music.[87] Nevertheless, Heylyn was alive to the ways in which 'the piety of these times' might not live up to the piety of Laudian times. In particular, he urged that the bishops should be restored to their secular, political powers. Without a full restoration of the bishops' powers and privileges, 'they must pass for Cyphers in the Church-Arithmetick, disabled from proceeding in the work of God; of less esteem amongst their freinds, and a scorn to their adversaries.' What Heylyn particularly had in mind was the restoration of bishops to the privy council. 'The State was never better served', he claimed, 'then when the Messengers of Peace were the Ministers of it: when Kings

---

[83] Heylyn, *Examen*, 269–78. See also *ibid.*, 219–20, 242–3; *Observations*, 135–9, 217–18; *Extraneus*, 56–68. In fairness, it should be noted that Heylyn sometimes defended Williams from scandalous accusations: e.g. *Respondet Petrus* (1658), 153–5; *Extraneus*, 17–18, 24.

[84] Heylyn, *Examen*, 276.

[85] Heylyn was appointed sub-dean on 9 July 1660: WAM Chapter Act Book III, f. 3.

[86] Heylyn, *A Sermon preached in the Collegiate Church of St Peter in Westminster, on … the Anniversary of his Majesties most joyful Restitution to the Crown of England* (1661), 39. It is notable that this phrase is italicized.

[87] *Ibid.*, 36–8.

asked Counsel of the Priests, and that the Priests were Counsellors, Officers and Judges'.[88]

Heylyn's anxieties about the limited secular powers of the Restoration church were not assuaged by the time of his death the following year.[89] Nevertheless, his period of greatest prominence as a writer arguably still lay in the future. Amid the tensions of the restored Church of England, Heylyn's voice was increasingly heard from beyond the grave. In the heat of the religious tensions of the late 1660s and early 1670s, and again at the height of the Exclusion Crisis, he was seized upon as an advocate of the Tory cause and a zealous opponent of the populist Whigs. His great apologia for the Laudian movement, *Cyprianus Anglicus* (his life of Archbishop Laud), appeared in 1668; 1670 saw the republication of his history of the English Reformation (*Ecclesia Restaurata*) and of his previously unpublished history of presbyterianism, *Aerius Redivivus*. The next year saw a reprinting of *Cyprianus Anglicus*, and the following year the republication of *Aerius Redivivus*, and two years later of *Ecclesia Restaurata*. These regular reprintings are all the more significant as the works in question are substantial folio volumes. In 1681 Heylyn's continuing importance was recognized with the publication of a substantial collection of some of his previous works, and subsequently of two biographies. While he doubtless had his enthusiastic readers, he also wielded an equally important influence in the opposition that he aroused. The extreme clericalism and anti-puritanism of Heylyn's histories made him a favourite target of writers such as Sidney and Locke, who used him as a spokesman for the high-church position, and also partly shaped Burnet's own *History of the Reformation*.[90] His influence may have been even more significant than this: James II possessed his own annotated copy of Heylyn's *Ecclesia Restaurata*, and reportedly claimed that his reading of it helped to sway him from his allegiance to Anglicanism.[91]

---

[88] *Ibid.*, 39.

[89] Heylyn had also expressed anxieties to Gilbert Sheldon that no meeting of convocation accompanied the Convention Parliament: Bodl. MS Tanner 49, ff. 146–7; cf. Heylyn, *Ecclesia Restaurata*, i, pp. clxxviii–clxxxi.

[90] M.A. Goldie, 'John Locke and Anglican royalism', *Political Studies*, xxxi (1983), 66, 69–70. Champion, *Pillars*, 75 & n. 89.

[91] Burnet described James when Duke of York showing him marked passages from his own copy of Heylyn's *Ecclesia Restaurata* 'to shew upon what motives and principles men were led into the changes that were then made': Burnet, *History of his Own Time* (Oxford 1833), ii, 24, quoted in Heylyn, *Ecclesia Restaurata*, i, p. clxxiii. J.S. Clarke, *The Life of James II, King of England ... collected out of Memoirs writ by His Own Hand* (1816), i, 630–1. (The other works alleged to have undermined James's allegiance, however, are Hooker's *Laws of Ecclesiastical Polity* and a treatise by 'a learned Bishopp

When compared with his substantial later influence as a historian of high-churchmanship, Heylyn's acrimonious exchanges with the dean of Westminster in the 1630s can appear by contrast to be simply another minor, ill-tempered personal tussle between a dean and a canon. Moreover, as we have seen, it was not a conflict that was necessarily driven by different styles of churchmanship. Nevertheless, it was a conflict that was to have important repercussions. The arguments of Williams and Heylyn over the communion table were revived two centuries later in a series of high-profile Victorian cases over church ritual, in which the two authorities were regularly invoked.[92] Moreover, in Heylyn's campaign against Williams and the puritan triumvirate of Burton, Bastwick and Prynne, he was not simply acting as a sort of clerical rottweiler, nourished by Charles and Laud to snarl at puritans and allowed to slip his lead whenever one was spied. On the contrary, he was also acting in essence as the main apologist for Caroline religious policy. It is important to remember that the appointed voice of the more elaborate ceremonialism of the 1630s was not Lancelot Andrewes, John Cosin, Jeremy Taylor, George Herbert, Nicholas Ferrar, or any of the other so-called 'Caroline divines' who inspired the later Anglo-Catholic movement. It was the oft-forgotten Heylyn who was the officially accredited voice of Personal Rule policies, and whose personal ambitions and animosities shaped the form in which those policies were articulated and defended.[93] If historians neglect to place him centre-stage in the 1630s then they miss an important, perhaps even a defining, feature of the period. Some clashes in cathedral cloisters are no more than that. But Peter Heylyn reminds us that at times the politics of religious polemic played an important role in shaping the history and identity of the Church of England.

---

of the Church of England'). See also Champion, *Pillars*, 70, on the use of Heylyn by Roman Catholic authors.

[92] Williams, *Work of Williams*, 20, 108–12.

[93] This point also holds good for another defender of the Caroline policies towards the altar and the sabbath – John Pocklington – who was motivated by just as deep a combination of personal antipathy towards Williams and clerical ambition. I hope to discuss Pocklington's career in more detail elsewhere.

CHAPTER NINE

The Lord of Jerusalem: John Williams as Dean of Westminster

C.S. Knighton

'A man odious to all the world'; 'a proud, restless, overweening spirit' ... 'that anti-prelatical archbishop'; 'the English Richelieu'; 'a slippery Welsh politician of ambiguous loyalty' who 'deviated into a clerical career merely by accident'; 'the prelate blessed with the sharpest hindsight of his day'; 'extravagant, learned, but wildly indiscreet'.[1]

The dean of Westminster from 1620 to 1644, who combined that office with the bishopric of Lincoln from 1621 to 1641 and then with the archbishopric of York, and who also headed the national administration as lord keeper of the great seal from 1621 to 1625, has never lacked epithets. He has not, however, found a substantial biographer since his friend and disciple John Hacket wrote the account of him on which much subsequent study (including some of what follows) is based.[2]

---

[1] *Cabala, sive Scrinia Sacra* (2nd edn 1663), 299 [quoting the duke of Buckingham]. E. Hyde (earl of Clarendon), *The History of the Rebellion and Civil Wars in England*, ed. W.D. Macray (Oxford 1848), i, 464, 476. Soden, *Goodman*, 138. H.R. Trevor-Roper (Lord Dacre of Glanton), *Renaissance Essays* (1985), 244, and *idem*, 'King James and his bishops', *History Today*, v (1955), 575. C. Carlton, *Charles I. The Personal Monarch* (1983), 68–9. R.L. Ollard, *Clarendon and his Friends* (1987), 40.

[2] Hacket, *Scrin. Res.* was revised by A. Philips as *The Life of John Williams* (1700. 2nd edn, Cambridge 1703). The standard modern life is B. Dew Roberts, *Mitre & Musket. John Williams, Lord Keeper, Archbishop of York, 1582–1650* (Oxford 1938). Williams, *Work of Williams*, which principally contains a facsimile of *The Holy Table, Name and Thing* (1637), Williams's defence of his altar policy, includes (pp. 39–41) a brief account of his career at Westminster. This is also treated by A. Tindal Hart in Carpenter, *House of Kings*, 151–67. On his political career see S.R. Gardiner in *DNB*; J. Campbell, *The Lives of the Lord Chancellors and Keepers of the Great Seal of England* (1845–7), ii, 434–500. By far the best account of Williams's life (though chiefly concerned with his work in chancery) is G.W. Thomas, 'Archbishop John Williams. Politics and prerogative law, 1621–1642' (Oxford DPhil dissertation 1974), and *idem*, 'James I, equity and lord keeper John Williams', *EHR*, xci (1976), 506–28. See also M. Hudson, 'The political and ecclesiastical activities of Bishop Williams' (London MA dissertation 1926); I. Bowen, 'John Williams of Gloddaeth ... ', *Transactions of the Honourable Society of Cymmrodorion*, session 1927–8 (1929), 1–91; H.T. Blethen, 'Bishop Williams, the altar controversy, and the royal supremacy, 1627–41', *WHR*, ix (1978–9), 142–54;

His achievements as dean of Westminster have been recognized in his benefactions to the fabric, the library, and to Westminster School. His stout defence of the Abbey and its treasures on the eve of the Civil War is also remembered. Certainly he had an affection for the place; he fought off repeated attempts to remove him from it, and he was an energetic upholder of its privileges. For much of his tenure he was absent, indeed under suspension. The deanship would nevertheless be exalted rather than diminished by his holding it along with his secular and other ecclesiastical dignities. In Dean Stanley's view Williams 'left more traces of himself in the office than any of his predecessors, and than most of his successors'.[3] It is clear, however, that Williams acquired the deanery and retained it principally because it gave him an ideal base from which to conduct his political operations.

Williams had been educated at Ruthin School in Denbighshire, Gabriel Goodman's foundation.[4] Williams would extend the association Goodman had established between North Wales and Westminster, bringing Welshmen to his service from which opportunities came for their own political careers.[5] From Wales Williams also brought a musicality which tempered the severity of his Calvinism.[6] He enjoyed and participated in the choral music which he found at Westminster, and this set him at odds with most of those whose political and religious opinions he supposedly shared. So too did his high view of the episcopal office, at least as exercised by himself. Williams was also a bachelor; this was the result

---

N.R.F. Tucker, *Prelate-at-arms. An account of Archbishop John Williams at Conway during the Great Rebellion, 1642–1650* (Llandudno, n.d.). Various selections of his letters are in *Cabala, sive Scrinia Sacra* (1654), i, 54–113, and 2nd edn (1663), 283–310; *Letters of Archbishop Williams, with Documents relating to him*, ed. J.E.B. Mayor (Cambridge 1866) [also in *Communications … of the Cambridge Antiquarian Society*, ii (1864), 25–66; iv (1879), 61–108]; B.H. Beedham, 'The unpublished correspondence between Archbishop Williams and the Marquis of Ormond', *Archaeologia Cambrensis*, 3rd ser. xv (1869), 305–43.

[3] Stanley, *Historical Memorials*, 415.

[4] K.M. Kenyon-Thompson, *Ruthin School. The First Seven Centuries* (Ruthin 1974), 87–8, accidentally promoted Williams to Canterbury; it also cites a claim that he was Shakespeare.

[5] At first it was thought he would take few Welshmen into his household: *Calendar of Wynn (of Gwydir) Papers, 1515–1690* (Aberystwyth 1926), 151 (no. 962), Sir Richard to Sir John Wynn, 25 June 1621. For the Welsh connexion see particularly J.K. Gruenfelder, 'The Wynns of Gwydir and parliamentary elections in Wales, 1604–40', *WHR*, ix (1978–9), 121–41.

[6] Williams's Calvinism is at its most explicit in a sermon before the House of Lords in February 1629: Tyacke, *Anti-Calvinists*, 209–10, referring to Hacket, *Scrin. Res.* i, 16. He is a rare 'enthusiastic ceremonialist' among 'conformist Calvinists': Fincham, *Early Stuart Church*, editor's introduction, 9.

of a childhood accident,[7] but it confusingly aligns him with ritualistic churchmen celibate by choice. Since to Williams religion was at best of secondary importance ('a mere parergon to his politics')[8] it matters little that he cannot be neatly labelled. It suited his style to shock his friends and court his enemies. Archbishop Laud was chief of the latter; but it was Williams who, at Lincoln College, Oxford, created the 'beau ideal of a Laudian chapel'.[9]

From Ruthin, Williams had proceeded (like Goodman) to St John's College, Cambridge. A sermon before the king at Newmarket gained him attention. He became chaplain to the marquess of Buckingham's mother, dissuaded the marquess's intended bride from converting to Rome, and officiated at the subsequent wedding.[10] The deanery of Salisbury came to him in 1619, though he coveted a post closer to the centre of affairs. None was more suitable to this purpose than the deanery of Westminster, then occupied by Robert Tounson. On 11 March 1620 the bishop of Salisbury, Martin Fotherby, died.[11] Next day (not having the advantage of the Electric Telegraph) Williams wrote to Buckingham proposing that if (as was expected) Tounson came to Salisbury as bishop, Williams might replace him at Westminster: 'Being unmarried, and inclining so to continue, I do find that Westminster is fitter by much for that disposition.'[12] These moves were known by 20 March to the gossipy John Chamberlain, who also noted that John Bowle (who had been promised the deanery of Westminster) would have to be content with that of Salisbury, thereby defeating another hopeful, John Donne, of *his* expectation.[13] Tounson was elected to the

---

[7] Hacket, *Scrin. Res.* i, 8. Philips, *Life*, 10, refutes a suggestion that he was born defective of pudenda. Cf. P. Collinson, *The Religion of Protestants* (Oxford 1982), 79 n. 54.

[8] H.R. Trevor-Roper, *Archbishop Laud, 1573–1645* (2nd edn 1962), 56.

[9] J. Newman, 'The architectural setting', in *Seventeenth-Century Oxford*, ed. N.R.N. Tyacke (History of the University of Oxford, iv, Oxford 1997), 165. Cf. Hacket, *Scrin. Res.* ii, 35; Trevor-Roper, *Laud*, 120, 179–80; J. Davies, *The Caroline Captivity of the Church. Charles I and the remoulding of Anglicanism* (Oxford 1992), 15.

[10] A.P. Kautz, 'The selection of Jacobean bishops', in *Early Stuart Essays in honor of David Harris Willson*, ed. H.S. Reinmuth jr (Minneapolis 1970), 155–6. Lockyer, *Buckingham*, 59, 60, 69–70, 111, 115. Hacket (*Scrin. Res.* i. 19) says the sermon gaining the king's attention was at Royston in 1610, but it took place at Newmarket on 19 Nov. 1611: *Letters of Williams*, 37, as noted in McCullough, *Sermons at Court*, supplementary 'Calendar'.

[11] Le Neve, *1541–1857*, vi, 2, 6.

[12] Hacket, *Scrin. Res.* i, 44.

[13] PRO, SP 14/113, no. 32 (*CSPD 1619–23*, 131; *Letters of Chamberlain*, ii, 296; Chamberlain to Sir Dudley Carleton, 20 March 1621). Cf. R.C. Bald, *John Donne. A Life* (Oxford 1970), 370.

see of Salisbury on 24 March, though still acting at Westminster on 23
May. He was consecrated on 9 July. Williams was appointed to Westminster on the following day, and installed on the 12th.[14]

He is said to have busied himself at once in surveying the Abbey's
properties.[15] The arrival of new deans had often been marked by innovations in regulation and record-keeping; but there is nothing of the
sort at Williams's first chapter meeting on 7 December.[16] An early
attempt to assert the authority of his office failed badly. In February
1621 parliament proposed to hold a corporate communion and nominated Archbishop Ussher to preach, but could not decide between the
Abbey and St Margaret's church; the latter had been used by the Commons since 1614 because of their aversion to ritual in the Abbey.
Williams sent a 'manerly message' by three or four of his chapter
colleagues telling the parliamentarians they were welcome in either
place – but since he was the ordinary of both, he would choose the
preacher. The king told the Commons to follow precedent and assemble
in St Margaret's, where Ussher gave them a dull sermon.[17]

This rebuff must soon have been forgotten as new vistas opened on
30 March with the death of the bishop of London, John King.[18] Williams
wrote at once to Buckingham seeking the nomination, on condition (1)
that since King had lived beyond Lady Day, Williams might keep all his
existing benefices until the following Michaelmas, (2) that thereafter he
might retain his rectory of Walgrave (Northants.) *in commendam*, and
(3) that if he were to be expected to assist the dean and chapter of St
Paul's in repairing the cathedral, he should be given a prebend there to
enable him to do so.[19] Within a week, however, it was expected that
Montaigne of Lincoln would be translated to London, Williams would
go to Lincoln, Bowle (now dean of Salisbury) would move to Westminster, and Donne would have the deanery of Salisbury.[20] But there are

---

[14] Le Neve, *1541–1857*, vi, 2; vii, 70 (installation date from Hacket, *Scrin. Res.* i, 44).
WAM Chapter Act Book II, f. 28 (*Acts 1609–42*, no. 35).

[15] Hacket, *Scrin. Res.* i, 43.

[16] WAM Chapter Act Book II , ff . 28v–29 (*Acts 1609–42*, no. 36).

[17] PRO, SP 14/119, nos 79, 90, 123 (*CSPD 1619–23*, 221, 222, 228; *Letters of
Chamberlain*, ii, 341, 346. Speaker's report, 6 February 1621. Chamberlain to Carleton,
10 and 27 February 1621). *Letters of Williams*, 82 (as SP 14/119, no. 90), 83 (Joseph
Mead to Carleton, 17 February 1621). Cf. D.C. Gray, *Chaplain to Mr Speaker* (House of
Commons Library Document no. 19, 1994), 23–5. The 1614 and 1621 controversies are
confused in Williams, *Work of Williams*, 39.

[18] Le Neve, *1541–1857*, i, 2.

[19] BL, Harleian MS 7000, f. 55 (*Cabala* [1654], i, 54–5) (undated).

[20] PRO, SP 14/120, no. 74 (*CSPD 1619–23*, 244; *Letters of Chamberlain*, ii, 360;
Chamberlain to Carleton, 7 April 1621). Williams is here said to have been promised
London 'almost a yeare since'. Trevor-Roper confuses the chronology by placing King's

better prizes even than bishoprics, and Williams's prospects improved yet further with the impeachment of Lord Chancellor Bacon in May. The king had determined to have no more lawyers keep his conscience, and (allegedly) chose Williams for the great seal on the strength of a report he submitted on chancery fees. The appointment was made public on 15 May, being greeted with astonishment and (especially among lawyers) outrage.[21] Even though Williams was given the lesser title of lord keeper, the House of Lords took exception that 'so meane a man as a deane shold so sodainly leape over all their heades'; it was felt that Williams should not take office until he had been consecrated bishop.[22] Nevertheless he was inaugurated on 10 July, and proceeded to the Abbey '*in pontificalibus*' with his mace and purse carried before him.[23]

Meanwhile another piece was being advanced on the board, chiefly by Buckingham's hand. William Laud, dean of Gloucester since 1616, had become a canon of Westminster in January 1621. His first appearance in the chapter minutes concerns a dispute over his prebendal house; Williams subsequently helped resolve the problem with a loan towards repair of the property.[24] On 3 June the king was persuaded (by Buckingham) to give Laud a hint of further promotion. On 19 June, when Williams was busy in London, Laud preached at Wanstead where the court was keeping the king's birthday. Four days later it was being said that Laud would be made dean of Westminster.[25] Williams, however, was finding that neither the official chancery residence in Holborn nor the second-best house in the Abbey precinct was an adequate exchange for the Deanery ('so fit and convenient for many

---

death in July, making it appear Williams grasped for London when he had already been nominated to Lincoln: *Laud*, 58.

[21] Thomas, 'James I, equity and lord keeper John Williams', 506–7, 522–3. Cf. Foster, 'Clerical estate', 141.

[22] PRO, SP 14/121, no. 121 (*CSPD 1619–23*, 267; *Letters of Chamberlain*, ii, 383; Chamberlain to Carleton, 23 June 1621). The last cleric not a bishop to have held the great seal was Thomas Langley, dean of York in his first year (1405–6) as lord chancellor: *HBC*, 85.

[23] *APC 1619–21*, 400. PRO, SP 14/122, no. 23 (*CSPD 1619–23*, 275–6; *Letters of Chamberlain*, ii, 387; Chamberlain to Carleton, 14 July 1621 [where *in pontificalibus* cannot refer to *pontificalia* proper, since Williams was not yet entitled to episcopal habit; doubtless the phrase simply contrasts his clerical dress with the secular insignia in his procession]). Cf. *Cal. Wynn Papers*, 151 (no. 966).

[24] Le Neve, *1541–1857*, vii, 79; viii, 45. WAM Chapter Act Book II, ff. 30, 33 (*Acts 1609–42*, nos 37, 43). For the issue of the house, see J.A. Robinson, 'Westminster Abbey in the early part of the seventeenth century', *Proceedings of the Royal Institution*, xvii (1904), 523–6.

[25] Laud, *Works*, iii, 136. Trevor-Roper, *Laud*, 57 & n. l.

purposes').[26] The prospect of surrendering this to Laud was particularly sour. Williams therefore decided to stay put and, with Buckingham's assistance, to find another and preferably distant place for Laud. At this point it was clear that neither Laud nor Bowle was coming to Westminster.[27] By 8 August this was known to Donne, once again left standing when the music stopped (he wished Williams had 'left a hole for so poore a worme as I ame to have crept in at').[28] By 18 August Williams had secured his *commendam* for the deanery and other benefices besides.[29] The actual process of his obtaining the see of Lincoln could not begin until Montaigne vacated it; that was effected by his nomination to London on 26 June. Williams was elected to the vacancy on 3 August.[30] Laud, for the moment, had to be content with the remote and modest dignity of bishop of St David's.

Consecration of both men was delayed as a result of the accidental killing of a Berkshire gamekeeper by Archbishop Abbot.[31] Williams at once wrote to Buckingham, helpfully offering to explain the canonical penalties which the archbishop had incurred. Williams hinted at the king's promise of a better bishopric even than Lincoln on his relinquishing the great seal, if not before.[32] He certainly had Lambeth Palace in his sights, though he was not yet (27 July) consecrated. There was no recent precedent in settled times for consecration to Canterbury from outside the existing episcopate (1533, 1556 and 1559 all being special cases). Having leapfrogged over the legal profession, Williams may have envisaged a similar ascent through the ecclesiastical hierarchy. It is inconceivable that he could have expected to retain the deanery of Westminster with the primacy of All England; but it is typical of him to have worked simultaneously on both options. It was, however, as bishop of Lincoln that Williams was consecrated in the Abbey on 11 November; the bishops of London, Norwich and Ely officiated because Abbot

---

[26] PRO, SP 14/122, nos 31, 46 (*CSPD 1619–23*, 277, 279; *Letters of Chamberlain*, ii, 388–9, 392; Chamberlain to Carleton, 21 and 28 July 1621).

[27] PRO, SP 14/122, no. 46. Cf. C. Carlton, *Archbishop William Laud* (1987), 29 (but details of Williams's preferments are here confused).

[28] *The Fortescue Papers*, ed. S.R. Gardiner (Camden Soc. new ser. i, 1891), 157–8. Bald, *Donne*, 371–2.

[29] PRO, SP 14/122, no. 77 (*CSPD 1619–23*, 283; *Letters of Chamberlain*, ii, 397; Chamberlain to Carleton, 18 August 1621).

[30] Le Neve, *1541–1857*, i, 2. *HBC*, 237.

[31] P.A. Welsby, *George Abbot. The unwanted Archbishop, 1562–1633* (1962), 91–104. HMC, *Cowper MSS*, i, 113.

[32] BL, Harleian MS 7000, f. 59 (*Letters of Williams*, 44–6. *Cabala* (1654), i, 55–6, [where it is printed after the undated letter applying for London *vice* King (above, n. 19), but these letters cannot have been written on successive days, as assumed in Trevor-Roper, *Laud*, 59]).

was still under a cloud.[33] It was not quite all Williams had wanted, but it represented nevertheless a concentration of dignity in church and state unmatched since Wolsey; and even he had not contrived to rest one buttock on the woolsack and the other in Westminster Abbey.

The four years following, during which Williams remained keeper, were those of his closest association with the Abbey and Westminster School, and saw his principal benefactions to both. He began a programme of restoration of the fabric. He redecorated the Jerusalem Chamber, the ancient room in the Deanery where the chapter meets, with panelling which survives. How much he spent cannot be assessed: Williams himself asserted in 1636 that he had so far laid out £5,000–£6,000 of his own money on repairs to the fabric and on the library, in addition to £700 on plate, ornaments, and the provision of scholarships; Hacket gives the sum for structural repairs as £4,500, and this has passed into succeeding histories.[34] Whatever the precise figure, it naturally includes some home improvements which cannot be regarded as philanthropy. Williams certainly repaired the north side of the church; on 8 December 1628 the chapter recorded their refutation of an 'unjust report' that the dean had financed this work 'out of the diett and bellies of the prebendaries and revennews of our said church, and not out of his owne revennewes'.[35] It is noteworthy that the chapter felt it necessary to disavow any corporate responsibility for this expenditure.

Williams envisaged a scheme of scholarships and fellowships linking Westminster with his old college of St John's in Cambridge. He purchased fee-farm rents worth £27 6s 8d in the manors of Sunbury and Great Stanmore, Middlesex, which he vested in the dean and chapter on

---

[33] PRO, SP 14/123, no. 100 (*CSPD 1619–23*, 308; *Letters of Chamberlain*, ii, 406; Chamberlain to Carleton, 10 November 1621).

[34] HMC, *Cowper MSS*, ii, 112 (Williams to Coke, 31 March 1636). Hacket, *Scrin. Res.* i, 46. Widmore, *Westminster Abbey*, 151. WAM 6612, f. 8 (payment of £14 17s 6d to Adam Browne, joiner, for 'making the chymney peice in Jerusalem chamber', following other expenses on furniture and glazing December 1628 x May 1629, ff. 7v–8). Jerusalem is first specified as the location of chapter meetings on 13 December 1638, when Williams was absent (WAM Chapter Act Book II, f. 67v; *Acts 1609–42*, no. 87), but it had probably been so used throughout Williams's time.

[35] WAM Chapter Act Book II, f. 45 (*Acts 1609–42*, no. 57). Cf. A. Milton above (p. 221) for Canon Heylyn's subsequent revival of the argument; what was in question was not the canons' stipends, but the additional perquisites from sealing fees and other dividends, which were necessarily reduced if that revenue was applied to the fabric or some other common purpose. Such expenditure by Williams's direction cannot be traced through the records, but his repairs to the north side (and other benefactions) are mentioned by the newswriter John Pory: BL, Harleian MS 7000, f. 340v (to Lord Brooke, 15 November 1632) and PRO, C 115/M.35, no. 8418 (to Lord Scudamore, 17 November 1632), reproduced in Powell, *Pory*, microfiche supp., 326–7, 329.

26 April 1624 to support four scholars in addition to the 40 of royal foundation in Westminster School. Four scholars were immediately elected, being paid 25s apiece for the remaining two quarters of the financial year, and a further sum for their gowns.[36] For the Cambridge part of the project he had meanwhile arranged for Sir Miles Sandys and his son to sell him 94 acres of pasture at Raveley in Huntingdonshire.[37] On 29 December 1623 he further acquired the advowsons of Souldern (Oxon.), Freshwater (Isle of Wight), St Florence (Pembs.) and Aberdaron in Caernarvonshire.[38] On 30 December he had licence from the crown to establish fellowships and scholarships at St John's and to make statutes for them.[39]

First details of his plans for St John's come in a letter from the Johnian bishop of Exeter, Valentine Carey, to the master of the college, Owen Gwyn, on 18 October 1623. Williams had offered £60 in rents to support two fellows (at £20) and four scholars (£5) a year. Carey realized that this was inadequate, but that the college would lose the prospect of 'further bounty' if it were refused. A particular difficulty was that Williams wished to evade a college statute which required all gifts to comprise capital worth four-thirds of the expected charge (the additional third was known as 'dead college').[40] The master and senior fellows shared Carey's doubts. Another prominent Johnian, Bishop Richard Neile (a former dean of Westminster) proposed linking Williams's endowment with his separate gift of £1,200 for the college library, thereby getting round the 'dead college' rule. He agreed that the stipends offered were minimal, but thought the college should not 'slight such a fayre offre'.[41] Williams was furious that this had been so coolly received, and it took a personal visit from Carey (clutching a model of the new college library) to pacify him. Neile's deal was accepted.[42]

---

[36] WAM Chapter Act Book II, f. 34v (*Acts 1609–42*, no. 46). WAM 33681, f. 7v.

[37] SJC Archives, D.21.139 (mortmain licence, 1 September 1623).

[38] SJC Archives, D.66.6 (original instrument).

[39] SJC Archives, D.5.23 (original instrument).

[40] SJC Archives, D.105.232, printed in *The Eagle*, xvii (1893), 148–9. A.C. Crook, *From the Foundation to Gilbert Scott. A History of the Buildings of St John's College, Cambridge, 1511 to 1885* (Cambridge, privately pr. 1980), 49. Williams's intention to augment the foundation at St John's had been alluded to in a letter to him from the college on 14 January 1624: SJC Archives, C.7.16, p. 248 (*Letters of Williams*, 29–30 [where misdated]).

[41] SJC Archives, D.105.235, D.105.236 (*The Eagle*, xvii [1893], 153–5; Neile to Gwyn, 9 November 1623, and Gwyn's reply, undated). Cf. H.F. Howard, *An Account of the Finances of the College of St John the Evangelist in the University of Cambridge, 1511–1926* (Cambridge 1935), 60–1.

[42] SJC Archives, D.105.237, D.105.238 (*The Eagle*, xvii [1893], 155–6, 343–5; Carey to Gwyn, 14 and 19 November 1623). Baker, *Hist. St John's*, i, 208–10.

The master was warned by his local agent that the Raveley lands were a poor investment.[43] Nevertheless the college accepted endowment of this property and the four advowsons on 24 March 1624. Williams gave a further £160 in cash so that the college might buy land worth £7 or £8 and increase the revenue from £55 to at least £62.[44] The statutes were sealed by Williams at Westminster on 29 June and by the college on 4 November 1624.[45] The St John's scholars were to be chosen from those of Williams's Westminster foundation; two were to be Welsh and two from the diocese of Lincoln, but if no such candidates were found, natives of Westminster or the dean and chapter's properties elsewhere might be chosen. Election was to be made at Midsummer by the dean, the head master and one of the fellows on the foundation at St John's (who was allowed 20s for travelling to Westminster). The two fellowships would be filled by normal college election. The original fellows and scholars were, however, to be named by Williams. The master of St John's was permitted to take one of the four livings of the endowment; the fellows, on resigning, could apply for the others. In a modest way Williams was thus following a pattern common to medieval episcopal founders, providing a conveyor-belt of patronage from the schoolroom to the pulpit.[46] But Williams was no Wykeham or Waynflete, and his cut-price *amicabilis concordia* would lose its top tier after twenty years.

As soon as all the formalities were completed, Williams proposed to name his first two fellows (none having been recommended to him by the college, as he was expecting). He could not observe the 'fundamentall orders' as yet because none of his scholars was graduate, and he knew of no suitable fellow-countrymen. He therefore nominated John Barrett, MA (an Old Westminster who had been at St John's since 1614) and William Mostyn of Queens' College (his kinsman). But if Mostyn were passed over as 'rawe', he would have Edward Baker, MA, of Trinity

---

[43] SJC Archives, D.94.185 (John Crosse, registrar of the archdeaconry of Huntingdon, to Gwyn [who was archdeacon], 6 January 1624).

[44] SJC Archives, D.5.12 (original instrument); D.59.3 (copy); C.8.1, pp. 1046–8 (registered copy). The Raveley lands were immediately let, but by October had proved an inadequate resource: D.66.3 (assignment, 24 March 1624); D.94.436 (William Boswell to Gwyn, 26 October 1624).

[45] SJC Archives, D.59.50 (original instrument; codex with Williams's seal); D.67.10 (copy as sealed by the college); C.8.1, pp. 1058–60 (registered copy). WAM 12962 (copy as sealed by St John's, 4 November 1624).

[46] Cf. M. Jewell, 'English bishops as educational benefactors in the later fifteenth century', *The Church, Politics and Patronage in the Fifteenth Century*, ed. R.B. Dobson (Gloucester 1984), 154–5; J.K. McConica, 'The collegiate society', in McConica, *Collegiate University*, 670–1.

College.[47] Barrett and Mostyn were duly admitted on 6 April 1625.[48] Only three further Williams fellows were elected. Williams knew well enough that the college had accepted his benefaction out of deference and in expectation of more. His secretary Thomas Wharton gives an affecting account of Williams finally drawing up plans for an additional £300 endowment on the night before he died.[49] St John's was left with arrears on the fellowship account rising from £160 2s 8d at the end of 1634 to £479 18s by 1651.[50] On 28 August 1651 the committee for reform of the university ordered an enquiry. On being told that, despite careful management, the endowment had never yielded more than £40 a year and had already put the college almost £500 in debt, the committee (18 September) instructed the college to abolish the fellowships and use the endowment to support the scholars alone.[51]

The scholarships, at Westminster and St John's, were more successfully planted. Among Williams's first choices for a college scholarship was his kinsman Richard Bulkeley, a youth 'of extraordinarie hopes for his yong yeares', already with expectation of a place at Trinity. Williams wanted him to stay at school longer than was quite necessary (in order to shine at the forthcoming examination) and then to be admitted to St John's ahead of the normal entry 'least he should loose a yeare by his lingring at Westminster'.[52] After his initial nominations Williams continued to recommend Westminsters for scholarships at St John's and to promote their further careers. Not every endorsement was effusive: in February 1640 he wrote of Richard Mattock, OW, elected his scholar at St John's in the previous November: 'he needes much, yeat whyther he

---

[47] SJC Archives, D.94.402 (*Letters of Williams*, 33–4; Williams to Gwyn, 30 December 1624). Barrett and Mostyn are assumed to have been at Westminster by virtue of this nomination; Baker is otherwise known to have been at school: *ROW*, i, 43, 56; ii, 671. A play by Barrett, *Stoicus vulpans*, performed at St John's, was published in a collection beginning with John Hacket's verse comedy *Loiola* and including a work by Thomas Vincent (1648: Wing H170); Hacket and Vincent were also Westminsters. For others elected to Williams's foundation see appendix, p. 259.

[48] SJC Archives, C.3.2, p. 300.

[49] Philips, *Life*, 352–6. An extract is written on the dorse of the Westminster copy of the foundation statutes: WAM 12962.

[50] SJC Archives, D.59.69.

[51] SJC Archives, D.59.62, D.59.63, D.59.64 (*The Eagle*, xxxiii [1912], 109–11).

[52] SJC Archives, D.105.200 (*Letters of Williams*, 31–2; Hacket to Gwyn: Westminster, 28 June 1624). Williams subsequently recommended Bulkeley for a fellowship. Neither of his own foundation was available, so he sought to place Bulkeley on the foundation of Gwyn's uncle (and therefore Williams's kinsman). Bulkeley was ineligible for this fellowship, but by virtue of the king's mandate (20 March 1629) was admitted on the foundress's foundation 25 March 1629: SJC Archives, D.105.201 (Williams to Gwyn, 24 November 1628; *Letters of Williams*, 40 & n. [on pp. 81–2]). Baker, *Hist. St John's*, i, 294.

deserves, I must referre wholye to you'.[53] This was written when Williams was a prisoner in the Tower; so too was his recommendation of a namesake in September 1640 who duly advanced from Westminster to St John's in the following November.[54] And in May 1642, free again but with other concerns impending, Williams scribbled a recommendation for Robert Jessup which secured his place on the college foundation.[55] There were 21 admissions to the Williams scholarships while the founder lived. Eight of those elected were from Wales, three from the diocese of Lincoln and the remainder from the home counties. Apart from one who entered royal service, all those whose careers are known became clergymen. Two of the scholars, Cardell Goodman and William Morgan, were elected onto the Williams fellowships and thereafter held livings with which the college had been provided. These two may be said therefore to have accomplished the founder's full intentions.[56]

While Williams made no formal provision for founder's kin, three of his nominees (Wynn, Bulkeley and Mostyn) were his relatives and others may also have been. In about 1659 Dorothy Watts, widow, petitioned the governors of Westminster School to place her son, already a pupil there, on the foundation of the late archbishop, to whom he was 'nearly allyed'. The boy's father, a luckless clergyman, had died in 1649 with Prince Rupert's naval squadron in Kinsale. These circumstances, tactfully omitted from the mother's petition, were doubtless known to the head master, Richard Busby, a discreet protector of royalist unfortunates.[57]

Williams's foundation had continuing difficulties. In November 1653 the Westminster governors found that the board and lodging of the scholars was costing £48 a year, £20 more than Williams's fee-farms covered.[58] In 1654 the new master of St John's, Anthony Tuckney, could not find the original deed relating to the scholarships at his college.[59]

---

[53] SJC Archives, D.67.7 (Williams to William Beale, master, 21 February 1640).

[54] SJC Archives, C.7.16, p. 377 (Williams to Beale, 23 September 1640).

[55] *Ibid.*, p. 402 (record of applicant's suit endorsed by Williams 23 May 1642).

[56] Goodman became rector of Freshwater in March 1641, Morgan of St Florence in September 1660: *ROW*, i, 383; ii, 665. Morgan had joined the royalist army and his employer, reflecting that 'perchance by occasion thereof he may runne summ hazzard concerning his degree, fellowship and other emoluments' permitted him to keep his college precedence and profits notwithstanding: SJC Archives, C.7.16, p. 406 (the king to the college, 28 February 1643).

[57] WAM 43102. *ROW*, ii, 974. Le Neve, *1541–1857*, v, 10. *Wells Cathedral Chapter Act Book 1666–83*, ed. D.S. Bailey (Somerset Record Soc. lxxii, 1973), p. xi. Watts senior had sought a dignity at Wells, of which Busby was canon. Watts junior would become precentor of Hereford and archdeacon of Llandaff.

[58] WAM 43485, 43486.

[59] WAM 43059 (Tuckney to Serjeant Bradshaw, 27 January 1654).

Nevertheless the 'Bishop's Boys' survived at Westminster until the nineteenth century; their distinctive purple gowns were abolished by a humourless head master in 1847 and the last scholar was elected in 1872. The endowment income, having soared to £72, was transferred to the school's general exhibition fund. The St John's scholarships were terminated by the university commission of 1856.[60]

Williams's most enduring monument at Westminster is the chapter library. This had since 1591 occupied the northern half of the former monastic dormitory.[61] On 27 January 1626 the chapter recorded the dean's re-edification of the room and the provision of £2,000 worth of books. At the same time Richard Gouland, who for two years had been re-ordering the collection, was confirmed as library keeper with a substantially increased fee (£20 a year), a house and a place at the canons' table.[62] When Williams vacated the keepership he asked the king to give Gouland the next vacant canonry; this was denied him, but he was able to make amends in 1631 by collating Gouland to the prebendal stall of North Kelsey in his cathedral church of Lincoln.[63] A catalogue had been made in 1623; the register of benefactors also begins this year.[64] A major if unwitting contributor was Sir Richard Baker, sometime sheriff of Oxfordshire. He had unwisely married into debt and his property was subsequently seized by the crown. Williams bought his entire library for £500 – 'a cheap peny worth for such precious war[e]' according to Hacket.[65] Williams persuaded his chapter colleagues and others to contribute a further £500 worth of books. Among the earliest benefactors recorded are Sir Julius Caesar (£128), Lord Russell (£10), Sir Ranulph Crew (£6 13s 4d), Sir Henry Spelman (£6 13s 4d) and John Selden (no sum mentioned). Lambert Osbaldeston, the head master,

---

[60] *ROW*, ii, 1109–10. G.F. Russell Barker, *Memoir of Richard Busby* (1895), 13 n. 2. L.E. Tanner, *Westminster School. A History* (1934), 11 (which suggests that the boys, not just their gowns, were abolished in 1847).

[61] *Acts 1543–1609*, no. 430. The room is oddly called 'the monks' old parlour' by A. Tindal Hart in Carpenter, *House of Kings* (p. 151), echoed in Williams, *Work of Williams*, 40. For the library and Williams's contribution to it see J.W. Clark, 'On ancient libraries', *Proceedings of the Cambridge Antiquarian Society*, new ser. iii (1899 for 1894–8), 53–6; Robinson and James, *MSS of Westminster Abbey*, 17–21; Tanner, *Library*, 5–8, 11–12.

[62] WAM Chapter Act Book II, f. 38 (*Acts 1609–42*, no. 51). WAM Reg. XIII, f. 24v. WAM 9815 (draft patent 27 January 1626, redated 18 December following).

[63] Hacket, *Scrin. Res.* ii, 25. Le Neve, *1541–1857*, ix, 99.

[64] WAM 33680, f. 5. WA Library, Register of Benefactors (no class mark); in fact begun after Williams's death, and said to be in progress in March 1651: WAM 57167 (I owe this reference to Dr T. Trowles).

[65] *CSPD 1628–9*, 383. *Notes and Queries*, 2nd ser. xi (1861), 384 (wrongly cited in *DNB*, i, 936). *Hist. Parl. 1558–1603*, i, 387. Hacket, *Scrin. Res.* i, 47.

paid £25 for the portrait of Williams which remains in place above the shelves and desks which the dean provided. Orlando Gibbons, the organist, gave two works by Speed, including an atlas.[66]

Not all the benefactors were disinterested. William Spicer, DCL, would complain that Williams and the chapter had (among other things) accepted from him £20 worth of books and a clock, on condition of his receiving a lease of a plot of land in the precinct, which had then been refused. In his reply Williams claimed that Spicer had defaulted by not building a house which would have reverted to the use of the library keeper. He observed that the books were freely given, and in any case were 'verie poore and imperfect'; while the clock, which Spicer claimed to be of 'rare and curious composition' was but 'an od thinge somwhat like the giver and of noe value or use at all'.[67] Spicer none the less received a lease in December 1632 for another property he had alleged the chapter were wrongly detaining from him, and most of the books he gave can be identified in the Abbey library.[68] In addition to the other furniture there, two covers were bought for the 'great globe' in 1627.[69] A separate library for the scholars was fitted up at the end of the school (the other part of the old dorter) in 1638.[70] The chapter library was not for the sole use of the dean and

[66] WA Library, Register of Benefactors, ff. 18, 26, 28, 29, 48, 59, 65. Selden had been released from prison in 1621 by Williams's means, and in the following year he was appointed auditor to the dean and chapter: WAM Chapter Act Book II, f. 32v (*Acts 1609–42*, no. 42). Thomas, 'Archbishop John Williams', 202–3. Russell and Crew were tenants of substantial houses in the Abbey precinct; Spelman was a neighbour in Tothill St; Caesar was Williams's colleague in chancery: WAM Reg. XII, ff. 269v–270v, 323v–325, 371–2. HMC, *9th Report* (1883–4), ii, 424. L.M. Hill, *Bench and Bureaucracy. The Public Career of Sir Julius Caesar, 1580–1636* (Cambridge 1988), 205–6.

[67] WAM 18150 (Spicer to Lord Keeper Coventry, 24 January 1632); WAM 18151 (Williams's reply, undated). As Dr Milton has illustrated (above, p. 210), Spicer carried the quarrel a stage further in July 1632 by leaking comments made to him by Williams during the time of their friendship.

[68] WAM Chapter Act Book II, f. 55 (*Acts 1609–42*, no. 68). WAM Reg. XIV, ff. 211–13. WAM 65064: N. Horsfall, 'William Spicer and the Westminster Abbey library' (1964). WA Library, Register of Benefactors, f. 68 (where Spicer is wrongly named 'John'). The books in question were [with press marks of those identifiable as extant]: Cesare Baronius, *Annales Ecclesiastici* (Cologne 1609–25), in 11 volumes, to which 2 published 1630 were subsequently added [V.2.21]; W. Camden, *Britannia*, with maps (1607; *STC* 4508) [R.1.49]; John Minsheu, *Guide into the Tongues* (1617; *STC* 17944) [0.3.41]; Jean Crespin, *Lexicon Græcolatinum* (1579) [not found]; Thomas Cooper, *Thesaurus Linguae Romanae et Britannicae* (1584; *STC* 5689) [0.3.18]. I am grateful to Dr Trowles for assistance in identifying these volumes.

[69] WAM 33683, f. 8.

[70] WAM 33688, f. 8.

canons, but was open to the public and particularly frequented by lawyers working in Westminster Hall. According to Hacket, Williams had turned 'a wast place ... into Plato's portico'.[71] This, however, is unjust to preceding deans and their chapters, who had by no means neglected this facility.

Williams also acquired a collection of manuscripts. In 1623 the dean and chapter of Worcester sent 20 duplicate volumes of canon law and theology for the 'newly erected' Westminster library.[72] These seem, however, to have been among 200 or so manuscripts which remained in Williams's study at Westminster after his departure in 1642.[73] The disposition of this whole collection was of concern to the parliamentary governors who took the place of the dean and chapter. On 17 April 1649 the governors deputed one of their number, Sir John Trevor, to deliver 'a study of bookes' in the Deanery to Williams or his agent, on condition that after the archbishop's death the books should go to St John's College, Cambridge, according to his former gift.[74] Custody was given to Richard Gouland. When Williams died in March 1650, the disposal of his books became the responsibility of his nephew and administrator, Griffith Williams. In the following July two fellows of St John's borrowed from Westminster a catalogue of such books remaining there as Williams had intended for them; but having scrutinized the list the master and fellows disclaimed all interest in the contents.[75] In 1651 Griffith relinquished any right he might have had to 'some manuscript bookes' which Williams had intended to give to Westminster

---

[71] Hacket, *Scrin. Res.* i, 47. Selden asked Sir Robert Cotton to procure for him a loan of 'the Talmud of Bablyon in divers great volumes' from the library which Williams was setting up ('for the Library is not yet so setled as that books may not be lent if the founder will'): BL, Cotton MS Julius C.3, f. 188v (*Original Letters of Eminent Literary Men*, ed. Sir H. Ellis [Camden Soc. xxiii, 1843], 143; Selden to Cotton, 4 July 1629). Selden seemingly sought the edition in 10 volumes (Venice 1570), which does not survive in WA Library.

[72] Worcester Cathedral Library, A.75, ff. 81v, 84v, cited and quoted in Lehmberg, *Cathedrals under Siege*, 252. Notes on this gift are in an interleaved copy of Robinson and James, *MSS of Westminster Abbey* in WA Library, reference collection.

[73] Tanner, *Library*, 8, gives 230 as the total of Williams's MS collection; this derives from Bernard's 1697 catalogue (see n. 81 below), and may include some later acquisitions. But c. 1651 the library keeper accounted for 237 MSS (along with 4,514 volumes received, 4,875 passed to his successor, and 28 'refuse' books): WAM 9832.

[74] WAM 12645B.

[75] WAM 12646 (receipt by Henry Eyre and Samuel Heron, fellows of St John's, 18 July 1650). SJC Archives, MR.57.118 (Baker, *Hist. St John's*, ii, 620–2; quitclaim by master and fellows 18 September 1650). The college had to dispose of many 'imperfect' or superfluous books which came to them from Williams's library at Buckden: SJC Archives, D.25.259, D.105.339. Cf. Philips, *Life*, 317–18.

library, which at this time were also in Gouland's custody.[76] Gouland, who had lost his place as keeper of the library but received a pension and some further work there, asked the governors to issue library regulations which Williams himself would have made but for 'his own and the late publique troubles'.[77] On 12 March 1653 Gouland was commissioned to catalogue the manuscripts.[78] In November the governors directed the collection to be housed in a room next to the library, and estimates were made for the furniture.[79] Here all but one of Williams's manuscripts was destroyed by fire in 1695.[80] Several lists of the collection survive, showing that the contents ranged from grammar and theology to astrology and alchemy. M.R. James, who collated the lists, thought most of the classical MSS were fifteenth-century Italian copies, but two were ancient and one '*may* have been valuable and interesting', if 'rather recent'.[81]

To bibliophiles at least, Williams was a paragon, to be spoken of in the same breath as Sir Thomas Bodley.[82] He loved to pose as the great patron of scholars, almost by way of demonstrating that he was too much the public man to write that much himself. He delighted in welcoming foreign visitors, be they Czech philosopher or Greek monk.[83] But there was always a political purpose. This was never more obvious than in the Spanish and French translations of the Book of Common Prayer which Williams provided to accompany successive marriage negotiations for Prince Charles. In March 1623, when the prince and

---

[76] WAM 9825 (Griffith Williams to the governors of Westminster College: Penrhyn, 28 June 1651). There was much uncertainty about the rights to Williams's property generally: cf. WAM 12648. Lists of his goods remaining at Westminster: WAM 12647, 12650–2. Cf. Philips, *Life*, 319, 320–1.

[77] WAM 9833 (undated). Cf. WAM 9816–18, 43165, 43296 (for Gouland's loss of income and subsequent payments to him); WAM 9826 (library rules).

[78] WAM 9831.

[79] WAM 9828, 43486, 43487. The room had been surveyed two years earlier: WAM 43292*. Extracts from these papers are in Robinson and James, *MSS of Westminster Abbey*, 20–1.

[80] WAM 56814, printed in Tanner, *Library*, 7 (John Nedham, receiver-general, to his son-in-law, 24 January 1695).

[81] Robinson and James, *MSS of Westminster Abbey*, 26–62, collating (1) BL, Harleian MS 694, ff. 20–9 (old pp. 38–56); (2) Trinity College, Cambridge, MS 0.5.38, pp. 59–66; (3) Bodl. MS Tanner 272, ff. 34–44; (4) WA Library, Register of Benefactors, ff. 122–9; (5) E. Bernard, *Catalogi Librorum Manuscriptorum Angliae et Hiberniae* (Oxford 1697), ii, 27–9; (1–3) yield 180+ entries, (4) 170, (5) 230. The item of possible interest to James (p. 28, his italics) was 'Expositiones SS. Patrum in Biblia, viz. Dionysii Ignatii Polycarpi Justini etc.'

[82] Robert Burton, quoted in Trevor-Roper, *Renaissance Essays*, 244.

[83] Cf. H.R. Trevor-Roper, *From Counter-Reformation to Glorious Revolution* (1992), 104, 222.

Buckingham were in Spain on their mission to cut through (as they supposed) the diplomatic obstacles to a Spanish match, Williams heard that in Spain it was understood that the English church had no formal liturgy. So he arranged for a renegade Dominican, Fray Fernando de Teleda, to translate Cranmer into Spanish, and forwarded the result to Madrid with King James's approval.[84] It was during the Spanish mission that Williams detached himself from adherence to Buckingham; his intrigues against his former patron would be conducted from his Westminster house.[85]

By December 1624 a French marriage was in prospect. Williams was, against his inclination, ordered to entertain the French negotiating team. He gave them dinner in Jerusalem Chamber and presented copies of the Prayer Book translated into French by Pierre Delaune, a protestant minister at Norwich. He also put on a show in the Abbey, with torches, anthems sung by the choir, and Gibbons at the organ. This was *son et lumière* not liturgy, though an interesting development in music as entertainment and in the use of the Abbey. One of the Frenchmen asked for more, and was (from behind a curtain) present on Christmas morning when Williams celebrated and preached at a 4½-hour service.[86]

These splendid occasions mark the high point of Williams's career. Early in the new year James I endowed him with an extra £2,000 a year.[87] The king's death on 27 March, with Williams alone of the clergy in attendance, prevented any further reward. Williams preached an eloquent oration at James's funeral in the Abbey on 7 May, likening him to

---

[84] Hacket, *Scrin. Res.* i, 126–7 (where the translator is called 'John Taxeda'). BL, Harleian MS 7000, f. 121v (Williams to Buckingham 15 July 1623; *Cabala* [1654], i, 79; [1663], 309 [both printed versions incomplete and without date]). The volume is *Liturgia Ingelsa* (1624 *recte* 1623; STC 16434). See *Spain and the Jacobean Catholics*, ii, 1613–1624, ed. A.J. Loomie (Catholic Record Soc., Records ser. lxviii, 1978), 185–6.

[85] R.E. Ruigh, *The Parliament of 1624. Politics and Foreign Policy* (Harvard Historical Studies, Cambridge, Mass. 1971), 273–8.

[86] PRO, SP 14/176, no. 65 (*CSPD 1623–5*, 411–12; *Letters of Chamberlain*, ii, 591–2; Chamberlain to Carleton, 18 December 1624), establishing date of event 18 December. Hacket, *Scrin. Res.* i, 209–12 (extracts in Carpenter, *House of Kings*, 156). Hacket says (p. 209) that Williams commissioned Delaune to translate the Prayer Book for the occasion, but *La Liturgie Angloise* was printed in 1616 (STC 16431, transl. attrib. to de Laune). Williams actually opposed the imposition of a translated Anglican liturgy on the stranger churches: Trevor-Roper, *Laud*, 182, 203.

[87] M.A. Van C. Alexander, *Charles I's Lord Treasurer. Sir Richard Weston, Earl of Portland (1577–1635)* (1975), 74. For Williams's total income see Thomas, 'Archbishop John Williams', 85, 333–40; he notes correctly (p. 337) that the £232 10s forming his official Westminster salary was a fraction of the real income he would have derived from dividends of fines and other casualties; at the peak of his career he may have commanded £12,500 a year from all sources.

Solomon in all but his vices.[88] The new king had no vices; Williams, however, was no more impressed by virtue than he was shocked by vice. He found it necessary to instruct Charles I in elementary constitutional aspects of the demise of the crown on the day after his accession. There was little prospect that he would remain in office, and on 23 October he was required to surrender the great seal. He was then ordered away to his diocese.[89] He returned to Westminster by 7 January, confidently looking forward to doing duty as dean of Westminster at the coronation on 2 February.[90] The king, however, meant Laud to take the dean's part in the ceremony, even though he was still only a very junior member of the chapter.[91] Williams was ordered to name a deputy. Since he 'had no mind to nominate ... his corrival and supplanter' (in Buckingham's favour), he returned a list of the whole chapter, from which the king selected Laud.[92] Parliament was due to assemble on 6 February, for which the writs had gone out on 20 December. Williams at first received no summons, and wrote to the king complaining that he was thus denied what even prisoners and condemned peers had been accorded in the previous reign. He particularly asked the king to 'mitigate and allay the causes and displeasure of my lord duke against me, who is so little satisfied with any thing I can do', and begged that rumours against him should not be credited.[93]

Six days before the coronation (27 January) the chapter blandly recorded that the dean had 'urgent occasions to be absent from his deanery' for a year, and he was dispensed from his residence and

---

[88] J. Williams, *Great Britain's Salomon. A Sermon preached at the magnificent Funerall of the most high and mighty King, James* (1625: STC 25723). The sermon was in print by 21 May: PRO, SP 16/2, no. 80 (*CSPD 1625–6*, 26; *Letters of Chamberlain*, ii, 619; Chamberlain to Carleton, that day). Cf. SP 16/1, no. 46 and SP 16/2, no. 55 (*CSPD 1625–6*, 8, 22; *Letters of Chamberlain*, ii, 608, 616; same to same, 9 April [news that Williams was to preach], 14 May [account of funeral]). For analysis of the sermon and the funeral ceremony see Woodward, *Theatre of Death*, 175–203, esp. pp. 175–6, 179, 184 (on the sermon), 195 & n. 98 (on its being the first royal funeral sermon printed).

[89] Hacket, *Scrin. Res.* ii, 4, 27. Alexander, *Weston*, 78–9, 89.

[90] BL, Harleian MS 7000, f. 191 (*Cabala* [1663], 310; *Letters of Williams*, 57–8; Williams to Buckingham, 7 January 1626).

[91] On coronation day Laud stood 10th in seniority of the 12 canons: Le Neve, *1541–1857*, vii, 72 x 83. On 31 July he was granted a further *commendam*, at Buckingham's suit, to retain his canonry with the bishopric of Bath and Wells: *CSPD 1625–6*, 570.

[92] Heylyn, *Cyprianus*, 144.

[93] WAM 57084, as printed in *Cabala* (1654), i, 108–9; undated, but said to be written four months after taking leave of the king at Salisbury, where the court had been 14 x 24 October 1625: *APC 1625–6*, 199 x 218. The WAM is a modern acquisition, once supposed to be the holograph original; it is actually a contemporary copy with a poor imitation of Williams's signature (Williams's hand is distinctive, and is helpfully authenticated by SJC Archives, D.67.7). Alexander, *Weston*, 97. *HBC*, 537. Williams is recorded as present from the opening of the session: *LJ*, iii, 492.

preaching obligations.[94] At the same meeting it was agreed that Buckingham, who had been high steward of Westminster since 1618, should have a lease of the largest block of the Abbey's country property, in Worcestershire and Gloucestershire. Buckingham paid a fine of £1,000, from which the dean and chapter bought lands worth £99 10s 11½d, of which £40 annually was bestowed on the choir.[95] Buckingham and Laud were now in effective control of the Abbey.

Williams spent the next eleven years mostly at Buckden in Huntingdonshire, his principal residence as bishop of Lincoln. He came to Westminster rarely: by his own account, only at the great festivals, the school election, and the two main chapters (the audit in December and the other in early summer). Even so he had to refute Abbot's allegation that he had called a chapter on 12 May 1626 as an excuse for returning to Westminster while parliament remained in session.[96] Later that year he asked Buckingham to procure the king's leave to spend two or three months at his 'poor house in Westminster'. But when in July 1627 he came down for a few days at the school election, he was ordered to return as soon as that business was done. He then more modestly petitioned to be allowed to return for 'these necessary occasions' if his 'sick and crazy state of body permitted'.[97] In fact he may have attended no more than five chapter meetings in these eleven years, since on all other occasions his signature in the Act Book appears to have been written in spaces left vacant for him.[98] About the only expenditure on

---

[94] WAM Chapter Act Book II, f. 38 (*Acts 1609–42*, no. 51).

[95] WAM Chapter Act Book II, ff. 25, 37–37v, 41 (*Acts 1609–42*, nos 32, 50, 53). WAM Reg. XIII, ff. 25–25v. WAM 1579, 32946–7. The Venetian ambassador reported on 15 January 1627 that Williams had arranged this transaction in the hope of regaining political favour, and that Buckingham had resold the lands at three times the price he had paid: *CSP Ven. 1626–8*, 93–4.

[96] Hacket, *Scrin. Res.* ii, 69. By an order of 1585 the summer chapter was fixed at the Monday in the second week of Easter term (*Acts 1543–1609*, no. 374), though meetings were mostly held on the Friday of that week; in 1626 this fell on 12 May, when no meeting is recorded. Williams attended parliament on 11 and 13 May (no sitting on 12th): *LJ*, iii, 591, 593. Visits to Westminster for Christmas (1628) and election (1634) are mentioned by Lord Clare: *Letters of John Holles 1587–1637*, ed. P.R. Seddon (Thoroton Soc. Record ser. xxxi, xxxv–vi (1975–86), iii, 389, 460; cf. ii, 325, 369; I am grateful to Dr Milton for drawing my attention to these references.

[97] PRO, SP 16/37, no. 87 (*CSPD 1625–6*, 455; Williams to Buckingham, 15 October 1626). HMC, *Cowper MSS*, i, 329 (Williams to Coke, 5 November 1627).

[98] Williams's signature is apparently retrospective for 21 of the 26 meetings between 25 February 1626 and 22 May 1637 (after which he was imprisoned until 1640): WAM Chapter Act Book II, ff. 38 x 63v. Signature may indicate presence on 16 May 1628, 3 May 1630, 17 and 23 May 1631, 13–14 December 1632: *ibid.*, ff. 43, 47v, 50v, 51v, 56. Signature is, however, never proof of attendance. Williams's signatures to nine chapters after his release, 14 December x 25 May 1642, also look retrospective: *ibid.*, ff. 75 x 81.

his presence was for a mat and pillow in the dean's stall 'for my lordes feet'.[99]

Since 1604 the dean of Westminster had been the customary preacher at court on Good Friday. It was reported that Williams was barred from this duty in 1627, and again in 1632; on the latter occasion his place was taken by William Warre, fellow of Trinity College, Cambridge. Exclusion from court itself rather than its pulpit was the more frustrating for Williams; though he occasionally fostered the image of himself as a preaching pastor, this was more by way of anti-Arminianism than for any positive purpose.[100] Court politics inter-related with those of the Abbey at many points. Buckingham was murdered at Portsmouth on 23 August 1628. By the time of his funeral in the Abbey on 18 September the king had selected the earl of Montgomery, lord chamberlain, to succeed the duke as high steward of Westminster. Williams had already offered the post to the earl of Holland: he grudgingly accepted the king's nomination, though the office was in his own gift. Charles was annoyed when the dean and chapter sent him a blank warrant for the appointment. On 19 September the chapter promised that a patent for Montgomery would be sealed as soon as a quorum could be assembled. In 1630 when Montgomery, having succeeded his brother as earl of Pembroke, sought to succeed him also as chancellor of Oxford University, Williams took his side against the alternative and successful candidate, Laud.[101]

---

[99] WAM 41584 (bill of 1635).

[100] McCullough, *Sermons at Court*, 148–9. *Letters of Williams*, 85 (Chamberlain to Joseph Mead, 9 March 1627; Good Friday was 23 March). PRO, C 115/M.35, no. 8398 (Powell, *Pory*, supp., 238; Pory to Scudamore, 31 March 1632; Good Friday was 30th). The dean of Westminster is listed as Good Friday court preacher for 1622–5 and 1628–30: WAM, Muniment Book 15, ff. 44, 45, 45v, 46, 46v, 47. PRO, LC 5/183, f. 1 (for 1625; as given in McCullough's supplementary 'Calendar'). There are no lists for other years of Williams's decanate, and he may not necessarily have exercised his duty in person even when specifically listed. In March 1631 Lord Clare expected that Williams 'will be at London for good fryday sake': *Letters of Holles*, iii, 425. Williams preached before the House of Lords in the Abbey on 6 April 1628 (on Galatians 6:14: STC 25729), and again before their lordships there on Ash Wednesday, 18 February 1629 (on Job 42:12: STC 25727). For his preaching generally see K.C. Fincham, *Prelate as Pastor. The Episcopate of James I* (Oxford 1990), 274. A collection of holograph sermon notes, with two complete sermons (on Genesis 3:15 and John 11:51) forms Magdalene College, Cambridge, Pepys Library, no. 1441.

[101] Lockyer, *Buckingham*, 457–8. CSPD 1628–9, 276, 277, 311, 327, 330–1. WAM Chapter Act Book II, f. 44 (*Acts 1609–42*, no. 56). Heylyn, *Cyprianus*, 208. No patent for Montgomery himself is registered, but his deputy was appointed bailiff of Westminster 8 December 1628: WAM Reg. XIII, ff. 266v–267v. Carlton (*Charles I*, 116) misunderstands Williams to have solicited the stewardship for himself.

Williams's kinsman Theodore Price had been a canon of Westminster since June 1623. When the bishopric of St Asaph became vacant in the following September, Price had hope of receiving this in reward for services to church and state in Ireland. Williams supported Price's candidacy, but the prince of Wales (affecting to believe that bishoprics in the principality were for service to him) had one of his chaplains appointed. Two years later Price aspired to the archbishopric of Armagh; this time Williams withdrew his endorsement when it was observed that Price had never once preached before the king (a major disqualification) and rarely occupied any pulpit. At which point Price fell out with Dean Williams, the chapter, and the Church of England generally. When he died at Westminster on 15 December 1631 he was given the last rites of the Roman church, whereupon he lay unburied for a week because none of the canons would conduct his funeral. Eventually Williams persuaded the precentor, John Frost, to officiate. Pembroke chided the king for having so much as considered appointing Price to a bishopric. Price's conversion seems plausible enough in the light of his disappointments. The suggestion supposedly made by the Laudian party that the whole story was invented by Williams to embarrass Laud seems notably but not untypically self-defeating.[102]

None of this seriously threatened Williams. But Laud, especially after he became archbishop of Canterbury in 1633, was always looking for ways to strike down his old rival. Williams's conduct as bishop of Lincoln was (or could be presented as) so correct that no grounds for deprivation would be found; indeed in many ways Williams displayed an attention to duty and decorum which accorded with Laud's model.[103] His continued occupancy of the deanery of Westminster was the more disagreeable to Laud because the peculiar status of the collegiate church was an affront to the uniform ecclesiastical order he was determined to impose. Laud had vacated the chapter himself in 1628 on becoming bishop of London, but since 1631 he had his personal nark there in the form of his chaplain, Peter Heylyn. By March 1634 Heylyn and the three other junior canons had concocted a 36–article indictment of

---

[102] Hacket, *Scrin. Res.* i, 207; ii, 97–8. Le Neve, *1541–1857*, vii, 78. PRO, C 115/M. 35, no. 8387 (Powell, *Pory*, supp., 190; Pory to Scudamore, 24 December 1631). Frost is there identified as a gentleman of the chapel royal, but he was also precentor of Westminster Abbey: *The Old Cheque-Book ... of the Chapel Royal, from 1561 to 1744*, ed. E.F. Rimbault [Camden Soc, new ser. iii, 1872], 7, 203). Cf. Soden, *Goodman*, 133–4; Thomas, 'Archbishop John Williams', 224 (accepting the theory that Williams deliberately publicised the event); M. Questier, *Conversion, Politics and Religion in England, 1580–1625* (Cambridge 1996), 42, 49, 192 n. 102.

[103] Cf. Trevor-Roper, *Laud*, 179–84; Carlton, *Laud*, 125–7; Davies, *Caroline Captivity*, 35–6, 235–9; K. Sharpe, *The Personal Rule of Charles I* (1992), 336–8.

Williams's activities, or lack of them, at Westminster. Minor matters of local precedence were mixed with more serious accusations of mal-administration and corruption. The petition was formally presented to the king on 31 March, and he referred the matter to a committee of the privy council.[104]

Williams drafted a magisterial reply finding fault in the premises of his opponents' claims and in the logic of their arguments. He had an answer for everything; though sometimes, and so the less convincingly, more than one.[105] It was said, for example, that he had not worn his full episcopal habit at all services as required by canon 25 and the local statutes of the church. He replied that (1) the particular occasion complained of was after the service proper had ended, (2) he could find no local statute on the subject, and the usage of previous deans was a matter of their personal preference, and (3) the canon cited was probably of no effect in the exempt church of Westminster.[106] He was said to have made deals with tenants which were unfavourable to the church. In particular he was accused over a lease to chief justice Heath of disafforested land in Gloucestershire. No fine had been paid, and the original rent of £100 a year was reduced to £60 by the dean, who had secured the chapter's agreement by the simple expedient of bringing the judge in to sit beside him. To this Williams answered that this was waste land, from which they had received no revenue before and the

---

[104] Vernon, *Life of Heylyn*, 67–81. The *Earl of Strafforde's Letters and Despatches*, ed. W. Knowler (1739), i, 360 (George Garrard to Wentworth, 11 January 1635). The four complainants were the juniors (by date of appointment): Thomas Wilson (1626), Lewis Wemys (1631), Heylyn (1631), and Gabriel Moore (1633). Heylyn's leading role is well established; cf. above, p. 211; I thank Dr Milton for his additional guidance on this issue. Wilson may have been a minor conspirator; Williams identified only the other three as his detractors: HMC, *Cowper MSS*, ii, 112 (Williams to Secretary Coke, 31 March 1636; by this time Wilson and Wemys had advanced in seniority because of new appoinments to the chapter). Dr Foster has also suggested to me that the sub-dean, Robert Newell, may well have quietly encouraged the opposition to Williams.

[105] WAM 25095: 'Heades for the deanes answer to the objections of the 4 junior prebendaries'; printed privately [by J.A. Robinson, c. 1906], and in Bowen, 'John Williams', 75–91. Williams refers to present year as '1634' (f. 12v), and to his being '16 yeares a deane of this churche', i.e. from his initial deanery of Salisbury, 1619 (f. 7); it was therefore presumably composed in the first months of 1635 n.s. No copy appears to survive of the canons' original petition. Hacket (*Scrin. Res.* ii, 91) speaks of 36 articles, though the 'Heades' responds to 39 numbered objections; in view of the prolonged controversy, it may well be supposed that the agenda lengthened.

[106] WAM 25095, f. 1. Neither the 1604 canon cited nor the only relevant act of the second collegiate church gave any direction on episcopal habit: *The Anglican Canons, 1529–1947*, ed. G. Bray (Church of England Record Soc. vi, 1998), 296/297. *Acts 1543–1609*, no. 262.

remission of £40 a year was reasonable in view of Heath's specified improvements. He said nothing to the further observation that Heath was in arrears for the residual £60 rent.[107] Williams's general response was that he knew more about estate management than the canons because 'churchmen are but poore survayors of land' (thus nicely distancing himself from the mere clergy).[108]

Even where he acknowledged an irregularity, he had an excuse; he had indeed presented Anthony Clopton to the vicarage of Stanford-in-the-Vale (Berks.) without consulting his colleagues – but at a time of plague, when a chapter could not be assembled, and he acted to prevent the right lapsing to the diocesan.[109] When on uncertain ground he turned on the chapter; if there had been no proper accounts kept of timber felled or other matters, that was the fault of the officers (treasurer, steward or receiver-general), not the dean. The school had apparently neglected to mark the last anniversary of the king's accession with the customary verses. Williams said he was away at the time, and that in any case the four complainants had not troubled to go up school to read the displayed poems in previous years.[110] Williams firmly defended other charges against standards in the school and the behaviour of the head master, Osbaldeston. Several of the charges related to the choir, perhaps with some hope of embarrassing Williams in the eyes of his low church friends. He was said to have lured one of the Abbey choirmen to sing in his chapel at Buckden, and to have placed one of his servants, a layman, in one of the minor canonries at Westminster. He denied any faults: the Abbey choirmen were welcomed to Buckden, but not permanently abducted there. The servant he had introduced into the minor canonry had become a deacon, and was 'a civill younge man, a good base'. To the accusation that he had

---

[107] WAM 25095, ff. 2v–3. For the lease (1633) see WAM Chapter Act Book II, f. 57v (*Acts 1609–42*, no. 71); WAM Reg. XIV, ff. 262–4, 265v–266. Heath was an energetically 'improving' landlord: P.E. Kopperman, *Sir Robert Heath, 1574–1649* (Royal Historical Soc. Studies in History, lvi, 1989), 251, 255–64.

[108] WAM 25095, f. 6.

[109] *Ibid.*, f. 4v. The presentation was in 1625, a year of prolonged epidemic; the chapter recorded only one meeting (6 May): Foster, *Alumni Oxon.* i, 293. Shrewsbury, *Plague*, 318–38. WAM Chapter Act Book II, f. 36v (*Acts 1609–42*, no. 48). Clopton was instituted on 1 September: Wiltshire Record Office, Trowbridge, Reg. Tounson and Davenant, f. 21.

[110] WAM 25095, f. 10. Reference is made to anniversaries of coronations generally, and specifically to 'the anniversarie of ... the kinge anno 1634'. The anniversary of the actual coronation was 2 February, but accession day (27 March) was popularly called coronation day; cf. J.E. Neale, 'November 17th', in his *The Age of Catherine de Medici, and Essays in Elizabethan History* (1963), 96. Even Laud used this misnomer: *Works*, iii, 213.

built a house for one of the choirmen out of chapter funds, he replied that this was very proper.[111]

He was supposedly rude to the canons; his defence was that he hardly ever spoke to them. He admitted losing his patience on one occasion when a canon, who had been visiting South Benfleet (Essex) and was told of an encroachment of the dean and chapter's boundaries there, returned to accuse the dean of mislaying some of the Abbey's 'bonds'. Williams had said the fellow was 'not well inhabited in his upper partes'.[112] The junior canons objected to the increase in charges of their commons – from £7 or £8 to £20 a week. This was because (Williams claimed) an arrangement originally designed for three or four residents had been swamped by all twelve canons 'thrustinge in'; he had therefore been obliged to discontinue the common table.[113] Most other objections were dismissed as trivial or not within the dean's direct responsibility.

In general Williams was accused of being autocratic and of failing to consult with his chapter colleagues; against this he maintained that the dean was not *primus inter pares*. Here he correctly interpreted the constitution of the collegiate church, where the dean (as in the kindred Henrician cathedrals) has much greater authority over his chapter than does the dean in the old foundation cathedrals. Williams was particularly scornful of the lowly status of his accusers who were, he implies, all or mostly young men and no more than masters of arts. In fact, of the four juniors in January 1635, only Heylyn was under 40 and had not held a doctorate on appointment (though he had since taken his DD). The only mere MA in the chapter was Williams's friend and ally, Osbaldeston. It is undoubtedly Heylyn whom Williams had allegedly called a 'sawcie fellow'. Williams did not deny this, adding that he might indeed 'hold it a sawcie part for a yonge man, a master of artes and a preist, to challenge his deane (a bishop by consecration) of perjurye'.[114]

On 20 April 1635 a commission under the great seal was issued to both archbishops, the bishop of London (Juxon), Lords Manchester and Cottington (lord privy seal and chancellor of the exchequer) and secretaries Coke and Windebank, directing them to enquire into Williams's conduct as dean. Since the commissioners were appointed by

---

[111] WAM 25095, f. 2. In May 1631 the chapter had recorded with satisfaction that all 16 singingmen had been provided with houses at the church's expense: WAM Chapter Act Book II, f. 51 (*Acts 1609–42*, no. 62).

[112] WAM 25095, ff. 8v–9 (quotation on f. 9).

[113] *Ibid.*, f. 12v. The common table was broken up in January 1632: WAM Chapter Act Book II, f. 53 (*Acts 1609–42*, no. 65).

[114] WAM 25095, f. 8.

the king in his capacity as visitor, no demurrer respecting Westminster's exemption could be entered. Laud could not visit Westminster as archbishop, but (as he was about to do in the similar case of the universities) he was ready to use royal authority where his metropoliticality failed him. However, it was not until the following January that a date was fixed for the hearing, and Laud had the satisfaction of nailing his citation on the Abbey's door. By this time Westminster's internal squabbles had been well broadcast. The proceedings finally began on 27 January, and on 1 February Heylyn was chosen to speak for the plaintiffs. The case continued until 15 April, when it was adjourned *sine die*.[115] In the event this weapon was not needed, as Williams was brought down by other means. He had much earlier been accused of leaking privy council secrets; the charges were in themselves feeble, but in defending himself Williams incidentally laid himself open to an authentic charge of perjury. At first he hoped to escape with a fine of £2,000, but his enemies brought further charges which threatened to deprive him of his benefices. In November 1635 an agreement kept him at Westminster and the other livings he held *in commendam* on payment of £4,000. Laud was particularly annoyed that Cottington and Windebank had contrived this.[116] Williams's opponents were unrelenting, and he was eventually obliged to offer a larger fine and to resign the deanery. All these deals were theoretical, and for the time being his Westminster stipend was still paid.[117]

When Williams was eventually convicted in star chamber on 11 July 1637 he was fined more than £10,000, suspended from his benefices and sent to the Tower. The king offered to release him if he would surrender the deanery and his other *commendam* benefices, and exchange Lincoln for an Irish or Welsh see. He would still have been liable to the fine, having lost most means to pay it. Williams did not think this a good bargain, and was particularly averse to Ireland, where he suspected Wentworth would 'cut off his head within one month'.[118]

On 21 November 1637 the Westminster chapter was authorized by letters patent to hold its annual audit, then imminent, in the dean's absence and to seal leases and patents of office without his assent. The

[115] WAM 12659, as printed in Rymer, *Foedera*, xix, 630–4. Seddon, *Letters of Holles*, iii, 476 (Lord Clare, writing from Westminster to his son, Lord Houghton, on 24 January 1636, expected 'a chrysis of the work' promoted by the '3 turbulent Prebends'); I am again grateful to Dr Milton for reference to this source.

[116] Knowler, *Strafforde's Letters*, i, 489, 490 (James Howell to Wentworth, 28 November 1635; Garrard to same, December). Laud, *Works*, vii, 214–15 (Laud to Wentworth, 30 November 1635). Cf. Trevor-Roper, *Laud*, 327–32.

[117] WAM 12634, 41828, 41829.

[118] Clarendon, *History*, i, 148.

dean's stipend and dividends were to be disposed of at the king's pleasure. The decapitated chapter duly met on 20 December under the presidency of Newell as sub-dean. Heylyn, who was treasurer for the year, no doubt had particular satisfaction on arranging for the sequestration of the dean's income in June 1638. During his absence some of Williams's arrangements were reversed; a house which he had given to the school was resumed as a canonical residence. Laud's influence is seen in the presentation, at his request, of a member of his old college of St John's, Oxford, to the Abbey's principal living of Islip (Oxon.) in 1639.[119]

Williams returned to star chamber for a further trial in February 1639 following the discovery at Buckden of letters written five years before from Williams to Osbaldeston. In these allusions were made to 'Leviathan' (apparently meaning Lord Treasurer Weston) and 'the little urchin' and 'medling hocus-pocus', whom everyone recognized as Laud. Needless to say by calling attention to these expressions, and by assuming himself to be thus described, Laud ensured that the names would for ever attach to him. Williams and Osbaldeston were prosecuted for libel: it was seriously maintained that Williams had published the letters by keeping them in a deed-box. Osbaldeston's defence was that the objectionable words were nicknames he and Williams gave to Chief Justice Richardson ('Leviathan') and Dr Spicer ('urchin'). Williams concurred. Spicer's connexion with the library was recalled, though now it was said he had defaulted on a promised gift of books worth £40 to the school. None of this was believed. Osbaldeston was fined and sentenced to the pillory; he escaped by hiding in London while announcing that he was gone 'beyond Canterbury', so sending Laud's unimaginative policemen to search the road to Dover. Williams received a further fine, and his household goods were now forfeit.[120] One of those who had informed against him, Richard Kilvert, acquired the right to his library; Sir Edward Hyde declined to purchase it.[121]

Williams's decision to stay in the Tower was not entirely quixotic. Although he was restricted to one meal a day, 'and that a spare one',[122]

---

[119] WAM Chapter Act Book II, ff. 64–5, 65v, 67, 67v, 69v, 70–1 (*Acts 1609–42*, nos 81, 82, 83, 87, 92, 93).

[120] PRO, SP 16/413, no. 56 (*CSPD 1638–9*, 491; Thomas Smith to Sir John Pennington, 21 February 1639). Heylyn, *Examen*, 221–2. Hacket, *Scrin. Res.* ii, 130–1. J. Rushworth, *Historical Collections* (1721), ii, 803–17.

[121] BL, Add. MS 4187, ff. 37–8 (Hyde to Falkland, copy, with date 1637), printed in K. Weber, *Lucius Cary, Second Viscount Falkland* (Columbia University Studies in English and Comparative Literature, cxlv, 1940), 71–2. Cf. Baker, *Hist. St. John's*, ii, 621.

[122] Knowler, *Strafforde's Letters*, ii, 167 (Garrard to Wentworth, 10 May 1638).

he remained at least geographically close to the political world, and was able to maintain contact with its leaders. In efforts to win his freedom on acceptable terms he asked the help of the opposition leader, Hampden, and of the earl of Arundel, once his opponent at court. He also corresponded with William Prynne in his remoter imprisonment. In the end it was the queen to whom Williams owed his release in November 1640.[123] He resumed his decanal duties and his arguments with Heylyn (who was obliged to release £187 18s 6d of the dean's dividends which had been paid into the exchequer during his suspension).[124] On 23 December the privy council ordered that all entries in the privy council against Williams should be expunged.[125]

For a year Williams was again at the centre of events, indeed straddling the political divide. In January 1641 he preached before the king and condemned the opposition as 'tailors and shoemakers', then reingratiating himself with them by regaling court gossip. Notoriously he advised the king to save his own neck by breaking Strafford's. In August he angered the Commons by devising a form of prayer for the peace with Scotland which prompted them to adjourn to the chapel of Lincoln's Inn rather than attend the Abbey.[126] For a time it seemed Williams might be the man to reconcile the opposing factions and, as Lord Russell suggests, preside over a 'revitalized Caroline church'.[127]

In March 1641, with Laud in turn in the Tower, Williams chaired the Lords' committee for reform of religion. One of its main recommendations was the revival of genuine episcopal election by deans and chapters. Williams's personal interest is evident from the exclusion of the dean of Westminster's civil jurisdiction from the provisions of the reform bill first read on 1 July.[128] Opposition schemes to seize capitular revenues finally aligned Williams with the king's cause. On 15 November he was elected (in the old fictitious fashion) archbishop of

[123] Trevor-Roper, *Laud*, 357, 386. Davies, *Caroline Captivity*, 36. LPL, MS 1030, f. 182 (Williams to Hampden, 29 April 1640). K. Sharpe, 'The earl of Arundel, his circle and the opposition to the duke of Buckingham, 1618–1628', in *Faction and Parliament. Essays on Early Stuart History*, ed. Sharpe (Oxford 1978), 212, 215–16. Thomas, 'Archbishop John Williams', 284–5.

[124] WAM 12664 (2 June 1641).

[125] WAM 12641. WAM 12640 gives the 25 entries concerned, beginning with Williams's dismissal from the council 22 February 1633. Cf. Hacket, *Scrin. Res.* ii, 138. Carlton, *Laud*, 198.

[126] Clarendon, *History*, i, 338–9, 385, 469. Sermon of 24 January 1641: BL, Harleian MS 6424, f. 9v.

[127] C.S.R. Russell, *The Fall of the British Monarchies, 1637–1642* (Oxford 1991), 437.

[128] *Ibid.*, 251–2. *The Constitutional Documents of the Puritan Revolution*, ed. S.R. Gardiner (3rd edn, Oxford 1906), 167–79 (Westminster reference p. 170).

York.[129] He was allowed three years more as dean of Westminster *in commendam*. It was in his Deanery there that he met his next crisis in late December. There were riots in the city, in which the bishops and their properties were principal targets. On 27 December Williams was jostled in the streets and had his clothes torn; he needed the protection of Manchester to reach his way to the deanery.[130] On the following day (Holy Innocents, the Abbey's foundation festival) the church itself was attacked. Williams ordered the doors to be locked and armed his servants. Some Westminster boys joined his little army, and one of them took out a leader of the mob with a well-directed slate.[131] On 29 December, perhaps aware of what befell another archbishop in his sanctuary on that day, Williams gathered eleven other bishops into the deanery and drafted a protest. The bishops would not attend parliament while the intimidation continued; neither would they acknowledge as valid any proceedings in their absence. It was typical of Williams to dictate his own terms, and it was a misjudgement. The protesting bishops were at once impeached and on the 30th they were taken to the Tower.[132] On 5 May 1642 he was released on bail of £5,000; this he broke in July by going to join the king, thereafter taking up a new career as a military commander.[133] He had time to sign the Chapter Act Book for the last time on 25 May.[134] He would remain dean until his *commendam* expired in 1644, and he died in 1650. Meanwhile, in Westminster a new Jerusalem would be built; but it was an unlovely place, and had no continuing.

---

[129] Le Neve, *1541–1857*, iv, 3. Clarendon, *History*, i, 470–1.

[130] *The Autobiography of Sir John Bramston*, ed. R. Neville (Lord Braybrooke), (Camden Soc. xxxii, 1845), 82. Clarendon, *History*, i, 454.

[131] Hacket, *Scrin. Res.* ii, 78. T. Fuller, *The Church History of Britain*, ed. J.S. Brewer (Oxford 1845), vi, 218–19.

[132] Soden, *Goodman*, 356–63.

[133] *Walker Revised*, ed. A.G. Matthews (Oxford 1948), 18.

[134] WAM Chapter Act Book II, f. 81 (*Acts 1609–42*, no. 109).

Appendix   Scholars and Fellows at St John's College, Cambridge on
the foundation of John Williams 1624–50

1. *Scholars*

Admitted	Scholar	County	Career	*ROW* ref.
12 Nov 1624	Cardell Goodman	Herts	church	i, 383
15 Nov 1624	Richard Bulkeley	Anglesey	church	i, 137
15 Nov 1624	Maurice Wynn	Denbighs	royal household	ii, 1031
15 Nov 1624	Thomas Bourne	Herts		i, 109
8 Nov 1626	Richard Riley	Middlesex		ii, 788
8 Nov 1627	John Chapman	Lincoln dioc.		i, 177
4 Nov 1629	Thomas Sparrow	Essex		ii, 871
9 Nov 1631	John Ramsay	Middlesex		ii, 771
9 Nov 1631	Rice Phillipps	Pembs		iii, 742
6 Nov 1634	Thomas Butler	Middlesex		i, 150
6 Nov 1634	Arthur Williams	Caernarvons		ii, 997
8 Nov 1636	Thomas Nelson	Surrey		ii, 686
8 Nov 1636	William Morgan	Monmouth	church; army	ii, 665
6 Nov 1639	Fulk Tydder	Herts	church	ii, 938
6 Nov 1639	Richard Mattock	Middlesex		ii, 632
4 Nov 1640	John Williams	Denbighs		ii, 999
9 Nov 1642	Robert Jessup	Lincoln dioc.		i, 517
10 Nov 1647	John Winne	Kent		ii, 1032
10 Nov 1647	William Hughes	Anglesey	church	[Venn, ii, 428]
7 Nov 1649	John Lewis	Anglesey		[Venn, iii, 81]
7 Nov 1649	Thomas Longland	Lincoln dioc.	church	[Venn, iii, 103]

Admission dates sources: SJC Archives, C.3.2, pp. 433, 436, 439, 441, 444, 445, 447, 448, 453, 454, 456, 461, 462, 463, 464 (register of officers, fellows and scholars)

2. *Fellows*

Admitted	Fellow	County	Vacated	*ROW* ref.
6 Apr. 1625	John Barrett		†[? Midsummer 1625]	i, 56
6 Apr. 1625	William Mostyn		†[? Midsummer1633]	ii, 671
31 Mar 1626	Cardell Goodman (*vice* Barrett)		Midsummer 1641	[see scholars]
19 Mar 1634	William Rogers (*vice* Mostyn)	Flints	Midsummer 1644	ii, 799
[27]*Mar 1642	William Morgan (*vice* Goodman)	Monmouth	Midsummer 1645	[see scholars]

Sources: SJC Archives, C.3.2, pp. 300, 301, 304, 307; D.59.69

---

† Assumed on basis of subsequent entries, for which date of vacancy is specified in D.59.69

* Date written in both the register (C.3.2, p. 307) and D.59.69 as '2µ' March '1642' (µ here representing an uncertain figure). Cannot be 20 March 1642/3 (as *The Eagle*, xxxiii (1912), 107) because Jessupp was admitted scholar in November 1642 by promotion of Morgan to fellowship (C.7.16, p. 402). Year must be 1642 by modern reckoning and day of month must therefore be 25 x 29. Also entry occurs between others for April 1641 and November 1642, although the MS register is not invariably in chronological order; Baker's calendar silently corrects to this generally, but his suggested date of ?27 March 1642 for Morgan's admission is the likeliest reading: Baker, *Hist. St John's*, i, 295.

Index